646

Manual of tropical housing and building
Part one: Climatic design

Manual of tropical housing and building

Part one: Climatic design

O. H. Koenigsberger
Professor and Head, Development Planning Unit,
School of Environmental Studies, University of London

T. G. Ingersoll
former Deputy Head of the Housing and Research Unit,
University of Science and Technology, Kumasi, Ghana

Alan Mayhew
Director of Development, University College of Cape Coast,
Ghana

S. V. Szokolay
Senior Lecturer in Environmental Science,
Polytechnic of Central London

Longman

Longman Group Limited
London

*Associated companies, branches and representatives
throughout the world*

© O. H. Koenigsberger, T. G. Ingersoll,
Alan Mayhew and S. V. Szokolay, 1973

First published 1974

ISBN 0582 44545 0 Cased
ISBN 0582 44546 9 Paper

*Printed in Hong Kong by
Dai Nippon Printing Co (H.K.) Ltd*

Contents

List of figures

Section 3

Section 4

Section 5

Acknowledgements

The following illustrations are based on those given in the publications listed. Most have been converted to S.I. units by S. V. Szokolay. Authorship of the originals and their use as a basis is gratefully acknowledged.

Fig 4   I. S. Groundwater: *Solar radiation in air conditioning* (Crosby Lockwood, 1957).

Fig 21   R. Geiger: *The climate near the ground* (Harvard University Press, 1957)

Fig 25   T. Lawson: Air movement and natural ventilation in *Architects' Journal*, 11 December 1968

Fig 30 & 31   T. Bedford: *Environmental warmth and its measurement* Medical Research Council, War Memorandum No 17 HMSO 1940/1961

Fig 42, 55 & 103   W. Burt *et al*: *Windows and environment* Pilkington Advisory Service, 1969

Fig 43   Inst. of Heat. Vent. Engr.: *Guide*, 1965.

Fig 99   J. Longmore: *BRS daylight protractors* HMSO 1968

Fig 101   Building Research Station, Digest No 42 *Estimating daylight in buildings*

Fig 105   C. G. H. Plant: *Tropical daylight and sunlight* University College, London, 1967 (duplicated)

Fig 107   D. Paix: *The design of buildings for daylighting* Commonwealth Exp. Bldg. Stn. (Sydney) 1962

Fig 109   Illuminating Engr. Society, Technical Report No 10 *Evaluation of discomfort glare*

Fig 128   Exp. Bldg. Stn. *Notes on the Science of Bldg* No 80: 'Some common noise problems'

Fig 129   P. H. Parkin and H. R. Humphreys *Acoustics, noise and buildings* Faber, 1958

List of symbols

A	absorption	g	glare (in general) or glare constant
A	area of surface	HSI	heat stress index
a	absorbance (absorption coefficient)	h	height
AH	absolute humidity	I	intensity
AMR	annual mean range	I_a	intensity of direct radiation
AMT	annual mean temperature	I_d	intensity of diffuse radiation
A_t	total surface area	I_o	reference intensity (sound)
b	thickness (breadth)	IRC	internally reflected component
C	conductance	K	thermal diffusivity
CET	corrected effective temperature	k	conductivity
CS	contrast sensitivity	L	luminance
Cnd	conduction	L_h	luminance at horizon
Cnv	convection	L_z	luminance at zenith
c	specific heat	L_γ	luminance at γ altitude angle
D	dirt factor	M	mass per unit surface
DBT	dry bulb temperature	Met	metabolism
DF	daylight factor	MF	maintenance factor
d	density	MRT	mean radiant temperature
d	distance (length)	N	number (of air changes per hour)
E	illumination (eclairage)	NC	noise criteria
E_i	illumination indoors (at defined point)	OT	operative temperature
		P4SR	predicted four hour sweat rate
ΔE_{max}	magnitude of illumination vector	P	pressure (atmospheric ~)
E_n	illumination of normal plane	P_a	partial pressure – dry air
E_o	illumination outdoors	P_s	stack pressure
E_s	scalar illumination	P_v	partial pressure – vapour
E_β	illumination on plane tilted by β degrees	P_{vs}	saturation point vapour pressure
		P_w	wind pressure
ECI	equatorial comfort index	p	position index
ERC	externally reflected component	Q	heat flow rate
ET	effective temperature	Q_c	conduction heat flow rate
EW	equivalent warmth	Q_e	evaporative cooling rate
Evp	evaporation	Q_i	internal heat gain, rate of ~
e	emittance	Q_m	mechanical heating/cooling rate
F	function of . . .	Q_s	solar heat gain, rate of ~
F	flux (flow) of light	Q_v	ventilation heat flow rate
F_l	flux emitted by lamps	q	heat flow rate, density of ~
F_r	flux received (on working plane)	**R**	red (hue designation)
FF	framing factor	Rad	radiation
f	frequency	RH	relative humidity
f	surface or film conductance	RT	resultant temperature
f_i	inside surface conductance	R	resistance
f_o	outside surface conductance	R_a	air-to-air resistance
G	glare index	R_c	cavity resistance
GF	glazing factor	r	reflectance

S	total surface area		v	velocity
s	component surface areas		WBT	wet bulb temperature
SC	sky component		a	solar azimuth angle
SH	saturation point humidity		β	angle of incidence
TI	transmission loss		γ	solar altitude angle
T_m	mean outside air temperature		δ	azimuth difference (=horizontal
T_i	inside air temperature			shadow angle)
T_o	outside air temperature		ϵ	efficiency
T_s	sol-air temperature		ϵ	vertical shadow angle
T_{se}	sol-air excess temperature		θ	solar gain factor
$_\Delta T$	temperature difference		λ	wavelength
t	transmittance (transmission coefficient)		μ	decrement factor
			ϕ	time-lag
U	air-to-air transmittance		ψ	visual angle (solid angle)
UF	utilisation factor		ρ	visual angle
V	Munsell value		ω	wall azimuth angle (orientation)
V	ventilation rate			

Preface and acknowledgements

This book is intended as a textbook for students, as a reference work for practitioners and as an aid for their clients — investors, administrators and politicians.

It is the result of the joint efforts of its authors, their fellow teachers and several generations of students who used successive drafts, recorded their reactions and experiences and provided material for revision and rewriting.

I started working on the manual in 1952 to record the experience of twelve years of planning and building in India. The first draft provided the nucleus for a course in tropical architecture started in 1953 with E. Maxwell Fry as director at the Architectural Association in London*. It was designed to meet the demands of students from tropical countries for a syllabus centred on their specific needs. Some twenty to thirty architects, planners and builders from as many different countries assembled every year for a period of joint studies. The first draft of the Manual served to structure their discussions and was gradually developed and changed in the 'give and take' between teachers and students.

After about ten years T. G. Ingersoll, a teacher in the department, revised and re-wrote the text to incorporate the most recent advances in a rapidly expanding subject. Alan Mayhew, also a former teacher, produced the third version designed especially to facilitate learning and teaching, and S. V. Szokolay prepared the manuscript for publication. He re-wrote some chapters and added others on the basis of his teaching experience in Africa and authoritative knowledge of building science. He also undertook and completed the — by no means negligable — task of translating and re-calculating formulas, tables, graphs and figures to fit into the new international system of measurements and notations.

My fellow authors join me in recording their gratitude to the many colleagues and students who helped during the long gestation period of this manual. My particular thanks go to the trustees of the Halley Stewart Trust who had the foresight of financing the beginning of the work.

August 1972   Otto Koenigsberger

*Later 'Department of Development and Tropical Studies' and, since 1971, 'Development Planning Unit' of the School of Environmental Studies, University College, London.

Introduction

For most of the tropics, traditional housing is rural housing. Some of the countries of the arid belt of the northern hemisphere, notably Iraq, Egypt and the Maghreb countries, Iran, Rajastan, the Punjab and southern China have town-house traditions from which new urban building forms could develop. Yet, these are exceptions in the tropical world where the process of·urbanisation has gathered momentum only in the last four or five decades. The majority of the people of the tropics still live dispersed in low density rural settlements and deal with their housing problems in the same manner as their fathers and forefathers have done.

Traditional house types have developed in response to the needs of a predominantly peasant population. The surrounding country provides the building materials: in the humid tropics timber, bamboo and thatch; in arid zones stone, earth and bricks; and in composite climates a mixture of organic and inorganic materials. The rhythm of country life includes time for building as much as for tilling, sowing and harvesting. Everybody is a house builder as much as he is cultivator or herdsman. Traditional rural building is based on low investment and high maintenance. Monetary transactions are minimal. The assistance of relations, friends and neighbours is rewarded by food, drink and mutual help.

Children and adults spend most of the day in the open. The functions of huts and houses are reduced to three: shelter from rain and spells of extreme heat or cold, minimal privacy and the safe storage of possessions. The safe storage of agricultural products receives as much — and often more — attention than shelter for human beings.

Space is plentiful. Growing family or tribal units can be accommodated easily by the addition of huts, stores and enclosures as the need arises. Waste disposal and health problems are solved, or at least mitigated, by dispersal. There are a few exceptions. In the Nile Valley, in the hinterland of Peshawar, and in parts of Bengal and southern China, for instance, land is so fertile and so much in demand that villagers have to be as careful in its use as townsfolk. Yet in most rural communities, the land needs for housing are negligeable compared to those of agriculture.

The traditional building forms of the rural tropics often include sound solutions of climatic problems. Given technological limitations and the always overriding considerations of safety, some of these solutions must be considered ingenious, and there can be no doubt that they deserve careful study.

Yet the most pressing housing needs of the tropics are urban, and traditional forms because of their origin in the life and economy of rural societies are seldom suited to urban conditions. This is demonstrated convincingly by going through the above-described features of rural life and noting how few of them apply in towns and cities.

Building materials for city needs cannot be taken from the surrounding countryside without, in the case of organic materials, denuding it of vegetation or, in the case of earth building, making borrow pits of dangerous dimensions. Building materials that have to be brought in over large distances cease to be cheap. The rhythm of city life does not include time for house building, least of all for the poorest, the unemployed, the casual or unskilled labourer who has to fight hard to stay alive and who cannot afford to miss a chance of finding a foothold in the urban economy. Even time for maintenance work becomes scarce and the towns-man soon learns to value durable materials and methods that do not need frequent attention. He receives money for his labour and is expected to pay cash for the services he requires including those of builders.

His family, like that of the villager, spends a good part of the day in the open, but space for outdoor living is not as plentiful and suitable. Safe storage of posses-sions is even more important than in the open country. So is privacy, but both are more difficult to achieve. Yet it is space, a commodity so plentiful and so little valued in rural life, that becomes a major concern for the town-dweller. It is not a matter of the total amount of land available — although that too can be a problem in certain urban areas — but rather a question of location. Because he wants to be near to work, schools and shops, the townsman must be content with a small piece of ground and adjust his life style, household size and building methods to proximity with others.

Proximity makes major issues out of problems that the villager can afford to neglect. Fire hazards, waste disposal, sanitation, and noise pollution are typical urban problems that cannot be solved by going back to essentially rural traditions.

They cannot be solved either by the adoption of Western technology and Western patterns that have their origin in different climates, different cultures and different economic conditions. It seems so obvious that house types and building materials from cold climates cannot solve the problems of cities where heat is the dominant problem and that solutions from communities with average per capita incomes of $7 000 per annum cannot work in communities where the income is less than $70. Yet the cities of the tropics are full of galvanised iron roofs, plate glass windows and buildings that could just as well stand in Manchester, Detroit or Montreal. The resulting urban environment is climatically and socially inadequate.

A wealthy elite can escape the consequences of poor design through mechanical air-conditioning. The others suffer from living conditions that permit neither efficient work nor rest or enjoyment. It is the purpose of this manual to demonstrate that this need not be so, that it is possible to create cities that have pleasant indoor and outdoor living spaces and are suited to the social conditions of their inhabitants.

Section 1   Climate: The given conditions

University of Strathclyde
SCHOOL OF ARCHITECTURE
INFORMATION ROOM

**1.1.1
Climate and
tropical
climates**

Climate (from Greek: *klima*) is defined by the Oxford dictionary as 'region with certain conditions of temperature, dryness, wind, light, etc.'. A somewhat more scientific definition is: 'an integration in time of the physical states of the atmospheric environment, characteristic of a certain geographical location.' As *weather* is the momentary state of the atmospheric environment at a certain location, climate could be defined as 'the integration in time of weather conditions'.

Tropical climates are those where heat is the dominant problem, where, for the greater part of the year buildings serve to keep the occupants cool, rather than warm, where the annual mean temperature is not less than 20°C.

Before tropical climates can be examined in detail, we must survey the factors shaping the climates, on a global scale.

**1.1.2
Solar
radiation:
quality**

The earth receives almost all its energy from the sun in the form of radiation, thus the sun is the dominating influence on climates.

The spectrum of solar radiation extends from 290 to 2300 nm (nanometre = 10^{-9} m). According to human means of perception we can distinguish:

a   *ultra-violet* radiation, 290 to 380 nm, producing photo-chemical effects, bleaching, sunburn, etc.
b   visible *light*, 380 (violet) to 700 nm (red).
c   short *infra-red* radiation, 700 to 2300 nm, radiant heat with some photo-chemical effects.

The spectral energy distribution varies with altitude, due to the filtering effect of the atmosphere. Some of the shorter wavelengths are absorbed by the atmosphere and reradiated at much longer wavelengths, e.g. long infra-red, up to 10 000 nm.

As the luminous efficiency of energy-radiation depends on its spectral composition, there is no constant relationship between radiation intensity and its lighting effect. However, as a general guidance, the value of 100 lumens/watt can be used for solar radiation. This would give an illumination of 100 lux for every W/m² intensity or 100 000 lux per kW/m².

1.1.3
Solar
radiation:
quantity

The intensity of radiation reaching the upper surface of the atmosphere is taken as the *solar constant*: 1 395 W/m², but it may actually vary ±2% due to variations in the output of the sun itself and it varies ±3·5% due to changes in the earth–sun distance.

The earth moves around the sun in a slightly elliptical orbit. One revolution is completed in 365 days, 5 hours, 48 minutes and 46 seconds. This orbit results from the gravitational pull of the sun and the centrifugal force due to the earth's inertia and momentum. At aphelion the solar distance is 152 million km and at perihelion is is 147 million km.

1.1.4
Tilt of the
earth's axis

The earth rotates around its own axis, each rotation making one 24-hour day. The axis of this rotation (the line joining the North and South Poles) is tilted to the plane of the elliptical orbit, at an angle of 66·5° (i.e. a tilt of 23·5° from the normal) and the direction of this axis is constant.

Maximum intensity is received on a plane normal to the direction of radiation. If the axis of earth were rectangular to the plane of the orbit, it would always be the equatorial regions which are normal to the direction of solar radiation. Due to the tilted position, however, the area receiving the maximum intensity moves north and south, between the tropic of Cancer (latitude 23·5°N.) and the tropic of Capricorn (latitude 23·5°S.). This is the main cause of seasonal changes.

On 21 June areas along latitude 23·5°N. are normal to the sun's rays, the sun's apparent path goes through the zenith at this latitude, and the longest daylight period is experienced. At the same time latitude 23·5°S. experiences the shortest day and a radiation minimum.

On 21 March and 23 September areas along the Equator are normal to the sun's rays and experience a zenith path of the sun. For all areas of the earth these are the equinox days (day and night of equal length).

Figure 1 clearly explains this relationship.

Fig 1
The earth–sun
relationship

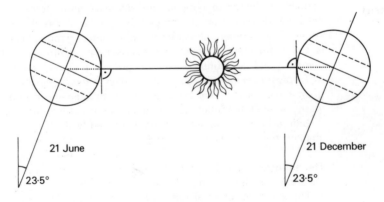

21 June   21 December

23·5°   23·5°

1.1.5
Radiation at
the earth's
surface

This earth–sun relationship affects the amount of radiation received at a particular point on the earth's surface three ways:

1 *the cosine law*, which states that the intensity on a tilted surface equals the normal intensity times the cosine of the angle of incidence. Figure 2 shows how the same amount of radiation is distributed over a larger area, therefore less radiation falls on unit area.

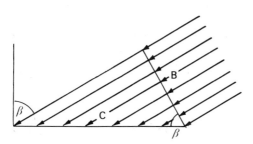

Fig 2
The angle of
incidence

$$\cos \beta = \frac{B}{C}$$

Area C > Area B
Intensity C < Intensity B
$I_C = I_B \times \cos \beta$

2 *atmospheric depletion*, i.e. the absorption of radiation by ozone, vapours and dust particles in the atmosphere (a factor of 0·2 to 0·7). The lower the solar altitude angle, the longer the path of radiation through the atmosphere, thus a smaller part reaches the earth's surface. Figure 3 indicates this geometrical relationship and Figure 4 shows this effect in quantitative terms for points at different heights above sea-level. This atmospheric depletion is also affected by the momentary state of the atmosphere: its purity, vapour, dust, smoke, etc., content
3 *duration of sunshine*, i.e. the length of the daylight period [1]*

1.1.6
The earth's
thermal
balance

The total amount of heat absorbed by the earth each year is balanced by a corresponding heat loss [2]. Without this cooling the thermal balance of the earth could not be maintained, the temperature of the earth and its atmosphere would increase

Fig 3
Length of path
through the
atmosphere

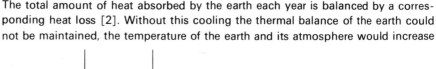
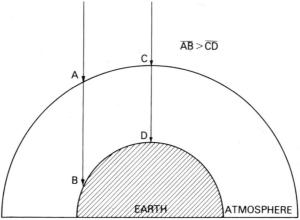

$\overline{AB} > \overline{CD}$

EARTH   ATMOSPHERE

and would soon cease to be favourable to most forms of life.

Figure 5 illustrates the distribution of incoming radiation and Figure 6 shows how the earth's surface releases heat by three processes:

a by long-wave radiation to cold outer space (some 84% of this reradiation is absorbed in the atmosphere, only 16% escapes to space)
b by evaporation: the earth's surface is cooled, as liquid water changes into vapour and mixes with air
c by convection: air heated by contact with the warm earth surface becomes lighter and rises to the upper atmosphere, where it dissipates its heat to space

Winds are basically convection currents in the atmosphere, tending to even out the differential heating of various zones.† The pattern of movements is modified by the earth's rotation.

1.1.7
Winds:
thermal
forces

At the maximum heating zone (which is somewhere between the tropics of

* Figures in square brackets refer to the bibliographical list on p. 275 *et seq.*
† It has been calculated [4] that if the atmosphere were still, the average temperature at the Equator would be 33°C in lieu of 27°C and at the North Pole it would be −40°C, instead of −17°C, as it is now.

6

Cancer and Capricorn) air is heated by the hot surface, it expands, its pressure is decreased, it becomes lighter, it rises vertically and flows off at a high level towards colder regions. Part of this air, having cooled down at the high level, descends to the surface in the subtropic regions, from where the cooler, heavier air is drawn in towards the Equator from both north and south.

Fig 4
Variation of direct
solar intensity with
height (Original by
I S Groundwater in
Btu/ft²h and ft units)

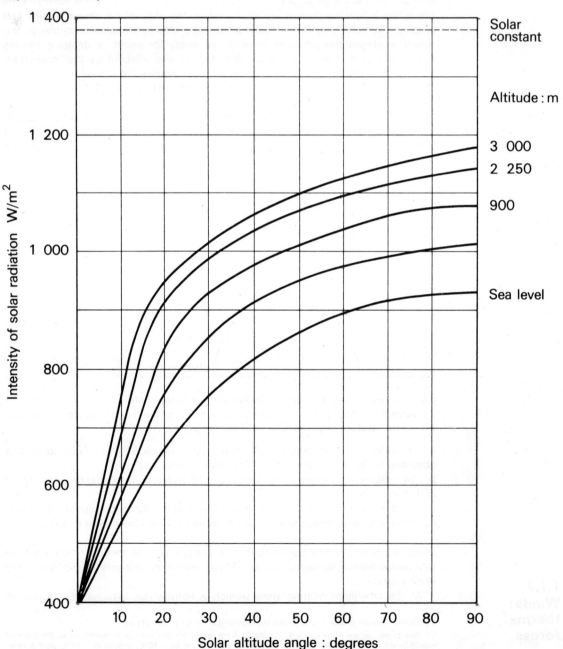

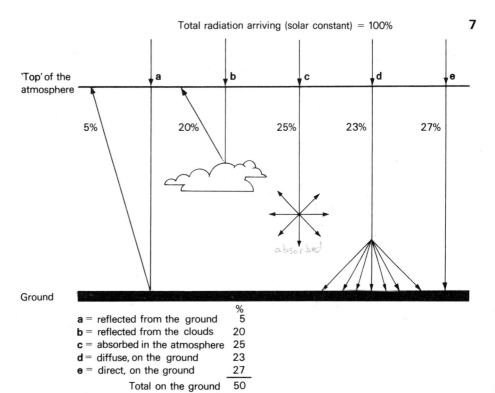

Fig 5
Passage of radiation
through the
atmosphere

Total radiation arriving (solar constant) = 100%

7

'Top' of the
atmosphere

5% 20% 25% 23% 27%

absorbed

Ground

		%
a =	reflected from the ground	5
b =	reflected from the clouds	20
c =	absorbed in the atmosphere	25
d =	diffuse, on the ground	23
e =	direct, on the ground	27
	Total on the ground	50

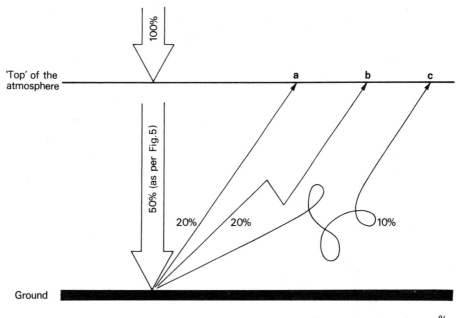

Fig 6
Heat release from the
ground and the
atmosphere

100%

'Top' of the
atmosphere

a b c

50% (as per Fig.5)

20% 20% 10%

Ground

		%
a =	long-wave radiation	20
b =	evaporation, thence radiation	20
c =	convection, thence radiation	10
	Total	50

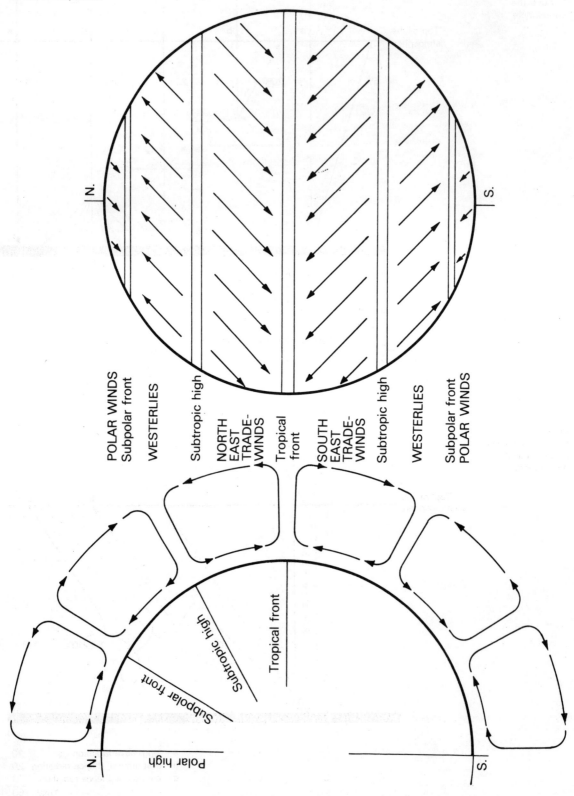

POLAR WINDS
Subpolar front
WESTERLIES
Subtropic high
NORTH EAST TRADE-WINDS
Tropical front
SOUTH EAST TRADE-WINDS
Subtropic high
WESTERLIES
Subpolar front
POLAR WINDS

N.
S.

Tropical front
Subtropic high
Subpolar front
Polar high
N.
S.

The area where the air rises, where these northerly and southerly winds meet, where the *tropical front* is formed, is referred to as the *inter-tropical convergence zone* (ITCZ). This area experiences either completely calm conditions or only very light breezes of irregular directions and is referred to by sailors as 'doldrums'.

The global pattern of thermal air movements is shown in Figure 7. The following explanation also relates to Figure 7.

1.1.8
Trade-winds:
the Coriolis
force

The atmosphere rotates with the earth. As it is light in weight and behaves as fluid, held against the earth's surface only by gravity and friction, it has a tendency to lag behind the earth's rate of rotation where this rotation is the fastest, i.e. at the Equator. There is a 'slippage' at the boundary layer between the earth and its atmosphere caused by what is known as the 'Coriolis force'. The effect is experienced as a wind blowing in a direction opposite to that of the earth's rotation.

The actual wind is the resultant of thermal forces and the Coriolis force (Figure 8): north-easterly winds north of the Equator and south-easterlies south of the Equator. These are known as North East and South East *trade-winds* [5], a term originated by round the world traders in the days of sailing-ships.

Fig 8
Wind parallelogram

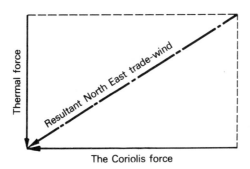

1.1.9
Mid-latitude
westerlies

Around 30°N. and S. there are two bands of continually high barometric pressure (descending air). Winds in these zones are typically light and variable. Between 30 and 60°N. and S., however, strong westerly winds prevail, blowing in the same direction as the earth's rotation.

The origin of these winds was for a long time in dispute, but it is now generally agreed that the mid-latitude westerlies can best be explained by the law of *conservation of angular momentum*.* The total angular momentum of the earth—atmosphere system must remain constant. If it is reduced at the Equator by easterly winds, this must be compensated for by westerly winds elsewhere. If the air is moving from about 30° where it has a substantial circumferential velocity, towards 60° where the earth's radius of rotation, thus its circumferential velocity is much less, the faster rotating air will 'overtake' the earth's surface.

1.1.10
Polar winds

Further towards the poles from latitudes 60°N. and S. the air flow patterns come once more under the influence of thermal factors. The pattern is similar to that near the Equator. Air at the surface moves from the coldest to the slightly warmer regions, i.e. away from the poles. As the circumferential velocity of air at the poles is almost nil, the air will lag behind the rotating earth as it moves away from the poles. The northerly is deflected into north-easterly and the southerly (near the South Pole) into south-easterly *polar winds*.

* 'Since the direction of the rotation of the earth is from west to east all easterly winds have a braking effect on the earth's surface, whereas all westerly winds have an accelerating effect. But the law of conservation of angular momentum requires that the sum of angular momentum in the system "earth + atmosphere" remains constant. In the easterly wind regions surface friction does indeed transfer westerly angular momentum from the earth to the atmosphere, whereas in westerly wind regions the opposite occurs, and the more rapidly rotating atmosphere transfers angular momentum to the earth. This is possible only when the atmosphere transfers angular momentum from the tropics and also to a much smaller extent from the polar caps to the middle latitudes.' [3]

At the meeting point of cold polar winds and the mid-latitude westerlies, a band of low pressure – a *subpolar front* – is formed, with highly variable and strong winds.

1.1.11 Annual wind shifts

During the course of each year the global wind pattern shifts from north to south and back again, remaining broadly symmetrical about the inter-tropical convergence zone. The location of the ITCZ follows the maximum solar heating, i.e. the zenith path of the sun, with a delay of about a month. Figure 9 gives the extreme north and south positions of the ITCZ in July (north) and in January (south).

As a consequence of this annual shift most regions of the earth experience seasonal changes not only in temperature but also in wind directions and in rainfall (as a result of air movements which carry water vapour).

1.1.12 Influence of topography

On a continental scale, wind and weather are the result of an interaction between broad global flow patterns and regional pressure and temperature patterns created by the sun's differential heating effect on land, forest and water.

The force, direction and moisture content of air flows are strongly influenced by topography. Air can be diverted or funnelled by mountain ranges. Air flow deflected upwards, as it cools, releases its moisture content. A descending air mass will very rarely give any precipitation, therefore rainfall characteristics vary sharply between locations on windward and leeward slopes of mountain ranges. The humidity of air will vary with the rate of evaporation of moisture from the surface below, i.e. it depends on the availability of water to be evaporated.

Air movements can be generated on quite a small scale, e.g. between a lake and its shores, between a quarry and a nearby forest, between a town and the surrounding countryside or even between the sunny and shaded sides of a large building, but this will be examined in more detail in 1.4.11 [6].

Fig 9
Seasonal shifts of the
inter-tropical
convergence zone

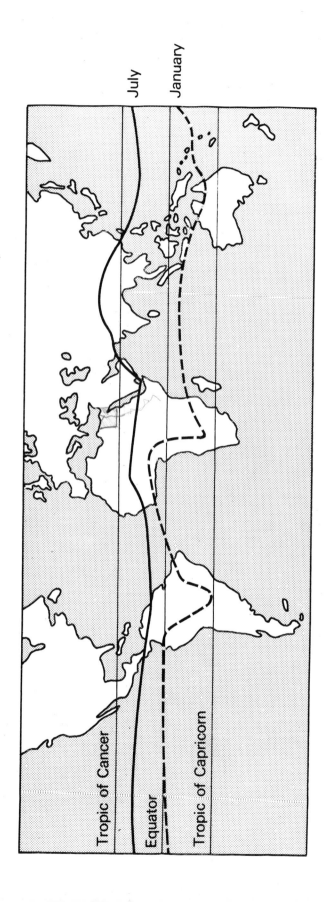

**1.2.1
Climatic
information**

The designer is interested specifically in those aspects of climate which affect human comfort and the use of buildings. They include averages, changes and extremes of temperature, the temperature differences between day and night (diurnal range), humidity, sky conditions, incoming and outgoing radiation, rainfall and its distribution, air movements and special features, such as trade-winds, thunder-storms, dust-storms and hurricanes.

Climatic records as gathered at airports and meteorological stations are not primarily intended for the use of designers. Publications frequently omit some of the aspects that interest the designer. It is often necessary to supplement such information with unpublished data obtained directly from meteorological stations.

It is the designer's task to analyse climatic information and present it in a form that allows him to identify features that are beneficial or harmful to the future occupants of his building.

**1.2.2
Temperature:
measurement**

The temperature of the air is measured in *degrees Celsius* ('C), most often with a mercury thermometer. The dry-bulb or 'true air temperature' is a value taken in the shade, the thermometer being mounted inside a louvred wooden box, known as the 'Stevenson screen' (Figure 10), at a height of 1·20 to 1·80 m above the ground [7]. Readings can be taken at specified times of the day, or if a *maximum–minimum thermometer* is used, one reading daily can give the momentary temperature as well as the maximum and minimum temperatures reached in the past 24 hours. Alternatively a *thermograph* can be used, which is based on a bimetallic thermometer and gives a continuous graphic recording of temperature variations.

1.2.3 Temperature: data

All these readings would produce an unmanageable mass of data, thus some simplification is necessary.

As a broad description, *monthly mean* temperatures can be given for each of the 12 months. The average is taken between each day's maximum and minimum and then the average of the 30 days' average is found (and possibly as many years' average for the same month). To give an indication of diurnal variations, this can be supplemented by *monthly mean maxima* and *minima*. (Monthly mean maximum is the average of 30 days' maximum temperatures.) These will establish the *monthly mean range* of temperatures.

It may be useful to indicate the highest and lowest temperatures ever recorded for each month, i.e. the *monthly extreme maxima* and *minima*, to establish the *monthly extreme range* of temperatures.

These five values for each of the 12 months would give a reasonably accurate picture of temperature conditions, on which the design work can be based (see Section 8).

1.2.4 Humidity: measurement

The humidity of air can be described as *absolute humidity* (AH), i.e. the amount of moisture actually present in unit mass or unit volume of air, in terms of gramme per kilogramme (g/kg) or gramme per cubic metre (g/m³).

The *relative humidity* (RH) is, however, a much more useful form of expression, as it gives a direct indication of evaporation potential. The amount of moisture the air can hold (the *saturation-point humidity*: SH) depends on its temperature (see appendix 1.1). Relative humidity is the ratio of the actual amount of moisture present, to the amount of moisture the air *could* hold at the given temperature — expressed as a percentage:

$$RH = \frac{AH}{SH} \times 100 \ (\%)$$

Humidity is usually measured with the *wet-and-dry-bulb hygrometer*. This consists of two ordinary mercury thermometers mounted side by side. The first one measures the air (*dry-bulb*) *temperature* (DBT). The bulb of the second one is covered with a gauze or wick and is kept wet. Moisture evaporating gives a cooling effect, thus the reading of the *wet-bulb temperature* (WBT) will be less than the DBT. As in dry air the evaporation is faster, the cooling is more pronounced and the difference between the two readings (the 'wet-bulb depression') is greater. In case of 100% RH the two readings will be identical, as there is no evaporation. The rate of evaporation, thus the wet-bulb depression, is a function of the relative humidity. Having made the two readings, the corresponding RH can be found from the psychrometric chart (Figure 12), from a table or a special slide-rule (see appendix 1.2).

Fig 10
The Stevenson screen

1.2.5 Vapour: pressure

Another indication or expression of atmospheric humidity is the *vapour pressure*, i.e. the partial pressure of water vapour present in the air. The 'atmospheric pressure' (P) is the sum of the 'partial pressure of dry air' (P_a) and the 'partial vapour pressure' (P_v):

$$P = P_a + P_v$$

The air is saturated when the vapour pressure (P_v) is equal to the pressure of saturated vapour of the same temperature (P_{vs}). Relative humidity can also be expressed as the ratio of actual vapour pressure to the 'saturation point vapour pressure':

Fig 11
A hygrograph

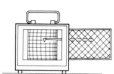

$$RH = \frac{AH}{SH} \times 100 = \frac{P_v}{P_{vs}} \times 100 \; (\%)$$

Vapour pressure is measured in the standard SI pressure unit, the Newton per metre square (N/m²):

1 millibar = 100 N/m².

The vapour pressure concept is rarely used in practical work.

The relationship of all these quantities, i.e. of dry-bulb and wet-bulb temperature, absolute and relative humidity and of vapour pressure is shown by the *psychrometric chart* (Figure 12).

1.2.6 Humidity: data

To give an indication of prevailing humidity conditions, it is sufficient to establish the monthly mean maximum (the average of 30 days' maximum) and the monthly mean minimum relative humidity values for each of the 12 months. This is only possible, where continuous *hygrograph** recordings are available. Where these are not available, readings are made just before sunrise, e.g. at 6.00 hours (which is likely to be the maximum value), and at 15.00 hours (which is near the minimum value).

As the early morning values are fairly high in any climate, the afternoon values are much more characteristic of a given location. They are often used alone, as a brief indication of humidity conditions.

1.2.7 Precipitation

Precipitation is the collective term used for rain, snow, hail, dew and frost, that is, for all forms of water deposited ('precipitated') from the atmosphere [8]. It is measured by rain-gauges, i.e. calibrated receptacles, and expressed in millimetre per a time unit (mm/month, mm/day).

Values indicating the total precipitation for each month of the year (and as many years' average) would show the pattern of dry and wet seasons. Ever recorded maxima and minima would give an indication of the reliability of rains or deviations from the average.

The maximum rainfall for any 24-hour period is a useful guide for the predication of flooding, and for the design of surface drainage (roofs, paved areas, gutters and downpipes) the maximum hourly rainfall intensity (mm/h) should be known.

1.2.8 Driving rain

The building designer may want to know whether intense rains are associated with strong wings, in other words what is the likelihood of *driving rain* [9].

The driving rain index [10] characterises a given location and expresses the degree of exposure. It is the product of annual rainfall (in m) and the annual average wind velocity (in metres per second: m/s) – thus its dimension is m²/s. Up to 3 m²/s the location can be considered as 'sheltered'. The exposure is 'moderate' if the index is between 3 and 7 m²/s and 'severe' if over 7 m²/s.

Obviously this index only broadly classifies the given location, the actual rain penetration will depend on the instantaneous rain intensity and the simultaneous wind velocity.

1.2.9 Sky conditions

Sky conditions are usually described in terms of presence or absence of clouds. On average, two observations are made per day, when the proportion of sky covered by cloud is expressed as a percentage (some records give cloud cover in 'tenths' or even in 'eighths' or 'octets', e.g. 50%, five-tenths or four-eighths would all indicate that half of the sky hemisphere is covered by cloud). Few records exist of night-time sky conditions [11].

It would be useful for the designer to know the time of day and frequency of observations. A single average figure giving the sky conditions for a typical day of

* This is an instrument based on the moisture movement of human hair, which is proportionate to the relative humidity. The expansion and contraction of this is transmitted through a lever mechanism to a pen, which draws a continuous graph of humidity variation on a paper stretched over a clockwork-driven cylinder (see Fig 11).

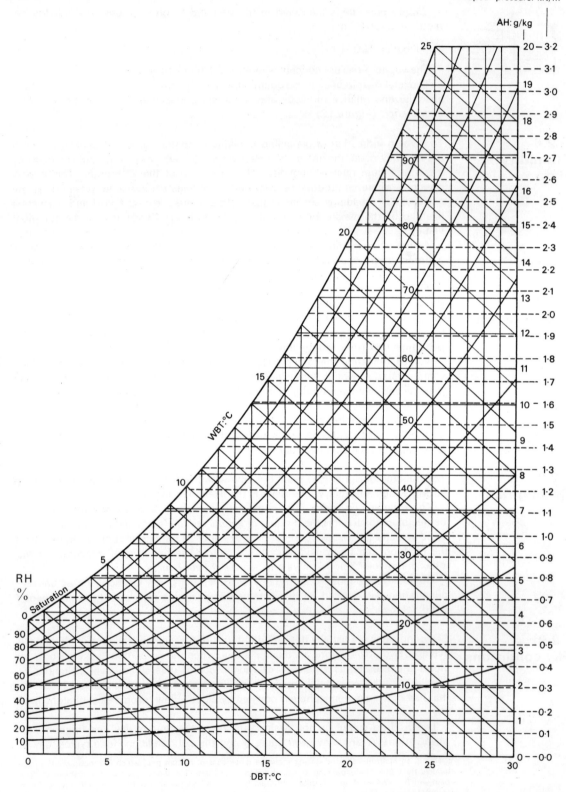

Vapour pressure: kN/m²

a given month may conceal significant differences, e.g. between morning and after-noon conditions, which may affect the design of roofs, overhangs and shading devices.

Sky luminance values are needed if daylighting in buildings is to be predicted.

1.2.10 Solar radiation: measurement

A simple *sunshine recorder* will register the duration of sunshine, which can be expressed in number of hours per day, as an average for each month.

A variety of more sophisticated instruments (solarimeter, heliometer, actino-meter and pyranometer) are used for the quantitative recording of solar radiation, but reliable and comparable data is few and far between. Much of the available literature gives recorded intensities in Btu/ft²h*, in kcal/m²h or in langleys (cal/cm²) per hour, but the now accepted international standard (SI) unit is the watt per metre square (W/m²). This is the instantaneous intensity, i.e. the incidence of energy in joules per square metre of the surface per second (W/m² = J/m²s, as W = J/s). Total radiation received over a longer period, one day, for instance, will be ex-pressed in J/m²day or the multiple MJ/m²day will be used (megajoule = 1 million joules) [12].

1.2.11 Solar radiation: data

Average daily amounts of solar radiation (MJ/m²day) for each month of the year would give a fair indication of climatic conditions, including seasonal variations. This could be supplemented by the highest and lowest daily totals for each month, to set the limits of variations which can be expected.

For the purposes of detailed design, hourly totals (MJ/m²h), or rather hourly average intensities (W/m²), must be known for a typical day of each month – or at least for a typically high and a typically low radiation day of the year.

Quantitative radiation data are not normally published by meteorological obser-vatories, but are sometimes available on request or can be found in special publica-tions [13]. The US Weather Bureau collects recordings of solar radiation intensity from all countries of the world.

Appendix 2 gives a series of protractors for the calculation of radiation intensities under clear sky conditions, to be used in conjunction with the stereographic sun-path diagrams. Appendix 3 gives a method for estimating daily radiation totals on the basis of sunshine duration records.

1.2.12 Wind: measurement

Wind velocity is measured by a cup-type or propeller *anemometer*, or by a *Pitot tube* (similar to the air-speed meters of aeroplanes), and its direction is measured by a wind vane. An *anemograph* can produce continuous recordings of wind velocity and directional changes.

Free wind velocities are normally recorded in open flat country at a height of 10 m [14]. Measurements in urban areas are often taken at a height of between 10 and 20 m to avoid obstructions. Velocities near the ground are a good deal lower than the free wind speed.

Directions can be grouped into eight or sixteen categories: the four cardinal (N., E., S. and W.) and four semi-cardinal compass points (NE., SE., SW. and NW.) and possibly the eight tertiary compass points (NNE., ENE., ESE., SSE., SSW., WSW., WNW. and NNW.). Velocities are measured in metres per second (m/s), but much data can still be found in obsolete units, such as ft/min, mph or knot (nautical mile per hour). A 'wind-force scale' developed by Beaufort in 1806, based on visual observation, is still in use in spite of its completely unscientific nature. The defini-tions of the twelve categories are given in appendix 4.

1.2.13 Wind: data

The designer must try to determine whether there is a prevailing direction of winds, whether predictable daily or seasonal shifts occur and whether there is a recognis-able pattern of daily or seasonal velocities. It is also important for him to note the calm periods in each month.

* For definition of units, see p. 69

All observatories record the occurrence of storms, hurricanes, typhoons or tornadoes. It is customary to tabulate winds according to their direction and velocity categories, in terms of their frequency of occurrence, over a significant time, generally 25 to 50 years.

Several methods of diagrammatic representation have been evolved, some of which are shown in Figures 13 and 14.

Fig 13
Monthly wind
frequency graph

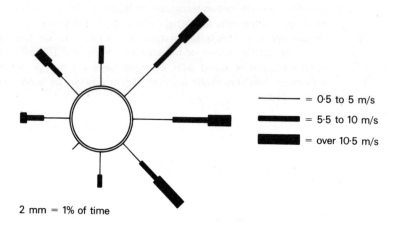

——— = 0·5 to 5 m/s

▬▬▬ = 5·5 to 10 m/s

████ = over 10·5 m/s

2 mm = 1% of time

1.2.14 Special characteristics

Most regions experience conditions which are particularly unfavourable, such as hail and thunder-storms, line or arched squalls, earthquakes, tornadoes, hurricanes and dust-storms. Although such events may be rare, it is important to extract from meteorological data their frequency, likely duration and nature. The designer must classify rare events into those which affect human comfort and those which may endanger the safety of buildings and the lives of inhabitants.

Discomfort — even if it impedes work or sleep — can be accepted if it is rare enough and lasts ohly for a few hours. Structural safety, on the other hand, must be guaranteed however infrequent the danger.

1.2.15 Vegetation

The picture of climate is incomplete without some notes on the character and abundance of plant life. Although generally regarded as a function of climate, vegetation can in its turn influence the local or site climate. It is an important element in the design of out-door spaces, providing sun-shading and protection from glare.

This section of the climatic survey may range from a few notes about local species of plant life to a lengthy compendium of the major native plants and trees — their shape and colour, also their preferred orientation and situation.

1.2.16 Graphic representation

It is not easy to understand the nature of a particular climate by merely looking at the vast amount of data published in the records of the nearest meteorological station. It is necessary to sort, summarise and simplify available data with reference to the objectives and requirements of climatic design. This is accomplished best by adopting a standardised method of graphic presentation. Figure 15 illustrates a graphic method that was developed especially to facilitate environmental design.

For the purposes of showing the diurnal variations of one climatic parameter (e.g. temperature) throughout the year, an isopleth chart can be used such as that shown in Figure 16.

Fig 14
Annual wind
frequencies (Nairobi)

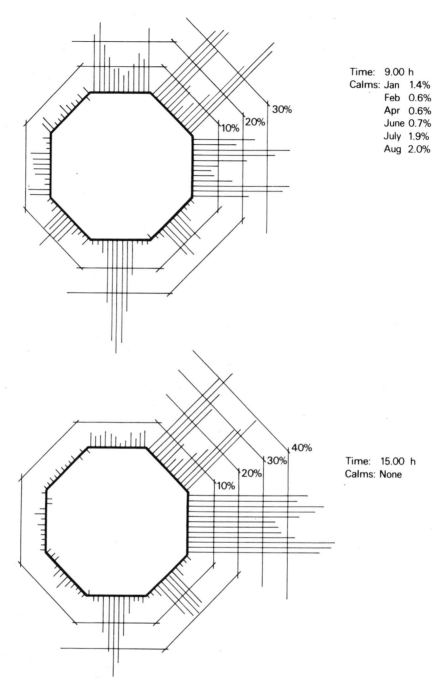

Time: 9.00 h
Calms: Jan 1.4%
            Feb 0.6%
            Apr 0.6%
            June 0.7%
            July 1.9%
            Aug 2.0%

Time: 15.00 h
Calms: None

To understand a new and unfamiliar climate one must relate it to a familiar one then measure and note essential differences. This is best done by using the standard graphic presentation first for the climate of one's own home-town and then for the strange climate being investigated. When the two graphs are placed side by side (or superimposed if one is transparent) similarities and differences become apparent and characteristic features can be identified. Even the comparison of simplified climate graphs (such as those shown in Figure 17) can reveal the most important differences.

Fig 15
Climate graph
(Nairobi) — tropical
upland climate

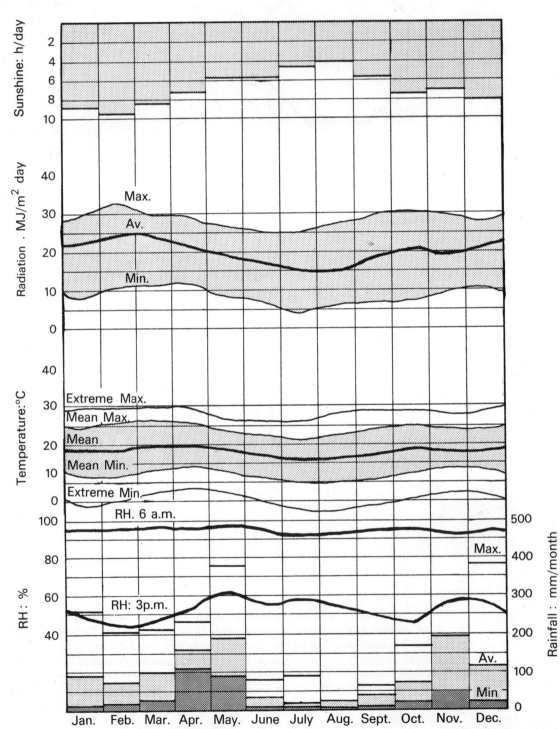

Fig 16
Temperature isopleths

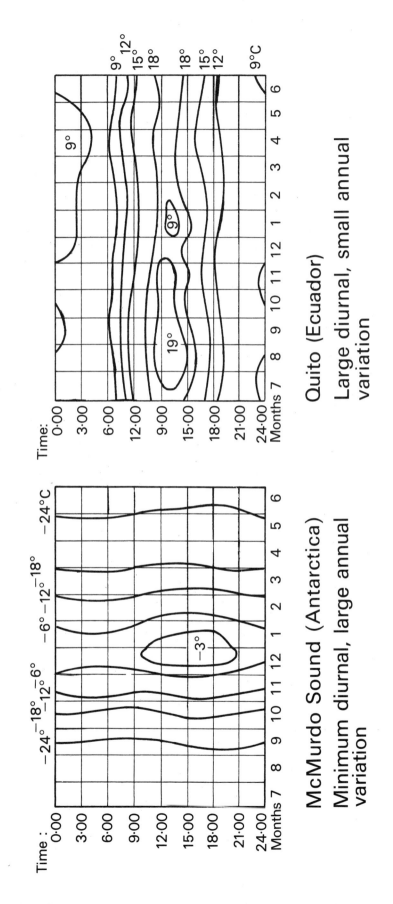

Quito (Ecuador)
Large diurnal, small annual variation

McMurdo Sound (Antarctica)
Minimum diurnal, large annual variation

Fig 17
Comparison of
climates

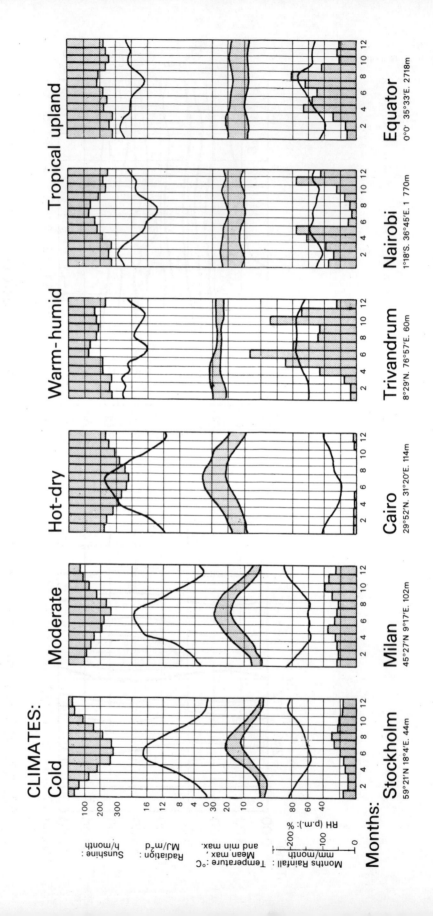

CLIMATES:

Cold — Stockholm 59°21'N 18°4'E. 44m

Moderate — Milan 45°27'N 9°17'E. 102m

Hot-dry — Cairo 29°52'N. 31°2'0'E. 114m

Warm-humid — Trivandrum 8°29'N. 76°57'E. 60m

Tropical upland — Nairobi 1°18'S. 36°45'E. 1 770m / Equator 0°0' 35°33'E. 2718m

Months:

Sunshine: h/month — 100 200 300

Radiation: MJ/m²d — 16 12 8 4 0

Temperature °C Mean max, and min max. — 30 20 10 0

Months Rainfall mm/month — 200 100

RH (p.m.): % — 80 60 40 0

1.3   Classification of tropical climates

1.3.1   Climatic zones
1.3.2   Tropical climates
1.3.3   Warm-humid climate
1.3.4   Warm-humid island climate
1.3.5   Hot-dry desert climate
1.3.6   Hot-dry maritime desert climate
1.3.7   Composite or monsoon climate
1.3.8   Tropical upland climate

**1.3.1
Climatic
zones**

The interaction of solar radiation with the atmosphere and the gravitational forces, together with the distribution of land and sea masses, produces an almost infinite variety of climates. However, certain zones and belts of approximately uniform climates can be distinguished. It is essential for the designer to be familiar with the character and location of these zones, as they are indicative of the climatic problems he is likely to encounter.

Boundaries of climatic zones cannot be accurately mapped. One zone merges gradually and almost imperceptibly into the next. It is, nevertheless, easy to identify the zone, or the transition area between two zones, to which a particular settlement belongs.

The present work concerns itself with tropical climatic zones only, as defined in 1.1.1. The subdivision of tropical climates into climatic zones should be looked upon as a useful tool of communication. It is a code that conveys a great deal of information for those who are familiar with it. Its usefulness increases with the increase of the number of people familiar with it, who accept and use it.

**1.3.2
Tropical
climates**

The classification given below was suggested by G A Atkinson in 1953. It has since been widely accepted and proven useful. The basis of this classification is given by the two atmospheric factors which dominantly influence human comfort: air temperature and humidity (as it will be shown in Section 2). The main criterion is: what extremes of these two factors are likely to cause discomfort. Accordingly the tropical regions of earth are divided into three major climatic zones and three subgroups:

1   Warm-humid equatorial climate – subgroup: warm-humid island or trade-wind climate

24 Fig 18
Climate graph
(Mombasa, Kenya) —
warm-humid climate

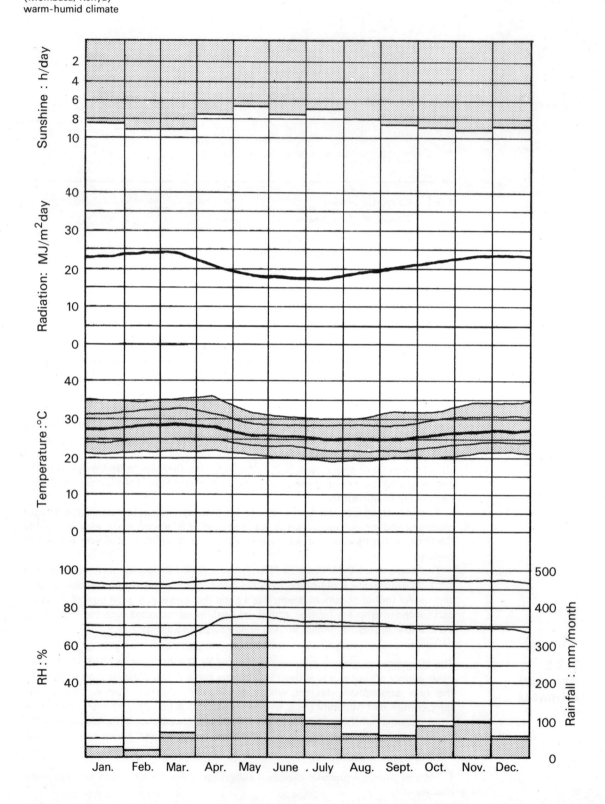

Fig 19
Climate graph
(Phoenix, Arizona) —
hot-dry desert climate

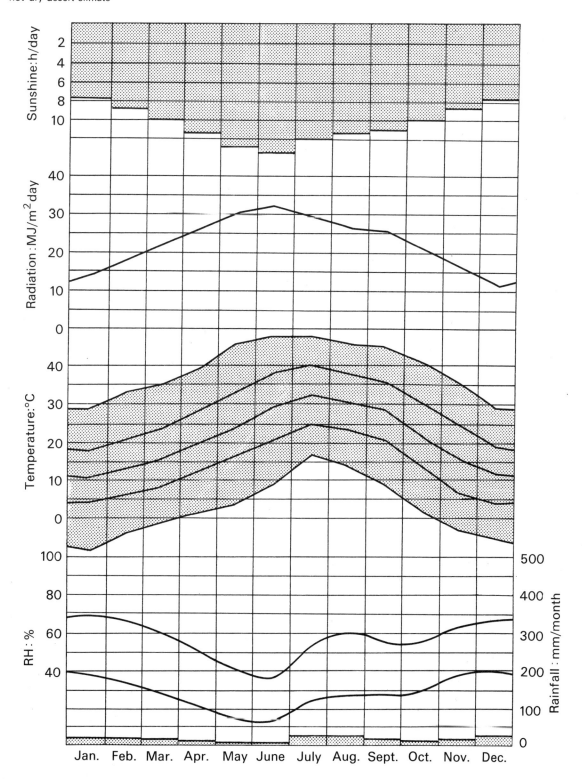

2   Hot-dry desert, or semi-desert climate – subgroup: hot-dry maritime desert climate

3   Composite or monsoon climate (combination of **1** and **2**) – subgroup: tropical upland climate

These groups are referred to throughout the text. Detailed description of each zone is given below (many of the values taken from Atkinson's publication) [15].

1.3.3 Warm-humid climate

Warm-humid climates are found in a belt near the Equator extending to about 15°N. and S. Examples of cities in this zone: Lagos, Dar-es-Salam, Mombasa, Colombo, Singapore, Jakarta, Quito and Pernambuco. Figure 18 shows a climate graph for Mombasa.

There is very little seasonal variation throughout the year, the only punctuation being that of periods with more or less rain and the occurrence of gusty winds and electric storms.

Air temperature, i.e. DBT, in the shade reaches a mean maximum during the day of between 27 and 32°C, but occasionally it may exceed the latter value. At night the mean minimum varies between 21 and 27°C. Both the diurnal and annual ranges of temperature are quite narrow.

Humidity, i.e. RH, remains high, at about 75% for most of the time, but it may vary from 55 to almost 100%. Vapour pressure is steady in the region of 2500 to 3000 N/m².

Precipitation is high throughout the year, generally becoming more intense for several consecutive months. Annual rainfall can vary from 2000 to 5000 mm and may exceed 500 mm in one month, the wettest month. During severe storms rain may fall at the rate of 100 mm/h for short periods.

Sky conditions are fairly cloudy throughout the year. Cloud cover varies between 60 and 90%. Skies can be bright, a luminance of 7000 cd/m² or even more when it is thinly overcast, or when the sun illuminates white cumulus clouds without itself being obscured. When heavily overcast, the sky is dull, 850 cd/m² or less.

Solar radiation is partly reflected and partly scattered by the cloud blanket or the high vapour content of the atmosphere, therefore the radiation reaching the ground is diffuse, but strong, and can cause painful sky glare. Cloud and vapour content also prevents or reduces outgoing radiation from the earth and sea to the night sky, thus the accumulated heat is not readily dissipated.

Wind velocities are typically low, calm periods are frequent, but strong winds can occur during rain squalls. Gusts of 30 m/s have been reported. There are usually one or two dominant directions.

Vegetation grows quickly due to frequent rains and high temperatures and it is difficult to control. The red or brown laterite soils are generally poor for agriculture. Plant-supporting organic substances and mineral salts are dissolved and washed away by rain-water. The subsoil water table is usually high and the ground may be waterlogged. Little light is reflected from the ground.

Special characteristics: high humidity accelerates mould and algal growth, rusting and rotting. Organic building materials tend to decay rapidly. Mosquitoes and other insects abound. The thunder-storms are accompanied by frequent air-to-air electrical discharges.

1.3.4 Warm-humid island climate

Islands within the equatorial belt and in the trade-winds zone belong to this climate type. Typical examples are the Caribbeans, the Philippines and other island groups in the Pacific Ocean.

Seasonal variations are negligible.

Air temperature, i.e. DBT, in the shade reaches a day-time mean maximum between 29 and 32°C and rarely rises above skin temperature. Night-time mean minima can be as low as 18°C, but it is normally between this figure and 24°C. The diurnal range is rarely more than 8 degC and the annual range is only about 14 degC.

Humidity, i.e. the RH, varies between 55 and almost 100%, the vapour pressure being between 1750 and 2500 N/m².

Precipitation is high, 1 250 to 1 800 mm per annum, and 200 to 250 mm in the wettest month. Up to 250 mm may fall in a single storm of a few hours' duration. Spray is driven nearly horizontally on windward coasts.

Sky conditions are normally clear or filled with white broken clouds of high brightness, except during storms, when the skies are dark and dull. Clear blue skies are of low luminance, between 1 700 and 2 500 cd/m².

Solar radiation is strong and mainly direct, with a very small diffuse component when the sky is clear, but varies with the cloud cover.

Winds: the predominant trade-wind blows at a steady 6 to 7 m/s and provides relief from heat and humidity. Much higher velocities occur during cyclones (see below).

Vegetation is less luxuriant and of a lighter green colour than in the warm-humid zones. It varies with the rainfall. Sunlight reflected from light coloured coral, sand and rock can be very bright. The soil is often dry with a fairly low water-table.

Special characteristics are the tropical cyclones or hurricanes with wind velocities from 45 to 70 m/s, which constitute a serious seasonal hazard. The high salt content of the atmosphere encourages corrosion in coastal areas.

1.3.5
Hot-dry
desert climate

These climates occur in two belts at latitudes between approximately 15 and 30° north and south of the Equator. Examples of settlements in this zone: Assuan, Baghdad, Alice Springs, and Phoenix. Figure 19 shows a climate graph for the last-named.

Two marked seasons occur: a hot and a somewhat cooler period.

Air temperature, i.e. DBT, in the shade rises quickly after sunrise to a day-time mean maximum of 43 to 49°C. The ever-recorded maximum temperature of 58°C was measured in Libya in 1922. During the cool season the mean maximum temperature ranges from 27 to 32°C. Night-time mean minima are between 24 and 30°C in the hot season and between 10 and 18°C in the cool season. The diurnal range is very great: 17 to 22 degC.

Humidity, i.e. the RH, varies from 10 to 55%, as the wet-bulb depression is large (rapid evaporation). The vapour pressure is normally between 750 and 1 500 N/m².

Precipitation is slight and variable throughout the year, from 50 to 155 mm per annum. Flash-storms may occur over limited areas with as much as 50 mm rain in a few hours, but some regions may not have any rain for several years.

Sky conditions are normally clear. Clouds are few due to the low humidity of the air. The sky is usually dark blue, with a luminance of 1 700 to 2 500 cd/m², and further darkened during dust or sand-storms to 850 cd/m² or even less. Towards the end of the hot period, dust suspended in the air may create a white haze, with a luminance of 3 500 to 10 000 cd/m², which produces a diffuse light and a painful glare.

Solar radiation is direct and strong during the day, but the absence of cloud permits easy release of the heat stored during the day-time in the form of long-wave radiation towards the cold night sky. Diffuse radiation is only present during dust haze periods.

Winds are usually local. The heating of air over the hot ground causes a temperature inversion, and as the lower warm air mass breaks through the higher cooler air, local whirlwinds are often created. Winds are hot, carrying dust and sand — and often develop into dust-storms.

Vegetation is sparse and difficult to maintain because of the lack of rain and low humidities. The soil is usually dusty and very dry. Strong sunlight illuminating a highly reflective light coloured and dry ground can create a luminance of 20 000 to 25 000 cd/m². Soils dry quickly after rain and would generally be fertile if irrigated. The subsoil water-table is very low.

Special characteristics: during certain months dust and sand-storms may be frequent. The high day-time temperatures and rapid cooling at night may cause materials to crack and break up.

1.3.6 Hot-dry maritime desert climate

Maritime desert climates occur in the same latitude belts as the hot-dry desert climates, where the sea adjoins a large land mass. These are regarded to be amongst the most unfavourable climates of the earth. Typical examples are Kuwait, Antofagasta and Karachi.

There are two seasons: a hot one and somewhat cooler one.

Air temperature, i.e. DBT, in the shade reaches a day-time mean maximum of about 38°C, but in the cool season it remains between 21 and 26°C. The night-time mean minimum temperatures of the hot season range from 24 to 30°C and of the cool season from 10 to 18°C. The diurnal mean range varies between 9 and 12 degC, the larger diurnal variation occurring during the cool season.

Humidity, i.e. the RH, is steadily high, between 50 and 90%, with vapour pressures of 1 500 to 2 500 N/m², as the strong solar radiation causes strong evaporation from the sea. The moisture is, however, not precipitated but remains suspended in the air, creating intensely uncomfortable conditions.

Precipitation, as in other desert regions, is very low.

Sky conditions are as for hot-dry desert climates, a little more cloud may occur in the form of a thin, transparent haze, which is likely to cause glare.

Solar radiation is strong, with a higher diffuse component than in desert climates, due to the thin clouds and suspended moisture.

Winds are mostly local, coastal winds, caused by the unequal heating and cooling of land and sea surfaces. These tend to blow off the sea towards the land during the day and in the reverse direction during the night.

Vegetation is sparse, not more than some dry grass. The ground and rocks are brown or red; it is dry and dusty throughout the year. Ground glare can be intense.

Special characteristics: dust and sand-storms may occur. The salt laden atmosphere accelerates corrosion.

1.3.7 Composite or monsoon climate

These climates usually occur in large land masses near the tropics of Cancer and Capricorn, which are sufficiently far from the Equator to experience marked seasonal changes in solar radiation and wind direction. Examples of cities with composite climates: Lahore, Mandalay, Asuncion, Kano and New Delhi. The latter is shown as an example in Figure 20.

Two seasons occur normally. Approximately two-thirds of the year is hot-dry and the other third is warm-humid. Localities further north and south often have a third season, best described as cool-dry.

Air temperature, i.e. DBT, in the shade is as follows:

seasons	hot-dry	warm-humid	cool-dry
Day-time mean max.	32–43°C	27–32°C	up to 27°C
Night-time mean min.	21–27°C	24–27°C	4–10°C
Diurnal mean range	11–22 degC	3–6 degC	11–22 degC

Humidity, i.e. the RH, is low throughout the dry periods at 20 to 55%, with a vapour pressure of 1 300 to 1 600 N/m². During the wet period it rises to 55 to 95%, with a vapour pressure of 2 000 to 2 500 N/m².

Precipitation: the monsoon rains are intense and prolonged; occasionally 25 to 38 mm can fall in an hour. Annual rainfall varies from 500 to 1 300 mm with 200 to 250 mm in the wettest month. There is little or no rain during the dry seasons.

Sky conditions markedly vary with the seasons. The sky is heavily overcast and dull during the monsoons, and clear, with a dark blue colour, in the dry seasons. Towards the end of the hot-dry seasons the sky becomes brighter with frequent dust haze. The intensity of sky glare varies accordingly.

Solar radiation alternates between conditions found in the warm-humid and the hot-dry desert climates.

Winds are hot and dusty during the dry period. Directional changes in the prevailing winds at the beginning of the warm-humid season bring rain-clouds and humid air from the sea. Monsoon winds are fairly strong and steady.

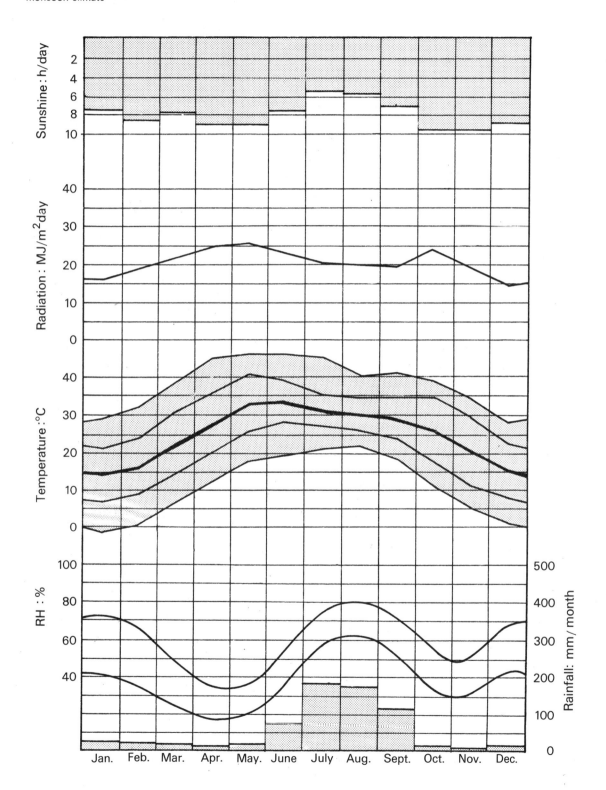

Fig 20
Climate graph (New
Delhi) — composite or
monsoon climate

Vegetation, which is sparse — characteristic of a hot-dry region — with brown and red barren ground, changes rapidly and dramatically with the rain. The landscape becomes green and fertile within a few days. Plants grow quickly. In the cooler period vegetation covers the ground, but diminishes as the temperature rises. The soil is damp during the rains but it dries out quickly. There is a risk of soil erosion during monsoons. In the dry season strong ground glare may be experienced.

Special characteristics: seasonal changes in relative humidity cause rapid weakening of building materials. Dust and sand-storms may occur. Termites are common. Occasional condensation problems.

1.3.8 Tropical upland climate

Mountainous regions and plateaux more than 900 to 1 200 m above sea-level experience such climates, between the two 20°C isotherms. Examples of cities in such regions: Addis Ababa, Bogota, Mexico City and Nairobi. A climate graph for Nairobi has been given in Figure 15.

Seasonal variations are small in upland climates near the Equator, but when further away from the Equator, the seasons follow those of the nearby lowlands.

Air temperature, i.e. the DBT, in the shade decreases with altitude. At an altitude of 1 800 m the day-time mean maxima may range from 24 to 30°C and the night-time mean minima are around 10 to 13°C. At some locations it may fall below 4°C and ground frost is not uncommon. The diurnal range is great. The annual range depends on latitude: at the Equator it is slight; but at the tropics of Cancer and Capricorn it may be 11 to 20 degC.

Humidity, i.e. the RH, varies between 45 and 99% and the vapour pressure between 800 and 1 600 N/m².

Precipitation is variable, but rarely less than 1 000 mm. Rain often falls in heavy concentrated showers, reaching an intensity of 80 mm per hour.

Sky conditions are normally clear or partly cloudy, to the extent of about 40%. During the monsoon rains the sky is overcast — and the clouds are heavy and low.

Solar radiation is strong and direct during the clear periods, stronger than at the same latitude, but at sea-level. Ultra-violet radiation especially is stronger than at lower altitudes. It becomes more diffuse as cloud cover increases.

Winds are variable, predominantly north-east and south-easterlies, but may be drastically deflected by local topography. Wind velocity rarely exceeds 15 m/s.

Vegetation is green although not very luxuriant during the wet season but it may wither in the dry season, when the ground can turn brown or red. The soil may be damp in the rains but dries quickly.

Special characteristics: heavy dew at night. Strong radiation loss at night during the dry season, which may lead to the formation of radiation fog. Thunder-storms with a fair proportion of electric discharges — air to ground. Hail may also occur.

1.4.1 Deviations within the zone

Knowledge of the climatic zone to which a town or settlement belongs and possession of published regional climatic data does not eliminate the need for careful investigation of site climatic conditions. It does, however, usually provide enough information for the designer to make a preliminary assessment of the climate and may be sufficient to form the basis of sketch designs.

Every city, town or village and even a precinct in a town may have its own climate, slightly different from the climate described for the region – the *macroclimate*. Information published by the nearest meteorological observatory describes the macroclimate. Such information may be a useful guide to the climate of the site, but is seldom sufficient in accuracy as conditions can vary considerably within a short distance from the point of observation.

1.4.2 Site climate

The term 'site climate' has been chosen deliberately rather than the synonymously-used term 'microclimate'. The latter can imply any local deviation from the climate of a larger area, whatever the scale may be. The botanist may consider the 'microclimate' of a single plant leaf, with its temperature and moisture conditions, its population of insects and micro-organisms, on the scale of a few centimetres. For the urban geographer the term 'microclimate' may mean the climate of a whole town.

'Site climate' establishes the scale: whatever the size of the project, it implies the climate of the area available and is to be used for the given purpose, both in horizontal extent and in height.

1.4.3
The designer's task

If a large site is available, the first task of the designer is to identify the area most suitable for habitation. In all cases, however, he must design the building(s) in such a way as to take advantage of the favourable and mitigate the adverse characteristics of the site and its climatic features.

The opportunity is rarely given to carry out on site observations and measurements for any length of time. The best approach is to start with regional data and assess the likely deviations. Valuable advice may be obtained from an expert, an experienced observer, who may be able to predict climatic deviations on the basis of visual inspection of the site. For a large project it is certainly worthwhile to seek expert advice, as many users of the building may have to endure the consequences of climatic design decisions for a long time.

The nature and extent of climatic deviations — also the likely effects of the intended building — should be assessed early in the design stage, before one is committed to a certain solution which may later prove to be difficult to rectify.

It is the purpose of the present section to give an understanding of local factors, which should enable the reader to make his own assessment of a given site climate with reasonable accuracy.

1.4.4
Local factors

The factors governing the climate of a zone have been surveyed in the previous sections. Factors which may cause local deviation from this are:

Topography, i.e. slope, orientation, exposure, elevation, hills or valleys, at or near the site.

Ground surface, whether natural or man-made, its reflectance, permeability and the soil temperature, as these affect vegetation and this in turn affects the climate (woods, shrubs, grass, paving, water, etc.).

Three-dimensional objects, such as trees, or tree-belts, fences, walls and buildings, as these may influence air movement, may cast a shadow and may subdivide the area into smaller units with distinguishable climatic features.

A logical method will be to follow the sequence of climatic elements examined in the previous section and see how each of these may be affected by the above mentioned factors.

1.4.5
Air temperature

At any point near the ground the air temperature is dependent upon the amount of heat gained or lost at the earth's surface and any other surfaces with which the air has recently been in contact.

Heat exchange at surfaces varies between night and day, with the season, latitude and the time of year, always influenced by the amount of cloud cover.

During the day, as surfaces are heated by solar radiation, the air nearest to the ground acquires the highest temperature. In calm conditions the air within 2 m of the ground remains stratified in layers of differing temperatures. Mixing of the hotter and cooler layers takes place as the heat build-up of the lowest layer becomes great enough to cause an upward eddy of warmer, lighter air [16].

At night, particularly on clear nights, the ground loses much heat by radiation and soon after sunset its temperature falls below that of the air. The direction of heat flow is reversed: from the air to the ground. The lowest layer of air becomes cooler. Figure 21 shows the typical diurnal changes at various heights.

1.4.6
Temperature inversion

This phenomenon is referred to as *temperature inversion*, as the day-time situation of decreasing temperature with increase of height is taken as normal. This is a much more stable situation than the 'normal' day-time temperature strata — there are no thermal forces tending to cause disturbances or upward eddies.

Cold air tends to settle in the deepest depressions and behaves as a liquid. It does not flow quite as readily as water, rather like a highly viscous liquid. If it flows down the hill and along the floor of a long, sloping valley it can add up to a 'katabatic wind': a concentrated and accelerating flow of a cold mass of air [17].

Fig 21
Formation of
temperature inversion

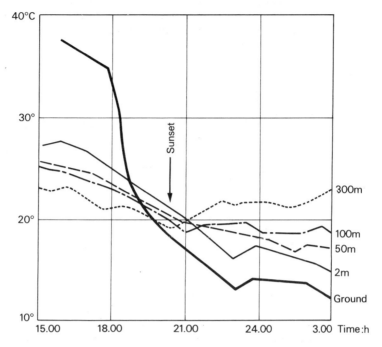

Topography can thus strongly influence air temperature [18], a difference of 7 to 8 m in height can cause a difference of 5 to 6 °C in air temperature, under still air conditions.

1.4.7 Humidity

The relative humidity depends as much on the air temperature as on the actual amount of water vapour present in the air.

During the day, as the lowest layer of air is being heated by the ground surface, its RH is rapidly decreased. With a lower RH the rate of evaporation is increased, if there is water available to be evaporated. An open surface of water or rich vegetation would provide an abundant supply of water – in such a case strong evaporation would increase the AH of the lower layers of air. The following situation is likely to arise, if the air is still:

	at ground	*at 2 m*
Temperature	high	lower
Relative humidity	low	higher
Absolute humidity	high	lower

With air movement the rate of evaporation is increased, but with the mixing of air the temperature and humidity differences tend to be evened out.

At night the situation is reversed. Especially on a clear night with still air, as the lowest layer (of the highest AH) cools, its RH increases, the point of saturation is soon reached and with further cooling the excess moisture condenses out in the form of *dew* (hence the term 'dewpoint').

When the dewpoint temperature is reached the formation of fog will start, and if there is no further rapid cooling and no air movement, a deep layer (up to 40 to 50 m) of fog can develop near the ground.

1.4.8 Precipitation

When moisture bearing winds occur frequently from the same direction, the effect of hills on rainfall patterns can be very pronounced. Where the ground changes level by more than 300 m, the windward slope can be expected to receive a rainfall more

34

than the regional average, and the leeward slope correspondingly less (Figure 22). With the increase of height or steepness of the hill formation, the effect will be more pronounced. In an extreme case it can happen that on a large site located on the top of a hill and extending down to both slopes, the leeward half receives only 25% of the rain received by the windward side.

Fig 22
Precipitation on hills

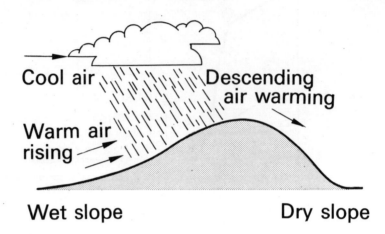

The cause of the above phenomenon is that the hill forces the air mass to rise, as it rises it cools and can no longer support the moisture carried. Conversely, a descending air mass increases in temperature and it can absorb more moisture, rather than to precipitate any. A similar situation can develop over towns, where the more absorbent surfaces reach a high temperature and can produce an upward air movement. Such an upward current may divert any horizontal air movement in an upward direction, with similar effects to a hill slope.

Fig 23
Precipitation over towns

Actually a number of workers have reported a higher frequency of rains of the cloudburst type over city centres (Figure 23). (A factor contributing to this, may be the presence of solid particles in urban atmospheres.) If rainfall generally occurs associated with high wind velocities, resulting in 'driving rain', the effect will be more pronounced on the windward side than on the leeward slope, as explained by the parallelogram of forces in Figure 24.

**1.4.9
Sky
conditions**

Normally sky conditions do not vary perceptibly over short distances, unless there is an abrupt and considerable change in topography, which may lead to an almost permanent cloud formation. The flag-like permanent cloud on the leeward side of the Rock of Gibraltar is a good example, but it is rather rare.

Fig 24
Driving rain
parallelograms

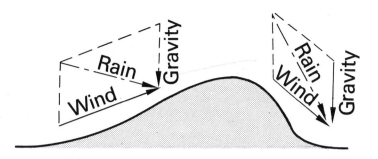

1.4.10
Solar radiation

The amount of solar radiation may be influenced by local factors three ways:

1 the intensity on a theoretical horizontal plane above the ground is affected by local variations in the *transparency of the atmosphere*. Atmospheric pollution, smoke, smog or dust and local cloud formations can produce substantial reductions
2 the intensity on the actual ground surface is influenced by the *slope and orientation* of the site, this effect being negligible around the Equator, but increasingly important towards higher latitudes. At mid-latitudes a site sloping towards the pole will receive much less radiation than one sloping towards the Equator
3 the daily total amount of radiation may also be influenced by the slope (later sunrise and earlier sunset for a northern slope on the northern hemisphere) but also by nearby *hills* or even *trees* and existing *buildings*, which may cast a shadow over the site at certain times of the day. This effect is most pronounced when such obstructions lie on the east or west of the site. When the sun is on these sides, it is at low angle and casts a long shadow

Radiation on a vertical building surface will be affected by *its* orientation, but not by the slope and orientation of the site. The factors under **1** and **3** above will still show an effect.

The magnitude of thermal effects of such incident radiation will, of course, depend on the surface qualities of the recipient ground or objects (see 1.4.5). If it is vegetation, some of the solar energy is converted into chemical energies and the heating is also mitigated by evaporation, but a stone, concrete or especially an asphalt surface can reach a temperature up to 44 degC higher than the surrounding air temperature.

1.4.11
Air movement

Wind speed can be reduced after a long horizontal barrier by 50% at a distance of ten times the height and by 25% at a distance of twenty times the height. In addition to this, air flowing across any surface is subject to frictional effects. The type of ground cover affects the wind speed gradient. Near the ground the wind speed is always less than higher up, but with an uneven ground cover the rate of increase in speed with height is much more than with an unbroken smooth surface, such as water (Figure 25).

On a hilly site the greatest wind speeds will be experienced at the crests of hills. Small valleys and depressions will normally experience low velocities, except in cases where the direction of the valley coincides with the direction of wind. The more pronounced the form of the valley, the greater is its effect both in sheltering the valley floor from cross-winds and in funnelling the parallel winds. The effect of long, tall slabs or rows of buildings may be similar to this.

In regions where wind can provide a welcome relief from sultry heat, the crests and windward slopes are preferable as building sites to the leeward sides of hills.

The day-time heating of air over barren ground often gives rise to local thermal winds, especially in hot-dry regions. These may be whirlwinds or local breezes, normally hot and carrying fine dust. Observations can usually reveal a pattern of their course during certain seasons of the year.

Large stretches of water can give rise to local coastal breezes. On-shore breezes (from water to land) during the day may lower the maximum temperature by as

36 Fig 25
Wind velocity
gradients

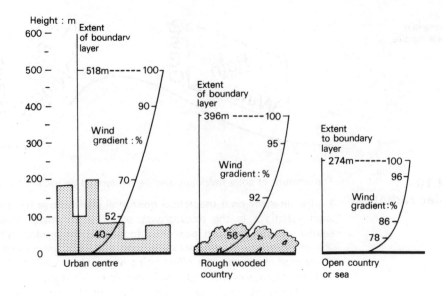

much as 10 degC, but are likely to increase the humidity. On lake shores these breezes are rarely effective beyond about 400 m inland, but on the sea coast the effect may reach much further inland if topography is favourable [9].

**1.4.12
Special
characteristics**

Thunder-storms are macroclimatic phenomena, but local topography can influence their path, their intensity and even their frequency. Local features particularly affect the accompanying electrical phenomena. Tops of hills are mostly subjected to lightning strikes and a tall building, which is the highest object of a large area, even on level ground, may be an attractive target for lightning. Precautionary measures must be taken accordingly.

Dust and sand-storms are influenced by local factors, both by the ground surface providing sand and dust to be carried by the wind, and by topography in funnelling or diverting the wind or by causing local eddies. Sand is only drifting along the surface even in strong winds, so small barriers will effectively stop its movement. It will be deposited at locations where the wind speed is reduced or where local turbulences or eddies are formed. Smaller dust particles being in suspension in the air stream are carried more freely and may reach a height of 1 500 m or more. Dust-storms of this magnitude are macroclimatic phenomena, not directly affected by local factors. Their effect is most adverse in positions exposed to high wind velocities. Barriers, natural or artificial, can provide adequate protection, but will exclude the possibility of utilising the air movement for cooling purposes.

Smaller dust-storms of the 'willy-willy' type may be generated on quite a small scale. At the time of maximum solar heating (14.00 to 15.00 h) the lowest and hottest layer of air may burst through the overlaying cooler air with violent suddenness in the form of a whirlwind and carry much dust with it. Both the birth and the path of such whirlwinds can depend on small-scale local features: topography and surface qualities.

Earthquakes, although not strictly climatic phenomena, must be considered here. They mostly occur in well-defined areas – seismic zones. Macroseismic information is available everywhere and, even in the absence of local instrumental recordings, in the light of geological evidence (e.g. location of fault lines), the seismic danger zones can be pinpointed on quite a small scale. 'Isoseismal maps', i.e. maps showing lines of equal earthquake risk, are available in many locations. If not, and if the given site is in or near a major seismic zone, expert advice should be sought, either regarding the least risky part of a large site or just to establish the degree of risk, so that appropriate precautionary measures can be taken.

1.4.13
Vegetation

Trees and vegetation form an intermediate layer between the earth's surface and the atmosphere. Their moderating effect on the site climate has already been referred to in the context of air temperature, humidity, radiation and air movement. By covering the ground with vegetation, the surface of contact is transferred to a higher layer and is increased four to twelve times. In all hot and dry regions of the earth the beneficial climatic effect of even the lightest plant cover is quite considerable.

Valuable information for siting and landscaping can be obtained from the observation of existing vegetation. With a working knowledge of the soil, water, sun and wind requirements of common plants, the designer should be able to identify the major areas of differences in site climate, as indicated by the existing vegetation.

1.4.14
Urban climate

Man-made environments can create microclimates of their own, deviating from the macroclimate of the region to a degree depending on the extent of man's intervention. Such intervention with the natural environment is greatest in large towns or cities, thus it is justifiable to speak of an 'urban climate'.

The factors causing deviations of the urban climate from the regional macroclimate are the following:

a *changed surface qualities* (pavements and buildings) – increased absorbance of solar radiation; reduced evaporation
b *buildings* – casting a shadow and acting as barriers to winds, but also channelling winds possibly with localised increase in velocity or by storing absorbed heat in their mass and slowly releasing it at night
c *energy seepage* – through walls and ventilation of heated buildings; the output of refrigeration plants and air conditioning (removing heat from the controlled space to the outside air); heat output of internal combustion engines and electrical appliances; heat loss from industry, especially furnaces and large factories
d *atmospheric pollution* – waste products of boilers and domestic and industrial chimneys; exhaust from motor-cars; fumes and vapours, which both tend to reduce direct solar radiation but increase the diffuse radiation and provide a barrier to outgoing radiation. The presence of solid particles in urban atmosphere may assist in the formation of fog and induce rainfall under favourable conditions

The extent of deviations may be quite substantial.

Air temperature in a city can be 8 degC higher than in the surrounding countryside and a difference of 11 degC has been reported.

Relative humidity is reduced by 5 to 10%, due to the quick run-off of rain-water from paved areas, to the absence of vegetation and to higher temperature.

Wind velocity can be reduced to less than half of that in the adjoining open country, but the funnelling effect along a closely built-up street or through gaps between tall slab blocks can more than double the velocity. Strong turbulences and eddies can also be set up at the leeward corners of obstructions.

1.4.15
Site climatic
data

Data relating to the regional macroclimate is available almost everywhere. A method of summarising such data in graphic and tabulated form has been given in 1.2.16.

Rarely will similarly reliable measured data be available for a given site. As the climatic parameters for a site are the same as for a region, it is best to start with the summary of regional data and, in a subsequent step, examine which of the parameters will be affected by local specific factors and what the extent of such deviations is likely to be. The climate graph and the values included in the tables can be changed accordingly. Where such deviations are not certain, this fact can be shown.

In most cases the regional data may be used with only some qualitative remarks regarding local deviations. This may be quite satisfactory, as the conclusions to be drawn from such information will most often be qualitative only.

Section 2   Comfort: The desirable conditions

2.1.1 Introduction

Our daily life cycle comprises states of activity, fatigue and recovery. It is essential that the mind and body recovers through recreation, rest and sleep to counterbalance the mental and physical fatigue resulting from activities of the day [19]. This cycle can be and is often impeded by unfavourable climatic conditions and the resulting stress on body and mind causes discomfort, loss of efficiency and may eventually lead to a breakdown of health. The effect of climate on man, is therefore, a factor of considerable importance [20].

The task of the designer is to create the best possible indoor climate (it is not feasible to regulate out-door conditions). The occupants of a building judge the quality of the design from a physical as well as an emotional point of view. Accumulated sensations of well-being or discomfort contribute to our total verdict on the house in which we live and the school, office or factory where we work. It is a challenge for the designer to strive towards the optimum of total comfort, which may be defined as the sensation of complete physical and mental well-being. Considerable information has by now been published on the physical side; but far less on the emotional aspects of our environment.

Criteria of total comfort depend upon each of the human senses. In the following paragraphs, while the subjective-emotional relationships with our environment may be mentioned, the main emphasis is placed upon human thermal comfort, which is the dominant problem in tropical climates. The physiological responses to specific climatic conditions, here described, can be verified by controlled experiments.

Interest in establishing thermal comfort criteria dates back in Europe about 150 years, to the beginning of the nineteenth century, when it started with the movement for the reform of conditions in industry and housing. Basic warmth criteria were first established in the mining, metal and textile industries, as accidents and illness due to heat and humidity stresses were formerly quite common.

Human response to the thermal environment does not depend on air temperature alone. It has been established beyond doubt that air temperature, humidity, radiation and air movement all produce thermal effects, and must be considered simultaneously if human responses are to be predicted. To appreciate the effect of these climatic factors, it is necessary to examine briefly the basic thermal processes of the human body.

2.1.2 The body's heat production

Heat is continuously produced by the body. Most of the biochemical processes involved in tissue-building, energy conversion and muscular work are exotherm, i.e. heat producing. All energy and material requirements of the body are supplied from the consumption and digestion of food. The processes involved in converting foodstuff into living matter and useful form of energy are known as *metabolism* [20].

The total metabolic heat production can be divided into *basal metabolism*, i.e. the heat production of vegetative, automatic processes which are continuous, and the *muscular metabolism*, i.e. the heat production of muscles whilst carrying out consciously controlled work. Of all the energy produced in the body, only about 20% is utilised, the remaining 80% is 'surplus' heat and must be dissipated to the environment.

This excess heat production varies with the overall metabolic rate, and depends on the activity. The following table indicates the rate of excess heat output of the body in various activities.

Activity	watts
Sleeping	min. 70
Sitting, moderate movement, e.g. typing	130–160
Standing, light work at machine or bench	160–190
Sitting, heavy arm and leg movements	190–230
Standing, moderate work, some walking	220–290
Walking, moderate lifting or pushing	290–410
Intermittent heavy lifting, digging	440–580
Hardest sustained work	580–700
Maximum heavy work for 30-minutes duration	max. 1100

(Average values of data published in many sources)

2.1.3 The body's heat loss

The deep body temperature must remain balanced and constant around 37 °C. In order to maintain body temperature at this steady level, all surplus heat must be dissipated to the environment [21]. If there is some form of simultaneous heat gain from the environment (e.g. solar radiation or warm air) that also must be dissipated.

The body can release heat to its environment by convection, radiation and evaporation – and to a lesser extent by conduction (Figure 26) [22].

Convection is due to heat transmission from the body to the air in contact with the skin or clothing which then rises and is replaced by cooler air. The rate of convective heat loss is increased by a faster rate of air movement, by a lower air temperature and a higher skin temperature.

Radiant heat loss depends on the temperature of the body surface and the temperature of opposing surfaces.

Evaporation heat loss is governed by the rate of evaporation, which in turn depends on the humidity of air (the dryer the air, the faster the evaporation) and on the amount of moisture available for evaporation. Evaporation takes place in the lungs through breathing, and on the skin as imperceptible perspiration and sweat.

Fig 26
Body heat exchange

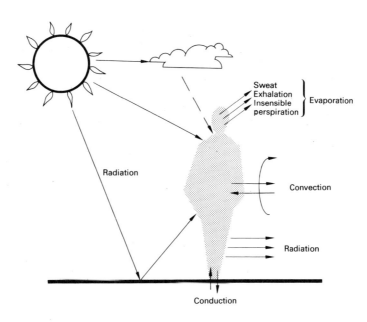

Sweat
Exhalation
Insensible
perspiration } Evaporation

Radiation

Convection

Radiation

Conduction

Conduction depends on the temperature difference between the body surface and the object the body is in direct contact with.

2.1.4 Regulatory mechanisms

The thermal balance of the body is shown by Figure 27 [22] and can be expressed by an equation. If the heat gain and heat loss factors are:

Gain: Met = metabolism (basal and muscular)
Cnd = conduction (contact with warm bodies)
Cnv = convection (if the air is warmer than the skin)
Rad = radiation (from the sun, the sky and hot bodies)

Loss: Cnd = conduction (contact with cold bodies)
Cnv = convection (if the air is cooler than the skin)
Rad = radiation (to night sky and cold surfaces)
Evp = evaporation (of moisture and sweat)

then thermal balance exists when

$$\text{Met} - \text{Evp} \pm \text{Cnd} \pm \text{Cnv} \pm \text{Rad} = 0$$

Fig 27
Thermal balance of
the body

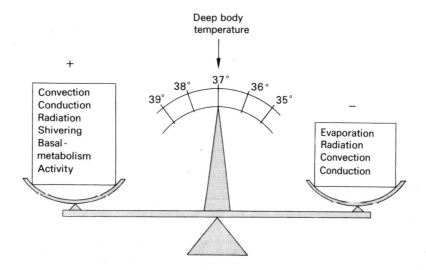

Deep body
temperature

+

Convection
Conduction
Radiation
Shivering
Basal-
metabolism
Activity

39° 38° 37° 36° 35°

−

Evaporation
Radiation
Convection
Conduction

As soon as this sum is more than zero, *vasomotor* adjustments will take place: blood circulation to the skin surface is increased, more heat is transported to the surface and the skin temperature is elevated — all forms of heat loss processes are accelerated. Conversely, if the sum of the above equation is less than zero, the blood circulation to the skin is reduced, skin temperature is lowered and the heat loss processes are slowed down.

If the vasomotor regulation is still insufficient, and overheating continues, sweating will start. The rate of sweating may vary from about 20 g/h to 3 kg/h during periods of physical effort combined with hot environmental effects [23].*

If, in a cold environment, underheating continues in spite of vasomotor adjustments, violent shivering may occur, which can cause a ten-fold increase in metabolic heat production for short periods.

Long-term, endocrine adjustments constitute the acclimatisation process. These may involve the change in the basal metabolic heat production, an increase in the quantity of blood (to produce and maintain a constant vaso-dilation) and an increase in sweat rate.

2.1.5
Heat loss in various thermal environments

In classifying tropical climates into six categories (1.3.2) and in discussing deviations of the site climate, the importance of the four basic factors has been emphasised which would directly affect human comfort, namely: air temperature, humidity, air movement and radiation. The importance of these factors should now be obvious: each influences in some way the heat exchange processes between the human body and its environment; each may aid or impede the dissipation of surplus heat from the body. For example, high air temperature is a definite obstacle to heat dissipation by convection (it may even produce a heat input, if warmer than the skin), and simultaneous high humidity may impede the heat loss by evaporation [24].

The following paragraphs will examine how these four climatic variables affect the heat dissipation processes of the human body for various indoor conditions.

2.1.6
Calm, warm air, moderate humidity

In a temperate climate, indoors, when the air temperature is around 18 °C, when the air is calm, i.e. air velocity does not exceed 0·25 m/s, and when the humidity is between 40 and 60%, a person engaged in sedentary work will dissipate the surplus heat without any difficulty, in the following ways:

by radiation   45%
by convection 30%
by evaporation 25%

if the temperature of bounding surfaces is approximately the same as the air temperature [25].

2.1.7
Hot air and considerable radiation

The normal skin temperature is between 31 and 34 °C. As the air temperature approaches skin temperature, convective heat loss gradually decreases. Vasomotor regulation will increase the skin temperature to the higher limit (34 °C), but when the air temperature reaches this point, there will be no more convective heat loss.

As long as the average temperature of opposing surfaces is below skin temperature, there will be some radiation heat loss, but as the surface temperature increases, radiation losses are diminished. Radiant heat from the sun or a hot body (a radiator or fire) can be a substantial heat gain factor.

When both the convective and radiant elements in the heat exchange process are positive, bodily thermal balance may still be maintained by evaporation (but only by evaporation) up to a limit, provided the air is sufficiently dry to permit a high evaporation rate.

---

* As the latent heat of water is 2 400 kJ/kg, the evaporation rate of 1 kg/h will produce a heat loss rate of 2 400 000/3 600 = 666 W.

**2.1.8
Hot air,
radiation and
appreciable
air movement**

When the air is hot (equal to or above skin temperature) so that the convection element is positive, when the surface temperatures are warm or there is a substantial radiant heat source, so that the radiant element is also positive, and when the air is humid (but less than 100% RH) the movement of air will accelerate evaporation, thus increase heat dissipation, even if its temperature is higher than that of the skin. The mechanism is as follows: if the air is at approximately 90% RH, it will take on some humidity by evaporation from the skin, but the thin (1 to 2 cm) layer of air in immediate contact with the skin soon will become saturated and this saturated air envelope will prevent any further evaporation from the skin. Moving air will remove this saturated air envelope and the evaporation process can continue. It has been estimated [26] that over 2000 N/m² vapour pressure, every 1 m/s increase in air velocity will compensate for an increase of 300 N/m² in vapour pressure.

When the air is completely saturated and warmer than the skin, air movement would only increase discomfort and heat gain. Fortunately such conditions are seldom met in nature. Even in warm-humid regions the highest humidities are experienced when air temperature is below skin temperature, whilst the highest temperatures are accompanied by moderate humidities.

**2.1.9
Saturated,
still air, above
body
temperature**

Let us assume a situation, where the air temperature and the temperature of surfaces are above the skin temperature (over 34°C), where there is no appreciable air movement (less than 0.25% m/s) and the relative humidity is near 100%. Sweating would be profuse, but there would be no evaporation. There will be a convective and radiation heat gain; therefore, however small is the metabolic heat production, all the elements in the thermal balance equation (2.1.4) would be positive.

The body temperature would begin to rise, and when the deep body temperature has increased 2 or (maximum) 3 degC only, heat stroke would occur. This is a circulatory failure, followed by a rapid increase in deep body temperature. When this reaches about 41°C, coma sets in and death is imminent. At about 45°C deep body temperature, death is unavoidable.

Such conditions rarely, if ever, occur in nature, but can quite easily be produced inside buildings of poor design and with bad management.

**2.1.10
Effects of
prolonged
exposure**

Even if the conditions are not bad enough to produce such immediate disastrous effects, prolonged exposure to discomfort conditions can produce adverse effects. Even if the physiological control mechanisms can maintain life (e.g. with a constant high rate of sweating and permanent vaso-dilation) there is considerable loss of efficiency in work coupled with physical strain.

Factors which may provide immediate relief, such as a high wind velocity, may themselves become causes of irritation and discomfort when of a long duration [27].

Conditions which are perfectly comfortable, may produce adverse effects if constant and there is no change at all over prolonged periods. One of the basic needs of humans is change and variation, a fact which has been ignored by early research workers. This point becomes particularly noticeable in mechanically controlled environments, such as in air conditioned buildings, where the environmental conditions can be and often are kept constant within very fine limits. What the designer should aim at, is a *range* of comfort conditions, within which considerable variations are permitted. Fortunately, in buildings without mechanical environmental controls, such variations will be produced by the diurnal variation of climatic factors.

**2.1.11
Subjective
variables**

The sensation of comfort or discomfort depends primarily on the four climatic variables discussed in the foregoing. Thermal preferences are however influenced by a number of subjective or individual factors.

Clothing can be varied at the discretion of the individual. A person wearing a normal business suit and cotton underwear* will require a temperature about 9°C lower than a naked body.

---

* This is taken as a unit of clothing, 1 *clo*. The maximum practicable, i.e. the heaviest arctic clothing is 4.5 clo.

Acclimatisation has been mentioned in 2.1.4. Exposed to a new set of climatic conditions, the human body will reach full adjustment in about 30 days and by that time the thermal preferences of the individual will change. (A person in London may prefer an average room temperature of 18°C, but after spending a few months in Lagos, may find the same temperature rather cool and would prefer a temperature around 25°C.)

Age and sex may influence thermal preferences: the metabolism of older people is slower, therefore they usually prefer higher temperatures. Women also have slightly slower metabolic rates than men; their preference is on average 1 degC higher than that of men.

Body shape, i.e. the surface to volume ratio, also has an effect. A thin person has a much greater body surface than a short, corpulent person of the same weight, can dissipate more heat and will tolerate and prefer a higher temperature.

Subcutaneous fat, i.e. fat under the skin, is an excellent thermal insulator. A fat person will need a cooler air to dissipate the same amount of heat.

State of health also influences thermal requirements. In an illness the metabolic rate may increase, but the proper functioning of the regulatory mechanisms may be impaired. The tolerable range of temperatures will be narrower.

Food and drink of certain kinds may affect the metabolic rate, which may be a reason for the difference in diet between tropical and arctic peoples.

Skin colour may influence radiation heat gain. It has been demonstrated [28] that the lightest skin reflects about three times as much solar radiation as the darkest — the light skin, however, is substantially more vulnerable to sunburn, ulcers, cancer and other sun-caused damage. Dark skin contains appreciably more melanin pigment, which prevents the penetration of damaging ultra-violet rays. Dark skin also increases the heat emission from the body in the same proportion as it affects absorption. Thus skin colour has no effect on thermal preferences, but is more resistant to the damaging effects of sunshine.

**2.2.1
Search for a
comfort scale**

When the designer wants to assess the effect of climatic conditions on the body's heat dissipation processes, he is faced with the difficulty of having to handle four independent variables simultaneously. During the past 50 years many attempts have been made and many experiments have been carried out in order to devise a single scale which combines the effects of these four factors. Such scales are collectively referred to as 'thermal indices' or 'comfort scales'.

In most of these experiments special rooms were built and used, in which any set of indoor climatic conditions could be produced at will. A number of experimental subjects were located in the room, and they were asked to record their subjective reactions on a questionnaire after each variation in the conditions, according to a set scale extending from 'very hot' to 'very cold'. The many answers were then evaluated statistically, and the results plotted on a graph, in most cases producing a nomogram which defines the experimentally found relationships. Various research workers have devised some thirty different thermal index scales.

The most important ones are described in the following paragraphs.

**2.2.2
Effective
temperature
(ET)**

The first such scale was produced by Houghton and Yaglou in 1923, working at the American Society of Heating and Ventilating Engineers. Their findings were plotted on a psychrometric chart, producing 'equal comfort lines' (Figure 28). They named the new scale as *effective temperature* and it can be defined as the temperature of a still, saturated atmosphere, which would, in the absence of radiation,

Fig 28
Psychrometric chart
with effective
temperature lines

(After Houghton and
Yaglou: converted to
metric units by S V
Szokolay)

Comfort zone after Macfarlane for NSW coastal and
inland conditions. Shaded area: for indoor workers.
Extended area: for outdoor workers.
U.K. comfort zone after Finniecome.

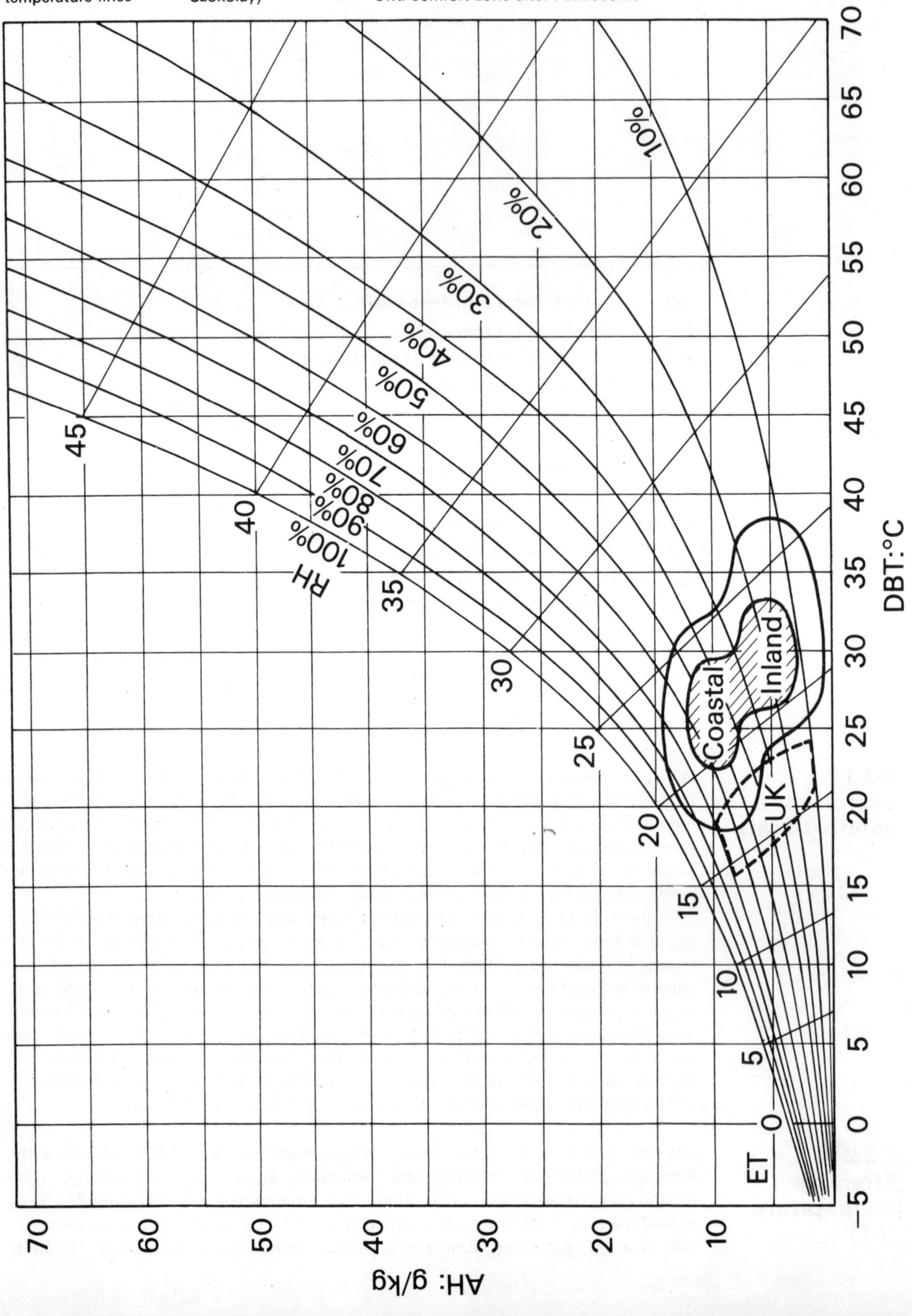

DBT:°C

AH: g/kg

produce the same effect as the atmosphere in question. In 1947 Yaglou slightly **49**
revised the scale, but other modifications also became generally accepted.

**2.2.3
Corrected
effective
temperature
(CET)**

Whilst the ET scale integrates the effects of three variables – originally of temperature and humidity but a later form included air movement – the *corrected effective
temperature* scale also includes radiation effects. This scale is at present the most
widely used one, therefore it will be described in much greater detail in the following
section.

**2.2.4
Equivalent
warmth (EW)**

Experiments were carried out by Bedford in England among over 2000 factory
workers. The subjects were engaged in light work, under varying indoor conditions.
Air temperature, humidity and mean radiant temperature were measured and
recorded together with the subjective responses of the workers. Surface temperatures of skin and clothing were also measured and recorded. After correlating the
findings, using statistical analysis methods, the *equivalent warmth* scale was
constructed and defined by a nomogram [28]. It is now thought to be reliable
within the comfort zone up to 35°C with low RH and up to 30°C with high RH, but
it underestimates the cooling effect of air movement with high humidities.

**2.2.
Operative
temperature
(OT)**

Another scale was developed in the USA, by Winslow, Herrington and Gagge, in
principle very similar to the scale of equivalent warmth. It combined the effects of
radiation and air temperature. Studies were carried out for a specific region with
cool conditions, where the effects of humidity were small and the rate of air movement also negligible [29].

**2.2.6
Equatorial
comfort index
(ECI)**

This was developed by C G Webb in Singapore during 1960. Subjective responses
of acclimatised subjects were recorded together with measurements of air temperature, humidity and air movement – the experimentally-found relationships were
organised into a formula and shown on a graph, very similar to the ET nomogram
[30].

**2.2.7
Resultant
temperature
(RT)**

Developed by Missénard, in France, this scale is a slight improvement on the ET
scale. The nomogram defining it is almost identical with the ET nomogram. It is
thought to be reliable for moderate climates but not for tropical conditions as it
does not allow sufficiently for the cooling effects of air movement over 35°C and
80% RH.

**2.2.8
Predicted four
hour sweat
rate (P4SR)**

This scale, which attempts to correlate subjective sensations with climatic measurement, is primarily concerned with the objective determination of physical stress, as
indicated by the rate of sweat secretion from the body, by the pulse and by internal
temperature.
  The method of measuring the rate of sweating was developed during experiments
carried out for the British naval authorities in 1947, intended to consider the
special heat stresses experienced by seamen. Metabolic rates as well as clothing,
air temperature, humidity, air movement and mean radiant temperature of the surroundings were considered. The sweat rate scale was established on the basis of
many different combinations of the above variables producing the same sweat rate,
thus presumably the same physiological stress [31].
  It seems to be the most reliable scale for high temperature conditions but not
suitable for temperatures below 28°C. The cooling effect of air movements at high
humidities is underestimated.

**2.2.9
Heat stress
index (HSI)**

On the basis of theoretical considerations similar to the above, a further scale was
developed in the USA. Several physiological assumptions were made and calculation methods evolved to find an indication of heat stress on the basis of environmental measurements. Metabolic heat production of subjects doing various kinds of
work was measured and taken as an indication of heat stress [32].
  It is thought to be reliable for still air between 27 and 35°C, 30 and 80% RH, and

for lower humidities if temperatures are higher, but unsuitable for the comfort zone.

2.2.10
The
bioclimatic
chart

Some Australian experiments [33] have shown that under overheated-conditions, when low metabolic rates (light activity) will already produce discomfort, the DBT values correlate much better with subjective judgements than ET values. On the basis of this and similar doubts V Olgyay arrived at the idea, that there is no point in constructing a single-figure index, as each of the four components are controllable by different means. He has constructed a bioclimatic chart (Figure 29), on which the comfort zone is defined in terms of DBT and RH, but subsequently it is shown, by additional lines, how this comfort zone is pushed up by the presence of air movements and how it is lowered by radiation [34]. Although his conclusions are seen to be perfectly valid, it is felt that a reliable comfort index still has its usefulness as a guide and as a means of concise communication.

2.2.11
Index of
thermal stress
(ITS)

After reviewing and checking the validity and reliability of many previously used thermal indices Givoni set out to establish a new index from first principles [35]. The *index of thermal stress* developed by him is the calculated cooling rate produced by sweating, which would maintain thermal balance under the given conditions. The calculation is based on a refined biophysical model of the man—environment thermal system. The index takes into account all the subjective and objective thermal factors. Its usefulness extends from comfortable to overheated conditions as far as the physiological adjustments are able to maintain thermal balance.

Due to the rather complex calculations involved, its use will probably be restricted to research workers and it will not be used by practitioners.

2.2.12
Comfort
scales and
design

Most existing indices have some limitations in their practical application and usefulness under different conditions. Some of these difficulties arise from the fact that the experiments were carried out under widely varying indoor climatic conditions — also the experimental methods were different. As a consequence of this, each of the indices is valid and useful for a limited range of conditions — not universally.

Perhaps the only exception is the CET scale, which is the result of a number of improvements on the original ET scale developed by Houghton and Yaglou. This is the most widely used and best understood scale — although its accuracy is doubted by some research workers [36] it is adequate under most conditions. It will be used throughout the following sections as a method for translating regional and site climatic data into a single index figure, to be used as a guide in establishing thermal comfort criteria for the indoor climate.

The word 'guide' is, however, emphasised, as no single figure index can be a substitute for detailed information relating to each of the four climatic factors.

Fig 29
Bioclimatic chart for men at sedentary work — wearing 1 clo. clothing — in warm climates (Original by V Olgyay in British units — some values revised according to Australian CEBS findings)

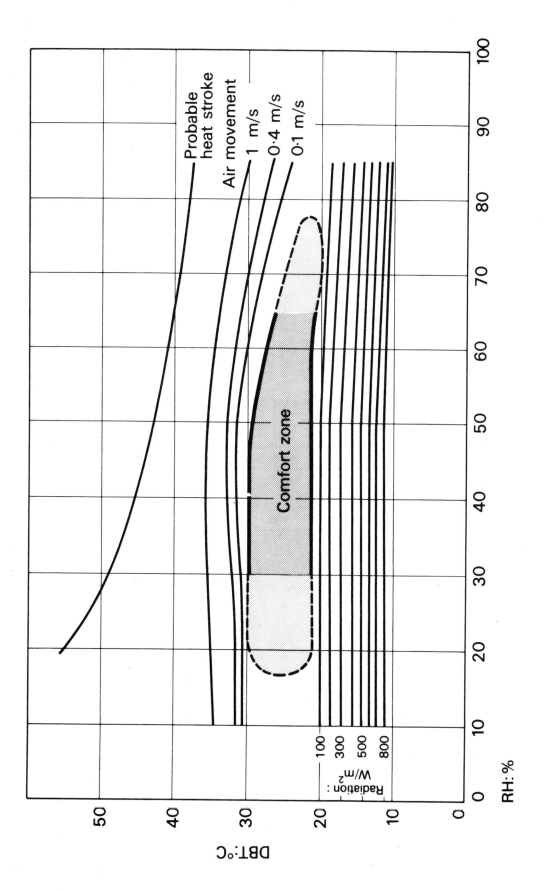

51

2.3.1   **Revisions of the ET scale**

2.3.2   **Mean radiant temperature**

2.3.3   **Finding the CET**

2.3.4   **The Kata thermometer**

2.3.5   **The comfort zone**

2.3.6   **The use of CET – an example**

2.3.7   **Climate analysis with CET**

2.3.8   **ET isopleths**

**2.3.1
Revisions of
the ET scale**

The ET scale was originally defined by the 'equal comfort lines' (straight lines) drawn on the psychrometric chart (Figure 28). Subsequent findings [36 and 39] have proved that this method underestimates the significance of moderate air movements at high temperatures and at the same time overestimates the adverse effect of higher humidities.

Incorporating the appropriate modifications, a nomogram has been constructed which defines the ET index directly from DBT and WBT readings. Figure 30 shows this nomogram at a scale large enough for practical work. This is the 'normal' scale, valid for persons wearing normal, light, indoor clothes. For persons stripped to the waist, the 'basic' scale should be used, which is given in Figure 31. (Both nomograms are reconstructed on the basis of those published in Bedford's work, in metric units.)

These scales still do not make any allowance for radiation heat exchange between the body and its environment. It has been found, however, that if globe thermometer readings (see 2.3.2) are used in these nomograms in lieu of the DBT values, the subjective reactions to radiant heat exchange are adequately allowed for. Values obtained in this case are referred to as *corrected effective temperature* or CET. The same nomograms can be used for the definition of either scale.

**2.3.2
Mean radiant
temperature
(MRT)**

Mean radiant temperature is defined as follows: if all surfaces in an environment were uniformly at this temperature, it would produce the same net radiant heat balance as the given environment with its various surface temperatures. It can be measured directly with the *globe thermometer* (Figure 32) which consists of an ordinary mercury thermometer enclosed in a matt black painted copper globe of 150 mm diameter. It has an inertia of some 15 minutes, but after this time, its

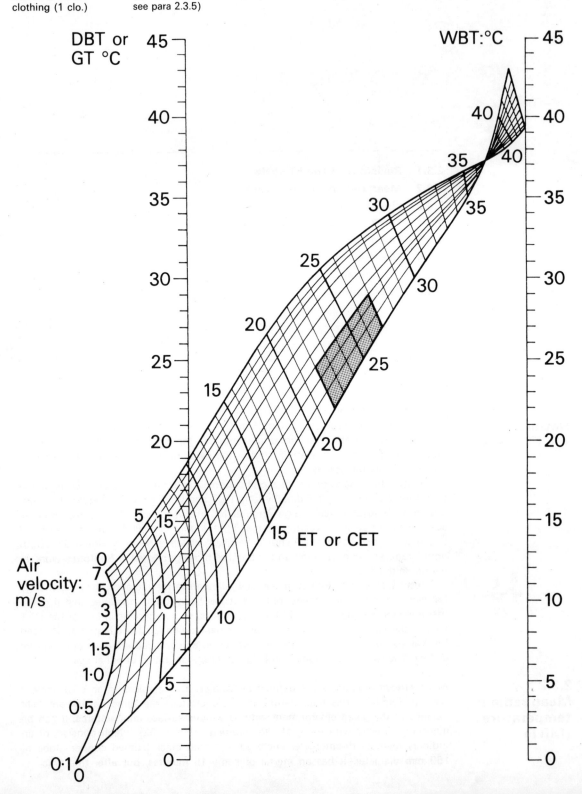

Fig 30
Effective temperature
nomogram for
persons wearing
normal business
clothing (1 clo.)

(shaded area: comfort zone,
see para 2.3.5)

DBT or
GT °C

WBT:°C

Air
velocity:
m/s

ET or CET

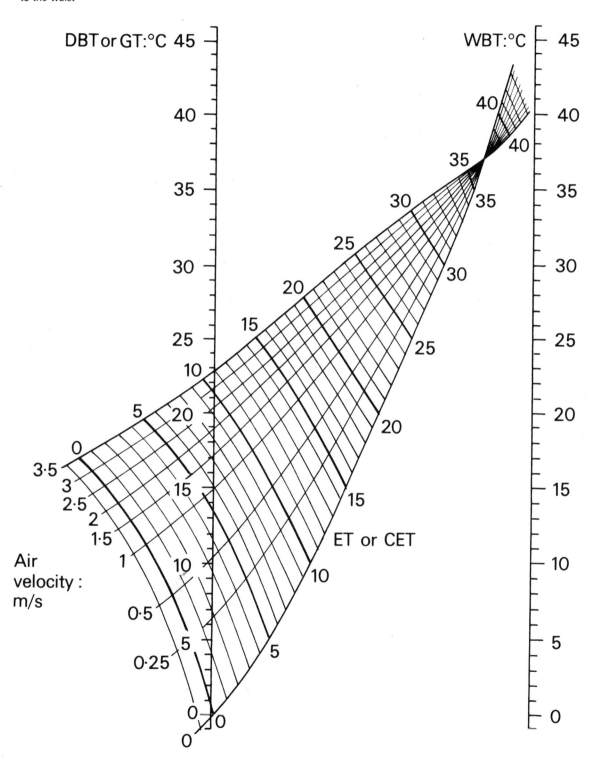

Fig 31
Basic effective
temperature nomogram
for persons stripped
to the waist

reading gives a combination of air temperature and the effect of any received or emitted radiation. If the air is warm, but the opposing surfaces (walls) are cold, some radiation will be emitted from the globe and the reading will be below the air temperature. If radiation is received the reading will be higher than the air temperature. Strictly speaking, the globe thermometer reading (*globe temperature* = GT) and the MRT are identical only if the air is completely still and there is no convective heat exchange between the globe and the air. For conditions other than this, corrections can be made by using another nomogram [21]. For the purposes of the CET nomogram the globe thermometer readings can be used without any correction.

2.3.3
Finding the
CET

When the CET is to be determined for a given situation, the following steps must be taken:

1 measure the globe thermometer temperature (Figure 32)
2 measure the WBT
3 measure the air velocity with an anemometer, or in case of low velocities with a Kata thermometer
4 locate the GT on the left-hand vertical scale of the nomogram (Figure 30 or 31)
5 locate the WBT on the right-hand vertical scale
6 connect the two points with a line (after some practise, laying a straight-edge across is sufficient)
7 select the curve appropriate to the air velocity (scale given on extreme left)
8 mark the point where the velocity curve intersects the line drawn (or the straight-edge)
9 read off the value of the short inclined line going through the same point: this is the CET value.

2.3.4
The Kata
thermometer

If there is no radiation loss or gain and the air is saturated, the globe and wet-bulb temperatures will be identical: the connecting line will be horizontal. If the air is still 0·1 m/s curve) the CET value will also be the same as the globe or wet-bulb temperatures — as it should follow from the definition of CET.

Anemometers with moving (mechanical) parts will rarely respond to air movements below 0·5 m/s. However, even small air speeds of random directions can be measured through their cooling effect. The *Kata thermometer* is an instrument used for this purpose. It is a glass tube, filled with a coloured spirit. The spirit is heated to expand to the small container at the top, usually by dipping it into hot water. When taken out of the water, it is wiped dry and hung on a stand: the level of the spirit starts dropping as it cools. There are two markings on the tube, one corresponding usually to 54·5°C and the other to 51°C (other types are marked at 38 and 35°C). The time it takes for the spirit to drop from the upper to the lower marking is measured by a stop-watch — this is the 'cooling time'. The specific properties of each thermometer are expressed by a number, the 'Kata factor' (between 250 and 600) which is marked on its back. The nomogram given on Figure 33 is now used as follows:

Fig 32
The globe
thermometer

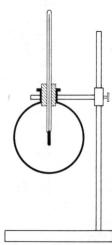

a mark the Kata-factor on the left-hand scale
b mark the cooling time on the inclined scale
c lay straight-edge across these two points and mark its intersection on the centre scale (the 'cooling power')
d mark the separately measured air temperature (DBT) on the right-hand inclined scale
e lay a straight-edge from the 'cooling power' across the DBT and read off the air speed on the right-hand vertical scale

The hot-wire anemometer works on similar principles but an electrical system replaces the use of nomogram or calculation, giving direct air speed reading.

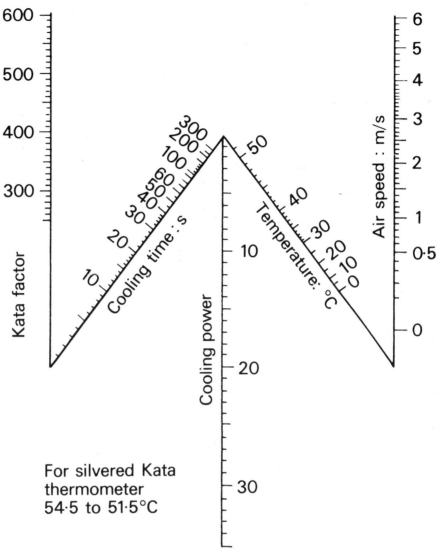

Fig 33
Kata air speed
nomogram

For silvered Kata
thermometer
54·5 to 51·5°C

2.3.5 The comfort zone

The range of conditions within which at least 80% of the people would feel comfortable, can be termed 'comfort zone'. This has been shown on the bioclimatic chart (Figure 29), and it is shown superimposed on the CET nomogram (Figure 30).

The following table compares the findings of several research workers and shows that there is considerable discrepancy between the various limits arrived at. All values are given in °C ET and the sources are indicated after the table.

location	minimum	optimum	maximum
UK, winter[1]	14	17	20
summer[2]	—	18	22
US, winter[3]	15	20	23
summer[3]	18	22	26
Sydney, summer[4]	—	22	25
Singapore[5]	24	—	27
Limits probably valid for most tropical regions	22	25	27

1. I. Bedford. *Warmth factor in comfort at work*. Medical Research Council, Industrial Health Research Board, Report No. 76. HMSO, 1936.
2. D E. Hickish. 'Thermal sensations of workers in light industry in summer' in *Journal of Hygiene*, **53**, 1955, No. 112.
3. C P. Yaglou. 'The comfort zone for man . . .' in *Journal of Industrial Hygiene*, **9**, 1927, 251.
4. E G A. Weiss. 'Air conditioning and working efficiency' in *Architectural Science Review*, July 1959, 68–76.
5. C G. Webb. *Ventilation in warm climates*. BRS Overseas Building Notes, No. 66, March 1960, 2.

On the basis of Singapore and Australian data it seems to be justified to adopt the values given in the last line of the table as valid for most tropical climates. The 22 and 27°C ET limits are indicated on the nomogram (Figure 30).

The comfort zone must also be limited in terms of air velocities. Below 0·15 m/s, even if all other conditions are satisfactory, most people would complain of 'stuffiness'. Above 1·5 m/s the air movement can produce secondary or side-effects which may be annoying, such as papers blown about, ashtrays swept clean and dust stirred up. This is not a rigid limit: under hot and humid conditions people may put up with such minor annoyances for the sake of some thermal relief, but not under less severe conditions. The average value is taken as 1·5 m/s.

Thus the shaded quadrangle in Figure 30, limited by the CET lines 22 and 27°C and by the velocity lines 0·15 and 1·5 m/s indicates the 'comfort zone' or the range of conditions found comfortable in most tropical climates.

2.3.6 The use of CET – an example

Assume that the globe thermometer reads 30°C and the wet-bulb reading is 26°C (these are day-time conditions often found in Freetown, on the west coast of Africa). Figure 35 shows the nomogram, with these points (A and B) indicated and connected by a line. It can be seen that with little or no air movement this condition is uncomfortable; with a velocity of 0·1 m/s it would give a CET of 27·5°C. With an air velocity of 0·5 m/s it would be tolerable, just on the limit of the comfort zone, and with a 1·5 m/s wind it would be well within the comfort zone, giving a CET of 26°C. An air velocity of 7 m/s would bring the CET down to below 23°C, but this wind itself would cause discomfort.

At night, in the same location, both the globe thermometer and the wet-bulb temperatures may be 23°C (indicating 100% RH), shown by the line C to D in Figure 34. This indicates that with air movements between 0·1 and 0·5 m/s most people would feel comfortable (CET 22 to 23°C), but with higher air velocities it would be too cool.

If the wet-bulb reading is not available, but the DBT and RH are known, the value of the corresponding WBT can be read off the psychrometric chart (Figure 12 and 1.2.5). For example, a DBT of 25°C and a RH of 70% would correspond to a WBT of 21°C.

2.3.7 Climate analysis with CET

If the globe thermometer temperature is not available but the DBT is known, in many cases it can be assumed that the surface temperatures are the same as the air temperature, thus the DBT can be taken as the globe thermometer value. If there is a strong radiation source, with a known intensity, the globe thermometer value can be roughly estimated as 1°C higher than the air temperature for every 90 W/m² radiation intensity.

If regional macroclimatic data has been collected (1.2.16) – if it has been modified according to deviations of the site climate (1.4.15) – it can now be further simplified by amalgamating air temperature, radiation humidity and air movement data into a single CET figure, by the use of the nomogram (Figure 30). This can be done for the mean maximum and mean minimum values for each month and shown graphically, with the comfort zone superimposed as in Figure 34.

A more detailed analysis of the climate of Islamabad is shown in Figure 36 as an example. It is a composite climate with three distinct seasons, thus three typical days of the year are selected for which climatic data is compiled at 2-hourly intervals. This data is converted into CET values and plotted on a diagram to show the diurnal changes on these three days. Distinctions are also made between spaces exposed to or protected from the wind, and for the cold season a sunlit space is also examined.

From local information it has been assumed that the comfort limits are 18 and 24°C CET and this comfort zone is shown superimposed on the diagram.

The diagram reveals that there is considerable 'underheating' in the cold season and practically constant 'overheating' in the hot-dry season. Wind could bring

Fig 34
Effective temperature
histogram (Baroda)

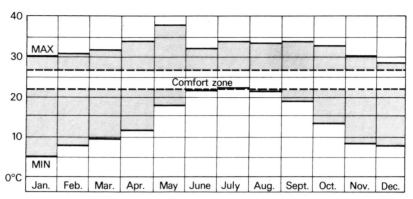

Location: Baroda (72°15'E. 22°15'N. 35m)
Maximum = ET based on monthly mean maxima of DBT and p.m. humidity.
Minimum = ET based on monthly mean minima of DBT and morning humidity
Assumed: MRT=DBT and air velocity less than 0·1 m/s

some relief, but in practice this is not often feasible, as the wind carries much dust.

Studies such as this assist the designer to define the control functions expected of the building and establish criteria for the design of the building fabric.

**2.3.8
ET isopleths**

Both annual and diurnal variation of effective temperature can be shown on an isopleth chart, similar to that shown for air temperature alone in Figure 16.

For the purpose of constructing such a chart, the air temperature, humidity, mean radiant temperature and wind velocity data should be known for a 'typical' day of each month of the year, at least at 2-hourly intervals. Such data is rarely available.

Several assumptions can however be made to simplify this task:

a for the consideration of indoor conditions, the effects of solar radiation can be excluded and the surface temperatures can be taken to be the same as the air temperature (i.e. DBT = GT).
b air movement can be considered at the monthly mean velocity for all hours to produce a set of ET values, but another set should be calculated for still air conditions, as the worst condition is still air
c when hourly or 2-hourly data is not available, only mean maximum and mean minimum, the *hourly temperature calculator* (Figure 37) can be used to estimate the missing values

The process of using this calculator is the following:

1 take the mean maximum temperature and the p.m. humidity and find the WBT (from psychrometric chart, Figure 12). From these define the maximum ET (using nomogram of Figure 30) – then locate this on the top scale
2 take the mean minimum temperature and the morning humidity, define the WBT; then the minimum ET – locate this on the bottom scale
3 connect these points with a line, the 'temperature line'
4 select the time required on one of the vertical scales and mark the intersection of the 'temperature line' with the time line
5 project this vertically to either the top or bottom scale and read off the corresponding ET value

Figure 38 shows a worked example using a tabulation of data. Mean maximum and mean minimum DBT values, a.m. and p.m. humidities are entered. WBT values are obtained from Figure 12. Maximum and minimum ET values are found from Figure 30. Figure 37 is used to interpolate 2-hourly values. Results are transferred to the isopleth chart.

Further use of this will be shown in 4.2.14.

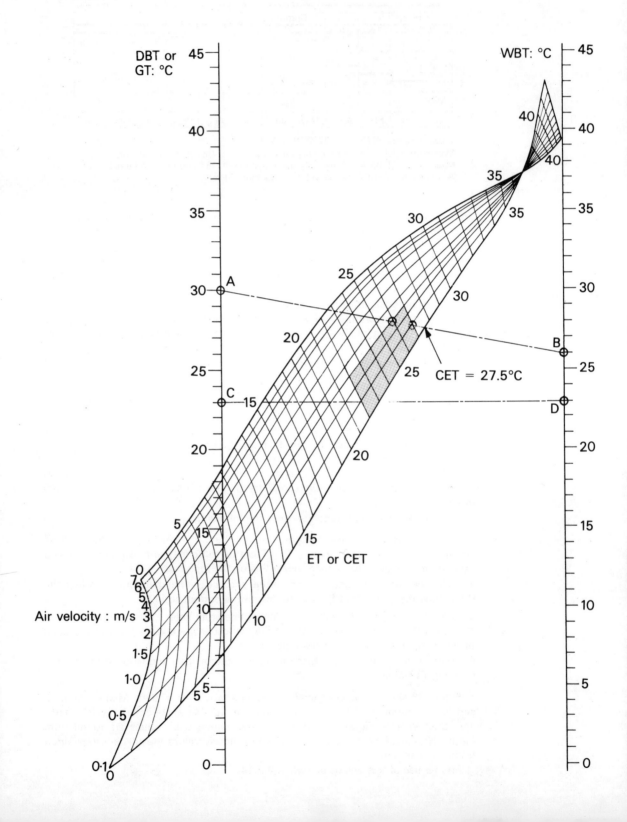

Fig 36
Climate analysis with
corrected effective
temperature

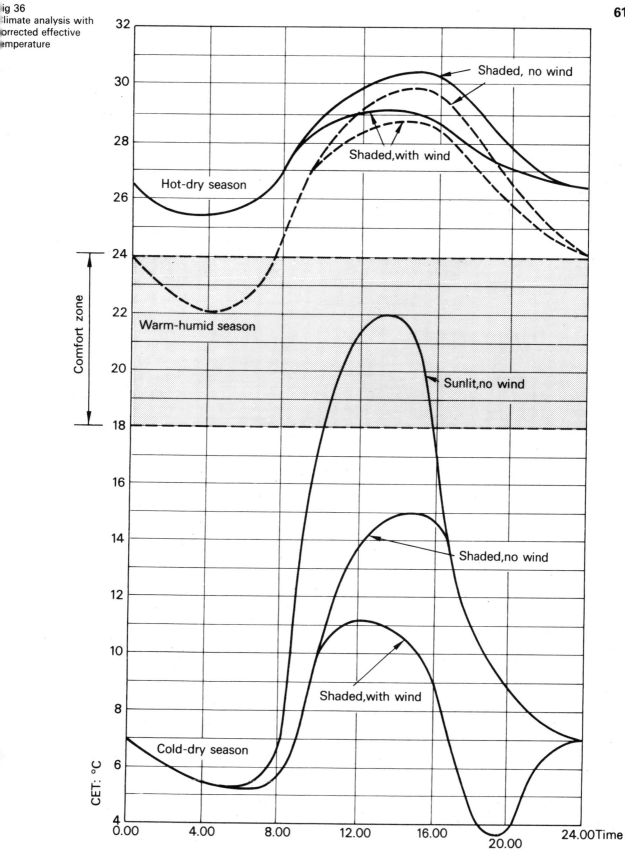

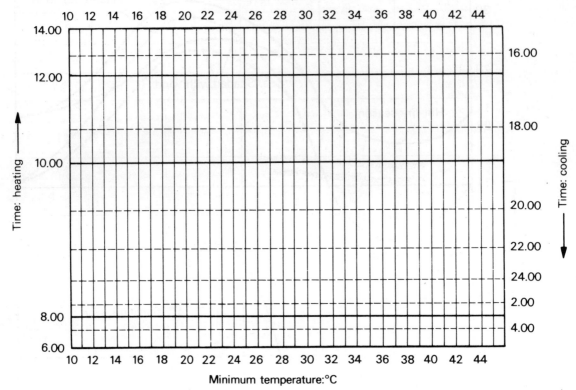

Fig 38
Effective temperature isopleth and its computation (New Delhi, India)

		Jan.	Feb.	Mar.	Apr.	May	June	July	Aug.	Sept.	Oct.	Nov.	Dec.
Data	Mean max. DBT °C	21	24	30·5	36	40·5	39	35·5	34	34	34	29	23
	RH p.m.: %	41	35	23	19	20	36	59	64	51	32	31	42
	WBT: °C	13·5	14·5	16·5	19	22	24·5	27	29	25	21	17·5	15
	ET: max.: °C	**18·5**	**20**	**24**	**26·5**	**28**	**29·5**	**30**	**30·5**	**28**	**26·5**	**23·5**	**20**
Data	Mean min. DBT °C	6·5	9·5	14·5	20	26	28·5	27	26	24	18·5	11	8
	RH a.m. %	72	67	49	35	35	53	75	80	72	56	51	69
	WBT: °C	4·5	5·5	9	12	16	21·5	24	23·5	20·5	13·5	6·5	5·5
	ET: min.: °C	**6·5**	**9·5**	**13·5**	**17·5**	**21·5**	**25**	**25**	**24·5**	**22·5**	**17**	**10·5**	**8**

			Jan.	Feb.	Mar.	Apr.	May	June	July	Aug.	Sept.	Oct.	Nov.	Dec.
Interpolation from Fig 37	Hours	0.00	9	12	16	19·5	23	26	26	25·5	23·5	19	13	10·5
		2.00	8	11	15	19	22·5	25·5	26	25	23	18	12	9·5
		4.00	7	10	14	18	22	25	25·5	25	23	17·5	11	9
		6.00	6·5	9·5	13·5	17·5	21·5	25	25	24·5	22·5	17	10·5	8
		8.00	7·5	10·5	14·5	18·5	22	25·5	25·5	25	23	18	11·5	9·5
		10.00	13·5	15·5	19·5	23	25·5	27·5	28	28	26	22·5	18	15
		12.00	17	18·5	22·5	25	27	29	29	29·5	27	25	21·5	18
		14.00	18·5	20	24	26·5	28	29·5	30	30·5	28	26·5	23·5	20
		16.00	17·5	19	23	26	27·5	29	29·5	30	27·5	26	22·5	19
		18.00	15	17	21	24	26	28	28·5	29	26	23·5	19·5	16
		20.00	12	14	18	21·5	24·5	27	27	27	25	21	16	13
		22.00	10	13	17	20·5	23·5	26·5	26·5	26·5	24	20	14·5	12

Computation of hourly effective temperatures: °C

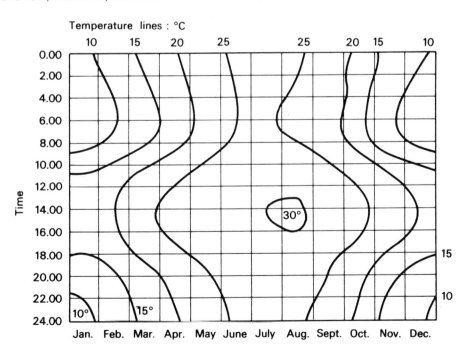

Temperature lines : °C

3.1.1
Introduction

At this point, after surveying the naturally given conditions and after showing the dependence of humans on appropriate thermal conditions, but before the means of thermal controls could be analysed, it is necessary to clarify some basic physical facts regarding the nature of heat and the ways of its propagation. For a more detailed treatment of physical principles refer to the works listed under item [40–42] of the bibliography. Only in possession of this knowledge and with a clear understanding of the principles involved can the designer avoid some of the popular misconceptions.

If the methods of control were to be learned in applied form only, without analysing the underlying principles, many more items of information would have to be memorised, the learning task would be far more difficult and the designer would still not be equipped to deal with unfamiliar situations.

**3.1.2
Temperature**

Temperature is actually not a physical quantity but it can be thought of as a symptom – as the outward appearance of the thermal state of a body. If energy is conveyed to a body, the molecular movement within that body is increased and it appears to be warmer. If this molecular movement is spreading to other bodies (e.g. to air), its intensity within the body decreases and the body appears to be cooling.

Temperature is measured by the *Celsius scale*. This has been constructed by taking the freezing and boiling points of water (at normal atmospheric pressure) as fixed points and dividing the interval into 100 degrees.

A position on this scale, i.e. the temperature of an object is denoted as: °C but an interval or difference in temperature is: **degC**.

Both should be pronounced as 'degrees Celsius'. (The popularly used name 'centigrade' should be avoided, because it is used as an angular measure in some places of the Continent: the rectangle is divided into 100 *grades* and each grade into 100 *centigrades*.)

Thus if the indoor temperature is	22°C
and the out-door temperature is	4°C
the temperature difference is	18degC

or if the day-time maximum is	36°C
and the night-time minimum is	12°C
the diurnal range is	24 degC

In scientific work the *Kelvin scale* may be used, on which an interval of temperature is the same as on the Celsius scale, but the starting point – the zero – is the 'absolute zero', which is $-273 \cdot 15°C$.

Thus $N \, degC = N \, degK$
but $N \,°C = N + 273 \cdot 15 °K$

**3.1.3
Heat**

Heat is a form of energy, appearing as molecular movement in substances or as 'radiant heat', a certain wavelength band of electromagnetic radiation in space (700 to 10 000 nm). As such, it is measured in general energy units: *joules* (J)

The joule is derived from the three basic units:

length = metre (m)
mass = kilogramme (kg)
time = second (s)

in a logical and coherent way, as follows:

a   *velocity* – a movement of unit length in unit time, metre per second: m/s

b   *acceleration* – a unit change in velocity in unit time, $\frac{m/s}{s}$ = metre per second square: m/s^2

c   *force* – that, which can cause unit acceleration of a body having a unit mass $m/s^2 \times kg = kg \, m/s^2$. This unit is given the special name 'Newton':   N

Note that as the gravitational acceleration is $9 \cdot 8 \, m/s^2$ the gravitational force acting on 1 kg mass, i.e. the 'weight' of 1 kg or 1 kgf (kilogramme–force), is 9·8 N. It would be advisable to completely delete the term 'weight' from the vocabulary (and speak either of *mass* or of *force*) as it blurs the fact that mass units kg or lb are not the same as force units kgf or lbf. Weight is actually the gravitational acceleration of a unit mass, a force unit, the use of which is to be discontinued.

d *work* – unit work is carried out if a unit force is acting over a unit length (i.e. if a body of 1 kg mass is given a velocity of 1 m/s in one second, with 1 m movement) thus the unit work is N ×m = kg m/s² ×m = kg m²/s² and this unit is given the special name 'Joule':   J

e *energy* – is the potential or capacity for carrying out a certain work, thus it is measured in the same unit as work: J

Previously special units were is use for the measurement of heat, even if the *joule* was used for measuring other forms of energy.

The British Thermal Unit (Btu) was defined as the amount of heat necessary to raise the temperature of 1 lb of water by 1 degF.

The kilocalorie (kcal) was defined as the amount of heat necessary to raise the temperature of 1 kg of water by 1 degC.

Both of these are now obsolete. Old data can be converted into SI units by using the following factors:

1 Btu   = 1 055·06 J
1 kcal   = 4 186·8 J

3.1.4 Other thermal quantities

Before proceeding further, several other thermal quantities must be defined, to which reference will have to be made in the following sections.

Specific heat of a substance is the amount of heat energy necessary to cause unit temperature increase of a unit mass of the substance. It is measured in: J/kg degC

The higher the specific heat of a substance, the more heat it will absorb for a given increase in temperature. Of all common substances water has the highest specific heat: 4 187 J/kg degC.

For gases often the *volumetric specific heat* is given in: J/m³ degC

The volumetric specific heat of air is around 1 300 J/m³ degC (varying with pressure and humidity).

Latent heat of a substance is the amount of heat energy absorbed by unit mass of the substance at change of state (from solid to liquid or liquid to gaseous) without any change in temperature. It is measured in: J/kg

For water the latent heat is:

of fusion (0°C ice to 0°C water)   335 kJ/kg
of evaporation at 100°C   2 261 kJ/kg
(of evaporation at around 20°C   2 400 kJ/kg)

At change of state in the reverse direction the same amount of heat is released.

Thermal capacity of a body is the product of its mass and the specific heat of its material. It is measured as the amount of heat required to cause unit temperature increase of the body, in units of   J/degC

Calorific value is the amount of heat released by unit mass of a fuel or food material by its complete combustion and it is measured in   J/kg

Calorific value per volume is measured in   J/m³

3.1.5 Heat flow

Heat energy tends to distribute itself evenly until a perfectly diffused uniform thermal field is achieved. It tends to flow from high temperature to lower temperature zones, by any or all of the following ways:

conduction
convection
radiation

The 'motive force' of heat flow in any of these forms is the temperature difference between the two zones or areas considered. The greater the temperature difference, the faster the rate of heat flow.

An outline of the physical principles and of the quantities involved is given in the following paragraphs, and methods of calculating the heat flow rate will be described in section 3.2.

**3.1.6
Heat flow rate**

Power is the ability to carry out a certain work in unit time: it is measured in joules per second, J/s, which is given a special name 'Watt':   W

If unit work is carried out in unit time, or unit energy is expended to unit time, we have unit power. Thus if we think of power as the rate of energy expenditure, it will be seen that the same unit can be used to measure the *rate* of energy flow. This energy flow may be the flow of heat through a wall, the heat removed by a cooling plant, the radiant heat flow from an electric radiator, the flow of electricity through a light bulb, sound (acoustical) energy emitted by a loudspeaker, the rotational (mechanical) energy output of an electric motor or, indeed, of a motor-car engine. In all these cases energy is flowing or expended, and it is the *rate* of this flow which we measure in watts.

Watt is of the same physical dimension at Btu/h, as kcal/h, as erg/s or as horsepower (hp). The following conversion factors can be used to convert old data into watts:

1 hp (British)   = 745·7 W
1 hp (metric)   = 735·5 W
1 Btu/h   = 0·293 W
1 kcal/h   = 1·163 W
1 erg/s   = 0·000 000 1 W (10^{-7} W)
1 ton of refrigeration = 3516 W (approximately 3·5 kW)

The common element in all these units is that all are energy units per a time unit, which may be a second, an hour or a day, as in the last item. (A ton of refrigeration is the cooling power of 1 ton (American 'short' ton of 2 000 lb) of ice melting in 24 hours. As a pound of ice requires 144 Btu of heat to melt it into water of the same temperature:

$$1 \text{ ton of refrigeration} = \frac{2000 \times 144}{24} = 12000 \text{ Btu/h} = 12000 \times 0.293 \text{ W} = 3516 \text{ W.})$$

In most practical applications the multiple of watt, 'kilowatt', will be used   kW (1 kW = 1 000 W):

**3.1.7
Density of
heat flow rate**

If the total rate of heat flow from an identifiable unit is to be measured (such as the heat loss from a given building, the output of a boiler, the radiation through a given window or the heat removed through a cooling plant) the unit of measurement is W or kW.

In many cases, however, there is no defined area through which the heat flow could be considered, e.g. solar radiation or flow of heat through a wall of un-specified size. In such cases the heat flow rate can be measured in relation to a unit area, i.e. the *density* of such heat flow rate (*per analogiam*: population density: numbers per unit area). The unit of measurement is watt per metre square: W/m^2
(The term *intensity* is often used synonymously with density, thus the intensity of a sound or the intensity of solar radiation is measured in W/m^2.)

**3.1.8
Conductivity**

In conduction through a body or through bodies in direct contact, the spread of molecular movement constitutes the flow of heat. The rate at which such molecular movement spreads varies with different materials and is described as a property of the material – its thermal *conductivity* (or '*k*-value'). It is measured as the rate of heat flow (flow of energy per unit time) through unit area of unit thickness of the material, when there is a unit temperature difference between the two sides. The unit of measurement would thus be W × m/m² degC, but this can be simplified by cancellation: W/m degC
Its value varies between 0·03 W/m degC for insulating materials and up to 400 W/m degC for metals. The lower the conductivity, the better insulator a material is.

Resistivity is the reciprocal of this quantity ($1/k$) measured in units of: m degC/W Better insulators will have higher resistivity values.

For conductivity and resistivity values of various materials see appendix 5.1

3.1.9 Relevance of density

It must be noted that density is often taken as an *indicator* of conductivity: higher density materials normally have a higher conductivity or *k*-value, but there is no direct or causal relationship between the two quantities. The apparent relationship is due to the fact that air has a very low conductivity value, and as lightweight materials tend to be porous, thus containing more air, their conductivity tends to be less. There are, however, many exceptions, for example:

	density kg/m³	conductivity W/m degC
Expanded ebonite	64	0·029
Glass wool mat	24	0·042
Foamed slag concrete	1 280	0·338
Expanded clay concrete	1 200	0·460
Steel	7 800	58
Aluminium	2 700	220

In all three pairs the second one is lighter, but has a higher conductivity value.

The relationship is true for materials of the same kind, but of varying densities, or for the same material with different densities, due to variations in moisture content.

Water has a conductivity of 0·580 W/m degC
whereas air has only 0·026 W/m degC

Therefore if air in the pores of a material is replaced by water, its conductivity rapidly increases. Tests on an asbestos insulating slab gave the following values [41]:

	density kg/m³	conductivity W/m degC
Dry	136	0·051
Wet	272	0·144
Soaked	400	0·203

The more porous a material, the greater the increase in conductivity with increased moisture content.

3.1.10 Conductance

Whilst conductivity and resistivity are properties of a material, the corresponding properties of a body of a given thickness are described as *conductance* (C), or its reciprocal, *resistance* (R): $C = \dfrac{1}{R}$

Conductance is the heat flow rate through a unit area of the body (i.e. the density of heat flow rate) when the temperature difference between the two surfaces is 1 degC. The unit of measurement is W/m² degC
and resistance is measured in m² degC/W

Resistance of a body is the product of its thickness and the resistivity of its material:

$$R = b \times \frac{1}{k} = \frac{b}{k}$$

where b is the thickness in metres (dimension: m × m degC/W = m² degC/W).

3.1.11 Multilayer body

If a body consists of several layers of different materials, its total resistance will be the sum of the resistances of the individual layers. The conductance of such a multilayer body (C_b) can be found by finding its total resistance (R_b) and taking its reciprocal:

$$R_b = R_1 + R_2 + R_3 \ldots = \frac{b_1}{k_1} + \frac{b_2}{k_2} + \frac{b_3}{k_3} \ldots$$

$$= \sum \frac{b}{k}$$

$$C = \frac{1}{R} = \frac{1}{\sum b/k}$$

Note that the conductances are not additive, only the resistances.

**3.1.12
Surface
conductance**

In addition to the resistance of a body to the flow of heat, a resistance will be offered by its surfaces, where a thin layer of air film separates the body from the surrounding air. A measure of this is the *surface* or *film-resistance*, denoted thus: $1/f$ (m² degC/W) f being the *surface* or *film-conductance* (W/m² degC).

Surface conductance includes the convective and the radiant components of the heat exchange at surfaces.

In the preceding paragraphs, heat flow from one surface of the body to the other surface was considered (thus the temperature difference was taken between the two surfaces). Conductance has been defined in these terms. If the heat flow from air on one side, through the body, to air on the other side is considered, both surface resistances must be taken into account.

The overall, *air-to-air resistance* (R) is the sum of the body's resistance and the surface resistances:

$$R_a = \frac{1}{f_i} + R_b + \frac{1}{f_o}$$

where $1/f_i$ = internal surface resistance
 R_b = resistance of the body
 $1/f_o$ = external surface resistance
(all resistance values in m² degC/W).

The magnitude of surface- or film-conductance (f) is a function of surface qualities and of the velocity of air passing the surface. Values valid for moderate climates, winter conditions, are given in appendix 5.2, but values given in appendix 5.3 are likely to be more reliable for warm climates.

**3.1.13
Transmittance**

The reciprocal of this air-to-air resistance is the *air-to-air transmittance*, or U-value:

$$U = \frac{1}{R_a}$$

Its unit of measurement is the same as for conductance – W/m² degC – the only difference being that here the air temperature difference (and not the surface temperature difference) will be taken into account.

This is the quantity most often used in building heat loss and heat gain problems, as its use greatly simplifies the calculations. Values for everyday constructions are given in appendix 5.4, but if the U-value of a particular construction is not found in the table, it can be computed from its component factors [40]. (See also 3.2.12)

**3.1.14
Cavities**

If an air space or cavity is enclosed within a body, through which the heat transfer is considered, this will offer another barrier to the passage of heat. It is measured as the *cavity resistance*, (R_c) which can be added to the other resistances described above.

At most the value of R_c for an empty cavity may be the sum of an internal and an external surface resistances (0·176 m² degC/W), but often it is less if the cavity is narrower than 50 mm, or if strong convection currents can develop inside the cavity. Its value can be improved significantly by hanging an aluminium foil freely, inside the cavity. The function of this will be explained when radiation effects are discussed.

Values of cavity resistances (and the reciprocals, the cavity conductances) are given in appendix 5.5.

3.1.15
Convection

In convection, heat is transferred by the bodily movement of a carrying medium, usually a gas or a liquid. This movement may be self-generating, i.e. due to thermal forces alone (temperature differences, thus different densities, causing convection currents, as in wind generation) or may be propelled by an applied force.

The rate of heat transfer in convection depends on three factors:

1 temperature difference (difference in temperature of the medium at the warmer and cooler points)
2 the rate of movement of the carrying medium in terms of kg/s or m³/s
3 the specific heat of the carrying medium in J/kg degC or J/m³ degC

These quantities will be used in ventilation heat loss or cooling calculations. (The convective heat flow from a body, through a medium, to another body is expressed by a more complex equation, not necessary for our purposes.)

3.1.16
Radiation

In radiation heat transfer the rate of heat flow depends on the temperatures of the emitting and receiving surfaces and on certain qualities of these surfaces: the emittance and absorbance.

Radiation received by a surface can be partly absorbed and partly reflected: the proportion of these two components is expressed by the coefficients *absorbance* (*a*) and *reflectance* (*r*). The sum of these two coefficients is always one:

$a + r = 1$

Light coloured, smooth and shiny surfaces tend to have a higher reflectance. For the perfect reflective theoretical white surface: $r = 1$, $a = 0$.

The perfect absorber, the theoretical 'black body', would have the coefficients: $r = 0$, $a = 1$.

(For values of some building surfaces see appendix 5.6.)

The coefficient *emittance* (*e*) expresses how much of the available heat will be emitted (in relation to the 'black body', for which $e = 1$). Its value is the same as for absorbance:

$a = e$

for the same wavelengths of radiation, but may differ for different wavelengths. The wavelength of emitted radiation depends on the temperature of the emitter. The sun with its surface around 5500 °C, emits short-wave infra-red (and on shorter wavelengths, light and ultra-violet) — but objects at terrestrial temperatures (0 to 50 °C) emit long-wave infra-red only. Thus the absorbance for solar radiation will not be the same as emittance at terrestrial temperatures; for example:

	a (solar)	e (terrestrial)
White painted surface	0·1–0·3	0·8–0·9
Bright metals	0·1–0·3	0·05–0·2

The practical significance of this is that if both surfaces are exposed to solar radiation, both will reflect and absorb the same amount of heat, but the white painted surface will re-emit much of the absorbed heat, whereas the bright metal surface will not. Therefore the latter will attain a much higher temperature.

Bright metal foils are successfully used for insulation in situations where heat is transmitted mainly by radiation. A loose foil in a cavity will reflect much of the incident radiant heat, but if it absorbs any, very little of it will be reradiated.

3.1.17
Measurement
of radiation

Radiation incident on a plane surface can be measured instrumentally and its intensity described in terms of W/m² (see 1.2.10). With many sources producing a complex pattern by inter-reflection, a description of the situation in these terms would be very lengthy and cumbersome. Such a situation can be described in terms of the mean radiant temperature (MRT) or globe thermometer readings (see 2.3.2).

**3.1.18
Sol-air
temperature**

For building design purposes it is useful to combine the heating effect of radiation incident on a building with the effect of warm air. This can be done by using the *sol-air temperature* concept. A temperature value is found, which would create the same thermal effect as the incident radiation in question, and this value is added to the air temperature:

$$T_s = T_o + \frac{I \times a}{f_o}$$

where T_s = sol-air temperature, in °C
$\quad\quad T_o$ = outside air temperature, in °C
$\quad\quad I$ = radiation intensity, in W/m²
$\quad\quad a$ = absorbance of the surface
$\quad\quad f_o$ = surface conductance (outside), W/m² degC

The concept of surface conductance has been explained in 3.1.12. However, it is necessary to point out, that whilst in a cold climate a lesser value of f_o would help reducing the heat loss, in a warm climate (in a solar heat gain situation) a greater value of f_o is desirable to reduce solar overheating. The reason is that the incident radiation increases the surface temperature far above the air temperature, thus some heat is dissipated to the out-door air immediately. The greater the f_o value, the more heat will be dissipated before it can be conducted away by the wall material.

**3.1.19
Solar gain
factor**

It might be useful to consider the combined effect of reflective surfaces and thermal insulation. For the reduction of solar heat gain a dark, highly absorptive surface with good insulation may be just as effective as a more reflective but less well-insulated element. (Good insulation with a highly reflective surface is of course, better than both.)

From the above sol-air temperature equation the temperature equivalent of the radiation gain (the 'sol-air excess') is:

$$T_s - T_o = \frac{I \times a}{f_o}$$

Thus the extra *heat flow rate* (q) per unit area (caused by the radiation) is:

$$q = \frac{I \times a}{f_o} \times U \quad \text{(in W/m}^2\text{)}$$

From this the 'solar gain factor' is:

$$\frac{q}{I} = \frac{a \times U}{f_o} \quad\quad \left(\frac{\text{W/m}^2}{\text{W/m}^2} = \text{nondimensional} \right)$$

This solar gain factor is defined as the heat flow rate through the construction due to solar radiation expressed as a fraction of the incident solar radiation. As this value can be related to the increase in the inner surface temperature, a performance requirement can be established on the basis of experience, in terms of this solar gain factor.

Its value should not exceed 0·04 in warm-humid climates or 0·03 in the hot-dry season of composite climates, when ventilation is reduced.

It is reasonable to assume a constant value for external surface conductance as: f_o = 20 W/m² degC, thus we can establish target values for the $a \times U$ product:

	solar gain factor	$a \times U$
For warm-humid climates	0·04	0·8
Hot-dry season (composite)	0·03	0·6

3.2.1
Heat exchange
processes

In section 2.1 (especially 2.1.4) the human body was considered as a defined unit and its heat exchange processes with the environment were analysed. The building can similarly be considered as a defined unit and its heat exchange processes with the out-door environment can be examined (see Figure 39):

Fig 39
Heat exchange of
buildings

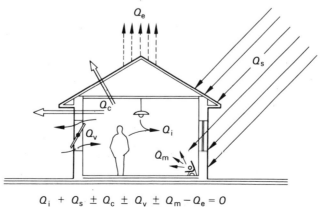

$$Q_i + Q_s \pm Q_c \pm Q_v \pm Q_m - Q_e = 0$$

a   *Conduction* of heat may occur through the walls either inwards or outwards, the rate of which will be denoted as Q_c (convective and radiant components in the transfer of the same heat at the surfaces are included in the term: transmittance)

b   The effects of solar radiation on opaque surfaces can be included in the above by using the sol-air temperature concept, but through transparent surfaces (windows) the *solar heat gain* must be considered separately. It may be denoted as Q_s

c   Heat exchange in either direction may take place with the movement of air, i.e. *ventilation*, and the rate of this will be denoted as Q_v

d   An *internal heat gain* may result from the heat output of human bodies, lamps, motors and appliances. This may be denoted as Q_i

e   There may be a deliberate introduction or removal of heat (heating or cooling), using some form of outside energy supply. The heat flow rate of such *mechanical controls* may be denoted as Q_m

f   Finally, if *evaporation* takes place on the surface of the building (e.g. a roof pool) or within the building (human sweat or water in a fountain) and the vapours are removed, this will produce a cooling effect, the rate of which will be denoted as Q_e

The thermal balance, i.e. the existing thermal condition is maintained if:

$$Q_i + Q_s \pm Q_c \pm Q_v \pm Q_m - Q_e = 0$$

If the sum of this equation is less than zero (negative), the building will be cooling and if it is more than zero, the temperature in the building will increase.

These factors will be examined in the following paragraphs.

3.2.2 Conduction

Conduction heat flow rate through a wall of a given area can be described by the equation:

$$Q_c = A \times U \times {_\Delta}T$$

where Q_c = conduction heat flow rate, in W
A = surface area, in m²
U = transmittance value, in W/m² degC
${_\Delta}T$ = temperature difference

For a whole building, enclosed by various elements and possibly the temperature differences varying from side to side, the above equation is solved for each element and the results are added.

If heat loss from a building is considered:

$${_\Delta}T = T_i - T_o$$

If heat gain in, say, an air conditioned building is calculated:

$${_\Delta}T = T_o - T_i$$

and if in the latter case a surface is also exposed to solar radiation:

$${_\Delta}T = T_s - T_i$$

where T_i = inside air temperature

3.2.3 Convection

Convection heat flow rate between the interior of a building and the open air, depends on the rate of ventilation, i.e. air exchange. This may be unintentional air infiltration or may be deliberate ventilation. The rate of ventilation can be given in m³/s.

The rate of ventilation heat flow is described by the equation:

$$Q_v = 1\,300 \times V \times {_\Delta}T$$

where Q = ventilation heat flow rate, in W
1 300 = volumetric specific heat of air, J/m³degC
V = ventilation rate, in m³/s
T = temperature difference, degC

If the *number of air changes per hour* (*N*) is given the ventilation rate can be
found as:

$$V = \frac{N \times \text{room volume}}{3\,600}$$

(3 600 is the number of seconds in an hour).

3.2.4 Radiation through windows

If the intensity of solar radiation (*I*) incident on the plane of the window is known – this itself being a value denoting a density of energy flow rate (W/m²) – it will have to be multiplied by the area of the aperture only (m²) to get the heat flow rate in watts.

This would be the heat flow rate through an unglazed aperture. For glazed windows this value will be reduced by a *solar gain factor* (*θ*) which depends on the quality of the glass and on the angle of incidence. Values of *θ* are given in Figure 55 (see 4.2.9).

The solar heat flow equation can therefore be established as:

$$Q_s = A \times I \times \theta$$

where A = area of window, in m²
I = radiation heat flow density, in W/m²
θ = solar gain factor of window glass

3.2.5 Internal heat gain

The heat output rate of human bodies has been given in 2.1.2. Heat output from a body (inside the building) is a heat gain for the building. Thus the heat output rate appropriate to the activity to be accommodated must be selected and multiplied by the number of occupants. The result, in watts, will be a significant component of Q_i.

The total rate of energy emission of electric lamps can be taken as internal heat gain. The larger part of this energy is emitted as heat (95% for incandescent lamps and 79% for fluorescent lamps) and the part emitted as light, when incident on surfaces, will be converted into heat. Consequently the total wattage of all lamps in the building (if and when in use) must be added to the Q_i.

If an electric motor and the machine driven by it are both located (and operating) in the same space, the total wattage of the motor must be taken as Q_i. (If the hp of a motor is known, its wattage can be found: W = 746 × hp.)

If the motor only is in the space considered and its efficiency is ϵ, then $W \times \epsilon$ useful power is utilised elsewhere, but $W (1-\epsilon)$ heat flow will contribute to Q_i.

3.2.6 Heating and cooling

Heating and cooling, i.e. mechanical controls will be dealt with in greater detail in Section 4.1. The heat flow rate of these systems is subject to the designer's intentions and it is deliberately controllable. It can thus be taken as a dependent variable in the equation, i.e. it can be adjusted according to the balance of the other factors.

3.2.7 Evaporation

The rate of cooling by evaporation can only be calculated if the rate of evaporation itself is known. If the evaporation rate is expressed in kg/h, the corresponding heat loss rate can be found:

$$Q_e = 666 \times \text{kg/h}$$

as the latent heat of evaporation of water around 20 °C is approximately 2 400 kJ/kg, this gives:

$$2\,400\,000 \text{ J/h} = \frac{2\,400\,000}{3\,600} \text{ J/s} = 666 \text{ W}$$

The estimation of evaporation rate is a more difficult task and it can rarely be done with any degree of accuracy (except under mechanically controlled conditions), as it depends on many variables, such as: available moisture, humidity of the air, temperature of the moisture itself and of the air and velocity of the air movement. It can be measured indirectly, e.g. by measuring the reduction in the quantity of water in an open vessel, or it can be estimated from the number of people in the room, their activity and thus their likely sweat rate (a value between 20 g/h and 2 kg/h).

Usually evaporation heat loss is either ignored for the purposes of calculations (except in mechanical installations), or it is handled qualitatively only: evaporative cooling will be utilised to reduce air temperature 'as far as possible'.

3.2.8
Heat loss
calculation

The purpose of heat loss calculation is usually for the design of a heating installation. Heat loss rate for a condition which is the coldest for 90% of the time is calculated. The heating installation is then designed to produce heat at the same rate.

Under less severe conditions the installation can work with a reduced output. Colder conditions in the remaining 10% of the time normally occur in short spells and may be bridged by the thermal inertia of the building (see Section 3.3) and by an 'overload capacity' of the installation. In the UK it is usual to take $-1\,°C$ or $0\,°C$ as the 'design out-door temperature' (T_o).

The calculation method is best illustrated by a simple example:

a 5×5 m and 2.5 m high office is located on an intermediate floor of a large building, therefore it has only one exposed wall facing south, all other walls adjoin rooms kept at the same temperature: $T_i = 20\,°C$

the ventilation rate is three air changes per hour,

three 100 W bulbs are in continuous use to light the rear part of the room, which is used by four clerical workers.

The exposed 5×2.5 m wall consists of a single glazed window, 1.5×5 m $= 7.5$ m^2
$U = 4.48$ W/m^2 degC
and a clinker concrete spandrel wall, 200 mm, rendered and plastered, 1×5 m $= 5$ m^2
$U = 1.35$ W/m^2 degC

Solution:
Temperature difference $(_\Delta T) = 20\,°C - (-1\,°C) = 21$ degC.

$Q_c = (7.5 \times 4.48 + 5 \times 1.35)\,21$
$\quad = (33.60 + 6.75)\,21 = 40.35 \times 21 = \underline{847\ W},$
the volume of the room is $5 \times 5 \times 2.5$ m $= 62.5$ m^3.
Thus the ventilation rate is:

$$\frac{62.5 \times 3}{3\,600} = \frac{187.5}{3\,600} = 0.052 \text{ m}^3/\text{s}$$

$Q_v = 1\,300 \times 0.052 \times 21 = \underline{1420\ W}$

The three light bulbs and four persons produce:

$Q_i = 3 \times 100 + 4 \times 140 = 300 + 560 = \underline{860\ W}$

As no solar radiation and no evaporative loss are considered (see 3.2.1), the thermal balance equation is:

$Q_i - Q_c - Q_v + Q_m = 0$

substituting the calculated values:

$860 - 847 - 1\,420 + Q_m = 0$

$-1\,407 + Q_m = 0$

$Q_m = 1\,407$ W

The heating installation should provide heat at this rate, or, rounded up, at the rate of 1.5 kW.

3.2.9
Heat gain calculation

Heat gain is usually calculated for the purposes of air conditioning design. It is **79** obvious that this installation should cope with the warmest conditions at its peak capacity. Again, the highest temperature for 90% of the time is taken as 'design out-door temperature' and a solar radiation intensity is taken on similar grounds.

The above example will be used, except:

T_o = 26°C and the incident radiation (I) = 580 W/m²
absorbance of the wall surface $\quad\quad a$ = 0·4
surface conductance $\quad\quad\quad\quad\quad\quad f_o$ = 10 W/m²degC
solar gain factor for window $\quad\quad\quad \theta$ = 0·75

Solution:

Temperature difference ($_\Delta T$) = 26°C −20°C = 6 degC for conduction through the window and for ventilation heat flow, but for the opaque surface the sol-air temperature must be found (see 3.1.18):

$$T_s = 26 + \frac{580 \times 0·4}{10} = 26 + 23·2 = 49·2°C.$$

Thus for the spandrel wall $_\Delta T$ = 49 −20°C = 29 degC.

$$Q_c = (7·5 \times 4·48 \times 6) + (5 \times 1·35 \times 29)$$
$$= (33·60 \times 6) + (6·75 \times 29) = 201·6 + 195·75 = \underline{397\ W}$$
$$Q_s = 7·5 \times 580 \times 0·75 = \qquad\qquad\qquad\qquad \underline{3\,270\ W}$$
$$Q_v = 1\,300 \times 0·052 \times 6 = \qquad\qquad\qquad \underline{405\ W}$$
$$Q_i = \text{(as before)} \qquad\qquad\qquad\qquad\qquad \underline{860\ W}$$

No evaporation loss is considered, thus the thermal balance equation is (see 3.2.1):

$$Q_i + Q_s + Q_c + Q_v + Q_m = 0$$

substituting the calculated values:

$$860 + 3\,270 + 397 + 405 + Q_m = 0$$
$$4\,932 + Q_m = 0$$
$$Q_m = -4\,932\ W$$

The air conditioning system must be capable of removing heat at this rate, or, rounded up, 5 kW.

3.2.10
Cooling by air

If heat is to be removed at this rate by circulating cooled air, the question is: What will have to be the rate of air exchange?

The supplied air, to avoid a chilly draught, can be approximately 16°C: this, mixing with the room air, is to keep the indoor temperature at 20°C. Therefore the temperature difference (return air minus supplied air)

$$_\Delta T = 20°C - 16°C = 4\ degC$$

Q_v is to be 5 000 W. Thus from the equation:

$$Q_v = 1\,300 \times V \times 4 = 5\,200 \times V$$

Therefore the rate of air supply (V) will have to be:

$$V = \frac{5\,000}{5\,200} = 0·962\ m^3/s$$

To avoid draughts, the air inlet velocity is to be limited to approximately 2 m/s and the size of the inlet opening will have to be:

$$\frac{0·962\ m^3/s}{2\ m/s} = 0·481\ m^2 \text{ (for example, 1 m} \times 481\ mm)$$

If the supplied air temperature can be lowered to approximately 12°C (by using an induction unit or a mixing box), the temperature difference is doubled (8 degC) and the rate of air supply can be reduced to half:

$$V = 0.481 \text{ m}^3/\text{s}$$

Comparing this rate of air flow with that necessary for ventilation, the supply of fresh air and the three air changes per hour (0.052 m³/s), it is obvious that the cooling function will set a much greater air flow requirement than the need for fresh air (removal of odours and supply of oxygen rich air).

3.2.11
Heating by air

If in the first example (3.2.8) the required heating rate of 1.5 kW is to be provided by warm air heating, the problem is similar: air is to be used as a heat carrying medium.

Here again, the return air temperature can be taken as the room temperature (20°C) but the supplied-air temperature will have to be higher if any heat is to be conveyed into the room. With normal air inlet diffusers a supplied-air temperature of 26°C will be acceptable, with induction (mixing-) units 30°C is quite normal. Thus, with a temperature difference of 10 degC, the air supply rate will have to be:

$$Q_v = 1\,300 \times V \times {}_\Delta T$$
$$1\,500 = 1\,300 \times V \times 10$$
$$V = \frac{1\,500}{13\,000} = 0.115 \text{ m}^3/\text{s}$$

3.2.12
Transmittance of composite walls

If the transmittance (U) value of the intended wall construction cannot be found in appendix 5.4, it can be calculated as shown in the following example:

assume a wall of a westerly, normal exposure, consisting of the following:

114 mm engineering brickwork	$k = 1.150$ W/m degC
50 mm cavity	$R_c = 0.176$ m² degC/W
100 mm dense concrete blocks	$k = 1.440$ W/m degC
25 mm wood wool slab	$k = 0.093$ W/m degC
12 mm plastering	$k = 0.461$ W/m degC
surface resistance	$1/f_o = 0.076$ m² degC/W
	$1/f_i = 0.123$ m² degC/W

As a first step, the above data has been obtained from tables in appendix 5. Resistances of the individual layers proceeding from the outside inwards will now be calculated (in m² degC/W):

surface: $\quad 1/f_o \qquad = 0.076$

brickwork: $\quad \dfrac{b}{k} = \dfrac{0.114}{1.150} = 0.099$

cavity: $\quad R_c \qquad = 0.176$

concrete: $\quad \dfrac{b}{k} = \dfrac{0.100}{1.440} = 0.069$

wood wool: $\quad \dfrac{b}{k} = \dfrac{0.025}{0.093} = 0.269$

plaster: $\quad \dfrac{b}{k} = \dfrac{0.012}{0.461} = 0.025$

surface: $\quad 1/f_i \qquad = 0.123$

total resistance: $R_a \qquad = \underline{0.837}$

$$U = \frac{1}{R_a} = \frac{1}{0.837} = 1.19 \text{ W/m}^2 \text{ degC}$$

3.2.13
Thermal
gradients

In some cases (e.g. for the prediction of condensation) it will be necessary to know the temperature at any point within the wall, i.e. the *thermal gradient* through the wall, or other constructional elements.

This can be established quite simply by a graphic method, as shown by an example, using the wall analysed in the preceding paragraph:

assume that the internal temperature T_i = 20 °C

and the out-door temperature T_o = 0 °C

Draw a cross-section of the wall (Figure 40) to a scale representing the resistances of the individual layers, instead of the thicknesses. A scale of 1 mm = 0·01 m² degC/W will be suitable, thus the external surface resistance is represented by 7·6 mm and the resistance of the brickwork is shown as 9·9 mm, etc. Alongside this, draw a cross-section of the wall to a physical scale of 1:10.

Set up a temperature scale vertically, which is to apply to both sections (3 mm = 1 degC).

Establish the T_o and T_i points at the faces of the resistance section, and connect these points with a straight line. The intersection points of this line with the various layers can now be projected across horizontally to the corresponding layers of the physical section. A line connecting the points thus derived will represent the thermal gradient through the wall.

Fig 40
Temperature gradient
through a composite
wall
(not to scale)

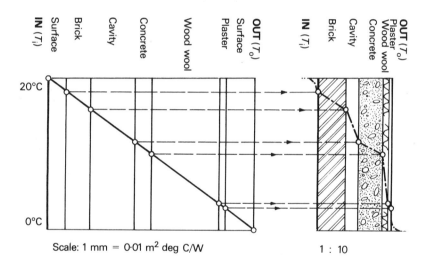

Scale: 1 mm = 0·01 m² deg C/W   1 : 10

3.2.14
Condensation

It has been mentioned (1.2.4 to 5) that relative humidity is a function of temperature, and that as the air is cooled, without changing the moisture content, its RH increases. When the RH reaches 100%, i.e. saturation, dew or condensation will appear. The temperature at which this happens is referred to as 'dewpoint temperature'.

By using the psychrometric chart (Figure 12) the dewpoint temperature for air with any defined moisture content or RH can be found. For example, for air at DBT = 20 °C and RH = 60%, find the intersection of the vertical 20 °C line with the 60% RH curve, project this point across to the left, to intersect with the 100% RH curve and read off the vertical line going through this point: 12·3 °C. This is the dewpoint temperature for the particular air.

If this air comes into contact with a surface having a temperature less than 12·3 °C, *surface condensation* will appear. This is a familiar occurrence on a bathroom mirror or on the inside of a cold window pane. On cold walls such surface condensation may be soaked up into the wall material, but if the surface is impervious, it will be 'dripping wet'.

Most building materials are porous and offer little resistance to the passage of vapours. If the inside humid air penetrates the wall, when it reaches a layer having a temperature less than its own dewpoint temperature, moisture will condense. This phenomenon is known as *interstitial condensation*. Its prediction (and avoidance) is an important concern of building designers in cold climates. The prediction technique [41 and 42] is based on establishing the dewpoint temperature of the air and finding where this will intersect with the thermal gradient of the wall.

**3.2.15
Thermal
design**

Mechanical engineers and heating or air conditioning designers often use calculation methods similar to those described in 3.2.8 to 11. These may become involved, refined and lengthy, but the principle is the same: they work within fixed parameters, i.e. in the thermal balance equation (3.2.1):

$$Q_i + Q_s \pm Q_c \pm Q_v \pm Q_m - Q_e = 0$$

all the factors are, or are assumed to be, fixed and determined, the only dependent variable (which is to be found) is the value of Q_m, the heat flow rate to be provided mechanically.

The building designer is faced with a much more indeterminate situation. He has to make decisions to determine the size, volume and construction of the building, the size and orientation of its windows, etc. – any of which will influence the magnitude of one or several of the thermal balance factors.

There is and there can be no set procedure for the decision sequence, but it may be useful to think of the thermal balance equation at any design decision, to see which of the factors (and in what direction) are affected by the particular decision, and to foretell the consequences of various alternative design solutions.

Q_m – that is, the mechanical controls – are expensive: therefore it should be the designer's aim to produce a zero sum without a Q_m component.

The means of controlling the various factors will be discussed in Section 4.

3.3.1
Steady state assumptions

The equation and calculation methods given in Section 3.2 are valid if, and only if, both out-door and indoor temperatures are constant. As perfectly static conditions do not occur in nature, the basis of the above methods is the *assumption of steady state* conditions. This is an obvious simplification of the actual situation but the results can be taken as reliable if the fluctuations of temperature do not exceed ±3 degC. Such a situation may prevail in the winter of moderate climates when the interior is heated and kept at a given temperature or in a warm-humid climate where the indoor temperature is kept constant by air conditioning.

Calculations based on steady state assumptions are useful to determine the maximum rate of heat loss or heat gain, also for the purpose of establishing the size and capacity of heating and cooling installations. Prediction of the thermal behaviour of the building is not the aim of the exercise — the mechanical controls will provide the necessary adjustments — the designer only has to make sure that enough capacity is provided in heating or cooling to cope with the reasonably likely worst conditions.

The steady state calculation methods can also be considered as preliminary studies, to lead up to the understanding of the more complex *non-steady-state* heat transfer problems.

3.3.2
Periodic heat flow

In nature the variation of climatic conditions produces a non-steady state. Diurnal variations produce an approximately repetitive 24-hour cycle of increasing and decreasing temperatures. The effect of this on a building is that in the hot period heat flows from the environment into the building, where some of it is stored, and at night during the cool period the heat flow is reversed: from the building to the environment. As the cycle is repetitive, it can be described as *periodic heat flow*.

The diagram given in Figure 41 shows the diurnal variations of external and

Fig 41
Time-lag and
decrement factor

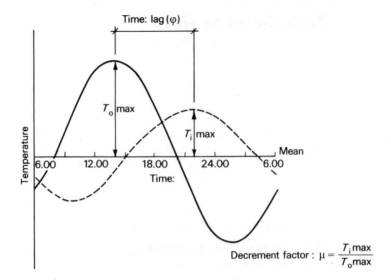

Decrement factor : $\mu = \dfrac{T_i \max}{T_o \max}$

internal temperatures in a periodically changing thermal regime. In the morning, as the out-door temperature increases, heat starts entering the outer surface of the wall. Each particle in the wall will absorb a certain amount of heat for every degree of rise in temperature, depending on the specific heat of the wall material (see 3.1.4). Heat to the next particle will only be transmitted after the temperature of the first particle has increased. Thus the corresponding increase of the internal surface temperature will be delayed, as shown by the broken line.

The out-door temperature will have reached its peak and started decreasing, before the inner surface temperature has reached the same level. From this moment the heat stored in the wall will be dissipated partly to the outside and only partly to the inside. As the out-door air cools, an increasing proportion of this stored heat flows outwards, and when the wall temperature falls below the indoor temperature the direction of the heat flow is completely reversed.

The two quantities characterising this periodic change are the *time-lag* (or phase shift, ϕ) and the *decrement factor* (or amplitude attenuation, denoted μ). The latter is the ratio of the maximum outer and inner surface temperature amplitudes taken from the daily mean.

3.3.3 Thermal diffusivity

Let us think of the situation described above, as the first particle of the wall starts receiving heat from the environment. The rate at which it will transmit heat to the next particle depends on two factors:

1 if it is of a high conductivity material, this rate will be faster
2 if it is a dense material and it has a high specific heat, the rate will be slower, as it will absorb much of the incoming heat before it can start transmitting any

Thus if k = conductivity (W/m degC)
d = density (kg/m³)
c = specific heat (J/kg degC)

the above relationship can be expressed as $k/(d \times c)$: this quantity is denoted as K and referred to as *thermal diffusivity*, or *temperature conductivity* (the latter term being more descriptive).*

The dimension of this quantity will be:

$$K = \frac{k}{d \times c} = \frac{\text{W/m degC}}{\text{kg/m}^3 \times \text{J/kg degC}} = \frac{\text{J/s m degC}}{\text{J/m}^3 \text{degC}} = \frac{\text{m}^2}{\text{s}}$$

* The product $d \times c$ has been referred to in 3.1.4 as 'volumetric specific heat' which has a dimension of kg/m³ × J/kg degC = J/m³ degC.

Fig 42
Decrement factor and
time-lag as a function
of conductance and
capacity

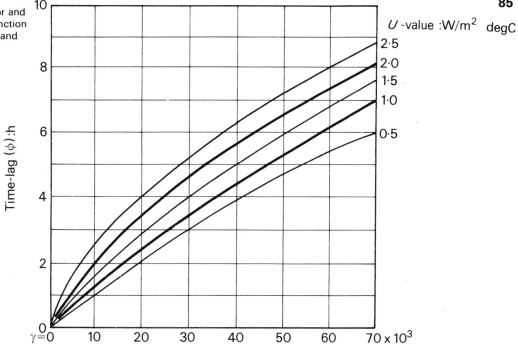

U -value :W/m^2 degC

2·5
2·0
1·5
1·0

0·5

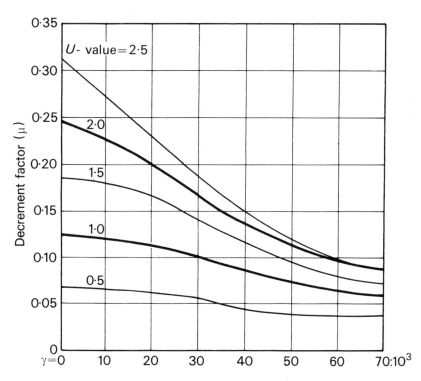

Conductance - capacity index : $\gamma = (\dfrac{d \times c \times b^2}{2k} = \dfrac{d \times c \times b}{2C}) = \dfrac{b^2}{2K}$

where d = density, kg/m^3

c = specific heat, J/kg deg C C = conductance (W/m^2 deg C) = $\dfrac{k}{b}$

b = thickness, m

k = conductivity, W/m deg C K = diffusivity (m^2/s) = $\dfrac{k}{d \times c}$

It can be visualised as the surface area of a sphere over which the temperature spreads in unit time. Figure 42 gives a method for defining ϕ and μ on the basis of diffusivity.

3.3.4
Practical use

In practical work the time-lag (ϕ) and the decrement factor (μ) values are used. These can be calculated for a particular construction [43], but the method is rather involved and not well tested.* Values of ϕ and μ can also be determined experimentally. Figure 43 gives a graphic indication of these values and appendix 6 lists the ϕ and μ values of several frequently used constructions.

A rule of thumb for massive masonry, earth and concrete walls is: $\phi = 10$ hours for each 0·3 m thickness.

Fig 43
Decrement factor and
time-lag values for
massive walls

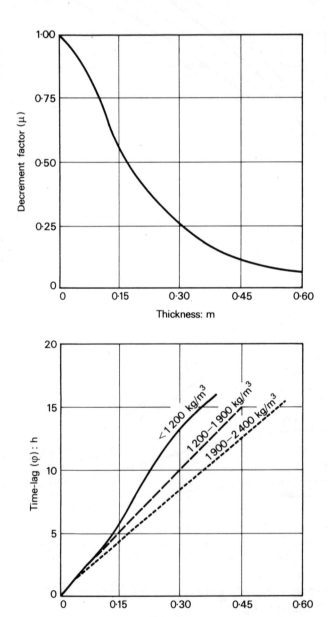

* The reader interested in periodic heat flow problems in more detail is referred to publications listed in the bibliography [44, 46, 47, 48 and 49].

3.3.5
Periodic heat flow calculation

The steady state equation $Q = A \times U \times {}_\Delta T$ can be used to find the balance of heat flow or average heat flow rate over a full cycle in a periodically changing thermal regime. To find the momentary rate of heat flow, it can only be used if the wall or element considered has a negligible thermal capacity.

If the indoor temperature is assumed to be constant (a reasonable assumption in controlled environments), the momentary rate of flow can be calculated fairly simply if it is split in two parts:

a   first, the average heat flow rate is found for the full cycle (one day), using the steady state equation, except that the temperature difference is taken between the daily mean out-door temperature and the indoor temperature:

$$Q' = A \times U \times (T_m - T_i)$$

b   the momentary deviation from the average heat flow rate is found: if the time-lag of the wall is ϕ hours, then the heat flow *now* will depend on the out-door temperature ϕ hours *previously*: T_ϕ. The deviation is found by using a temperature difference value between this T_ϕ and the mean. The transmittance, or U-value, is modified by the decrement factor (μ).

$$Q'' = A \times U \times \mu (T_\phi - T_m)$$

The two equations can be added to get the equation describing the periodic heat flow rate:

$$Q = A \times U \times [(T_m - T_i) + \mu (T_\phi - T_m)]$$

where
Q = momentary heat flow rate in W
A = area in m²
U = transmittance, W/m² degC
T_m = daily mean out-door temperature, °C
T_i = indoor temperature (constant), °C
T_ϕ = out-door (sol-air) temperature
        ϕ hours earlier, °C
μ = decrement factor
ϕ = time-lag in hours

3.3.6
Application

Knowledge of the decrement factor (μ) and time-lag (ϕ) for different materials, thicknesses and combinations of materials in various constructional elements, is important for the designer. He aims at permitting heat gain through the enclosing elements *when* there are heat losses by other channels (e.g. ventilation) but avoids such heat gain *when* there is already a surplus of heat flow into his building. Thus the selection of a construction with an appropriate time-lag is an essential factor in the design. The process could be described as 'balancing in time'.

Section 4.2 will further examine the use of thermal capacity as one of the means of thermal control.

The thermal capacity is a factor to be considered also in moderate climates. Low thermal capacity or 'quick response' structures warm up quickly but also cool rapidly. Large thermal capacity structures will have a longer 'heat-up time' but will conserve heat after switching off the heating.

3.3.7
Effect of insulation

The data given in appendix 6 shows that the position of insulation relative to the high thermal capacity mass has a very significant effect on the time-lag and decrement factor. With a 100-mm concrete slab, the placing of a 40 mm glass wool insulation gives the following variation:

	time-lag:h	decrement factor
Under the slab	3	0·450
On top of slab	11·5	0·046

The reason for this is obvious if the mechanism of the process is observed (e.g. in a hot-dry climate):

1 insulation on the outside reduces the heat flow rate into the mass — less heat will enter the mass in a given time, or, it will take much longer to 'fill up' the thermal storage capacity of the mass

2 insulation on the inside will not affect the 'filling up' process and, although it will reduce the heat emission to the inside space, it will not change the periodicity

In hot climates the aim is not only to store during the day as much of the heat, that has entered the outer surface as possible, but also to dissipate during the night all (or most) of this stored heat, so that by the morning the whole structure should contain as little heat as possible — to have all (or most) of its thermal capacity 'empty', as it were, ready to absorb the next heat wave.

Applied insulation will restrict not only the entry, but also the dissipation of heat. If this insulation is on the outside, heat stored can only be dissipated effectively to the inside. To remove it, good ventilation of the inner surface by the cool night air will be necessary.

3.3.8 Effect of cavity

An unventilated cavity is a good insulator ($R = 0{\cdot}15$ m^{2}degC/W), equal to about 180 mm brick wall. As it has been shown that the insulation should be outside of the main mass, it follows that the main mass should be located in the inner leaf of a cavity wall. The outer leaf should be of a lightweight construction. G K Kuba [45] suggests that the outer leaf should be constructed of hollow blocks or bricks, improving its thermal insulation but reducing its mass. He has also tested the effect of ventilating the cavities and arrived at the conclusion that ventilation during the day is undesirable; but night-time ventilation of the cavity would assist in the cooling of the wall.

Air flow in the cavity at night would be upwards and during the day downwards. Both lower and upper openings should be on the same side and should be closed during the day. If no provision is made for closing the ventilators, they should open to the inside of the building, which itself must be adequately ventilated at night. As, however, an opening to the cavity would admit insects and vermin it is better to have the cavity closed, unventilated.

4.1.1
Objectives

The objective of thermal controls can be stated briefly as follows:

1   When cold discomfort conditions prevail:
    a   to prevent heat loss
    b   to utilise heat gain from the sun and internal sources
    c   to compensate for any net loss, by heating which uses some form of energy supply

2   When hot discomfort conditions prevail:
    a   to prevent heat gain
    b   to maximise heat loss
    c   to remove any excess heat by cooling, which uses some form of energy supply

3   When conditions vary diurnally between hot and cold discomfort:
    a   to even out variations
    b   (**1**) in the cold phase and (**2**) in the hot phase (as above)
    c   to compensate for both excesses by a flexible heating-cooling system

Objectives listed under **a** and **b** in each group can be achieved by structural or constructional (passive) means, item **c** in each group is the task of mechanical or energy-based (active) controls.

4.1.2
Degree of control

Under extreme conditions, when human existence is at risk, mechanical controls are positively necessary. When the conditions are such that only the degree of comfort is in question — when the risk is a slight discomfort — the use of mechanical controls is optional.

As D H K Lee expressed it [50] 'the degree of sophistication (in environmental controls) is largely a socio-economic question'. In other words, we are capable of creating and maintaining any specified set of indoor conditions, but both our preferences and the refinement of control-installations will depend on our social status, on the standards of the society we live in and on the financial means at our disposal. A value judgment will be involved in deciding what degree of comfort we want to achieve and how much we are prepared to pay for it.

The environment immediately outside and between buildings can be influenced by the design of a settlement and by the grouping of buildings to a minor extent (see 1.4.14: urban climate). Figure 44 shows that the extremities of climatic variations can be attenuated by such means.

Fig 44
Potential of climatic controls

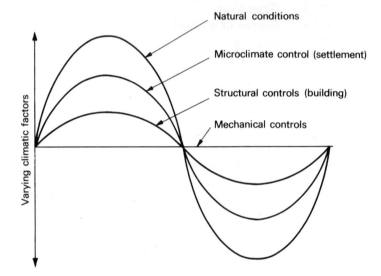

Natural conditions

Microclimate control (settlement)

Structural controls (building)

Mechanical controls

Varying climatic factors

Structural (passive) means of control can provide a further levelling out of the climatic variations, and often even comfort conditions can be achieved by such means.

Precisely controlled indoor climate can only be achieved by mechanical (active) controls (the straight line in Figure 44), but this may not be our aim, and even if it is, with adequate structural controls, the task of mechanical controls is radically reduced and it becomes more economical.

4.1.3
Heating

As the problems of tropical climates are our main concern, only a brief survey of heating is given.*

Heating can be provided locally, i.e. by the conversion of some form of energy (usually the chemical energy of some fuel material) into heat, where it is required. All the various fireplaces, stoves and ovens — burning wood, coal, coke or oil — fall into this category. The gas and electric heaters can be considered as using a processed fuel: the energy of coal, mineral gas, oil or hydraulic and atomic energy is processed centrally (by gas-works or generating plants), converted into a readily usable form and distributed through a network of pipes or cables to the points of use.

Central heating is the term used to describe an installation where heat is produced at a central point (the boiler or furnace), using any of the above mentioned fuel materials, and is subsequently distributed by some conveying medium. This

* A more extensive coverage of the topic can be found in items listed under [51] and [52] in the bibliography.

conveying medium is most often water or air, but it can be steam (or, theoretically, any other liquid or gas).

The level of centralisation can vary, from central heating of a single flat, of a house, of a block of flats or offices, through a hospital consisting of many buildings to an extensive 'district heating' scheme.

Any central heating system consists of three distinct elements:

1   the 'heat raising plant' (boiler or furnace)
2   the distribution network (ducting or piping)
3   the heat emitter units (diffusers, radiators or convectors)

4.1.4
Size of installation

The size and capacity of the heating installation depends on the rate of heat loss from the building. Increased insulation would reduce the heat loss rate, thus both the installation and running costs of heating would be reduced. To optimise the insulation versus heating expenditure, extensive cost-benefit analyses have been carried out [53]. (see 8.2.8)

In tropical climates the need for heating will rarely arise. Tropical upland climates are probably the only climates where cool discomfort conditions may prevail for such a length of time that the thermal storage capacity of the structure is insufficient to ensure indoor comfort. Even here the heat deficit is so small that in a suitably designed and built building, the incidental internal heat gain (from human bodies, lighting, etc.) will bring the temperature up to a level acceptable with warm clothing. At most, some local heating appliances may be provided, but will rarely be used.

4.1.5
Problems associated with heating

Heating may be the answer to an environmental problem, but it will create some of its own problems.

Distribution of heat, evenly, throughout the heated space is not an easy task. The temperature gradient between areas of concentrated heat loss (e.g. windows) and zones of the heat output units may be so steep that strong convection currents (draughts) are generated, adversely affecting comfort conditions and causing, for instance, discoloration of surfaces.

Dryness (very low humidity) is a result of heating. When cool air of medium humidity is heated, its relative humidity is decreased (see psychrometric chart: Figure 12). For example, air at 0°C DBT and 60% RH, heated to 20°C DBT, will cause the RH to drop to 15%.

Condensation can be caused indirectly. The warm indoor air will readily take on moisture from any available source: human exhalation (around 45 g/h per person), cooking, kettles, baths, etc. Its RH increases, consequently its dewpoint temperature is also increased. *Air* at 20°C DBT and 80% RH will have a dewpoint temperature of 16·5°C. It only needs to come into contact with a surface of 16°C and condensation will appear. Interstitial condensation may soak the wall material and increase its conductivity, thus lowering the wall surface temperature, which in turn further increases the condensation.

None of these problems is likely to arise in tropical climates (except with artificial cooling), but it is useful to understand the principles involved, which may be relevant under any sort of conditions.

4.1.6
Ventilation

Humans consume oxygen, taken from the air by breathing, and exhale carbon dioxide. An average person, depending on his activity, inhales about 0·5 to 5 m^3/h. In a closed environment oxygen content is reduced and the carbon dioxide content is increased by man's presence. Biologically the limit of existence is 0·5% CO_2 content (by volume) but a 0·15% content already gives a markedly 'used air' effect. Body smells, fumes and vapours produced by a variety of processes, such as smoking, all add to the deterioration of an enclosed volume of air. A supply of fresh air at a rate substantially higher than the volume of actually inhaled air will be necessary.

In many situations an adequate air supply can be ensured simply by keeping the windows and doors open. If, however, there is a large difference between externally given and internally created (comfort) conditions, the air exchange rate must be regulated, particularly if the interior is heated or cooled by the expenditure of energy. Often a certain degree of control can be achieved by the occupants opening and closing the windows at will, but in many cases there are no windows or a more precise and centralised form of control is necessary — therefore mechanical ventilation should be installed. This should supply air at the rate of 12 to 28 m³/h per person, depending on the volume of space and the activities carried out.

In mechanical ventilation the air is moved by motor driven fans, which can be:

4.1.7 Mechanical ventilation systems

a   propellor type or axial flow fans
b   impeller type, centrifugal or tangential flow fans

These can be local, e.g. built into a window or a wall, or may be central, in which case ducts will be necessary to deliver and distribute the air to where it is required.
   The installation can take the following forms:

1   an exhaust system — removing the used air and letting fresh air find its way in through grilles and openings (room under reduced pressure)
2   a plenum system — supplying air into the space and forcing out used air through grilles, etc. (slight overpressure in room)
3   a balanced system — both supplying and removing air. The most dependable, but most expensive, system used when combined with warm air heating, as it permits partial recirculation.

With a plenum or balanced system the air will normally be filtered at the point of intake, by one of the following means:
a   dry filters, fibrous or porous materials (paper, cloth or glass fibres), usually disposable
b   wet filters, metal turning or some loose material with a large specific surface, where all surfaces are coated with oil, normally by dipping. These can be cleaned and reused
c   washing, by a curtain of water flowing down the face of a metal or porcelain grille, or a spray through which the air is drawn
d   electrostatic filters, in which the suspended dust particles are ionised by a high static electrical charge and stick to the face of electrode plates

4.1.8 Cooling by ventilation

The moving air can be utilised as a heat conveying medium. Warm air heating is usually combined with a mechanical ventilation system. Ventilation can also provide a cooling effect simply by replacing the warm inside air with cooler outside air.
   In cold climates the need for cooling rarely arises. In warm climates the intention is to keep the indoor air cooler than the out-door air, thus there can be no cooling by ventilation. It can, however, be used quite successfully in a situation where the out-door air is at a comfortable temperature or just below that, but there is a significant internal heat gain (e.g. in a meeting room or a dance hall) which would cause indoor overheating.
   As an example, let us assume that the out-door temperature is 18°C; the indoor temperature has risen to 28°C and there is an internal heat gain of 5 kW, which would cause a further increase of indoor temperature.
   The temperature difference ($_\Delta T$) is 28°C −18°C = 10 degC. The specific heat of air is 1300 J/m³ degC. Using the ventilation heat loss equation (3.2.3):

$$Q_v = 1\,300 \times V \times {_\Delta T}$$
$$5\,000 = 1\,300 \times V \times 10$$

We must provide a ventilation rate of:

$$V = \frac{5\,000}{13\,000} = 0 \cdot 385 \text{ m}^3/\text{s}$$

With an air velocity of 2 m/s the necessary duct cross-sectional area should be: **95**

$$\frac{0.385 \text{ m}^3/\text{s}}{2 \text{ m/s}} = 0.192 \text{ m}^2, \text{ e.g. } 0.30 \times 0.64 \text{ m}$$

A fan giving the above ventilation rate can be selected from catalogues.

Note. The above is an approximate calculation only: a mechanical engineer would make allowances for frictional losses in ducts (velocity and pressure gradients).

Another form of cooling by air movement is the 'physiological cooling' (2.1.4) by directing an air stream of substantial velocity at the body surface. This is achieved by table-top or ceiling-mounted fans (punkahs), which do not provide air exchange, but generate an air movement.

4.1.9 Evaporative cooling

It has been mentioned (3.2.7) that evaporation of water absorbs a significant amount of heat. The latent heat of evaporation, at normal temperatures, is around 2 400 kJ/kg of water. This phenomenon can be successfully utilised for the cooling of air when the air itself is dry, so that the moisture does not cause inconvenience – and it may even improve the conditions. This is likely to be the case in hot-dry climates.

In a mechanical installation, a very fine spray of water may be put across an air intake duct to achieve maximum surface contact between air and water. (It must be followed by a set of 'eliminator plates' which would trap and drain away any small droplets of water carried by the fast moving air stream.) It may serve three purposes:

1 'washing the air', that is water droplets will stick to dust particles, which can thus no longer remain in suspension; they fall down and are washed away by the surplus water (4.1.7)
2 evaporative cooling, as described above
3 humidification, i.e. the increase of relative humidity

In a warm-humid climate the first of these functions could be performed; the second one only to a limited extent (as the air is already humid, it will not take on much extra moisture, especially if its temperature is lowered at the same time) – but the third one would definitely be undesirable: it would increase the humidity, which is already too high.

Such water sprays can be utilised in warm-humid climates only as a preliminary treatment of air if it is to be subsequently dehumidified.

4.1.10 Mechanical cooling

The simplest example of mechanical cooling is the domestic refrigerator, shown diagrammatically in Figure 45. A suitable gas, the 'refrigerant', is circulated in a closed circuit by a compressor. This is most often a gas called Freon (CF_2Cl_2); at least in small installations. In large plants, such as cold storage buildings, ammonia (NH_3) or carbon dioxide (CO_2) is often used: the former is toxic, therefore any leakage may be troublesome; the latter requires very high pressure.

The circuit consists of two coils:

Fig 45
A refrigeration (heat-pump) circuit

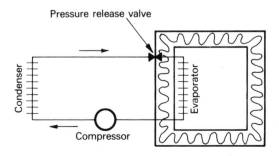

the warm coil or condenser, and
the cold coil or evaporator.

The two coils are connected on one side through a compressor and on the other side through a pressure release valve. The warm coil is thus kept under high pressure and the cold coil under a negative pressure. The refrigerant is in a liquid state under compression and in a gaseous state under low pressure. Without changing the heat content, compression increases the temperature; expansion decreases it. When liquefying, the refrigerant releases its latent heat of evaporation, and when evaporating, it absorbs a similar amount of heat.

The cycle can be described as follows:

a compressor   (i) increases pressure
                          (ii) no change in heat content
                          (iii) temperature from, say, 0 °C to 30 °C

b condenser   (i) no change in pressure
                          (ii) in condensation latent heat released and dissipated to the environment
                          (iii) temperature from 30 to, say, 26 °C

c pressure   (i) admits liquid only above a set pressure, thus guarantees a
   valve   low pressure in evaporator
                          (ii) no change in heat content
                          (iii) temperature from 26 to, say, −4 °C

d evaporator   (i) no change in pressure
                          (ii) in evaporation latent heat absorbed
                          (iii) heat taken from environment
                          (iv) temperature from −4 to, say, 0 °C

If the evaporator coil is placed into an air supply duct (instead of into a refrigerator cabinet) the air blown across it will be cooled (Figure 46).

Fig 46
Air cooler
arrangement

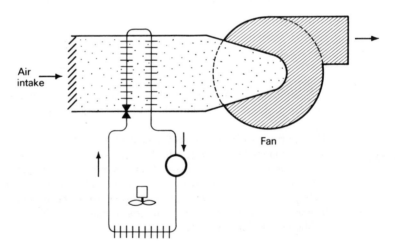

Air
intake

Fan

4.1.11 Measurement of cooling capacity

The 'ton of refrigeration' is an obsolete unit for the measurement of cooling capacity or rate of heat flow in cooling, but much of the existing literature still uses it. Its meaning and derivation has been explained in 3.1.6, but it is useful to recall that:

1 ton of refrigeration = 3 516 W
or, approximately   3·5 kW

In looking at manufacturers' information sheets, it should not cause any confusion to see an item such as:

cooling capacity   50 kW
compressor power 23 kW

It is not a question of 50 kW power being produced by 23 kW! In the refrigeration plant the 23 kW electric motor is working to cause the *removal* of heat at the rate of 50 kW.

**4.1.12
Problems
associated
with cooling**

If the air in a space is to be cooled, the space must be fully enclosed, otherwise the cooled inside air and the warm outside air would mix. If doors and windows are closed, the fresh air needed by the occupants must be supplied mechanically. Thus cooling must be combined with some form of mechanical ventilation system.

If the outside air is at a high temperature (30 °C DBT) and of a medium humidity (60%), this will be its condition at the point of air intake. If it is to be cooled to 18 °C DBT, its RH will increase. It will actually reach saturation point at 21·5 °C, so with further cooling some moisture will condense and at the end we will have an 18 °C DBT air of 100% RH. As the AH at 21·5 °C is 16 g/kg, and at 18 °C and 100% RH it is 13 g/kg, 3 g of moisture will condense out of every kg of air passing through the cooler. This condensate may be drained away, but the 100% RH of the supplied air would be the cause of acute discomfort.

	T_o: °C	RH: %	AH: g/kg	
cooled	30	60	16	
	21·5	100	16	condensation
	18	100	13	

**4.1.13
Dehumidifica-
tion**

What we would like to get, is air at 18 °C DBT and 60% RH. The only way to remove moisture from the air is to force it to condense out. This can only be done by cooling. When air is cooled to its dewpoint, the point indicating its condition on the psychrometric chart (Figure 12) would be moving horizontally across to the left. When it reaches the extreme curve, the 100% RH line, it has reached its dewpoint. Further cooling would cause it to move along the 100% RH curve, downwards and to the left. The downwards movement indicates that moisture is being condensed out, i.e. the absolute humidity is being reduced.

What must be done here, is to cool the air far below the required 18 °C DBT to get rid of moisture and then reheat it to 18 °C, without any addition of moisture, thus reducing the relative humidity. The question now is: 'How far is it to be cooled?' First we have to establish what value of AH corresponds to the desired condition, then find from the psychrometric chart at what temperature this AH would saturate the air.

All this can be done by using the psychrometric chart without any calculations. If any two of the DBT, RH, AH and WBT are known, the other two quantities can be found from the chart.

The method is best illustrated by an example. The values in **bold** type are the ones found from the psychrometric chart:

	DBT °C	RH %	AH g/kg
Given condition:	25	65	**13**
Desired condition:	18	60	**7·8**
Cooled to:	**10·5**	100	7·8
Reheated to:	18	**60**	7·8

Incidentally it can be established that the 13 − 7·8 = 5·2 g/kg of moisture will condense.

**4.1.14
Air
conditioning**

It has been shown that air, supplied to a room or to a building by mechanical means, is or can be:

propelled or moved
filtered

washed
humidified
cooled
dehumidified
heated or reheated

The collective term for the machinery which carries out all these functions is 'air handling plant', and the installation is referred to as *air conditioning*. Without dehumidification the system is not air conditioning.

Figure 47 shows the schematic arrangement of an air conditioner. As an actual piece of machinery, this may be available in the form of a box or 'unit conditioner' which can be built into a wall or a window, or, for a large plant, each section can be a separate unit and such sections of the appropriate size and capacity can be combined in the desired sequence.

Fig 47
An air conditioner

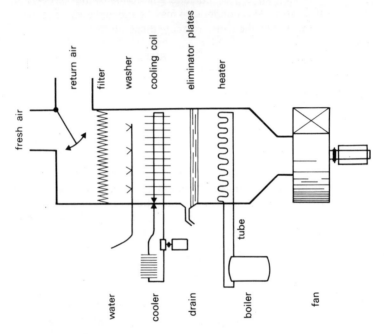

In principle a building installation can take one of the following three forms:

1   *central handling*, i.e. all the above functions are performed by a central plant and all the required air is distributed through a duct system
2   *local handling*, where the boiler and refrigeration plant is central, hot and chilled water is circulated to local air handling units, each serving a certain section of the building (much less ductwork is necessary)
3   *an induction system*, where only a small proportion of the required air quantity is treated centrally but it is dried or heated or cooled far beyond the required level. It is distributed through small size circular ducts usually at high velocity and before being discharged it is mixed with the room air through an induction unit (Figure 48)

Fig 48
Induction units

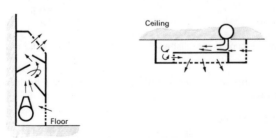

**4.1.15
Control
systems**

In its simplest form the unit conditioner can be controlled by manually turning a
few knobs. In its more refined form the air conditioning installation becomes a
self-regulating (homeostatic) system. Such a control system has three major types
of components:

1 *sensors*; thermometers and hygrometers, constantly monitoring the conditions
and sending information to the control unit
2 the *control unit*, which receives the above information and according to a set
programme issues 'instructions' for compensatory adjustments
3 *servo-mechanisms*: motorised valves, switches and dampers, which carry out
the above instructions and regulate all the processes, such as fan speed, rate of air
flow, temperature of cooling or heating, thus the rate of working for the boiler or
the cooling plant, etc.

Variations of solar heat gain differ from elevation to elevation. Heat losses may
depend on the direction of wind. Internal heat gains may vary from one part of the
building to another. Clearly, various parts or zones of the building may require
different thermal adjustments at the same time. Thus, a sophisticated system requires the building to be subdivided into several or many zones, each of which is
monitored and conditioned independently.

In an extreme case it can happen that the northern part of a building requires
heating, whilst the south facing part is overheated and requires cooling. For such
extremes, the recently developed 'total energy concept' requires the various zones
to be interconnected, and if the situation so requires, the surplus heat of one zone
to be utilised in heating the underheated zone.

**4.2.1
The need for
structural
controls**

'The use of massive air conditioning plants to correct an ill-conceived environment does not differ in principle from the use of a masonry facade to hide an unnecessarily ugly concrete structure' [54].

'The climate . . . presents a challenge to the architect not satisfied with substituting mechanical equipment for good design' [55].

These statements express an unequivocal ethical attitude to architectural design. V Olgyay arrives at a similar conclusion by way of a pragmatic approach: 'We do not expect to solve the problems of uncomfortable conditions by natural means only. The environmental elements aiding us have their limits. But it is expected that the architect should build the shelter in such a way as to bring out the best of the natural possibilities' [56].

E T Weston sums it up most poignantly: 'The less plant and fuel, the more satisfactory the result' [57].

Referring back to Figure 44 (4.1.2), we could summarise the task of environmental controls as follows:

to ensure the best possible indoor thermal conditions by relying on structural (passive) controls, which may obviate the need for any mechanical (active) controls, but even if mechanical controls do have to be resorted to, their task will thereby be reduced to a minimum.

The various structural (passive) means of controlling the thermal environment will be examined in the following paragraphs.

4.2.2 Thermal insulation

A construction with a low *U*-value (air-to-air transmittance) will reduce all forms of conduction heat transfer through the building envelope. Such a conduction heat flow would be large, if the temperature difference were large. With small temperature differences between the inside and outside, the heat flow would be small anyway; an improvement in thermal insulation would not bring any significant reduction.

However, it is worth remembering, that in a heat gain situation, with strong solar radiation, it is the sol-air temperature value which must be used to find the temperature difference, thus even if the air temperature difference is small, the actual temperature difference acting as a motive force for heat flow may be large, consequently insulation may be important.

Insulation will be most effective under steady state conditions, or if at least the direction of the heat flow is constant for long periods of time — especially for heated or air conditioned buildings. Where the direction of heat flow is twice reversed in every 24-hour cycle, the significance of insulation will be diminished.

4.2.3 Thermal capacity

Under conditions with large diurnal temperature variations the significance of thermal capacity will be much greater than of insulation. Some authors refer to the effect of thermal capacity as *capacitive insulation*, as opposed to *resistive insulation* provided by low conductivity materials and low transmittance constructions.

The theory of periodic heat flow and the concepts of time-lag and decrement factor have been introduced in Section 3.3. Here we can set the question: 'How much thermal capacity, what length of time-lag, is desirable?' A point often overlooked is that the thermal capacity can be too much, the time-lag can be too long. For example, a wall facing east receives its maximum heating at 10.00 hours. A time-lag of 10 hours would put the inside surface temperature maximum at 20.00 hours, when it is likely to be too hot anyway and the occupants may want to sleep but cannot.*

The question can be answered by drawing a graph of the out-door (sol-air) temperature variations for each wall and establishing from this at what time will the maximum indoor heating effect be required or tolerated. Figure 49 shows an example of such a graph and explains the reasoning for the selection of an appropriate time-lag.

4.2.4 Solar control

The effect of radiation on *opaque surfaces* can be combined with the effect of warm air by using the sol-air temperature concept (3.1.18). The magnitude of sol-air temperature is influenced by factors within the designer's control: absorbance and surface conductance. Appendix 5.6 shows that the selection of colour has little effect; the selection of materials is, however, of greater significance (see 3.1.16). Variations in surface conductance are even less, but a lesser absorbance and a greater surface conductance would reduce the solar heating effect.

However, even from a simple example, such as that given in 3.2.9, it is quite obvious that by far the greatest source of heat gain can be the solar radiation entering *through a window*. This could, in fact, increase the indoor temperature far above the out-door air temperature, even in moderate climates, through what is known as the 'greenhouse effect'. Window glasses are practically transparent for short-wave infra-red radiation emitted by the sun, but almost opaque for long-wave radiation emitted by objects in the room. The consequence of this is that the radiant heat, once it has entered through a window, is trapped inside the building. If solar overheating is a problem, as in all tropical climates, there are four methods available

---

* In fact it often happens, that people in hot-dry climates sleep on the roof or in a lightweight shelter constructed on top of a massive building, at least for the first half of the night. After midnight they may go indoors, as by then the out-door temperature will have dropped to cool discomfort and indoors it may have cooled to be just comfortable.

for the reduction of solar heat gain through windows, four variables which are **103**
within the control of the designer:

1   orientation and window size
2   internal blinds, curtains
3   special glasses
4   external shading devices

Each of these is examined in more detail in the following paragraphs.

Fig 49
Determining the
desirable time-lag

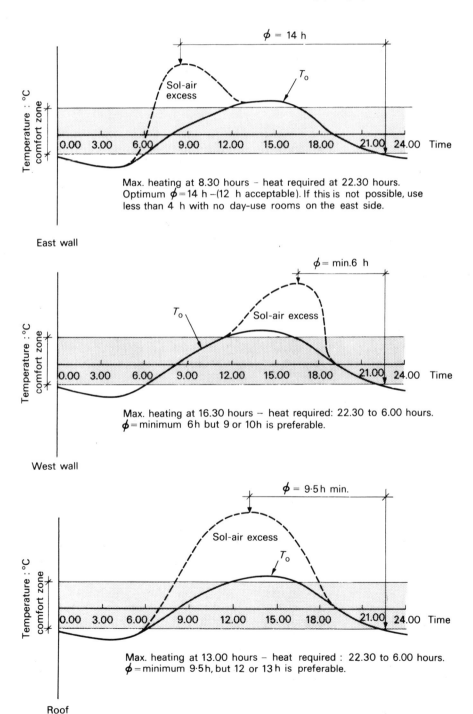

Max. heating at 8.30 hours – heat required at 22.30 hours.
Optimum ϕ = 14 h –(12 h acceptable). If this is not possible, use
less than 4 h with no day-use rooms on the east side.

East wall

Max. heating at 16.30 hours – heat required: 22.30 to 6.00 hours.
ϕ = minimum 6h but 9 or 10h is preferable.

West wall

Max. heating at 13.00 hours – heat required : 22.30 to 6.00 hours.
ϕ = minimum 9·5h, but 12 or 13 h is preferable.

Roof

Fig 50
Solar radiation
intensities for latitude
1° South (Nairobi) —
measured values

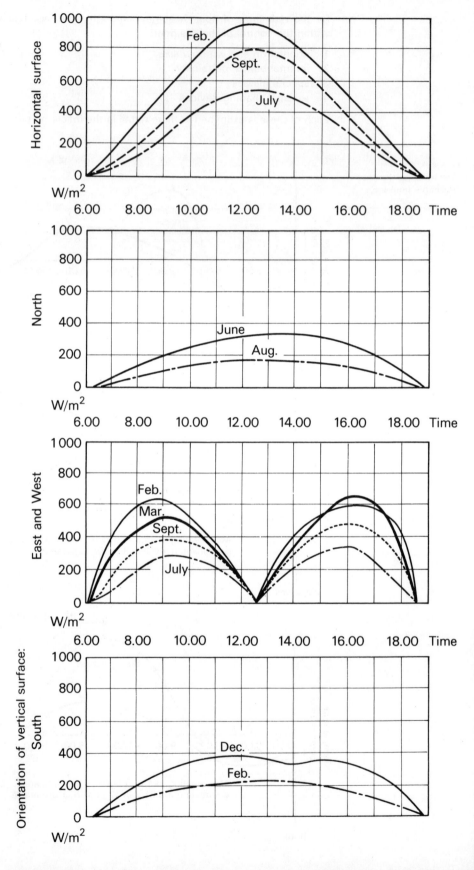

4.2.5
Orientation

It is useful to compare the variations of solar radiation intensities on a horizontal surface and on vertical walls of different orientations in graph form, as shown for two locations: latitude 1 °S. and latitude 33 °S. (Figures 50 and 51). The former is based on measured values, the latter is calculated, giving the possible maximum (assuming clear skies). Irregularities in the former are the effects of clouds. Nevertheless, the following facts will be apparent from the graphs:

a In both locations, but especially near the Equator, the horizontal surface receives the greatest intensity
b At the higher latitude the wall facing the Equator receives the next highest intensity in the winter (when the sun is low) but it receives very little in the summer
c In the equatorial location north and south walls receive the least intensity and that only for short periods of the year
d East and west facing walls receive the second highest intensities in the equatorial location and consistently large intensities even at the higher latitude

The conclusion can now be drawn that in the equatorial location, if solar heat gain is to be avoided, the main windows should face north or south. At the higher latitude, an orientation away from the Equator would receive the least sunshine, but here it may be desirable to have some solar heat gain in the winter, when the sun is low – so an orientation towards the Equator may be preferable. In both locations only minor openings of unimportant rooms should be placed on the east and west side. Solar heat gain on the west side can be particularly troublesome as its maximum intensity coincides with the hottest part of the day.

Proviso: the above conclusions are valid, all other factors being equal. If wind is to be captured or a pleasant view is to be utilised, etc., these considerations may, at times, override the solar considerations.

4.2.6
Internal blinds and curtains

Internal blinds and curtains are not very effective ways of solar control. It is true that they stop the passage of radiation, but they themselves absorb the solar heat and can reach a very high temperature. The absorbed heat will be partly convected to the indoor air and partly reradiated. Half of this reradiation is outwards, but as it is of a long wavelength, it is stopped by the window glass. The usual narrow space between the window and the blind will thus be quite substantially overheated. The hot surface of the blind causes the indoor MRT to rise far above the air temperature.

As a broad generalisation the daily average solar gain factor* of a single glazed window will be:

θ = 72% without any solar control device, and
θ = 55% with an internal venetian blind [58], i.e. the reduction is only 17%.†

4.2.7
Heat absorbing glasses

Whilst on opaque surfaces the incident radiation is partly absorbed and partly reflected (3.1.16):

$a + r = 1$

with transparent bodies, it may be absorbed reflected or transmitted. The proportion of the latter is expressed by the coefficient *transmittance* (t), thus:

$a + r + t = 1$

An ordinary window glass transmits a large proportion of all radiation between 300 and 3000 nm, i.e. both visible light and short-wave infra-red, but very little around and outside the 300 to 3000 nm range. Its transmittance is selective. This selective transmittance can be modified by varying the composition of the glass to reduce substantially the infra-red transmission, whilst only slightly affecting the light transmission (Figure 52). Such a product is referred to as *heat absorbing glass.*

---

* Solar gain factor is defined in 4.2.9
† For a more detailed treatment of this topic the reader is referred to publications listed in the bibliography under [56] and [58].

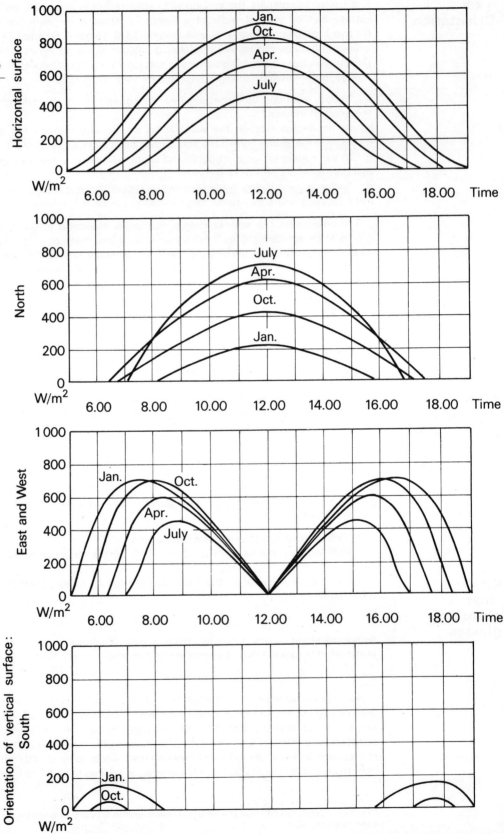

Fig 51
Solar radiation
intensities for latitude
33° South (Sydney) —
calculated values

The transmittance may be reduced from $t = 74\%$ to less than $t = 42\%$. One difficulty is that the reduction in transmittance is accompanied by a corresponding increase in absorbance, therefore an increased amount of heat is absorbed by the glass itself and it can reach a very high temperature. The absorbed heat will be reradiated and convected partly to the outside and partly to the inside, thus the net improvement will not be as great as the reduction in transmittance. The total amount of heat admitted, i.e. the total solar gain, is reduced from 83 only to 68% — as shown by Figure 53.

Fig 52
Transmittance of glasses

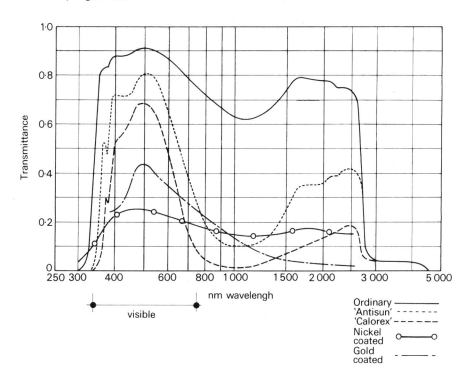

Ordinary ————
'Antisun' - - - - -
'Calorex' – – – –
Nickel coated o———o
Gold coated – —— -

Fig 53
Heat transfer through glass

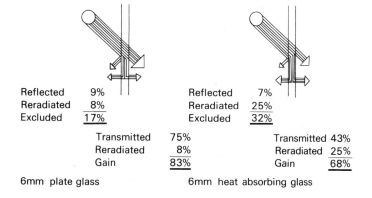

Reflected	9%		Reflected	7%	
Reradiated	8%		Reradiated	25%	
Excluded	17%		Excluded	32%	
	Transmitted	75%		Transmitted	43%
	Reradiated	8%		Reradiated	25%
	Gain	83%		Gain	68%

6mm plate glass   6mm heat absorbing glass

One way to overcome this absorption heat gain is to mount the heat absorbing glass at some distance (0·5 to 1 m) in front of an ordinary glazed window. This would reduce the transmission, and the absorbed heat would be dissipated on both faces to the outside air. Any heat reradiated towards the window would be at long wavelengths, for which the ordinary glass window is opaque.

**4.2.8
Other special
glasses**

Whilst the heat absorbing glasses achieve a selective transmittance by selectivity in absorption, the *heat reflecting glass* achieves a similar selective transmittance by selectivity in reflection [60]. The glass is coated by a thin film of metal (usually nickel or gold), applied by vacuum evaporation: the effect is shown in Figure 54. Such glasses absorb very little heat, therefore the improvement in reducing the total solar gain is far greater, but unfortunately they are still rather expensive. Appendix 7 gives a summary of transmission characteristics of various glasses.

Fig 54
Transmittance of
coated glasses

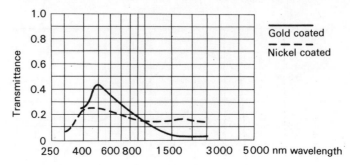

Recently, several types of photochromatic or *light-sensitive glasses* have been developed, containing submicroscopic halide crystals [61], which turn dark when exposed to strong light and regain their transparency when the light source is removed. Their transmittance may thus vary between 74 and 1%. When the technique is more developed and more economical, these glasses may have a future in solar control.

**4.2.9
Effects of
angle of
incidence**

The transmittance, etc., values mentioned above and in appendix 7 are valid for normal incidence. When the angle of incidence is other than normal, the transmittance (t) is reduced. For diffuse radiation the coefficients do not change with the angle of incidence.

To determine the total heat gain through a glazed window, one should establish:

incident direct radiation	I_a (W/m²)
incident diffuse radiation	I_d (W/m²)
angle of incidence	β
transmittance for given incidence	t
transmittance for diffuse radiation	t'
absorbance for given incidence	a
absorbance for diffuse radiation	a'

and find the sum of the following components:

direct radiation × transmittance	$I_a \times t$
diffuse radiation from half of the sky hemisphere × diffuse transmittance	$\dfrac{I_d \times t'}{2}$
half of the absorbed direct radiation	$\dfrac{I_a \times a}{2}$
half of the absorbed diffuse radiation	$\dfrac{I_d \times a'}{2} \times \dfrac{1}{2}$

thus

$$Q_s = A\left(I_a \times t + \frac{I_d \times t'}{2} + \frac{I_a \times a}{2} + \frac{I_d \times a'}{4}\right)$$

To simplify this lengthy calculation, the concept of *solar gain factor* (θ) has been introduced which expresses the proportion of the total solar heat admitted by a window by whatever means. The value of this for different angles of incidence can be read from the graphs given in Figure 55 [60] and the total incident radiation is to be multiplied by this single value, thus:

$$Q_s = A \times I \times \theta$$

as given in 3.2.4.

Fig 55
Solar gain factors (θ)

Above top line: reflectance (r)
Below lower line: transmittance (t)
Between two thin lines:
    absorbance (a)
Up to heavy line:
solar gain factor
(including transmittance plus
part of absorbed energy
emitted inwards)

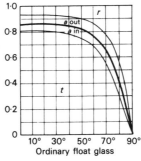

Ordinary float glass

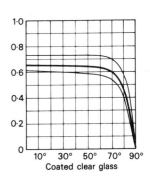

Coated clear glass

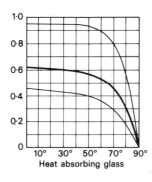

Heat absorbing glass

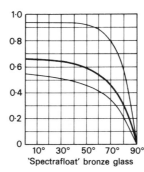

'Spectrafloat' bronze glass

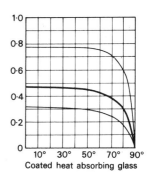

Coated heat absorbing glass

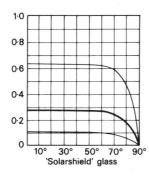

'Solarshield' glass

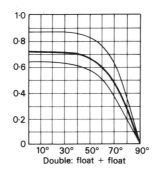

Double: float + float

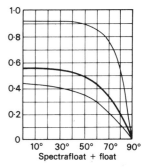

Spectrafloat + float

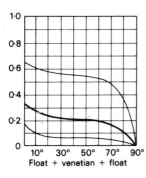

Float + venetian + float

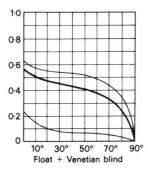

Float + Venetian blind

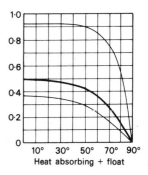

Heat absorbing + float

Fig 56
Stereographic
projection

(Hour lines are marked in
British Standard Time.
With Greenwich Mean
Time noon would be
12.00)

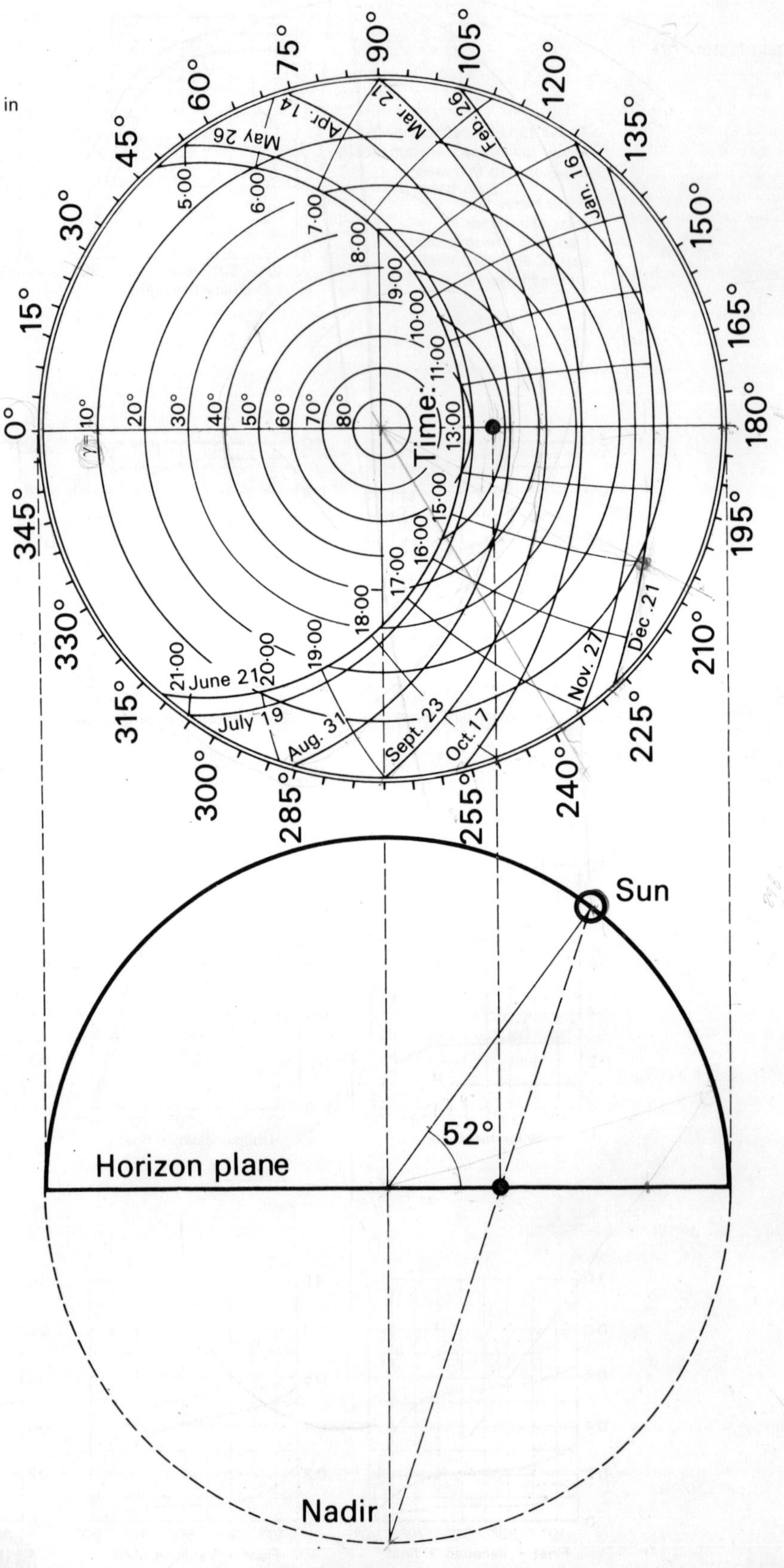

Horizon plane

52°

Sun

Nadir

4.2.10
The sun's
positions

To find the angle of incidence of solar radiation, the position of the sun in relation to the building elevation must be established for the given point in time.

The sun's position on the sky hemisphere can be specified by two angles:

- the *solar altitude angle* (γ), i.e. the vertical angle at the point of observation between the horizon plane and the line connecting the sun with the observer.

the *solar azimuth angle* (a), i.e. the angle at the point of observation measured on a horizontal plane between the northerly direction and a point on the horizon circle, where it is intersected by the arc of a vertical circle, going through the zenith and the sun's position. Thus

north $a = 0°$ or $360°$
east $\quad a = 90°$
south $a = 180°$
west $\quad a = 270°$ etc.

These two angles can be read directly for any date of the year and any hour of the day from the *solar charts* or sun-path diagrams, given in Appendix 8.

There are several methods of projection for representing the sun's apparent movement two-dimensionally but the 'stereographic' method of projection here adopted is by far the most generally used. Figure 56 shows the method of projection. The 'nadir' point is taken as the centre of projection and the sun's position on the apparent sky-hemisphere is projected onto the horizon plane represented by a horizontal circle.

The sun's paths at various dates are shown by a group of curves extending from east to west (the 'date lines') which are intersected by the short 'hour lines'.

The series of concentric circles establish a scale of altitude angles and the perimeter scale gives the azimuth angle.

Example:

Find the sun's position in an equatorial location at 15.00 hours on 22 December:

a select the chart marked latitude 0°
b select the 22 December date line
c select the 15.00 hour line and mark its intersection with the date line
d read off from the concentric circles the altitude angle – 40°
e lay a straight-edge from the centre of the chart through the marked time point to the perimeter scale and read off the azimuth angle – 239°

4.2.11
Angle of
incidence

From these two angles the sun's position in relation to the wall surface of any orientation (thus the angle of incidence) can be established.

The horizontal component of the angle of incidence (δ) will be the difference between the solar azimuth and the wall azimuth. If, for the above example, the wall is facing west (270°):

$$\delta = 270 - 239 = 31°$$

The vertical component is the same as the solar altitude angle itself (γ).

Referring to Figure 57, the angle of incidence (β), i.e. the angle between a line perpendicular to the wall and the sun's direction, can be found by the 'spherical cosine equation':

$$\cos \beta = \cos \delta \times \cos \gamma$$

In our example:

$$\cos \beta = \cos 31° \times \cos 40° = 0.8572 \times 0.7660 = 0.6566$$
$$\beta = 49°$$

This angle of incidence will be required both for selecting the appropriate solar gain factor in heat gain calculations through windows and for calculating the incident radiation on an opaque surface, e.g. when the sol-air temperature is to be established.

Fig 57
The angle of incidence

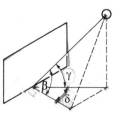

$\cos \beta = \cos \delta \times \cos \gamma$

The intensity of radiation measured on a plane normal to the direction of radiation must be multiplied by the cosine of this angle of incidence (see 1.1.5).

4.2.12 Shadow angles

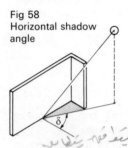

Fig 58
Horizontal shadow angle

δ = horizontal shadow angle

Fig 59
Vertical shadow angle

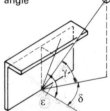

γ = solar altitude angle
ε = vertical shadow angle
tan ε = tan γ × sec δ

The performance of shading devices is specified by two angles: the horizontal and the vertical shadow angle. These are both measured from a line perpendicular to the elevation, and indicate the limit, beyond which the sun would be excluded, but within which the sun would reach the point considered.

The *horizontal shadow angle* (δ) characterises a vertical shading device (Figure 58), and it is the difference between the solar azimuth and wall azimuth, same as the horizontal component for the angle of incidence.

The *vertical shadow angle* (ε) characterises a horizontal shading device, e.g. a long horizontal projection from the wall, and it is measured on a vertical plane normal to the elevation considered (Figure 59).

The distinction between solar altitude angle (γ) and the vertical shadow angle (ε) must be clearly understood. The first describes the sun's position in relation to the horizon; the second describes the performance of a shading device. Numerically the two coincide (γ = ε) when, and only when, the sun is exactly opposite the wall considered (i.e. when solar azimuth and *wall azimuth angle* (ω) are the same, when α = ω), when the azimuth difference δ = 0. For all other cases, that is, when the sun is sideways from the perpendicular, the vertical shadow angle is always larger than the solar altitude angle for which it would still be effective ε > γ. The relationship is expressed as

$$\tan \epsilon = \tan \gamma \times \sec \delta$$

Thus if one is known, the other can be calculated, provided that the azimuth difference (δ) is given.

The *shadow angle protractor* (enclosed in a pocket inside the rear cover, for use with the solar charts given in appendix 8) gives a representation of these shadow angles on a horizontal plane in stereographic projection and to the same scale as the sun-path diagrams or solar charts. In more precise terms this protractor shows the various combinations of azimuth differences (δ) and solar altitude angles (γ) for which a particular shadow angle would be effective.

The perimeter scale gives the horizontal shadow angle (δ) up to −90° to the left and +90° to the right of the centre line. The arcuate lines indicate the vertical shadow angle (ε) from 0°, given by the horizon circle, to 90°, the zenith point. If laid over a solar chart, the corresponding sun-position angles can be read.

The following table summarises the various angles used in the foregoing paragraphs:

Angles with reference to 'objective' coordinates:

Solar altitude angle (from horizontal)	γ
Solar azimuth angle (from north)	α
Wall azimuth angle (orientation)	ω

Angles with reference to a wall:

Azimuth difference (horizontal shadow angle)	δ
Angle of incidence	β
Vertical shadow angle	ε

4.2.13 Shading devices

Internal devices have been considered under the heading of blinds and curtains (4.2.6). Here we will only consider external devices. These can be of three basic types:

1 vertical devices
2 horizontal devices
3 egg-crate devices

Vertical devices consist of louvre blades or projecting fins in a vertical position. **113** The horizontal shadow angle (δ) measures their performance. Narrow blades with close spacing may give the same shadow angle as broader blades with wider spacing.

Using the shadow angle protractor, the 'shading mask' of a given device can be established. For vertical devices this is the characteristic sector shape, as shown in Figure 60. If this is done on the same scale as the protractor, on tracing paper, it can be laid over the appropriate solar chart and the 'shading times' for the particular device (dates and hours) can be read off directly. This is a very quick short-cut, obviating the need to establish solar position angles.

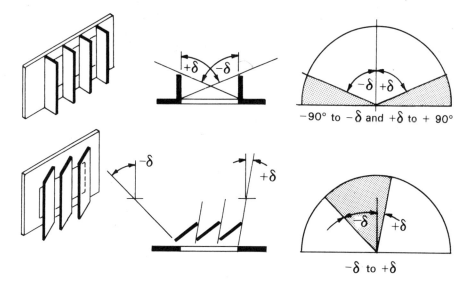

It will be seen that this type of device is most effective when the sun is to one side of the elevation, such as an eastern or western elevation. A vertical device to be effective when the sun is opposite to the wall considered, would have to give almost complete cover of the whole window.

Horizontal devices may be canopies, horizontal louvre blades or externally applied venetian blinds. Their performance will be measured by a vertical shadow angle (ϵ). The shading mask is of a segmental shape as shown in Figure 61. These will be most effective when the sun is opposite to the building face considered and at a high angle, such as for north and south facing walls. To exclude a low angle sun, this type of device would have to cover the window completely, permitting a view downwards only.

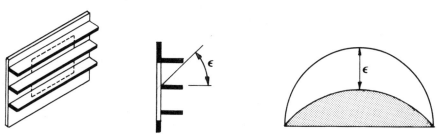

Egg-crate devices are combinations of horizontal and vertical elements (Figure 62). The many types of grille-blocks and decorative screens may fall into this category. Figure 63 shows the method of constructing the shading mask for a moderately complex shape. These can be effective for any orientation depending on detail dimensions.

114 Fig 62
Egg-crate shading
devices

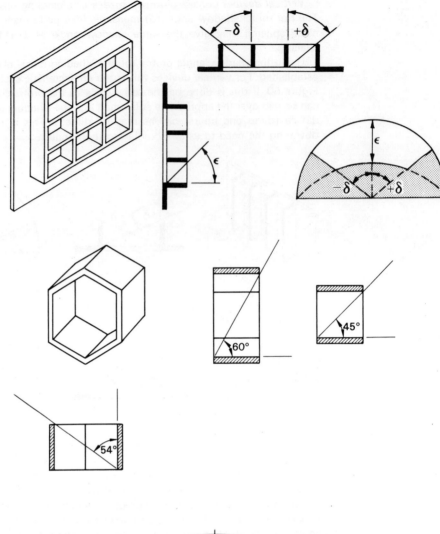

Fig 63
Construction of a
shading mask

4.2.14
Design of
shading
devices

As a first step, it must be decided *when* shading is necessary, at what times of the year and between what hours of the day. The best guide to this is the definition of the *overheated period*. This should be quite easy, if the climatic data has been compiled. Reference can be made to the ET analysis, shown in Figure 36, which shows the daily progress of temperature changes, with separate lines for each season. Alternatively, a temperature isopleth chart can be used, such as that shown in Figure 38.

The latter is a set of coordinates, with month lines horizontally and hour lines vertically, on which time points of equal temperatures are connected by a curve. The solar charts also have month (date) lines horizontally and hour lines vertically; the fact that these are curves and not straight lines should make no difference: the overheated period outlined on the isopleth chart, together with other ET lines can be transferred to the solar chart (Figure 64).

As on the solar chart each date line represents two different dates, an isopleth chart will be divided into two such diagrams: one for January to June; the other July to December.

Fig 64
Transfer of isopleth to the solar chart, to give effective temperature overlays

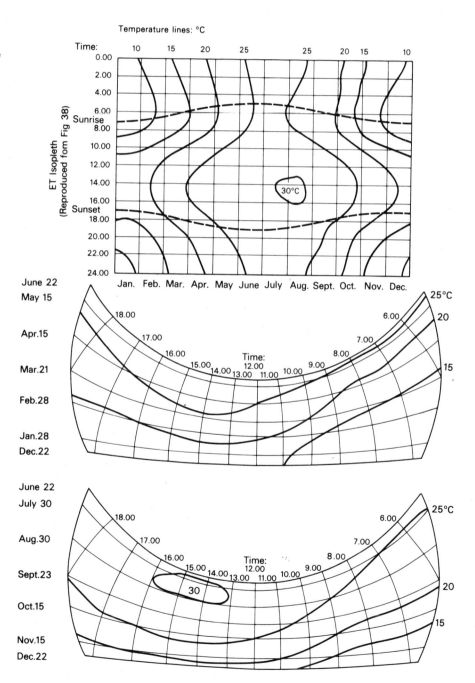

These can be produced on a transparent medium in the form of an overlay and preserved for future reference.

It should be noted, that radiation heat gain can never be eliminated completely, therefore it is advisable to define the 'overheated period' for the purposes of shading design, by the temperature isopleth corresponding to the *lower limit* of the comfort zone.

When a building elevation is considered from the point of view of shading, it will be represented (in plan) by a line crossing the centre point of the solar chart.

Fig 65
Fitting a shading mask

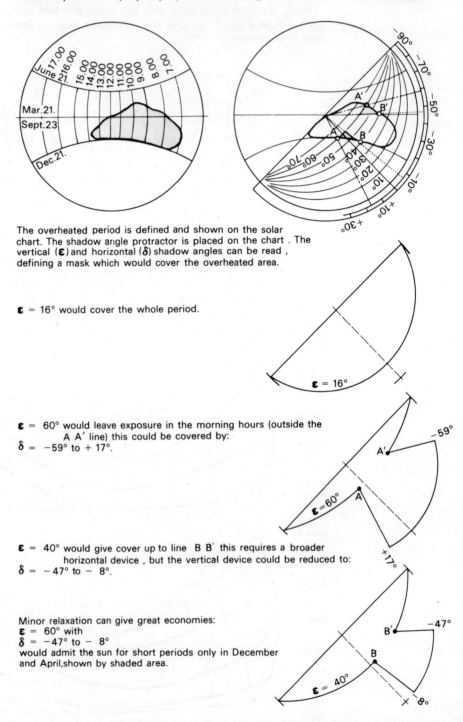

The overheated period is defined and shown on the solar chart. The shadow angle protractor is placed on the chart . The vertical (ε) and horizontal (δ) shadow angles can be read , defining a mask which would cover the overheated area.

$\varepsilon = 16°$ would cover the whole period.

$\varepsilon = 60°$ would leave exposure in the morning hours (outside the A A' line) this could be covered by:
$\delta = -59°$ to $+17°$.

$\varepsilon = 40°$ would give cover up to line B B' this requires a broader horizontal device , but the vertical device could be reduced to:
$\delta = -47°$ to $-8°$.

Minor relaxation can give great economies:
$\varepsilon = 60°$ with
$\delta = -47°$ to $-8°$
would admit the sun for short periods only in December and April,shown by shaded area.

Any part of the the overheated period behind this line can be ignored: when the sun is in these positions, it will not strike the elevation considered. The design of a suitable shading device is basically the finding of a shading mask which overlaps the overheated period with as close a fit as possible. Many combinations of vertical and horizontal shadow angles may achieve the same purpose. Minor compromises may be acceptable, i.e. for short periods the sun may be permitted to enter, if this results in substantial economies (Figure 65).

Once the necessary shadow angles have been established, the design of the actual form of the device will be quite a simple task and it can be postponed to a later stage, when it can be handled together with other considerations, structural or aesthetic, daylighting or air movement.

4.3 Ventilation and air movement

4.3.1 Functions of ventilation

Natural ventilation and air movement could be considered under the heading of 'structural controls' as it does not rely on any form of energy supply or mechanical installation, but due to its importance for human comfort, it deserves a separate section.

It has three distinctly different functions:

1 supply of fresh air
2 convective cooling
3 physiological cooling

There is a radical difference in the form of provisions for **1** and **2** and for **3**: therefore, the first two functions will be considered as 'ventilation' but the last function is considered separately as 'air movement'.

4.3.2 Supply of fresh air

The requirements of fresh air supply are governed by the type of occupancy, number and activity of the occupants and by the nature of any processes carried out in the space – as explained in connection with mechanical ventilation (4.1.6). Requirements may be stipulated by building regulations and advisory codes in terms of m³/h person, or in number of air changes per hour, but these are only applicable to mechanical installations. Nevertheless, they can be taken as useful guides for natural ventilation.

For natural ventilation usually certain limited solutions are prescribed and not the expected performance. The provision of 'permanent ventilators', i.e. of openings which cannot be closed, may be compulsory. These may be grilles or 'air bricks' built into a wall, or may be incorporated with windows. The size of openable windows may be stipulated in relation to the floor area or the volume of the room. The aim of all these rules is to ensure ventilation, but the rigid application of such rules may often be inadequate. To ensure a satisfactory performance the principles involved must be clearly undsrstood.

4.3.3 Convective cooling

As mentioned in the context of mechanical ventilation (4.1.8), the exchange of indoor air with fresh out-door air can provide cooling, if the latter is at a lower temperature than the indoor air. The moving air acts as a heat carrying medium.

A situation where this convective cooling is a practical proposition, can arise in moderate or cold climates, when the internal heat gain is causing a temperature increase, but also in warm climates, when the internal heat gain or solar heat gain through windows would raise the indoor temperature *even* higher than the out-door air temperature.

4.3.4 Provision for ventilation: stack effect

Fig 66
Ventilation duct arrangements

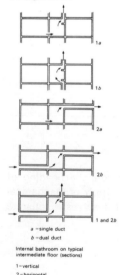

a = single duct
b = dual duct

Internal bathroom on typical intermediate floor (sections)

1 = vertical
2 = horizontal

Ventilation, i.e. both the supply of fresh air and convective cooling, involves the movement of air at a relatively slow rate. The motive force can be either thermal or dynamic (wind).

The stack effect relies on thermal forces, set up by density difference (caused by temperature differences) between the indoor and out-door air. It can occur through an open window (when the air is still): the warmer and lighter indoor air will flow out at the top and the cooler, denser out-door air will flow in at the bottom. The principle is the same as in wind generation (1.1.7).

Special provision can be made for it in the form of ventilating shafts. The higher the shaft, the larger the cross-sectional area and the greater the temperature difference: the greater the motive force therefore, the more air will be moved.

The motive force is the 'stack pressure' multiplied by the cross-sectional area (force in Newtons – area in m²). The stack pressure can be calculated from the equation:

$$P_s = 0 \cdot 042 \times h \times {}_\Delta T$$

where P_s = stack pressure in N/m²
   h = height of stack in m
   ${}_\Delta T$ temperature difference in degC
(the constant is N/m³ degC)

Such shafts are often used for the ventilation of internal, windowless rooms (bathrooms and toilets) in Europe. Figure 66 shows some duct arrangements for multistorey buildings, with vertical or horizontal single or double duct systems. Figure 67 gives a quick guide for establishing the size of ventilating shafts. These systems operate satisfactorily under winter conditions when the temperature difference is enough to generate an adequate air flow.

4.3.5 Physiological cooling

The movement of air past the skin surface accelerates heat dissipation in two ways:

1   increasing convective heat loss
2   accelerating evaporation

Both the bioclimatic chart (Figure 29) and the ET nomograms (Figures 30 and 31) show the cooling effect of air movement, i.e. how much higher temperatures can be tolerated with adequate air velocity:

For example, from Figure 30: 30°C DBT and 25°C WBT will give an ET of 27°C with still air (less than 0·1 m/s); and 22°C with a 7·5 m/s air velocity.

Or from Figure 29: the upper comfort limit at 40% RH is 30 °C with still air but 36 °C with a 1 m/s air movement.

In very low humidities (below 30%) this cooling effect is not great, as there is an unrestricted evaporation even with very light air movement. In high humidities (above 85%) the cooling effect is restricted by the high vapour pressure preventing evaporation, but greater velocities (above 1·5 to 2 m/s) will have some effect. It is most significant in medium humidities (35 to 60%).

Cooling by air movement is most needed where there are no other forms of heat dissipation available, when the air is as warm as the skin and the surrounding surfaces are also at a similar temperature.

Fig 67
Duct design graph

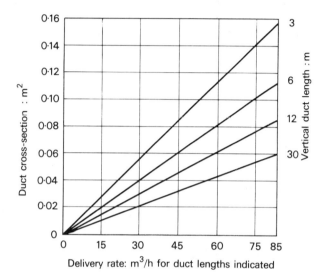

Delivery rate: m³/h for duct lengths indicated

4.3.6 Provision for air movement: wind effects

Thermal forces will rarely be sufficient to create appreciable air movements. The only 'natural' force that can be relied on is the dynamic effect of winds. When the creation of air movements indoors is the aim, the designer should try to capture as much of the available wind as possible. Negative control – when the wind is too much – is easy, if windows and openings can be shut.

Winds at the macroclimatic level have been considered in section 1.1 and it has been shown in 1.4.11 how local conditions can change the wind pattern on a microclimatic scale. Here we must extend this analysis and examine how the flow of air through a building will be influenced and by what factors.

In the same way as wind is generated by pressure differences – so an air flow through the building is the result of a pressure difference between the two sides.

Air – although light – has a mass (around 1·2 kg/m³), and as it moves, has a momentum, which is the product of its mass and its velocity (kg m/s). This is a vectorial quantity, which can be changed in direction or in magnitude only by another force. When moving air strikes an obstacle such as a building, this will slow down the air flow but the air flow will exert a pressure on the obstructing surface. This pressure is proportionate to the air velocity, as expressed by the equation:

$$P_w = 0.612 \times v^2$$

where P_w = wind pressure in N/m²
v = wind velocity in m/s
(the constant is Ns²/m⁴)

This slowing down process effects a roughly wedge-shaped mass of air on the windward side of the building, which in turn diverts the rest of the air flow upwards and sideways. A separation layer is formed between the stagnant air and the building on the one hand and the laminar air flow on the other hand. The laminar air flow itself may be accelerated at the obstacle, as the area available for the flow is narrowed down by the obstacle, as it were (Figure 68). At the separation layer, due to friction, the upper surface of the stagnant air is moved forward, thus a turbulence or vortex is developed.

Due to its momentum, the laminar air flow tends to maintain a straight path after it has been diverted, therefore it will take some time to return to the ground surface after the obstacle, to occupy all the available 'cross-section'. Thus a stagnant mass of air is also formed on the leeward side, but this is at a reduced pressure. In fact, this is not quite stagnant: a vortex is formed, the movement is light and variable and it is often referred to as 'wind shadow'.

Consequently vortexes are formed wherever the laminar flow is separated from the surfaces of solid bodies. On the windward side such vortexes are at an increased pressure and on the leeward side at a reduced pressure. If the building has an opening facing a high pressure zone and another facing a low pressure zone, air movement will be generated through the building.

Fig 68
Air flow around a building

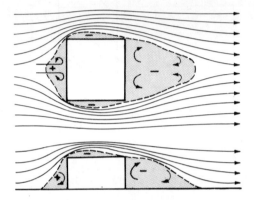

4.3.7
Air flow through buildings

As no satisfactory and complete theory is available, air flow patterns can only be predicted on the basis of empirical rules derived from measurements in actual buildings or in wind tunnel studies. Such empirical rules can give a useful guide to the designer but in critical cases it is advisable to prepare a model of the design and test it on a wind simulator.*

Fig 69
An open-jet wind simulator

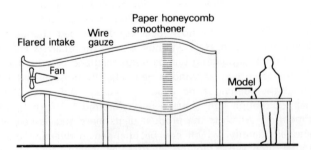

Wind simulators may be of the open-jet type (Figure 69) or the wind tunnel type (Figure 70). The former type is in use with the Architectural Association School of Architecture which has been developed with the cooperation of the Department of Fluid Mechanics, University of Liverpool. The latter type is best represented by an economical model developed by the Building Research Station which is described in BRS Current Paper 69/1968.

For qualitative studies a smoke generator can be used and the smoke traces can be photographed. This gives a convincing picture of flow patterns, position of laminar flow and turbulences. With some practise the wind tunnel operator can

* Scale models must be constructed with detailed precision. Inaccuracies of 2 to 3 mm may cause radical changes in the air flow pattern [62].

Fig 70
A closed wind tunnel

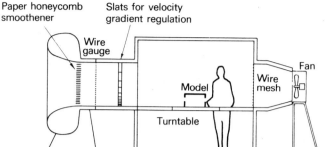

estimate velocity ratios from smoke traces with quite reasonable accuracy. For quantitative analyses air velocity or air pressure measurements must be taken with miniature instruments at predetermined grid points.

On the basis of such experimental observations the following factors can be isolated which affect the indoor air flow (both patterns and velocities):

a orientation
b external features
c cross-ventilation
d position of openings
e size of openings
f controls of openings

Each of these will be examined in the following paragraphs.

4.3.8 Orientation

The greatest pressure on the windward side of a building is generated when the elevation is at right angles to the wind direction, so it seems to be obvious that the greatest indoor air velocity will be achieved in this case. A wind incidence of 45° would reduce the pressure by 50%.

Thus the designer must ascertain the prevailing wind direction from wind frequency charts of wind roses* and must orientate his building in such a way that the largest openings are facing the wind direction.

It has, however, been found by Givoni [63] that a wind incidence at 45° would increase the average indoor air velocity and would provide a better distribution of indoor air movement. Figure 71 shows his findings: the relative velocities (with the

Fig 71
Effect of wind direction and inlet opening size on air velocity distribution

34	27	39	32	41
32	38	56	30	61
39	42	69	34	52
38	32	79	33	44
38	27	137	30	32

Average : 44%

68	36	37	31	72
44	44	29	29	50
37	25	29	29	36
33	25	31	29	30
34	29	31	29	37

Average : 35%

86	54	30	63	77
54	29	31	25	63
43	32	30	34	78
49	35	35	37	78
59	34	32	30	62

Average : 47%

36	24	24	28	84
31	26	25	24	93
29	24	27	39	78
30	27	27	109	28
24	28	71	152	29

Average : 44%

38	32	27	52	121
42	42	29	61	128
56	35	29	71	103
56	28	48	61	118
57	32	56	56	137

Average : 59%

44	35	56	67	77
56	32	30	85	88
59	32	30	85	88
67	34	43	102	109
55	52	76	78	115

Average : 65%

* It is useful to have information on wind direction in the most overheated period and not just frequency distribution for the whole of the time.

free air speed taken as 100%) measured at a height of 1·2 m above floor level. This seems to contradict common-sense and the findings of others, but it can be explained by the following phenomenon.

Figure 72**a** shows the outline of air flow at 90° and Figure 72**b** at 45°, to a building square in plan. In the second case a greater velocity is created along the windward faces, therefore the wind shadow will be much broader, the negative pressure (the suction effect) will be increased and an increased indoor air flow will result. The size of outlet opening was not varied in his experiments: it was fixed at the maximum possible so that the suction forces had full effect. It is justified to postulate that with smaller outlet openings this effect would be reduced, if not reversed.

Fig 72
Effect of direction on
the width of wind
shadow

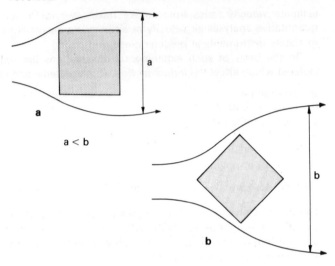

If often happens, that the optimum solar orientation and the optimum orientation for wind do not coincide. In equatorial regions a north–south orientation would be preferable for sun exclusion but most often the wind is predominantly easterly. The usefulness of the above findings is obvious for such a situation – it may resolve the contradictory requirements.

4.3.9
External
features

Wind shadows created by obstructions upwind, should be avoided in positioning the building on the site and in positioning the openings in the building. The wind velocity gradient is made steeper by an uneven surface, such as scattered buildings, walls fences, trees or scrub (Figure 25) – but even with a moderate velocity gradient, such as over smooth and open ground, a low building can never obtain air velocities similar to a taller one. For this reason (or to avoid specific obstructions) the building is often elevated on stilts.

External features of the building itself can strongly influence the pressure build-up. For example, if the air flow is at 45° to an elevation, a wing-wall at the downwind end or a projecting wing of an L-shaped building can more than double the positive pressure created. A simlar 'funnelling' effect can be created by upward projecting eaves. Any extension of the elevational area facing the wind will increase the pressure build-up. If a gap between two buildings is closed by a solid wall, a similar effect will be produced.

The air velocity between free-standing trunks of trees with large crowns can be increased quite substantially due to similar reasons.

The opposite of the above means will produce a reduction of pressures: if a wing wall or the projecting wing of an L-shaped building is upwind from the opening considered, the pressure is reduced or even a negative pressure may be created in front of the window.

4.3.10
Cross-
ventilation

Figure 73 shows that in the absence of an outlet opening or with a full partition there can be no effective air movement through a building [64] even in a case of strong winds. With a windward opening and no outlet, a pressure similar to that in front of the building will be built up indoors, which can make conditions even worse, increasing discomfort. In some cases oscillating pressure changes, known as 'buffeting' can also occur. The latter may also be produced by an opening on the leeward side only, with no inlet.

Fig 73
Lack of cross-
ventilation

Air flow loses much of its kinetic energy each time it is diverted around or over an obstacle. Several right-angle bends, such as internal walls or furniture within a room can effectively stop a low velocity air flow [65]. Where internal partitions are unavoidable, some air flow can be ensured if partition screens are used, clear of the floor and the ceiling.

Fig 74
Effect of opening
positions

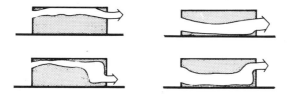

4.3.11
Position of
openings

To be effective, the air movement must be directed at the body surface. In building terms this means that air movement must be ensured through the space mostly used by the occupants: through the 'living zone' (up to 2 m high). As Figure 74 shows, if the opening at the inlet side is at a high level, regardless of the outlet opening position, the air flow will take place near the ceiling and not in the living zone.

Fig 75
Pressure build-up at
inlet

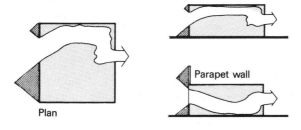

Plan

Parapet wall

The relative magnitude of pressure build-up in front of the solid areas of the elevation (which in turn depends on the size and position of openings) will, in fact, govern the direction of the indoor air stream and this will be independent of the outlet opening position. Figure 75 shows that a larger solid surface creates a larger pressure build-up and this pushes the air stream in an opposite direction, both in plan and in section. As a result of this, in a two storey building the air flow on the ground floor may be satisfactory (Figure 76) but on the upper floor it may be directed against the ceiling. One possible remedy is an increased roof parapet wall.

Fig 76
Air flow in a two
storey building

**4.3.12
Size of
openings**

With a given elevational area – a given total wind force (pressure × area) – the largest air velocity will be obtained through a small inlet opening with a large outlet. This is partly due to the total force acting on a small area, forcing air through the opening at a high pressure, and partly due to the 'venturi effect': in the broadening funnel (the imaginary funnel connecting the small inlet to the large outlet) the sideways expansion of the air jet further accelerates the particles.

Such an arrangement may be useful if the air stream is to be directed (as it were focused) at a given part of the room. When the inlet opening is large, the air velocity through it will be less, but the total rate of air flow (volume of air passing in unit time) will be higher. When the wind direction is not constant, or when air flow through the whole space is required, a large inlet opening will be preferable.

The best arrangement is full wall openings on both sides, with adjustable sashes or closing devices which can assist in channelling the air flow in the required direction, following the change of wind.

**4.3.13
Controls of
openings**

Sashes, canopies, louvres and other elements controlling the openings, also influence the indoor air flow pattern.

Sashes can divert the air flow upwards. Only a casement or reversible pivot sash will channel it downwards into the living zone (Figure 77).

Fig 77
Effect of sashes

Canopies can eliminate the effect of pressure build-up above the window, thus the pressure below the window will direct the air flow upwards. A gap left between the building face and the canopy would ensure a downward pressure, thus a flow directed into the living zone (Figure 78).

Fig 78
Effect of canopies

Louvres and shading devices may also present a problem. The position of blades in a slightly upward position would still channel the flow into the living zone (up to 20° upwards from the horizontal) (Figure 79).

Fig 79
Effect of louvres

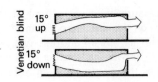 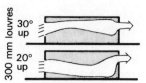

Fly screens or *mosquito nets* are an absolute necessity not only in malaria infested areas, but also if any kind of lamp is used indoors at night. Without it thousands of insects would gather around the lamp. Such screens and nets can substantially reduce the air flow. A cotton net can give a reduction of 70% in air velocity. A smooth nylon net is better, with a reduction factor of only approximately 35%. The reduction is greater with higher wind velocities and is also increased with the angle of incidence, as shown by the findings of Koenigsberger *et al.* [10]:

outside velocity	normal incidence		67·5° incidence	
	inside velocity	reduction	inside velocity	reduction
m/s	m/s	%	m/s	%
0·75	0·49	35	0·40	47
1·23	0·87	29	0·75	40
2·50	1·33	30	1·00	60
3·30	1·79	47	1·33	50
3·80	2·64	46	2·23	43
Average		37·4		50·0

4.3.14 Air movement and rain

Exclusion of rain is not a difficult task and making provision for air movement does not create any particular difficulties, but the two together and simultaneously is by no means easy. Opening of windows during periods of wind-driven rain would admit rain and spray; while closing the windows would create intolerable conditions indoors. The conventional tilted louvre blades are unsatisfactory on two counts:

1   strong wind will drive the rain in, even upwards through the louvres
2   the air movement will be directed upwards from the living zone

Verandahs and large roof overhangs are perhaps the best traditional methods of protection.

    Koenigsberger, Millar and Costopoulos [10] have carried out some experimental work, testing four types of louvres (Figure 80). Only type 'M' was found to be capable of keeping out water at wind velocities up to 4 m/s and at the same time ensuring a horizontal air flow into the building. The air velocity reduction varies between 25 and 50%.

Fig 80
Louvres for rain exclusion

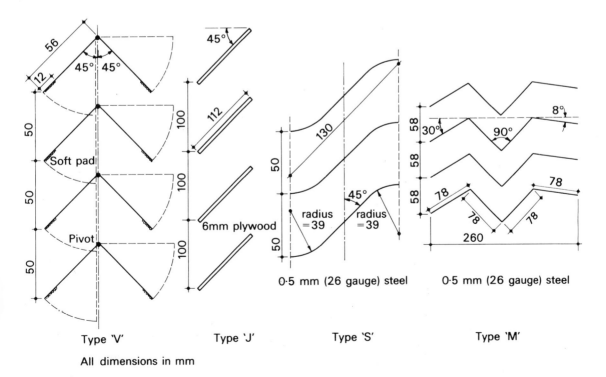

Type 'V'   Type 'J'   Type 'S'   Type 'M'

All dimensions in mm

4.3.15 Air flow around buildings

When the architect's task is the design of more than one building, a cluster of buildings or a whole settlement, especially in a warm climate, in deciding the lay-out, provision for air movement must be one of the most important considerations. After a careful analysis of site climatic conditions a design hypothesis may be produced on the basis of general information derived from experimental findings, such as those described below. A positive confirmation (or rejection) of this hypothesis can only be provided by model studies in a wind simulator. If the construction of adjustable or variable layout models is feasible, alternative arrangements can be tested and the optimum can be selected.

The effect of tall blocks in mixed developments has been examined in experiments conducted by the Building Research Station at Garston [66]. Figure 81 shows how the air stream separates on the face of a tall block, part of it moving up and over the roof, part of it down, to form a large vortex leading to a very high pressure build-up. An increased velocity is found at ground level at the sides of the tall block. This could serve a useful purpose in hot climates, although if the tall block is not fully closed but is permeable to wind, these effects may be reduced.

Fig 81
Air stream separation
at the face of buildings

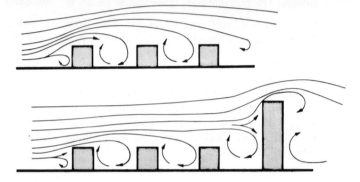

A series of studies in Australia [67], relating to low industrial buildings, produced the surprising (but *post facto* obvious) result that if a low building is located in the wind shadow of a tall block (Figure 82), the increase in height of the obstructing block will increase the air flow through the low building in a direction opposite to that of the wind. The lower (return-)wing of a large vortex would pass through the building.

Fig 82
Reverse flow behind a
tall block

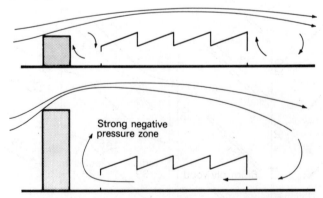

Strong negative
pressure zone

In Texas [68] a series of experiments was directed at finding the downwind extent of a turbulence zone, which was found to depend on building size, shape, type and slope of the roof, but practically unaffected by wind velocity.

Experiments at the Architectural Association Department of Tropical Studies yielded the following results:

a if in a rural setting in open country, single storey buildings are placed in rows in a grid-iron pattern, stagnant air zones leeward from the first row will overlap the second row (Figure 83). A spacing of six times the building height is necessary to **129** ensure adequate air movement for the second row. Thus the 'five times height' rule for spacing is not quite satisfactory

Fig 83
Air flow: grid-iron
lay-out

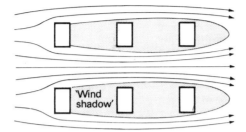

b in a similar setting, if the buildings are staggered in a checker-board pattern, the flow field is much more uniform, stagnant air zones are almost eliminated (Figure 84)

Fig 84
Air flow: checker-
board lay-out

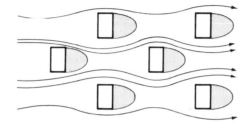

4.3.16 Humidity control

Dehumidification is only possible by mechanical means (4.1.13); without this, in warm-humid climates, some relief can be provided by air movement. In hot-dry climates humidification of the air may be necessary, which can be associated with evaporative cooling. In these climates the building is normally closed to preserve the cooler air retained within the structure of high thermal capacity, also to exclude sand and dust carried by winds. However, some form of air supply to the building interior is necessary.

All these functions:
controlled air supply
filtering out sand and dust
evaporative cooling
humidification
are served by a device used in some parts of Egypt [69] — the wind scoop. Figure 85 illustrates an example of this. The large intake opening captures air movement above the roofs in densely built up areas. The water seeping through the porous pottery jars evaporates, some drips down onto the charcoal placed on a grating, through which the air is filtered. The cooled air assists the downward movement — a reversed stack effect.

This device is very useful for ventilation (the above four functions), but it cannot be expected to create an air movement strong enough for physiological cooling.

Fig 85
A wind scoop

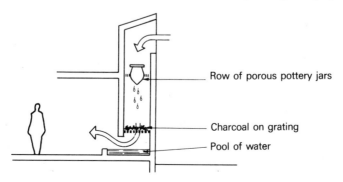

Row of porous pottery jars

Charcoal on grating
Pool of water

In some parts of India a curtain made of *cascas* grass is often hung in front of windows on the windward side. This is wetted by throwing a bucket of water against it from time to time. The grass is highly absorptive and retains the moisture for a long time. The wind passing through the loose textured mat curtain is both cooled and humidified.

In recent years the cascas mat is often hung from a perforated water pipe, which keeps it uniformly moist at all time.

Architects in Israel have used a porous honeycombed brick grill, with a perforated water pipe at the top, for a similar purpose. The water pipe may be supplied by an automatic flush-cistern, of the type used for urinals.

The 'desert cooler' developed in Delhi, is a cube shaped frame, of 500 to 600 mm sides. The top and bottom are shallow tanks. The sides are covered with cascas mats, the top of which is immersed in the upper tank. Water seeps down through the mat and is collected in the lower tank. Inside the box is an ordinary table fan, which blows air through the cascas mat, cooling and humidifying it. The fan motor may also drive a small pump, which lifts the surplus water back to the upper tank. If the box is mounted in or near a window, it is quite effective during the dry season. It is not used during the monsoon period.

5.1.1 Introduction

If the building envelope is thought of as a barrier between the internal, controlled environment and the external, perhaps undesirable conditions, it must be realised that it should be a selective barrier, or rather a filter, which excludes the unwanted influences whilst admits those which are desirable. One such desirable effect is *daylight*.

Perhaps the most important communication channel of man with his environment is vision. The eye is stimulated by light reflected from objects, thus light is a prerequisite of seeing. Light can be produced artificially (e.g. electric light), but if it is available — as it were 'free of charge' — it should be utilised.

In artificial lighting the light source itself is under the designer's (user's) control. In daylighting the source (sun and sky) is given, thus if control is necessary, it must be in transmission and distribution. Artificial lighting is practically independent of location, climate or even of the building fabric; daylighting, however, strongly depends on the externally given conditions and its control is only possible by the building itself. For this reason the present section will deal with daylight and sunlight — electric lighting will only be mentioned as far as it is interconnected with daylighting, or in relation to its heating effect.

The ultimate source of daylight is the sun, from which we receive also a large amount of thermal radiation together with the light. When in bright sunshine the illumination is around 100 klux (100 000 lux), the intensity of thermal radiation is likely to be about 1 kW/m² (see 1.1.2) [69*a*]. In climates where the heat balance

134

is negative, i.e. overheating is not likely, thermal considerations will rarely restrict the amount of daylight to be admitted.* In the tropics, however, the situation is not quite as simple. Here the admission of an abundant quantity of daylight will be accompanied by radiant heat which is probably excessive. Thus the 'filter' function of the envelope will be even more important. We must attempt to exclude radiant heat whilst admitting daylight. Where this cannot be done, thermal considerations will restrict the amount of light which can be admitted. This means that there must be a fundamental difference in approach to daylighting design, as will be shown in 5.2.6 *et seq.*

For a comprehensive treatment of the psychophysics of seeing the reader is referred to items [70] and [72] of the bibliography. It is, however, necessary to review some of the basic principles before the methods of daylighting design are described. Such methods developed for moderate climates will be described and then it will be examined to what extent are these applicable to tropical conditions.

Fig 86
Radiation spectrum

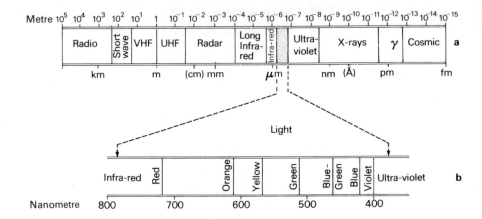

5.1.2
The nature of light

What we perceive as light, is a narrow wavelength band of electromagnetic radiation from about 380 to 780 nm (1 nanometre = 10^{-9} m) (Figure 86a). This energy radiation shows dual characteristics: it consists of energy particles — photons — but also shows transverse wave motion properties (for full explanation see item [73] of the bibliography). The wavelength determines its colour (Figure 86b). Light containing all visible waves is perceived as white. The human eye's sensitivity varies with the wavelength, it is greatest around 550 nm (yellow) as shown by Figure 87.

Fig 87
Spectral sensitivity of the eye

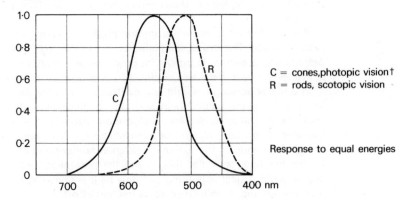

C = cones, photopic vision†
R = rods, scotopic vision

Response to equal energies

* It has been shown [100] that even in England the use of large windows leads to quite substantial overheating of buildings.

† The retina of the eye has two kinds of receptors: some 6·5 million cones, which perceive colour and over 100 million rods, which perceive only black and white, but respond to minute quantities of light.

about 3×10^8 m/s (300 000 km/s). More precisely (in m/s):

in vacuo	299 792 000
in air	299 724 000
in water	224 915 000
in glass	198 223 000

**5.1.3
Transmission**

Some materials when exposed to light, transmit a large part of it – these are referred to as 'transparent'. Others, the 'opaque' materials, block the passage of light. Behind an opaque object there will be no light (no direct light), i.e. it will cast a shadow. The term 'translucent' is applied to materials which transmit a part of the incident light, but break its straight passage, scatter it in all directions, creating 'diffuse' light.

Light incident on an object can be distributed three ways: reflected, absorbed and transmitted. Some important properties of the object and its material are described by the proportions of these three components:

reflectance	(r)
absorbance	(a)
transmittance	(t)

In all cases: $r + a + t = 1$
In case of opaque objects: $t = 0$, thus $r + a = 1$

**5.1.4
Reflection**

If parallel rays of incident light remain parallel after reflection from a surface, the surface is a 'plane mirror' and we speak of 'specular reflection' (Figure 88a). The rules of geometrical optics apply to such surfaces: the angle of reflection is the same as the angle of incidence; from a convex mirror the reflected rays will be divergent and from a concave mirror they will be convergent.

Light reflected from a matt surface will be diffused (Figure 88d). Most often a mixture of the two kinds of reflections will occur, termed as 'semi-diffuse' or 'spread' reflection, depending on the relative magnitude of the two components (Figure 88**b** and **c**).

Fig 88
Types of reflection

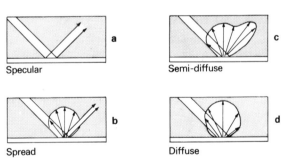

Specular · a

Semi-diffuse · c

Spread · b

Diffuse · d

Some materials have practically the same reflectance for all wavelengths of light. These do not change the wavelength composition of light after reflection. Surfaces with such 'neutral reflection' properties will be seen in white light as:

white	if r is above	0·75
grey	if r is between	0·05 and 0·75
black	if r is below	0·05

Other materials are selective in their reflectance. They may absorb certain wavelengths of the incident light, thus the remainder reflected will show a colour effect. Colour pigments are such selective absorbers, their colour being due to a subtractive process. In mixing coloured pigments the absorptions are additive and the reflections will be subtractive, for example:

yellow paint	absorbs blue;	reflects red, yellow, green
blue paint	absorbs red and yellow;	reflects blue and green
a mixture of the two	absorbs blue, red and yellow;	reflects only the green

A mixture of all kinds of pigments will be black, as it will absorb all wavelengths. No mixture of pigments can give white, as there will always be some absorption in certain wavelengths.

5.1.5
Coloured light

Coloured lights from different sources can be mixed in which case the resultant colour will be of a wavelength range which is the sum of the wavelength ranges of components. It is an additive process. Colours which add up to form white light are termed 'complementary colours', for example:

red and green, or yellow and blue

Coloured light can also be produced by filters. These are materials with a high, but selective transmittance. They may reflect or absorb most of the wavelengths, transmitting only the specified narrow band. This is again a subtractive process.

5.1.6
The Munsell system

The most generally used classification of surface colours is the *Munsell system*. It distinguishes three colour concepts (Figure 89) [81].

Fig 89
The Munsell colour-system

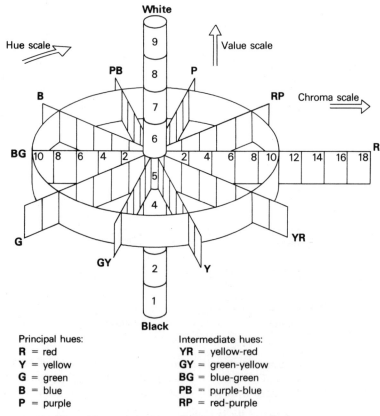

Principal hues:	Intermediate hues:
R = red	YR = yellow-red
Y = yellow	GY = green-yellow
G = green	BG = blue-green
B = blue	PB = purple-blue
P = purple	RP = red-purple

For example: 5R – 4/10 = red of hue 5–value 4/chroma 10

1 *hue* – the concept of colour, using the common colour terms: red, yellow, green, blue and purple, but further subdividing each into five subcategories
2 *value* – the subjective measure of reflectance, light or dark appearance, according to a scale from 0 (absolute black) to 10 (absolute white). In practice values from 1 to 9 are encountered. Convertible into reflectances:

$r = \mathbf{V}(\mathbf{V} - 1)$

3 *chroma* – the degree of colourfulness or intensity of colour, distinguishing 14 classes. A low chroma would be almost grey; the brightest colours have a chroma of 12 to 14

The Munsell notation is given in three facets:

hue – value/chroma, for example:
5R – 4/10

Of the three facets the *value* (**V**) is directly relevant to lighting design.
A selected range of colours is given in BS 4800: 1972 [82].

5.1.7
Photometric
quantities

The *intensity* of a light source (symbol: *I*) is measured in units of *candela* (cd). This is the basic assumed and agreed unit in the Système International (defined as the intensity of a 1/60 cm² uniformly emitting black body radiator at the melting point temperature of platinum) – all other units are derived from this.

The *flux* (or flow) of light (symbol: *F*) is measured in *lumens* (lm). One lumen is the flow of light emitted by a unit intensity (1 cd) point source, within a unit solid angle. As the surface of a sphere subtends at its centre 4π (= 12·56) units of solid angle, a 1 cd point source will emit a total of 12·56 lm in all directions.

Illumination (symbol, *E*) is measured as the amount of flux falling on unit area, i.e. lm/m² which is the *lux*, the unit of illumination in the Système International.

Luminance (symbol: *L*) is the measure of brightness of a surface. Units for its measurement can be derived two ways:

1 if a light source of 1 cd intensity has a surface area of 1 m² (1 cd is distributed over 1 m²) its luminance is 1 cd/m². This is the official SI unit
2 if a completely reflecting and diffusing surface ($r = 1·00$) has an illumination of 1 lux, its luminance is 1 asb (*apostilb*)

The two units measure the same quantity and are directly convertible – 1 cd/m² = 3·14 asb.

5.1.8
Illumination

Illumination from a point source reduces with the square of the distance.

A source of *I* candela emits a total flux of $4\pi I$ lumens. At a *distance* (d) this flux will be distributed over a sphere of radius d, i.e. a surface of $4\pi d^2$. Thus the illumination at a distance d is:

$$E = \frac{4\pi I}{4\pi d^2} = \frac{I}{d^2}$$

This is known as the inverse square law and is applicable when the illuminated plane is normal (perpendicular) to the direction of light, that is when the angle of incidence, $\beta = 0°$. When the plane is tilted, the same flux is distributed over a larger area, thus the illumination is reduced. The reduction is proportionate to the cosine of the angle of incidence:

$$E_\beta = E_n \times \cos\beta$$

where E_n = illumination on a normal plane
E_β = illumination on a plane tilted by β degrees
β = angle of incidence

Illumination of a surface from several sources will be the simple sum of the component illuminations:

$$E = E_1 + E_2 + E_3 \ldots$$

Illumination from a linear source of infinite length reduces in direct proportion to the distance (and not the square of distance) and from an infinitely large luminous surface (e.g. the sky) the illumination does not vary with the distance.

**5.1.9
Scalar
illumination**

Lighting conditions are usually described, measured or specified in terms of illumination on a given plane, most often the horizontal 'working plane' (taken at desk or bench height), but possibly a vertical or inclined plane. In other words, we usually speak of 'planar illumination'.

This, however, does not describe all the luminous qualities of a space. Even if the illumination on a horizontal plane is adequate, the vertical surfaces may remain dark, and if the visual task is other than two-dimensional, qualities other than the planar illumination must be considered.

Scalar illumination (or mean spherical illumination) is the average illumination received on the surface of a small sphere from all directions. It is denoted E_s and measured in lux. It measures the total quantity of light present regardless of its direction.

The *illumination vector* is a composite quantity having both magnitude and direction. Its magnitude is the maximum difference in illumination between two diametrically opposed points on the surface of a small sphere (denoted $_\Delta E_{max}$ and measured in lux). Its direction is given by the diameter connecting the two points between which its magnitude is measured. This direction is defined in terms of two angles: one horizontal (from a reference direction) and one vertical (from a horizontal up).

The *vector/scalar ratio* is a measure of the directionality of light and a good indicator of its modelling qualities.

When $\frac{\Delta E_{max}}{E_s} = 4$, we have a completely mono-directional light. In practice this value is always less than 4. A value of 0 would indicate a perfectly diffuse omni-directional lighting.

**5.1.10
Visual
efficiency**

The purpose of lighting is twofold:

a practical — to facilitate the performance of a visual task and ensure visual comfort
b artistic (for lack of a better term) — to create certain emotional effects

For practical purposes we need to measure visual efficiency, as this strongly depends on lighting. It can be measured on its three facets:

1 *visual acuity*, or sharpness of vision, measured as the reciprocal of the visual angle ρ (expressed in minutes) subtended at the eye by the least perceptible detail. For example, if the least perceptible detail subtends an angle of 2′ the acuity will be

$$\frac{1}{\rho} = \frac{1}{2} = 0.5$$

2 *contrast sensitivity* (CS), measured as the ratio of the least perceptible luminance difference $(L_2 - L_1)$ to the lower of the two luminances:

$$CS = \frac{L_2 - L_1}{L_1} \times 100 \quad (\%)$$

3 *visual performance*, i.e. the time required for seeing, expressed possibly as the number of characters perceived per second or on any comparative scale

All three facets, consequently visual efficiency itself, depend on the level of illumination, as shown by the graphs in Figure 90.

**5.1.11
Illumination:
quantity**

The eye responds to a range of illumination levels extending over a million orders of magnitude:

from   0·1 lux   (full moonlit night)
to   100 000 lux   (bright sunshine)

For practical situations and various activities (thus various visual tasks), detailed

illumination requirements are given in publications such as [71] and [76]. The **139**
following values (in lux) can provide some general guidance:

casual seeing	100
ordinary tasks, medium detail (e.g. wood machining, general office work)	400
severe, prolonged tasks (e.g. fine assembly, silk weaving)	900
exceptionally severe tasks (e.g. watchmaking)	2 000–3 000

Fig 90
Visual efficiency

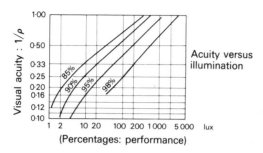

Acuity versus
illumination

(Percentages: performance)

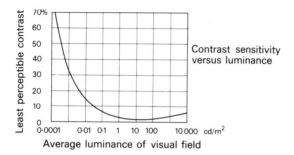

Contrast sensitivity
versus luminance

Average luminance of visual field

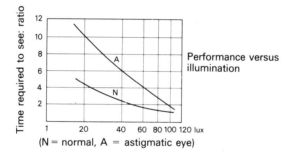

Performance versus
illumination

(N = normal, A = astigmatic eye)

For more detailed recommendations see appendix 9.1

As it can be seen from the graphs in Figure 90, visual efficiency increases with the
increase of illumination but the curve flattens out at higher levels. The 'law of
diminishing returns' applies. The decision regarding the level to be adopted
depends, to a large extent on socio-cultural and economic factors — in other words,
on 'how much light we can afford'. A comparison of recommendations in various
countries is rather revealing.

	drawing offices (fairly severe tasks) lux	exceptionally severe tasks lux
USSR*	50–150	150–300
Hungary*	150–300	300–500
UK [76]	600	2 000–3 000
USA [86]	1 500	5 000–10 000

* Farago, G and Maroti, G, *Vilagitastechnika* (Lighting techniques). Muszaki Konyvkiado, Budapest, 1962.

140 **5.1.12**
The visual field

With stationary head and eyes the visual field of an average person extends to 180° horizontally and 120° vertically. Within this the 'central field' is limited to 2° and the immediate 'background' extends to about 40°.

Visual comfort and efficiency can be ensured by the control of luminance distribution within the visual field.

The luminance ratios should be:

central field : background : environment
            5 :   2   : 1
but   10 :   3   : 1   should in no case be exceeded, as this may create *glare*.

The eye will adjust itself to the average luminance of the visual field (adaptation). With large contrasts this may lead to loss of seeing the less luminous areas (under-exposure) and discomfort caused by the bright areas (overexposure).

Glare may also be caused by a saturation effect, even without any contrast, when the average luminance exceeds about 25 000 cd/m² (80 000 asb).

The magnitude of glare can be indicated by the terms 'discomfort glare' (in a less severe case) and 'disability glare' (in a severe situation).

5.1.13
Illumination: quality

In lighting design the designer must ensure light which is both adequate and suitable for the visual task. Suitability in this context would mean the following qualities:

a   colour of light
b   colour rendering
c   light distribution (direct or diffuse; modelling)
d   freedom from glare
e   luminance distribution (consideration of surface qualities together with the lighting of these surfaces)

The first two depend on the light source: subject to choice in electric lighting but given in daylighting.

Distribution in electric lighting depends on the fittings and their position, in daylighting it depends on windows and reflective surfaces.

In daylighting the problem of glare is normally handled in qualitative terms only, but in electric lighting design the *glare index* concept gives a quantitative evaluation method (see 5.3.15).

**5.2.1
Sources of
light**

The ultimate source of daylight is, of course, the sun, but the light arriving at the earth from the sun may be partly diffused by the atmosphere and the locally prevailing atmospheric conditions will determine how this light will reach a building.

If we consider a point inside a building, light may reach it from the sun the following ways (Figure 91):

a diffused or *skylight*, through a window or opening
b *externally reflected light* (by the ground or other buildings), through the same windows
c *internally reflected light* from walls, ceiling or other internal surfaces
d *direct sunlight*, along a straight path from the sun, through a window to the given point

Fig 91
Daylight entering a
building

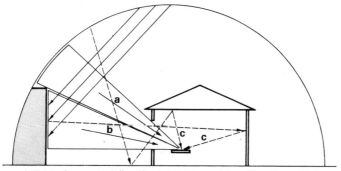

a = skylight   b = externally reflected light c = internally reflected light

Climatic conditions will greatly influence both the total quantity of light and the relative magnitude of the above components.

5.2.2 Climate and light

In high latitude moderate climates, where the sky is typically overcast, the whole of the sky hemisphere acts as a light source. Direct sunlight may occur, but cannot be relied on. The sky itself has a luminance sufficiently high to provide lighting in normal rooms. On the basis of many observations the Commission Internationale de l'Eclairage (CIE) has established the luminance distribution of a typical overcast sky, as varying according to the function:

$$L_\gamma = L_h \times (1 + 2 \times \sin\gamma)$$

where L_γ = luminance at γ altitude angle
L_h = luminance at the horizon
Thus the *zenith luminance* $(L_z) = 3 \times L_h$ [75].

Hot-dry desert climates are characterised by strong direct sunlight from cloudless skies. Direct sunlight is usually excluded from buildings for thermal reasons. The sky is typically of a deep blue colour and its luminance may be as low as 1 700 cd/m² – not enough to ensure adequate daylighting. This clear sky usually has the highest luminance near the horizon and the lowest luminance at right angles to the sun. The bare, dry, sunlit ground and light coloured walls of other buildings will reflect much light which will be the main source of indoor daylighting. It may, however, also be the source of glare, when these strongly lit light surfaces are within the visual field. Light dust suspended in the air may create a haze and increase the apparent sky brightness up to 10 000 cd/m², but the frequent heavy dust and sand-storms can reduce it to below 850 cd/m².

In warm-humid climates the sky is typically overcast, with a luminance often exceeding 7 000 cd/m². The proportion of diffused or skylight is predominant and the very bright sky viewed from a moderately lit room can cause discomfort glare.

In composite climates wide variations occur in natural lighting, between over-cast and clear sky conditions.

5.2.3 The daylight factor concept

Due to the variability of out-door lighting levels it is difficult (and perhaps meaning-less) to calculate interior lighting in photometric illumination terms. However, in a given building, at a certain point, the *ratio* of the illumination to the simultaneous out-door illumination can be taken as constant. This constant ratio, expressed as a percentage, is the *daylight factor* (DF):

$$DF = \frac{E_i}{E_o} \times 100 \ (\%)$$

where E_i = illumination indoors, at the point taken
E_o = illumination out-doors from an unobstructed sky hemisphere

The daylight factor concept is valid (the ratio remains constant) only under over-cast sky conditions when there is no direct sunlight. Thus, according to 5.2.1 above, three components will contribute to the daylight factor:

1 *sky component* (SC)
2 *externally reflected component* (ERC)
3 *internally reflected component* (IRC)

Thus: DF = SC + ERC + IRC

5.2.4 Design variables

The magnitude of each of these components depends on the following design variables:

a SC – the area of sky visible from the point considered and its average altitude angle (i.e. the luminance of sky at that angle), therefore: window size and position in relation to the point, thickness of window frame members, quality of glass and its

b   ERC – the area of external surfaces visible from the point considered and the reflectance of these surfaces

c   IRC – the size of room, the ratio of wall, etc., surfaces in relation to window area and the reflectance of these indoor surfaces

The technique of calculating each of these components is described in Section 5.3.

5.2.5
The design sky
concept

When the daylight factor for a given point has been established, it can be converted into an illumination value, if the out-door illumination is known.

For example, if DF = 8% and E_o = 6 000 lux

$$DF = \frac{E_i}{E_o} \times 100$$

$$8 = \frac{E_i}{6\,000} \times 100$$

$$E_i = \frac{8 \times 6\,000}{100} = 480 \text{ lux}$$

By statistical evaluation of long-term illumination records an out-door illumination level (E_o) can be established for a given location, which is exceeded in 90% (or 85%) of the time of daylight hours (the ninetieth or eighty-fifth percentile illumination level). This is taken as the 'design sky' illumination value for the particular location. With this the above calculation can be reversed and used as a basis of design, according to the following steps:

1   establish required illumination level, E_i (see appendix 9.1) – e.g. 300 lux
2   ascertain local 'design sky' illumination, E_o – e.g. 9000 lux
3   calculate necessary daylight factor:

$$DF = \frac{300}{9\,000} \times 100 = 3\cdot 33\%$$

4   manipulate the design variables (window size, etc.) to achieve this daylight factor

This method ensures that the required indoor illumination level will be reached or exceeded in 90% of the time. The remaining 10% of the time is likely to occur in short spells, fairly rarely, when human adaptability may be relied on; the visual task may be taken closer to a window or artificial lighting may be used. To provide for such rare occurrences would be uneconomical and unduly restrictive, resulting in excessive lighting most of the time.

Some typical 'design sky' illumination values (in lux) are:

London	lat. 52° –	5000
Hobart	lat. 43° –	5500
Sydney	lat. 33° –	8000
Brisbane	lat. 27° –	10000
Darwin	lat. 10° –	15000
Nairobi	lat. 1° –	18000

5.2.6
Daylighting in
the tropics

The above method ensures adequate daylight, even with a very low level of out-door lighting, thus most of the time the specified illumination levels will be exceeded.

Physically – physiologically this is advantageous (visual efficiency is improved) and in temperate climates the psychological effect of such over-lighting is likely to be an increased sense of well-being.

By contrast, in warm climates both the physical and the psychological effects would be disadvantageous. Due to the accompanying thermal radiation over-lighting would mean overheating. And overheating would cause much greater discomfort than under-lighting. Furthermore, a slightly under-lit room would be psychologically more acceptable, as light is mentally associated with warmth and reduced lighting with coolness.

This, however, requires great skill in handling, partly to ensure an adequate illumination for the necessary visual efficiency and partly to avoid creating a gloomy effect. Visual 'gloominess' is a subjective effect, created by excessive contrast between the very bright out-doors and the dimly lit interior. It can be strengthened by factors affecting the other senses: dampness, stale air, smells, even by untidiness.

The task and problems of daylighting in tropical climates can be summarised as follows:

a to provide adequate daylight, even if the windows are protected by louvres or grilles for thermal reasons
b to exclude from the visual field excessively bright (light coloured, sunlit, etc.) surfaces, which would cause glare

How these problems can be solved under various climatic conditions, will be examined in the following paragraphs.

5.2.7 In hot-dry climates

Direct sunlight must be excluded from buildings partly for thermal reasons, partly as it would unavoidably create glare.

As windows in this climate tend to be small, not much sky would be visible from any point indoors, thus, especially with low luminance blue skies, the sky component would be insufficient [77]. On the other hand, luminance of the sky near the horizon is greater and it may be a source of glare if not screened. Both the ground and the external surfaces of other buildings are usually light coloured: in the strong sunshine these may also create glare (Figure 92). Therefore externally reflected light can only be used providing that great care is taken to avoid glare.

Fig 92
Glare from sunlit surfaces

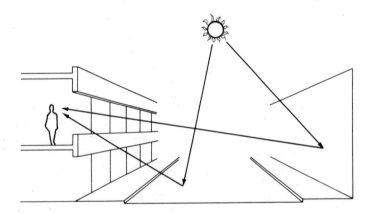

Internally reflected light would be the most convenient form of daylighting. One suitable arrangement is a high level window (with cill above eye-level), which would admit reflected light to the ceiling. If the ceiling is white, this method would ensure adequate and well diffused interior lighting, through a comparatively small window (Figure 93).

Fig 93
Reflected light, diffused by the ceiling

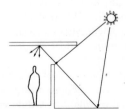

If shading devices are used, sunlit reflective surfaces of these devices can them-selves become sources of glare. These surfaces should either be non-reflective, or positioned so that they are not directly visible.

Low level windows are acceptable if they open onto a shaded and planted courtyard.

When a sunlit view through a window is unavoidable, the strong luminance contrast between the view and the window surround can be reduced by:

1 painting the adjacent wall a light colour
2 painting the inside of window frames white
3 as the walls tend to be thick in this climate, the deep reveals should be splayed (and light coloured) to provide 'contrast grading'
4 other openings may be placed in opposite or flanking walls, to throw some light onto the wall surrounding the window

One solution for the avoidance of an excessively bright view is the use of a vertical strip-window at the corner of the room (Figure 94). This would throw light onto the wall surface (as a 'wash') thus providing a larger apparent source of a lesser luminance.

Fig 94
A corner window

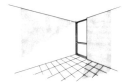

5.2.8
In warm-humid climates

Buildings in these climates are typically of lightweight construction, with large openings to ensure cross-ventilation and air movement, usually with wide over-hanging eaves or other shading devices.

Direct sunlight is excluded for thermal reasons. The sky is bright, could provide sufficient light, but its high luminance would also cause glare.

For this reason, view of the sky should be screened by shading devices or plants. As, however, the sky luminance is much less near the horizon than at higher altitude angles, a view of the sky up to about 15° from the horizon may be permissible.

The foregoing establishes rather specific requirements for the design of shading devices. The criteria, far more stringent than just the exclusion of sunlight, can be summarised as follows:

a permit view of sky and ground near the horizon only, within about ±15° (up and down)
b exclude view of bright ground and sunlit blade or louvre surfaces
c daylight is to be reflected from ground and blades up to the ceiling, which itself should be of a light colour

Figure 95 shows an arrangement which would satisfy these requirements, whilst ensuring adequate ventilation [78].

5.2.9
Supplementary artificial lighting

In moderate climates it is practically impossible to provide adequate daylight (DF = 2%) in side-lit rooms, to a depth greater than three times the window head height (above the working plane). In an average office or class-room this would correspond to a depth of 6 m (max.). For rooms deeper than this, a system has been developed, known as PSALI, (*permanent supplementary artificial lighting of the interiors*). With this, as the name implies, the interior parts of the room are lit permanently by electric lights, to provide the necessary illumination in such a way that the overall impression of day-lighting is maintained.

From this it was only one step to the use of PAL (*permanent artificial lighting*), which ignores daylight altogether, possibly leading to windowless environments. It has been claimed that, the window being the weakest point of the building

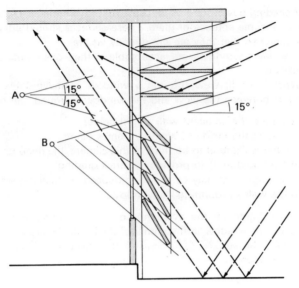

Two critical points (nearest to window) are taken as:
A = standing – 1·70m height , 1·10 m to window
B = sitting –1·20m height, 0·80m to window

envelope (in both thermal and noise insulation), great economic benefits would be obtained with a windowless building and the use of PAL. The saving on heating or air conditioning would be greater that the cost of artificial lighting.

The counter-argument is that the purpose of windows is not only to provide daylighting, but also to give a visual link with the outside world. With the use of PSALI this need would be satisfied with reduced sized windows, and the insufficient daylight would be supplemented by artificial means.

If the above is true in moderate climates, it must be even more so in hot climates. Particularly in hot-dry regions, where the windows would be small for thermal reasons and where some form of shading must be provided, the daylight reaching the interior is likely to be insufficient.

As probably the thermal controls are of primary importance, there would be only two choices open: either to accept a below standard lighting or to use PSALI.

5.2.10
Electric lamps

Two types of electric lamps are most generally used in electric lighting:

1 *incandescent lamps*, in which a current is passed through a tungsten filament, which will thus be heated and its light emission will be due to thermo-luminescence
2 *fluorescent lamps*, in which an electric discharge takes place between two electrodes through low pressure mercury vapour (mixed with some auxiliary gases) and the excited gas molecules emit an ultraviolet radiation. This is absorbed by the fluorescent coating on the inside of the glass tube end and re-emitted at visible wavelengths

Incandescent lamps have a luminous efficacy of 10 to 16 lm/W, whilst fluorescent lamps give 40 to 70 lm/W. Thus, to achieve the same output, a much lesser lamp wattage will be necessary with fluorescent, than with incandescent lamps.

For example, a 200 W incandescent lamp may give about 2 500 lm, but a 40 W fluorescent tube will give almost the same output (the ballast coil necessary to the latter would give a load of about 8 W, thus the total circuit wattage would be 48 W).

Or, to put it another way: the total emission of energy from the two lamps is distributed as follows:

incandescent: 5% light   95% heat
fluorescent: 21% light   79% heat

From a thermal point of view the total lamp wattage is taken into account as a **147**
heat gain rate. The bulk of the energy emitted is heat, but even the emitted light,
when incident on surfaces in the room, will be converted into heat. With fluorescent
lamps the total circuit wattage must be taken into account, not just the tubes, as
the ballast also produces heat.

If it is decided to use PSALI in a hot-dry climate, the heat produced by electric
lighting will increase the indoor temperature. It is therefore advisable to minimise
such heat production by using fluorescent tubes. In a critical situation it may be
worth while to separate the ballasts from the lamps and put them into an isolated
and independently ventilated space. This would save the 8 W heat gain with each
40 W fluorescent tube, giving a reduction of some 17% in the heat gain due to
lighting.

5.3.1
Local lighting

In electric lighting design the illumination on a given surface from a single point source of light (i.e. local lighting) can be predicted by using the inverse square law. Lamp or fitting catalogues usually give a set of curves (the *polar curves*) describing the light distribution characteristics of the fitting. Two examples of this are given in Figure 96.

From these curves it is possible to read the apparent intensity (I) of the source from various directions in candelas (cd). If d is the distance of the illuminated point from the source (in m) and β is the angle of incidence (Figure 97), the illumination on the given plane will be:

$$E = \frac{I}{d^2} \times \cos \beta \text{ (in lux)}$$

Normally the polar curves give the intensity (I) value for every 1 000 lm of lamp output, thus the value read must be divided by 1 000 and multiplied by the actual lamp lumens. Appendix 9.2 gives some lamp lumen outputs.

If several sources contribute to the illumination of a point, the illumination values must be calculated from each source separately and the results added.

Fig 96
Polar curves

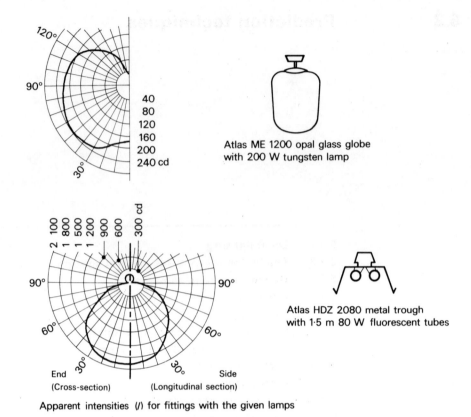

40
80
120
160
200
240 cd

Atlas ME 1200 opal glass globe
with 200 W tungsten lamp

2 100
1 800
1 500
1 200
900
600
300 cd

90°   90°

60°   60°

End   Side
(Cross-section)   (Longitudinal section)

Atlas HDZ 2080 metal trough
with 1·5 m 80 W fluorescent tubes

Apparent intensities (*I*) for fittings with the given lamps

Fig 97
Illumination from
point source

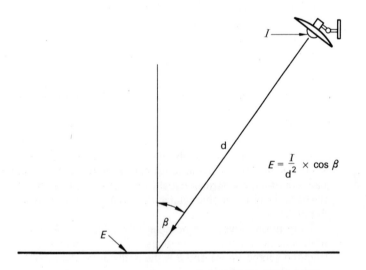

I

d

$$E = \frac{I}{d^2} \times \cos \beta$$

β

E

5.3.2
The lumen
method for
general
lighting

When a room is illuminated by many lamps and fittings the above method would
lead to a very lengthy and cumbersome calculation. If the fittings are positioned in
a regular array, an entirely different, much simpler method can be followed, based
on the concept of *utilisation factor* (UF).

This is simply the ratio of the total *flux received* on the working plane (F_r), to
the total *flux emitted by all the lamps* (F_l).

For example, if all lamps together emit 10 000 lm, and a plane 0·8 m high over the
whole of the room receives 5 000 lm, the utilisation factor is:

$$UF = \frac{F_r}{F_l} = \frac{5000}{10000} = 0.5$$

The illumination will, of course, be the flux received divided by the area (A). If the room is 50 m², the illumination is:

$$E = \frac{5000}{50} = 100 \text{ lux (lm/m}^2)$$

Given the UF, we can use it two ways:

1 if we know the lamps' output, we can calculate the illumination:

$$E = \frac{F_l \times UF}{A}$$

2 if we know what illumination we want to get, we can find the lamp output necessary to achieve this:

$$F_l = \frac{A \times E}{UF}$$

So the method can be used either as a checking tool or, directly, as a design tool.

The critical step is to establish the value of the UF. This will depend on the geometrical proportions of the room, the mounting height of the lamp, on surface reflectances and on the type of fitting used. Values of UF can be found in fitting catalogues or in specialist publications [71] where the method is also fully described. For general guidance it can be stated that its value ranges:

for downward direct lighting	0·4 to 0·9
for diffusing fittings	0·2 to 0·5
for indirect lighting	0·05 to 0·2

A further allowance should be made for dirt on the fitting or deterioration of lamp output: the UF should be multiplied by a *maintenance factor* (MF) usually taken as 0·8.

**5.3.3
Daylighting
requirements**

As has been mentioned (5.2.3), it would be difficult to calculate the daylight received at a point in the room in photometric terms. The concept of *daylight factor* (DF) has been introduced in 5.2.3. The concept is used to establish desirable or minimum daylighting requirements in rooms of various uses. Appendix 9.3 lists some recommended minimum DF values, on the basis of BS CP*3, chapter 1, part 1.

It should be remembered, that the minimum illumination received, with a given DF is related to the established 'design sky' illumination. If (as in the UK) this is taken as 5000 lux, e.g. a DF of 2% would mean a minimum illumination of:

$$E = \frac{5000}{100} \times 2 = 100 \text{ lux}$$

This value would be exceeded most of the time, whenever the out-door illumination is more than 5000 lux. Figure 98 gives the frequency distribution of various out-door illumination levels for London.

Fig 98
Frequency of out-
door illuminations
(London)

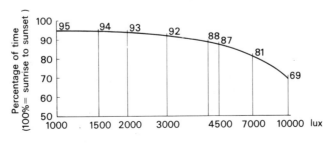

* British Standard Code of Practice.

5.3.4
Daylight protractors

The daylight prediction technique developed by the BRS [79] is based on the calculation of the three components of the daylight factor, separately.

The *sky component* (SC) and the *externally reflected component* (ERC) are found by using the daylight protractors, whilst the *internally reflected component* (IRC) is estimated with the help of a set of nomograms.

There are two series of protractors, one for a sky of uniform luminance and one for a CIE sky luminance distribution. In high latitudes, under predominantly overcast sky conditions, series 2 protractors should be used, but series 1 protractors must be used for the prediction of the sky component under a clear sky, tropical conditions.

Each series consists of five protractors, to be used for various glazing situations, as explained by the following tabulation, giving the numbering of the protractors:

	series 1 uniform sky	series 2 CIE sky
Vertical glazing	1	2
Horizontal glazing	3	4
Slope 30° to horizontal	5	6
Slope 60° to horizontal	7	8
Unglazed openings	9	10

Each protractor consists of two scales: 'A' giving an initial reading (from sections of the room) and 'B' giving a correction factor (from plans). The initial reading would give the sky component for infinitely long windows, but for a window of finite length (width) a correction factor (scale B) must be applied.

Protractor 2 is illustrated in Figure 99.

5.3.5
Sky component

The steps to be taken in establishing the sky component are described with reference to Figure 100, using a 4 × 4 m room: lit by one window, as an example:

1 take a section of the room, mark the 'working plane' and on it the point to be considered (O)

2 connect the limits of aperture (or edges of obstruction) to point O, i.e. lines $\overline{PO}$ and $\overline{RO}$

3 place the protractor with scale A uppermost, base line on the working plane with the centre on point O

4 read the values where lines $\overline{PO}$ and $\overline{RO}$ intersect the perimeter scale: the difference of the two values is the *initial sky component*

5 read the altitude angles where lines PO and RO intersect the 'angle of elevation' scale and take the average of the two readings

6 take the room plan and mark position of the point to be considered (O)

7 connect the limits of aperture with point O, i.e. lines $\overline{MO}$ and $\overline{NO}$

8 place the protractor with scale B towards the window, base line parallel to the window with the centre on point O

9 four concentric semi-circles are marked on the protractor: 0°, 30°, 60° and 90°. Select the one according to the corresponding elevation angle obtained in step **5**, if necessary interpolating an imaginary semi-circle

10 where lines $\overline{MO}$ and $\overline{NO}$ intersect this semi-circle read the values along the short curves on the scale of the inner semi-circle

11 if the two intersection points were on either side of the centre line, add the two values obtained; if both were on the same side, take the difference of the two values. This will be the *correction factor*

12 multiply the initial sky component (step **4**) by the correction factor to obtain the *sky component*

Fig 99
Building Research
Station daylight
protractor No. 2

153

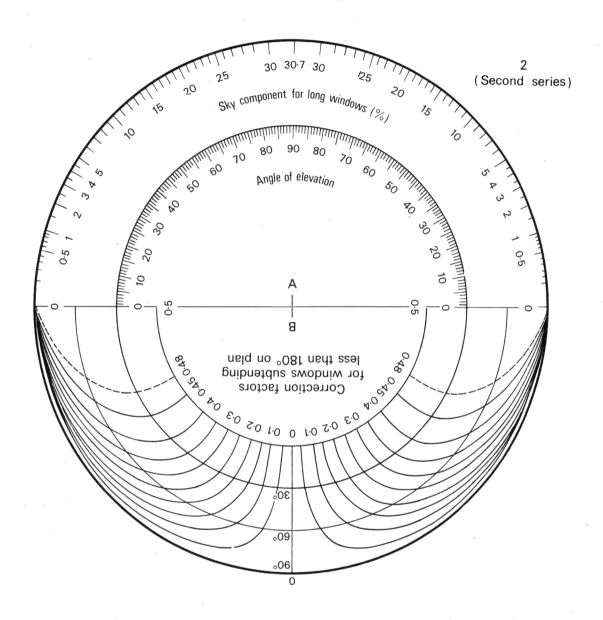

2
(Second series)

Sky component for long windows (%)

Angle of elevation

A
B

Correction factors
for windows subtending
less than 180° on plan

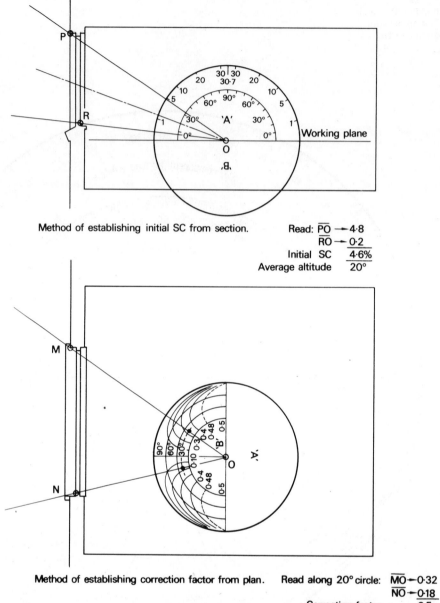

Method of establishing initial SC from section.

Read: $\overline{PO}$ → 4·8
$\overline{RO}$ → 0·2
Initial SC   4·6%
Average altitude   20°

Method of establishing correction factor from plan.

Read along 20° circle: $\overline{MO}$ → 0·32
$\overline{NO}$ → 0·18
Correction factor   0·5

$$SC = 4·6 \times 0·5 = 2·3\%$$

5.3.6 Externally reflected component

If there are no obstructions outside the window, there will be no ERC. If, however, there are objects higher than the line RO, the light reflected from these objects will reach the point considered, and will contribute to the lighting at that point. The magnitude of this contribution is expressed by the ERC, which can be found as follows:

a find the equivalent sky component, which would be obtained from the same area of sky were it not obstructed, following the steps described above
b multiply this value:
   (i) if series 1 (uniform sky) protractors were used, by 0·5 times the average reflectance of opposing surfaces, or if this is unknown, by a factor of 0·1
   (ii) if series 2 (CIE sky) protractors are used, by the average reflectance of opposing surfaces, or a value of 0·2.

Much of the light entering through the window will reach the point considered only after reflection from the walls, ceiling and other surfaces inside the room. The magnitude of this contribution to the lighting of the point considered is expressed by the IRC. This will normally be fairly uniform throughout the room, thus for most problems it is sufficient to find the average IRC value. The simplest method uses the nomogram given in Figure 101 [80]. Steps to be taken in using this nomogram are as follows:

5.3.7 Internally reflected component

1   find the window area and find the total room surface area (floor, ceiling and walls, including windows) and calculate the ratio of window:total surface area. Locate this value on scale A of the nomogram

2   find the area of all the walls and calculate the wall:total surface area. Locate this value in the first column of the small table (alongside the nomogram)

3   locate the wall reflectance value across the top of this table and read the average reflectance at the intersection of column and line (interpolating, if necessary, both vertically and horizontally)

Note. The table assumes a ceiling reflectance of 0·70 and a floor reflectance of 0·15.

4   locate the average reflectance value on scale B and lay a straight-edge from this point across to scale A (to value obtained in step 1)

5   where this intersects scale C, read the value which gives the average IRC if there is no external obstruction

6   if there is an external obstruction, locate its angle from the horizontal, measured at the centre of window, on scale D

7   lay the straight-edge from this point on scale D through the point on scale C and read the average IRC value on scale E

Due to the deterioration of internal finishes, a 'maintenance factor' should be applied to the IRC value thus obtained, either an average factor of 0·75 or one of the following:

type of location	type of work	maintenance factor
Clean	clean	0·9
Dirty	clean	0·8
Clean	dirty	0·7
Dirty	dirty	0·6

The minimum IRC can be obtained by multiplying the average IRC value thus obtained, by a conversion factor, depending on the average reflectance:

average reflectance	conversion factor
0·3	0·54
0·4	0·67
0·5	0·78
0·6	0·85

5.3.8 Further corrections

The DF will thus be obtained as a sum of SC + ERC + IRC, but it may be necessary to multiply this by the product of three further correction factors: GF, FF and D:

1   glazing (GF) — if this is other than clear glass, the appropriate one of the following factors:

wired plate glass	0·95
patterned or diffusing glasses	0·90–0·95
heat absorbing glasses	0·60–0·75
translucent fibreglass (GRP*) or acrylic plastic	0·65–0·90

2   framing (FF) — this could be calculated as the ratio of net glass area to window aperture, but an average value of 0·75 may generally be used

* Glass reinforced plastic.

Fig 101
Nomogram for the
average internally
reflected component
of the daylight factor

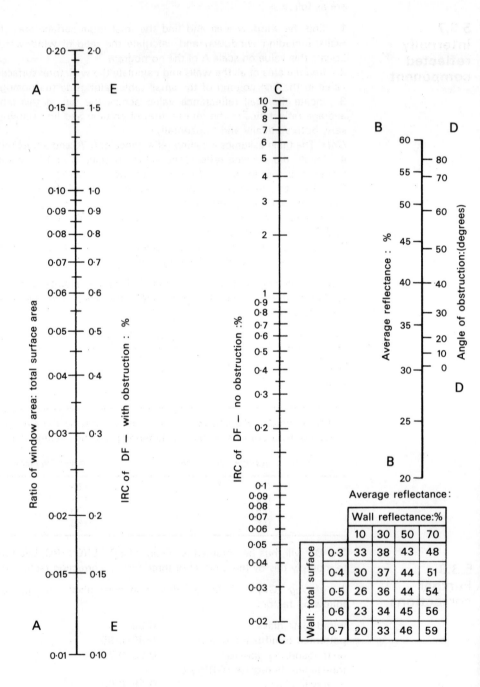

A	E
0·20	2·0
0·15	1·5
0·10	1·0
0·09	0·9
0·08	0·8
0·07	0·7
0·06	0·6
0·05	0·5
0·04	0·4
0·03	0·3
0·02	0·2
0·015	0·15
0·01	0·10

Ratio of window area: total surface area

IRC of DF — with obstruction : %

IRC of DF — no obstruction :%

Average reflectance : %

Angle of obstruction:(degrees)

Average reflectance:

Wall: total surface	Wall reflectance:%			
	10	30	50	70
0·3	33	38	43	48
0·4	30	37	44	51
0·5	26	36	44	54
0·6	23	34	45	56
0·7	20	33	46	59

3 *dirt on glass* (D) — a factor depending on the type of location and frequency of cleaning. A horizontal or sloping glass is more susceptible to deposition of dirt than a vertical one, thus the following D factors should be used:

location	vertical	sloping	horizontal
Clean	0·9	0·8	0·7
Industrial	0·7	0·6	0·5
Very dirty	0·6	0·5	0·4

**5.3.9
Distribution of
daylight**

If daylighting is to be predicted not only at a specified point, but throughout the room (i.e. its distribution), a reference grid should be set up on the plan and the daylight factor should be calculated for each grid point. In a subsequent step, daylight factor contours can be drawn by interpolation between the grid point values.

A systematic approach can save much work, therefore it may be advisable to use a form similar to that shown in Figure 102, which gives a worked example for the room shown in Figure 100.

**5.3.10
Perspective
projection**

The method described above is actually a checking tool, to be used with a design hypothesis, for the prediction of daylighting. Thus a trial-and-error process is unavoidable. There is, however, another perhaps less accurate method, which can be used directly as a design tool [74 and 83]. The method is based on using the 'pepper-pot' diagram (Figure 103) and involves the following steps:

a construct an interior perspective of the window (on tracing paper), as viewed from the point, for which the DF is to be established. The perspective distance (from the viewpoint to the picture plane) must be 30 mm (Figure 104)
b draw any external obstructions in the same projection
c place the pepper-pot diagram under the tracing paper drawing, with the centre of perspective coinciding with the centre of the pepper-pot diagram
d count the number of dots falling on the visible sky area and divide this number by 10 to obtain the SC
e count the number of dots falling on the area of the obstructions and divide this number by 100 to obtain the ERC
f apply the necessary correction factors (GF, FF and D), as with the protractors
g find the IRC by using the nomograms, as before

The usefulness of this method lies in the fact that the consequences of changing the window size or position can be assessed immediately, just by counting the dots.

**5.3.11
Clear sky
conditions**

Both the protractor and the pepper-pot diagram methods are useful and valid for overcast sky conditions. As the design in moderate climates aims at providing a level of daylight which would be exceeded most of the time (i.e. there is no upper limit) — direct sunlight need not be taken into account. If and when it occurs, it will be an extra bonus.

In the tropics, especially in hot-dry climates, the skies are clear and there is a strong, direct sunlight most of the time. Sun penetration must be limited for thermal reasons, thus an upper limit in lighting will be more important than a minimum.

Under such clear sky conditions direct light is received from the sun and a varying amount of diffuse light is received from the whole of the sky hemisphere. Furthermore, both the direct and the diffuse light will be reflected from the same surfaces outside and inside the room. The two components can only be quantified separately, but they should also be treated separately, as the performance of the various control devices and reflective surfaces is different for diffuse light and sunlight. Such separation, however, is not easy. Whilst full daylight with no sunlight does occur in reality with an overcast sky, with a clear sky it does not occur, and the separation is only theoretical.

158 Fig 102
Daylight factor
calculation

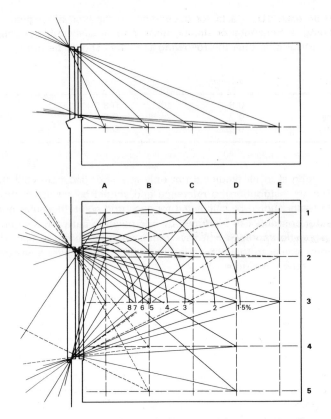

Assumed: no obstruction — no ERC.
If there is an obstruction, repeat
columns **1** to **12** of table .

IRC:
Window : $2 \cdot 5 \times 1 \cdot 5m = 3 \cdot 75m^2$
Total surface:
$19 \times 2 \cdot 7 + 2 \times 5 \times 4 \cdot 5 = 96 \cdot 3\ m^2$

$\dfrac{\text{window}}{\text{total}} = \dfrac{3 \cdot 75}{96 \cdot 3} = 0 \cdot 039$

Wall surface: $19 \times 2 \cdot 7 - 3 \cdot 75 = 47 \cdot 55\ m^2$

$\dfrac{\text{wall}}{\text{total}} = \dfrac{47 \cdot 55}{96 \cdot 3} = 0 \cdot 49$

If wall $r = 50\%$
Average $r = 44\%$ (from table)

From homogram:

IRC $= 0 \cdot 88\%$

Grid point reference		Scale 'A'						Scale 'B'			SC 3 × 9	GF = 1 FF = 0.75 D = 0.9 GF × FF × D	Corrected SC 10 × 11	IRC	DF 12 + 13
		Readings		Initial SC 1–2	Angles		Average altitude $\frac{4+5}{2}$	Readings		Correction factor 7 ±8					
		Upper	Lower		Upper	Lower		Left	Right						
		1	**2**	**3**	**4**	**5**	**6**	**7**	**8**	**9**	**10**	**11**	**12**	**13**	**14**
A	1–5							0·49	0·43	0·06	1·14		0·77		1·65
	2–4	21·4	2·4	19	66	24	45	0·49	0·12	0·61	11·60		7·83		8·71
	3							0·45	0·45	0·90	17·10		11·50		12·38
B	1–5							0·27	0·48	0·21	1·97		1·33		2·21
	2–4	9·7	0·3	9·4	45	11	28	0·07	0·44	0·51	4·80		3·24		4·12
	3							0·34	0·34	0·68	6·40		4·32		5·10
C	1–5							0·43	0·18	0·25	1·15	0·675	0·78	0·88	1·66
	2–4	4·7	0·1	4·6	33	6	20	0·38	0·05	0·43	1·98		1·34		2·22
	3							0·25	0·25	0·5	2·30		1·55		2·43
D	1–5							0·14	0·39	0·25	0·60		0·41		1·29
	2–4	2·5	0·1	2·4	25	5	15	0·04	0·32	0·36	0·86		0·58		1·46
	3							0·2	0·2	0·4	0·96		0·65		1·53
E	1–5							0·35	0·11	0·24	0·37		0·25		1·13
	2–4	1·6	0·05	1·55	20	4	12	0·27	0·03	0·3	0·46		0·31		1·19
	3							0·16	0·16	0·32	0·50		0·34		1·22

Fig 103
The 'pepper-pot'
diagram

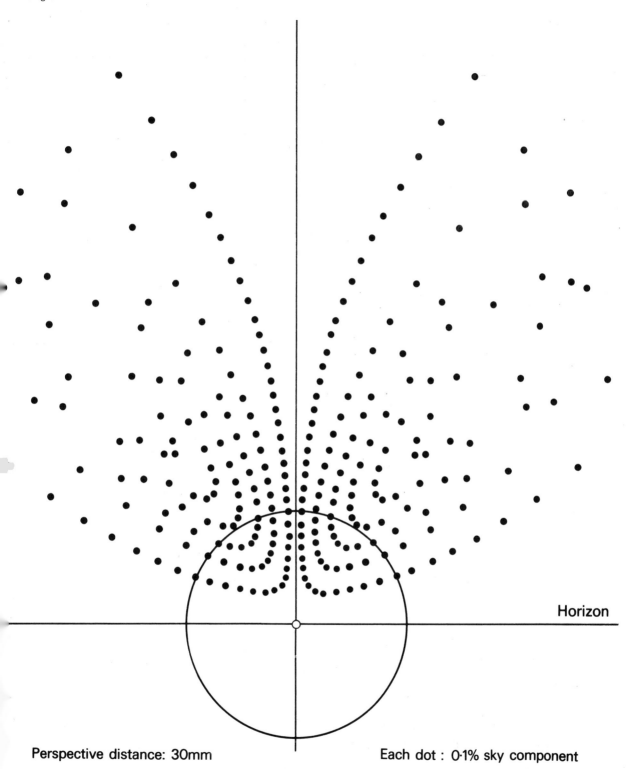

Horizon

Perspective distance: 30mm   Each dot : 0·1% sky component

Circle indicates the visual field within 45° *from* line of vision

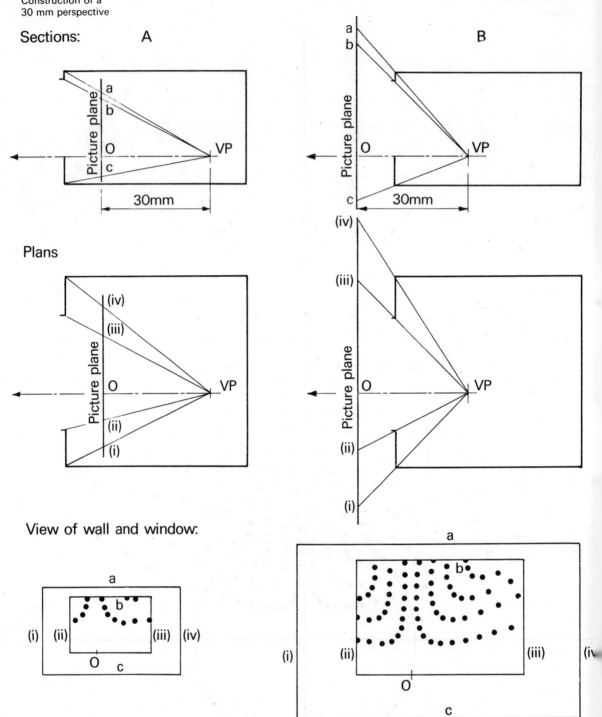

Sections: A   B

Plans

View of wall and window:

For a viewpoint (VP) 1·5 m from the window an internal elevation to 1:50 scale
would give the same view (30 mm = 1·5 m)

For a viewpoint 3m from the window an internal elevation to 1:100 scale would give
the same view (30 mm = 3 m)

Fig 105
Illumination from clear
sky plus sun

161

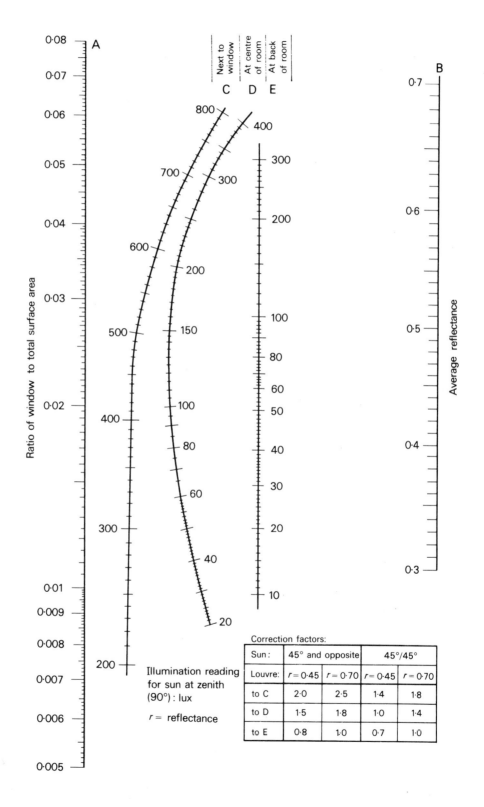

Ratio of window to total surface area

Average reflectance

Next to window
At centre of room
At back of room

C D E

Illumination reading
for sun at zenith
(90°) : lux

r = reflectance

Correction factors:

Sun:	45° and opposite		45°/45°	
Louvre:	*r* = 0·45	*r* = 0·70	*r* = 0·45	*r* = 0·70
to C	2·0	2·5	1·4	1·8
to D	1·5	1·8	1·0	1·4
to E	0·8	1·0	0·7	1·0

It has been established that the brightness distribution of a clear sky hemisphere is much closer to uniform than to the CIE distribution (5.2.2), thus the uniform sky (series 1) protractors can be used for the prediction of lighting due to the diffuse component.

Most of the methods for daylighting prediction under clear sky conditions are based on this separation of the diffuse and direct components, treating the two separately (each through its path of multiple reflections) and adding the results [59 and 59a]. Most of these methods are rather complicated and lengthy and, due to the large number of variable factors, not very reliable.

There is no comprehensive theory and calculation method for the prediction of the joint effect of diffuse (sky) and direct (sun)light, but on an empirical basis a method has been established through laboratory experiments which has a practical (although limited) usefulness [84 and 85]. It is only valid under the specified narrow range of conditions, as given below. The method uses a set of nomograms and tables (Figure 105) and is described in the following paragraph.

5.3.12 Sun plus clear sky nomograms

The following assumptions are made:

the sun is at 90° altitude
the angle of 20° is subtended at the window sill by an obstruction opposite the window
ground luminance is 3 400 cd/m²
sky luminance is 1 000 cd/m²
the window is fitted with louvres giving a 45° vertical shadow angle
louvre reflectance: 0·70
glass reflectance: 0·15

The method is illustrated using the following example (Figure 106):

room: 7·5 × 10·5 × 3 m
window: 3·6 × 2·4 m (in short wall)
reflectance: ceiling — 0·80
　　　　　　　walls　 — 0·65
　　　　　　　floor　 — 0·30

Fig 106
Example room for clear sky plus sun illumination

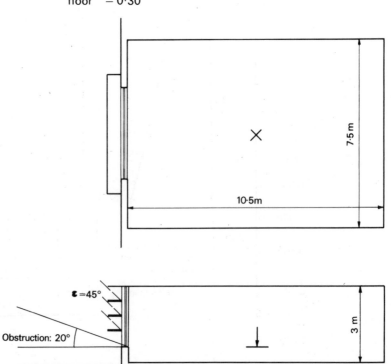

1   calculate surface areas (in m²):

floor	78·75
ceiling	78·75
walls (net)	99·35
windows	8·65
Total	265·50

2   calculate ratio of *window* (W) to total surface (A_t):

$$\frac{W}{A_t} = \frac{8·65}{265·5} = 0·0325$$

3   calculate average internal reflectance:

$$r = \frac{78·75 \times 0·8 + 78·75 \times 0·3 + 99·35 \times 0·65 + 8·65 \times 0·15}{265·5} = \frac{152·5}{265·5} = 0·574$$

4   take nomogram, locate the value of W/A_t on scale A and the value of r on scale B. Lay straight-edge across these points. Select the appropriate one of three centre scales: C – for next to the window, D – for centre of the room, E – for back of the room. Thus where straight-edge intersects scale D, read the illumination value: 199 lux

This is the illumination for the specified condition. Conversion factors are given with the nomogram (for louvre reflectances of 0·45 and 0·70) for two further sun positions: altitude 45° opposite and altitude 45° with 45° azimuth difference.

The method has obvious limitations and should be considered as the first attempt to construct a simple prediction tool.

5.3.13
The lumen method for daylight

The lumen method of lighting design (5.3.2) has been adapted for the prediction of daylighting [86]. In the first step the total flux of light entering through the window(s) is found, then this is multiplied by a utilisation factor (UF) to get the illumination on the working plane. So the method is based on the concept of the total light flux, as opposed to the daylight factor method, which uses the 'split flux' concept (split into its three components: SC + ERC + IRC).

If the illumination on the window is known (lux, which is actually lm/m²), this multiplied by the window area (m²) will give the total flux (in lm).

The magnitude of the UF depends on the relative size of the window, its position in relation to the point considered, any louvres or other controls, interior reflectances and room proportions. Its value can be read from tables included in the American IES Lighting Handbook [86].

This is a rather cumbersome method and the results much less accurate than those of the daylight protractor method.

An Australian publication [88] gives a simplified version of this. From a basic graph (Fig. 107) the illumination levels can be read for points at various distances from the window (expressed as multiples of the window head height above the working plane), for continuous strip window. Correction factors can then be applied for narrow windows and for outside obstructions.

Results obtained with this method will be approximate only, but it is simple and quick to use, therefore it should become a useful tool in the sketch-design stage.

5.3.14
Model studies

As the out-door illumination is constantly changing, it has been necessary to construct 'artificial skies', i.e. a lighting arrangement which simulates the illumination obtained from a sky hemisphere, under which daylighting studies can be carried out on models. Two basic types of such artificial skies exist, the hemispherical and the rectangular (mirror-) type (Figure 108) [89].

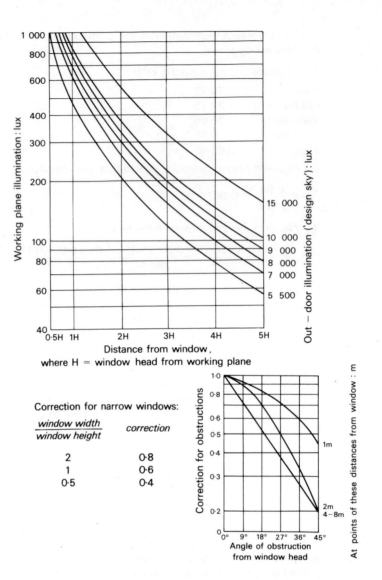

Correction for narrow windows:

window width / window height	correction
2	0·8
1	0·6
0·5	0·4

The hemispherical one has the advantage of close visual resemblance to the real sky, as seen. This makes it a useful tool for teaching and demonstration purposes.

The rectangular type has all lamps above a diffusing ceiling and all four walls are lined with mirrors. This creates an advantage over the hemispherical one: an apparent horizon is developed at infinity, thus the interior illumination in a model will more precisely follow the real situation.

Models used can be of two types:

1   for *quantitative studies* the models need not be realistic, shades of grey can be substituted for actual colours (with appropriate reflectance) and a scale of 1:20 may be sufficient

2   for *qualitative studies*, i.e. for the assessment of lighting quality (as well as quantity), a more realistic model should be built, visually sufficiently representative of the room, its furniture and furnishings — a scale of 1:10 would normally be necessary

For measurements of 'daylighting' in models, it is usual to establish a grid of approximately 1 m and measure the illumination at each of the grid points. On this basis isolux lines (or daylight contours) can be constructed by interpolation — similar to those mentioned in 5.3.9 (see Figure 102).

Fig 108
Artificial skies

165

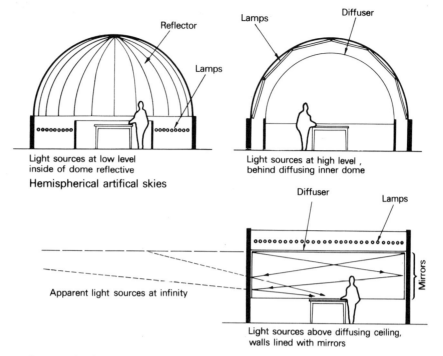

Light sources at low level
inside of dome reflective

Light sources at high level ,
behind diffusing inner dome

Hemispherical artifical skies

Apparent light sources at infinity

Light sources above diffusing ceiling,
walls lined with mirrors

Rectangular (mirror-type) artificial sky

The various calculation methods described were largely developed by using model studies under artificial skies. Now, even if such calculation methods are available, for more complex or non-typical building situations it will still be useful to carry out model studies under artificial skies at an early stage of the design.

5.3.15 Glare in electric lighting

The problem of glare has been mentioned in 5.1.12. By definition, *glare* (*g*) is a function of luminance ratios:

$$g = \mathbf{F}\,\frac{L_1}{L_2}$$

where L_1 = the higher luminance value
L_2 = the lower luminance value

(**F** indicates 'function of')

On the basis of experiments two further factors have been identified:

a glare is increased with the increase of the apparent area of the glare source, measured as a *visual angle* (*ψ*) in steradians
b glare also depends on the position of the glare source in relation to the direction of vision, as expressed by a *position index* (*p*)

The function, i.e. the nature, of this dependence is specified by the empirical formula:

$$g = \frac{L_1{}^{1.6} \times \psi^{0.8}}{L_2 \times p^{1.6}}$$

where g = glare constant
L_1 = luminance of glare source (cd/m²)
L_2 = luminance of environment (cd/m²)
$$\psi = \frac{\text{area of glare source}}{\text{square of distance}}\left(\frac{\text{m}^2}{\text{m}^2} = \text{steradians}\right)$$
p = position index

To describe the 'glariness' of an electric light installation, the concept of *glare index* (G) has been devised:

$$G = 10 \times \log g$$

Limiting glare index values are included with recommended illumination levels in publications such as [71 and 76] and appendix 9.1 gives some typical values. It has a value between 10 (for the most critical visual task) and 28 (for a non-critical situation), in increments of 3. This limiting glare index value should not be exceeded by the installation.

The IES report [87] describes the theoretical basis and gives a detailed method for the calculation of glare index, providing all the necessary data in tables and graphs. A slightly simplified method, together with the relevant data is given in *Interior lighting design* [71].

5.3.16 Glare in daylighting

The problem of glare in daylighting, particularly in sunny climates, has been mentioned in qualitative terms in 5.2.6 to 8. In most practical cases the analysis would not go beyond such a qualitative assessment — partly because quantitative analysis is lengthy and difficult, partly because glare is a very subjective phenomenon — depending very much on human expectation, adaptability and even on mood.

Should, however, a quantitative analysis be necessary, the following method could be used:

1 establish the limiting glare index for the given visual task, as a target, from appendix 9.1, or rather from [71 or 76]

2 take nomogram (Figure 109) and establish luminance of glare source (L_1) in cd/m² (e.g. of the window, or of the view seen through the window). Values given in 5.2.2 or in 1.3.3 to 8 can provide some rough guidance — locate this value on scale A of the nomogram

3 establish the solid angle subtended by the glare source at the viewing point, in steradians, dividing the projected area of the glare source by the square of its distance — locate this on scale B of the nomogram

4 connect the values on scales A and B and mark the intersection with the reference scale C,

5 establish the environmental luminance (L_2), i.e. the luminance of surfaces adjacent to the glare source, in cd/m² — locate this value on scale D

6 project a line from this, through the point marked on scale C to scale E — to get the initial glare constant

7 find position index from the table attached to the nomogram, locate its value on scale F

8 connect this point of scale F to the initial glare constant of scale E and read the final glare constant (g) on scale G.

Repeat the same process for each glare source within the visual field to get g_1, g_2, g_3, etc.

Find the glare index from the sum of these glare constants:

$$G = 10 \times \log (g_1 + g_2 + g_3 + \cdots)$$

If this glare index is greater than the target value (established in step **1**) — it is likely that discomfort would be caused in the real situation, therefore corrective measures should be taken.

Some difficulty may be experienced in ascertaining or predicting the luminance values of the potential glare sources (L_1) and of its surroundings (L_2) with any degree of accuracy, on the basis of a design. One could argue that if such luminance prediction is not reasonably accurate, there is not much use in carrying out this calculation — if the variables are handled sensitively in a purely qualitative way, the result is just as likely to be satisfactory. So the above method will be useful only if the luminances can be predicted with reasonable accuracy.

Fig 109
Glare constant
nomogram

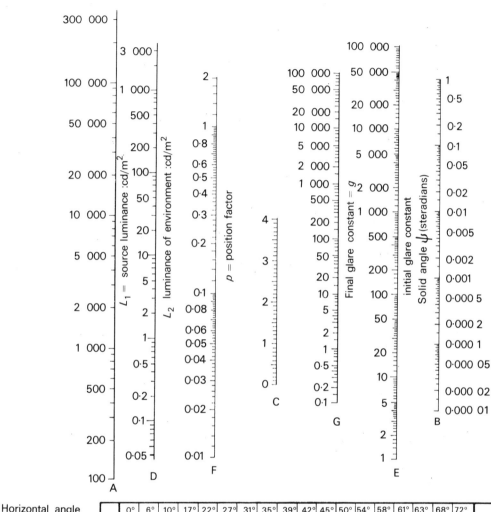

Horizontal angle
$\phi = \tan\ L/R$

L = lateral displacement
V = vertical displacement
R = horizontal distance

V/R	0°	6°	10°	17°	22°	27°	31°	35°	39°	42°	45°	50°	54°	58°	61°	63°	68°	72°	Vertical angle
1.9	—	—	—	—	—	—	—	—	—	0.02	0.02	0.02	0.02	0.02	0.02	0.02	0.02	0.02	62°
1.8	—	—	—	—	0.02	0.02	0.02	0.02	0.02	0.02	0.02	0.02	0.02	0.02	0.02	0.02	0.02	0.02	61°
1.6	0.03	0.03	0.03	0.03	0.03	0.03	0.03	0.03	0.03	0.03	0.03	0.03	0.03	0.03	0.03	0.03	0.03	0.03	58°
1.4	0.04	0.04	0.04	0.04	0.04	0.04	0.04	0.04	0.04	0.04	0.04	0.04	0.04	0.04	0.04	0.04	0.03	0.03	54°
1.2	0.05	0.05	0.06	0.06	0.06	0.06	0.06	0.06	0.06	0.06	0.06	0.05	0.05	0.05	0.05	0.04	0.04	0.04	50°
1.0	0.08	0.09	0.09	0.10	0.10	0.10	0.10	0.09	0.09	0.09	0.08	0.08	0.07	0.06	0.06	0.06	0.05	0.05	45°
0.9	0.11	0.11	0.12	0.13	0.13	0.12	0.12	0.12	0.12	0.11	0.10	0.09	0.08	0.07	0.07	0.06	0.06	0.05	42°
0.8	0.14	0.15	0.16	0.16	0.16	0.16	0.15	0.15	0.14	0.13	0.12	0.11	0.09	0.08	0.08	0.07	0.06	0.06	39°
0.7	0.19	0.20	0.22	0.21	0.21	0.21	0.20	0.18	0.17	0.16	0.14	0.12	0.11	0.10	0.09	0.08	0.07	0.07	35°
0.6	0.25	0.27	0.30	0.29	0.28	0.26	0.24	0.22	0.21	0.19	0.18	0.15	0.13	0.11	0.10	0.10	0.09	0.08	31°
0.5	0.35	0.37	0.39	0.38	0.36	0.34	0.31	0.28	0.25	0.23	0.21	0.18	0.15	0.14	0.12	0.11	0.10	0.09	27°
0.4	0.48	0.53	0.53	0.51	0.49	0.44	0.39	0.35	0.31	0.28	0.25	0.21	0.18	0.16	0.14	0.13	0.11	0.10	22°
0.3	0.67	0.73	0.73	0.69	0.64	0.57	0.49	0.44	0.38	0.34	0.31	0.25	0.21	0.19	0.16	0.15	0.13	0.12	17°
0.2	0.95	1.02	0.98	0.88	0.80	0.72	0.63	0.57	0.49	0.42	0.37	0.30	0.25	0.22	0.19	0.17	0.15	0.14	11°
0.1	1.30	1.36	1.24	1.12	1.01	0.88	0.79	0.68	0.62	0.53	0.46	0.37	0.31	0.26	0.23	0.20	0.17	0.16	6°
0	1.87	1.73	1.56	1.36	1.20	1.06	0.93	0.80	0.72	0.64	0.57	0.46	0.38	0.33	0.28	0.25	0.20	0.17	0°
	0	0.1	0.2	0.3	0.4	0.5	0.6	0.7	0.8	0.9	1	1.2	1.4	1.6	1.8	2	2.5	2	

Vertical displacement V/R

Vertical angle : $\theta = \tan\ V/R$

Horizontal displacement
L/R

**6.1.1
Introduction**

Hearing is one of man's most important communication channels, perhaps only second to vision. But, whilst the eyes can be shut when there is too much light or an unwanted scene to view, the ears are open throughout life to unwanted noises as well as to wanted sounds. Protection, if necessary, will have to be provided in the environment.

Noise is the term used for any unwanted sound, thus the definition of noise is subjective. One man's sound is another man's noise.

In rural life sounds rarely become noise: partly because they provide a sense of participation in the social life of the community and partly because they hardly ever reach intolerable levels. Urbanisation brings about a rapid increase of noise sources (industry, traffic, aircraft, radio, etc.), but also a change in social attitudes: in a village one knows everyone else, every sound originates from a known source and conveys some meaningful information; but a town is full of strangers and un-identified noises, for which we have little tolerance. The low density of rural areas ensures a greater distance between noise source and listener, thus reducing the disturbance, while in high density towns there are more potential noise sources in a given area — also the distances between sources and listeners are much less.

As the noise sources multiply, so the problems increase and defensive measures must follow.

The science of sound — acoustics — can be broadly divided into two major areas:

1   the handling of *wanted sound*, i.e. creating of the most favourable conditions for listening to a sound we want to hear: room acoustics
2   the handling of *unwanted sound*, i.e. the control of noise

The former is a rather specialised task and is considered to be outside the scope of this book. The control of noise is, however, closely related to other factors influencing a design, thus it will be dealt with in some detail in the following sections.

In tropical climates, even if today the given noise is much less than in the highly industrialised regions of moderate climates, tomorrow's problems will be no less severe. When this stage is reached, the designer's task will be much greater in the tropics than in moderate climates, for several reasons:

a a greater part of life in the tropics goes on out-of-doors, where noise control is not possible, as opposed to the predominantly indoor living of moderate climates
b there will be a conflict between thermal and aural requirements, especially in warm-humid climates, where the building is of lightweight construction with large openings, therefore it cannot effectively control noise penetration

In tropical climates the design of buildings will be strongly influenced by noise considerations. Noise control performance will depend on planning and basic design decisions, rather than on constructional details. Remedial measures will rarely be possible. Far greater foresight and skill will be demanded of the designer. He will have to possess a much clearer understanding of noise problems and the means of their control, than his colleagues operating in moderate climates. For this reason, before we can examine the specific problems of tropical climates, we must review the available means of control which are applicable under any conditions. This will establish a vocabulary of means, which can subsequently be drawn on as the circumstances demand. But even before that, a brief review of the physical and psychophysical principles will be necessary.

6.1.2 The nature of sound

Sound is, strictly speaking, the sensation caused by a vibrating medium acting on the ear, but the term is usually applied to the vibration itself.

The source of sound is most often some vibrating solid body (e.g. a string or a sheet) which in turn generates vibrations in the air, but it may be generated by vibrations of a gaseous medium, such as the air in a whistle or flute.

The medium conveying it to the ear can be a gas (air) or a liquid, in which the vibrations are transmitted as a longitudinal wave motion, i.e. successive compressions and rarefications of the molecules. Figure 110 shows how these longitudinal waves are represented graphically by a sine curve. If the conveying medium is a solid body, the vibration may be transmitted as lateral wave motion (an actual sine-curve type movement).

Fig 110
Sound waves

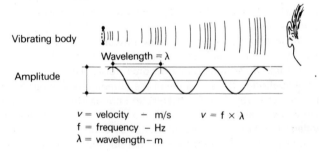

v = velocity – m/s $\quad v = f \times \lambda$
f = frequency – Hz
λ = wavelength – m

The wavelength (or the frequency, which is the number of waves per unit time) determines the pitch of the sound. Its strength is indicated by the amplitude of the sine curve.

Some typical frequencies (in Hz):

bottom note of bass singer   100
top note of soprano singer   1 200
range of grand piano   25 to 4 200
top note of piccolo flute   4 600

(1 Hz, i.e. one Hertz = one wave per second)

6.1.3
Sound waves

This wave motion can be described in terms of the following three quantities:

λ = wavelength (m) — see Figure 110
f = frequency (Hz) — number of vibrations per second
v = velocity (m/s)

The relationship of these quantities is $v = f \times \lambda$:
therefore if any two are known, the third one can be found.

The value of v is constant for a conveying medium of a given density. As the density of air changes rapidly with temperature, the velocity of sound also varies with air temperature. Some typical velocities in various media (in m/s) are:

air at	−20°C	319·3
	0°C	331·8
	20°C	343·8
	30°C	349·6

(for rough calculations taken as 340 m/s)

gases:	hydrogen	1 284
	oxygen	316
	carbon dioxide	259

liquids:	water	1 437
	sea-water	1 541
	petrol	1 166

solids:	steel	6 100
	timber (pine)	5 260
	brick	3 650

6.1.4
Power and intensity

The output of a source is measured as the rate of energy flow (i.e. power) in units of *watt* (W).

The average output of some sources (in watts) is:

jet airliner	10 000	(10^4)
pneumatic riveter	1	
50 kW axial fan	0·1	(10^{-1})
large orchestra	0·01	(10^{-2})
conversational speech	0·000 01	(10^{-5})

In a carrying medium (e.g. in air) the 'strength' of sound is usually measured as *intensity*, that is the density of energy flow rate through unit area, in W/m².

When a point source emits sound (or any other form of energy) uniformly in all directions in a free field, it is spreading over the surface of a sphere of increasing radius. The same amount of energy is distributed over a larger and larger area, therefore the intensity will decrease. At a distance of d metres from the source it will be [90]:

$$I = \frac{W}{4\pi d^2} \text{ (as the surface of the sphere is } 4\pi d^2 \text{)}$$

where I is in W/m²
      W is the source power in watts

This is known as the inverse square law.

6.1.5
The ear's sensitivity

The average person can hear frequencies from about 20 to 16 000 Hz, but this range is reduced with age and other subjective factors.

The lowest intensity perceived as a sound is:

10^{-12} W/m² (or 1 pW/m² = 1 picowatt per metre square)

and this limit is taken as the standard *threshold of audibility*.

The upper limit is the *threshold of pain*, at 1 W/m². Vibrations above this intensity would cause pain and could damage the ear.

Figure 111 shows the audible range of sounds in terms of frequency and intensity.

Fig 111
Audible range of
sounds

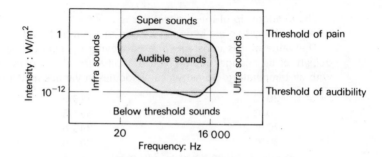

The ear has a built-in defence mechanism: its sensitivity decreases for higher intensity sounds. In fact its response is proportionate to the logarithm of intensity. The logarithm of the ratio of the measured sound intensity to the intensity at the threshold of audibility gives the *sound level scale* or *decibel* (dB) *scale*.

The number of decibels (N) [91]:

$$N = 10 \log \frac{I}{I_o}$$

where I = the measured intensity
I_o = reference intensity: 10^{-12} W/m²

Thus the intensity (in W/m²) and sound level (in dB) can be compared:

jet aircraft at 1 km	0·01	= 100
heavy traffic at 10 m from kerb	0·001	= 90
in office with ten typewriters	0·000001	= 60

Fig 112
Equal loudness
contours

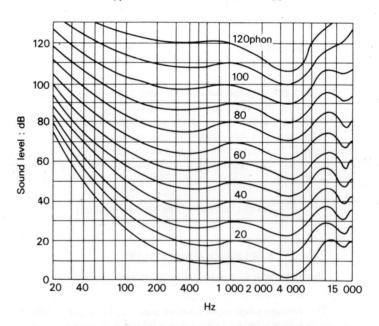

As it can be seen from Figure 111, sensitivity of the ear varies with the frequency of the sound. Levels of sounds of various frequencies, which are perceived as of the same loudness, are shown in Figure 112 by the *equal loudness contours*. This graph establishes the *loudness* or *phon scale*. By agreement, the dB and phon values coincide at 1 000 Hz, but differ at all other frequencies.

Loudness cannot be measured directly by instruments. Various electronic weighting circuits have been constructed to modify the readings of a sound level meter. The 'A' weighting (as shown by Figure 113) approximates the shape of the equal loudness contours, thus the reading in dBA will give the phon value:

$$1.05 \times dBA + 10 = phon \qquad e.g. \quad 80\ dBA = 94\ phon$$

Fig 113
Weighting to produce dBA

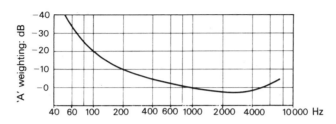

6.1.6 Frequency spectra

A single value in dB will only approximately describe a sound. The value in dBA will give an indication of the subjective effects of that sound. For a complete description of a sound a *frequency spectrum graph* would be necessary, which would show the sound level (in dB) for every octave band (or third octave band) measured separately.

An octave difference between two sounds means doubling of the frequency, e.g. 75 to 150 Hz, or 1 000 to 2 000 Hz. The range of all frequencies within an octave is referred to as the 'octave band'. For most practical purposes the following octave bands (in Hz) are used:

```
  37·5—    75
   75—   150
  150—   300
  300—   600
  600—1 200
1 200—2 400
2 400—4 800
4 800—9 600
```

When measuring a sound, a 'band-pass filter' is used in conjunction with the sound level meter, admitting only one octave band at a time. With successive measurements the full spectrum can be built up by plotting the sound level measured in each octave band (see Figure 132).

6.1.7 Effects of noise

Noises of various levels may produce both psychological and physiological effects:

65 dBA – up to this level noise or unwanted sound may create annoyance, but its result is only psychological (nervous effects). Above this level physiological effects, such as mental and bodily fatigue, may occur.

90 dBA – many years of exposure to such noise levels would normally cause permanent hearing loss.

100 dBA – with short periods of exposure to this noise level, the aural acuity may be impaired temporarily, and prolonged exposure is likely to cause irreparable damage to the auditory organs.

120 dBA – causes pain.

160 dBA – causes instantaneous loss of hearing.

The acceptable level of noise depends not only on objective, physical factors but also on subjective, psychological factors. Whether a noise is disturbing or not depends on the state of mind or expectation of the listener. In a sleeper train the monotonous noise, even at 70 to 80 dBA, will not be disturbing; but in a quiet home, if the listener is badly 'tuned', even the ticking of a clock at 20 dBA may cause great annoyance.

Noise may adversely affect concentration, particularly if the noise or unwanted sound has some information content.

Furthermore, as habits, expectations and attitudes depend on the socio-cultural environments, the noise tolerance of people may vary with the kind of society of which they are a part.

6.1.8
Noise in free field

The inverse square law (6.1.4) is applicable only to free field conditions, where there is no obstruction, no solid objects from which the sound could be reflected. Open air conditions approximate the theoretical free field.

According to the inverse square law, every doubling of the distance will decrease the intensity to one quarter. Due to the logarithmic relationship, in sound level this will correspond to a reduction of 6 dB for every doubling of the distance, regardless of the magnitude of intensity, e.g.:

a sound at 1 km from source: $I' = 0.01$ W/m²
at 2 km: $I'' = 0.0025$ W/m²

$$N' = 10 \log \frac{10^{-2}}{10^{-12}} = 10 \log 10^{10} = 10 \times 10 = 100 \text{ dB}$$

$$N'' = 10 \log \frac{25 \times 10^{-4}}{10^{-12}} = 10 \log (25 \times 10^8) = 10 (1.4 + 8) = 94 \text{ dB}$$

or:

speech at 2 m: $I' = 10^{-8}$ W/m²
at 4 m: $I'' = 25 \times 10^{-10}$ W/m²

$$N' = 10 \log \frac{10^{-8}}{10^{-12}} = 10 \log 10^4 = 10 \times 4 = 40 \text{ dB}$$

$$N'' = 10 \log \frac{25 \times 10^{-10}}{10^{-12}} = 10 \log (25 \times 10^2) = 10 (1.4 + 2) = 34 \text{ dB}$$

Distance also affects sound by the molecular absorption of energy in the carrying medium. This molecular attenuation in air is only significant for high frequency sounds. For every 300 m distance this reduction is:

1 dB at 1 000 Hz
40 dB at 9 000 Hz

Hence loud noises from a great distance (e.g. thunder) are heard at a lower pitch than from nearby: the higher frequency components have been filtered out by the air.

Fig 114
Effect of a wind
velocity gradient

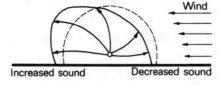

Wind

Increased sound   Decreased sound

In moving air (wind) there is usually a velocity gradient (see Figure 25), so the spherical wavefront is distorted. Figure 114 explains how this will result in an increased sound downwind and a decreased sound upwind.

Fig 115
Effect of temperature
gradients

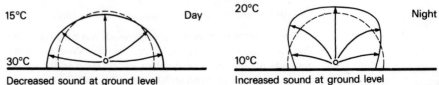

15°C   Day   20°C   Night

30°C   10°C

Decreased sound at ground level   Increased sound at ground level

As the velocity of sound increases with air temperature, a temperature gradient will also distort the spherical wavefront. Figure 115 shows how this will produce an increased sound effect for a ground level observer at night and a decreased sound effect during day-time temperature inversion.

Fig 116
Acoustic shadow at
high frequencies

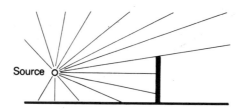

Screening or barriers in the path of sound can create an 'acoustic shadow' (Figure 116) — if the sound is of a high frequency. At low frequencies diffraction will occur at the edge of the barrier (Figure 117) — thus the 'shadow' effect will be blurred. If the dimension of the barrier (in a direction perpendicular to the sound path) is less than the wavelength of sound, the shadow effect disappears. As at 30 Hz the wavelength is over 10 m, any barrier less than 10 m will be ineffective for such low frequency sounds [92].

Fig 117
Diffraction at low
frequencies

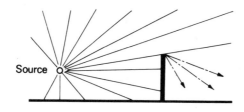

6.1.9
Noise in
enclosed
spaces

Sound incident on the surface of a solid body (e.g. a wall) is partly reflected, partly absorbed (converted into heat) and partly transmitted to air on the opposite side (Figure 118). The term 'absorption coefficient' is used normally to indicate all the sound *that is not reflected* (that is, it includes the part actually absorbed and that which is transmitted). The *absorption coefficient* is denoted by *a*: it is a decimal fraction — a non-dimensional quantity.

Fig 118
Airborne sound
transmission

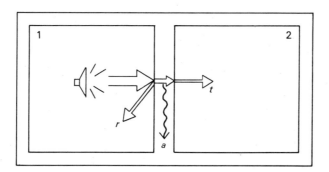

r = reflected   If source I =1
a = absorbed $r+a+t=1$
t = transmitted

For room 1: 'absorption coefficient' = $a + t$
         (all that is not reflected: $1 - r$)

For room 2: 'transmission coefficient' = t
         ($r+a$ is not transmitted)

When the sound is in an enclosed space, reflection will occur from the bounding surfaces: the reflected part will reinforce the sound within the space and the remainder will be lost for the system.

Absorption (**A**) is the product of the absorption coefficient and of the *area of a given surface* (s):

A $= a \times s$

It is measured by the 'open window unit', which is the absorption of a l m² opening having an absorption coefficient of 1 (i.e. zero reflectance).

In an enclosed space, even from a single source, there will be a complex pattern of interreflected sound, which is usually referred to as 'reverberant sound'. Thus at any point in the space the total sound received will consist of two parts:

a   the direct component
b   the reverberant component

as shown by Figure 119. The first reduces with the distance, but the second can be taken as constant throughout the space.

Fig 119
Direct and reverberant
sound

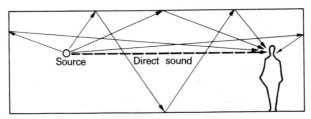

Reverberant sound: sum of an infinite number of paths

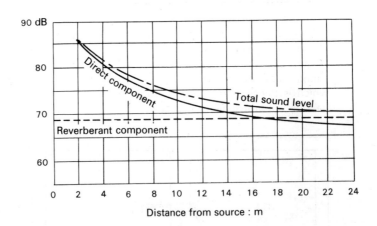

Distance from source : m

6.1.10
Transmission

The magnitude of the reverberant component depends on the absorbent qualities of room surfaces. The more absorbent these surfaces are, the lesser the reverberant component will be. A good rule of thumb is that every doubling of the total absorption in the space will reduce the reverberant sound level by 3 dB. If all surfaces in the space were perfect absorbers, conditions would be the same as in a free field: zero reverberant component.

When airborne sound impinges on a solid body, some of the energy of vibrating air molecules will be transmitted to the solid material and induce a vibration of its molecules. This vibration will spread in the body as 'structureborne sound' and may be re-emitted to air on other surfaces.

Figure 120 shows some possible sound paths from a source in one room to a listener in another room. Of the five paths 1 is airborne, 2, 3 and 4 are structureborne. Path 5 is strictly speaking also structureborne, but for practical purposes the transmission through a wall of a sound perpendicular to its plane is considered as 'airborne sound transmission'.

The only way to reduce structureborne transmission is to prevent the spread of vibrations by introducing structural discontinuity, i.e. a physical separation or flexible connections only.

Structureborne sound can also be generated by mechanical means: by a vibrating piece of machinery or by physical impact. In the latter case the result is referred to as 'impact sound'.

Fig 120
Sound transmission
paths

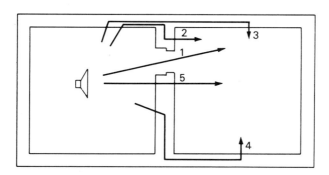

**6.2.1
Means of
noise control**

From the point of view of a building which is to be designed, it is useful to distinguish:

a   external noises
b   internal noises

Against external noise the following means of protection are available to the designer [95]:

1   distance
2   avoiding zones of directional sound
3   screening
4   planning: using non noise-sensitive parts of the building as barriers
5   positioning of openings away from the noise source
6   noise insulating building envelope

Against noises generated within the building, the designer can take the following measures:

1   reduction at source
2   enclosing and isolating the source, or use of absorbent screens
3   planning: separating noisy spaces from quiet ones, placing indifferent areas in between
4   placing noisy equipment in the most massive part of the building (e.g. in a basement)
5   reduce impact noises by covering surfaces with resilient materials
6   reduce noise in the space where it is generated by absorbent surfaces
7   reduce airborne sound transmission by airtight and noise insulating construction
8   reduce structureborne sound transmission by discontinuity

All these means will be examined in more detail in the following paragraphs.

6.2.2
Distance and
screening

If a site is given, on which the positioning of a building is subject to the designer's choice, and there is a noise source to one side of the site (e.g. a busy road), it will be advisable to place the building as far from the noise source as possible. It is worth remembering that every doubling of the distance will reduce the noise level by 6 dB. For example if 65 dB is measured at the boundary, 5 m from the centre of the road (the source), it will reduce to:

59 dB at 10 m
53 dB at 20 m
47 dB at 40 m

which is quite acceptable even in residential areas.

Some sources are strongly directional, as shown on Figure 121. It may occur that there is a band of maximum noise across the site, (particularly if it is a large site), either due to such directional sources or to the funnelling effect of local topography. Its existence can be discovered by a 'noise climate' survey of the site. The building(s) should then be placed away from such noise bands.

Fig 121
Directional tendencies
of some sound sources

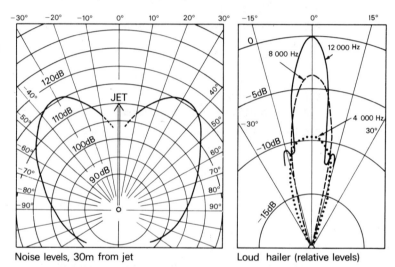

Noise levels, 30m from jet   Loud hailer (relative levels)

The screening effect of walls, fences plantation belts, etc., can be utilised to reduce the noise reaching the building. These should be positioned in such a way as to fit in with any advantageous effects of local topography. Figure 122 shows some possibilities. As a general rule it can be established that a given barrier will be most effective when it is as near to the source as possible. The second best position would be near the building which is to be protected: it would be least effective half-way between the source and the building.

Screening can rarely be relied on as a positive means of noise protection, but it will help to ameliorate an otherwise critical situation.

6.2.3
Planning

Planning of the building will obviously be governed by a whole series of factors other than noise, but noise protection should be included amongst the factors taken into account. The relative importance or weighting of the noise-control aspect will depend on the particular design task: it may be dominant in case of a school class-room near to a motorway, or it may be quite subordinate.

External noises can be controlled by planning in two ways:

a separating areas which are not noise-sensitive, where noise would not cause disturbance, and placing them on the side of the building (possibly in a separate block or wing) nearest to the noise source. Thus the areas or block would provide screening and protection to the more critical areas

Fig 122
The screening effect
of barriers

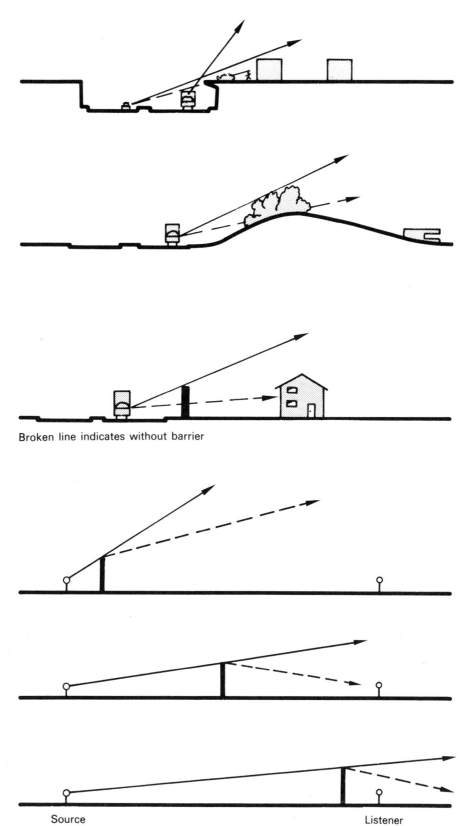

Broken line indicates without barrier

Source

Listener

Broken line indicates the same degree of diffraction.
Best position for barrier : nearest to the source.
Worst position: half-way between source and listener

b positioning or orientating the major openings away from the noise source. Usually in the external envelope of a building the openings (doors and particularly windows) are the weakest points for noise penetration, so it is logical to place them in the least exposed positions. Furthermore, the plan shape can be so adjusted as to provide protection or screening from the sides. Possibly special elements (wing-walls and screens) can be introduced to provide additional sideways protection

6.2.4
Reduction at
or near source

Although not strictly an architectural task, it is worth looking into how a particular source emits noise. Very often the source is some vibrating machinery. Here the unavoidable vibration may be below the audible range: it is not a sound. Some non-essential part, however, such as a sheet metal cover, may have a resonant frequency which coincides with one of the upper harmonics of the vibration. (Harmonics are frequencies 2, 4, 8, 16, etc., times the original frequency.) This part would thus come into vibration which is already in the audible range: it would become a noise source. It may be quite simple to change the resonant frequency of the noise emitting part, by modifying its fixings, using some form of stiffener, or replacing it by a heavier element.

Below audible frequency vibrations can be transmitted through the structure, and noise may be generated at a remote part of the building, where an element occurs with a corresponding resonant frequency. Here again the general principle of noise control is applicable: the nearer to the source, the easier the protective measures will be.

It is best to place the vibrating machinery on flexible mountings (Figure 123), which will isolate it from the building structure, so that the vibration is not transmitted. To be effective, the resonant frequency of the mounting itself must be lower than the frequency of vibration to be isolated.

Fig 123
Flexible mountings

Flexible connections

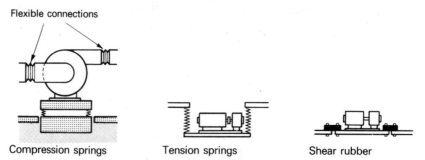

Compression springs   Tension springs   Shear rubber

Airborne sound emitted by a source can also be tackled most readily near the source. If the actual situation permits this, the source could be surrounded or covered by an insulating enclosure, e.g. a machine could be covered by a box. The box should be of massive construction, with absorbent lining on the inside, to prevent the build-up of reverberant noise level. It could be removable for access to the machine, or if larger, it could have a door. If usage of the machine does not permit enclosure, any transition between full enclosure and a simple screen may reduce the noise emission.

6.2.5
Reduction
within a space

Noise in the space where the source is located can be divided into two components (6.1.9): direct and reverberant noise.

Direct noise can be reduced by placing a screen between the source and the listener. The closer this screen is to the source, the better the result will be (optimum is the full enclosure – see 6.2.4).

Reverberant noise can be reduced by using absorbent materials on critical surfaces of the room.

Absorbent qualities of different materials vary with the frequency. Four basic types of absorbents can be distinguished:

1 porous absorbents (Figure 124) – best in the higher frequencies

2 membrane absorbents (Figure 125) – best in low frequencies

3 resonant absorbers (Helmholz resonators) (Figure 126) can be 'tuned' to a very narrow band of any frequency

4 perforated panel absorbents – a combination of resonant and porous absorbers (Figure 127), best in medium frequencies – can be 'tuned' to some extent by variation of hole size, shape and spacing and of backing material and space

Fig 124
Porous absorbents

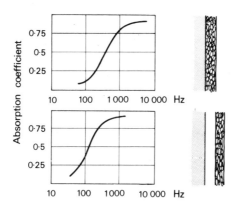

Fig 125
Membrane absorbents

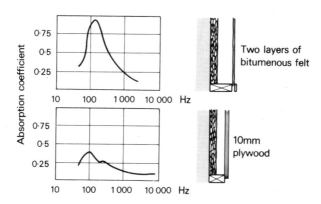

Two layers of bitumenous felt

10mm plywood

Fig 126
A resonant absorber

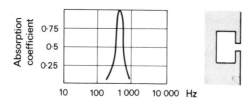

Fig 127
Perforated panel absorbents

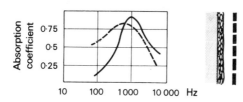

It must be obvious that the type of absorbents to be used must be selected according to the frequency of sound which is to be reduced.

The most likely surface to receive absorbent treatment is the ceiling — for two reasons:

a especially in low and extensive spaces, the ceiling would cause multiple reflections of the sound, thus it is the most critical surface
b most absorbents are rather vulnerable, and the surface least exposed to mechanical damage is the ceiling

6.2.6 Noise insulation

One form of expression used to describe the noise insulating qualities of an element is the *transmission coefficient* (*t*) — a decimal fraction, expressing the proportion of sound energy (intensity) transmitted.

Another form, more widely used, is the *transmission loss* (TI), or sound reduction index, the reduction effect of an element expressed in dB.

e.g., a wall with TI = 30 dB will reduce a noise of
90 dB to 90 −30 = 60 dB, or
70 dB to 70 −30 = 40 dB

The relationship between the two quantities is reciprocal and logarithmic:

$$TI = 10 \log \frac{1}{t}$$

$$t = \text{antilog} \frac{-TI}{10}$$

For solid, homogeneous walls (or roofs) the insulating quality is a function of the mass. An approximate value can be obtained from the formula:

$TI = 18 \log M + 8$
where M = mass per unit surface (kg/m²)

For walls less than 100 kg/m² the formula is modified into:

$TI = 14 \cdot 5 \log M + 13$

A good rule of thumb is that every doubling of the wall mass increases the TI by 5 dB.

'The chain is as good as its weakest link.' The overall insulating effect of quite a good insulating wall can be radically reduced by a relatively small area of low insulating material — as shown by the following example (which also shows the method of calculating the average transmission loss):

in a 12 m² 230 mm solid brick wall there is a 0·1 ×0·1 m opening. What is the average TI?

$S = 12$ m² $s' = 11 \cdot 99$ m² $s'' = 0 \cdot 01$ m² $t'' = 1$

$TI' = 50$ dB $t' = \text{antilog} \dfrac{-50}{10} = \text{antilog} -5 = 0 \cdot 00001$

$$\bar{t} = \frac{11 \cdot 99 \times 0 \cdot 00001 + 0 \cdot 01 \times 1}{12} = 0 \cdot 0008433$$

$$TI = 10 \log \frac{1}{0 \cdot 0008433} = 10 \log 1185 = 31 \text{ dB}$$

The TI value is reduced from 50 to 31 dB. Thus if noise insulation is to be improved, first of all the weakest points should be identified and improved.

6.2.7 Noise control requirements

The performance required of a noise barrier depends on two factors:

1 'sensitivity' of the space to be protected, depending on type of use. Appendix 10.1 gives some acceptable noise levels for various room usages
2 magnitude of the noise which is to be excluded, whether external or in an adjoining room

Fig 128
Noise control
nomogram

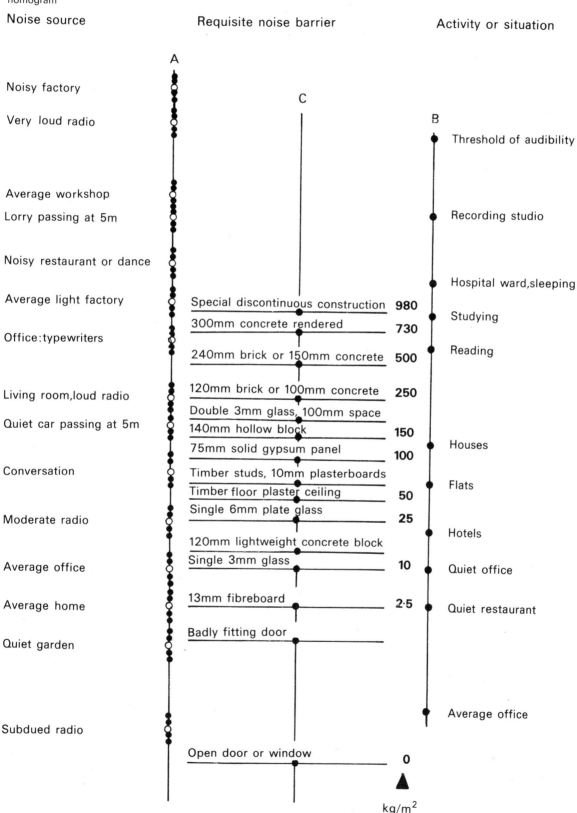

Noise source

Requisite noise barrier

Activity or situation

A

C

B

Noisy factory

Very loud radio

Threshold of audibility

Average workshop

Lorry passing at 5m

Recording studio

Noisy restaurant or dance

Average light factory

Hospital ward, sleeping

Barrier	kg/m²
Special discontinuous construction	980
300mm concrete rendered	730
240mm brick or 150mm concrete	500
120mm brick or 100mm concrete	250
Double 3mm glass, 100mm space	
140mm hollow block	150
75mm solid gypsum panel	100
Timber studs, 10mm plasterboards	
Timber floor plaster ceiling	50
Single 6mm plate glass	25
120mm lightweight concrete block	
Single 3mm glass	10
13mm fibreboard	2·5
Badly fitting door	
Open door or window	0

Studying

Office: typewriters

Reading

Living room, loud radio

Quiet car passing at 5m

Houses

Conversation

Flats

Moderate radio

Hotels

Average office

Quiet office

Average home

Quiet restaurant

Quiet garden

Average office

Subdued radio

kg/m²

A nomogram (Figure 128) shows this relationship: it gives the requisite noise barrier on scale C, where it is intersected by a straight line connecting the noise source on scale A and the receiving space on scale B [93]. Figures 129 and 130 show two similar nomograms for schools and for offices [92].

Fig 129
Suggested sound
insulation for schools

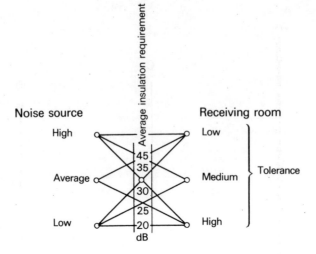

Fig 130
Suggested sound
insulation for offices

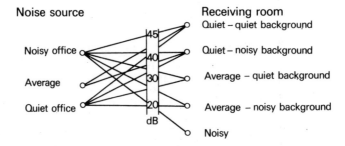

These nomograms will only give approximate values. A more precise definition of acceptable or permissible noise conditions is given by the NC curves (*noise criteria*) shown in Figure 131. The requirement for a particular space will be given as, for example:

'noise should not exceed NC 45.'

This establishes the limits which should not be exceeded in any octave band. If the externally given noise is measured in every octave band and is represented by a frequency spectrum graph, the established NC curve can be superimposed, and the distance between the two lines gives the insulation requirement for the enclosure (Figure 132).

Now, if this graph is redrawn, showing the sound insulation requirement in each octave band, relative to a straight base line, this will be directly comparable with the noise reduction data or graphs of various constructions (see Figure 133 and appendix 10.2).

For some building types, e.g. for residential buildings, such noise reduction requirements are established, based on the frequency composition of noises likely to be encountered in or around such buildings (Figure 134).

Rarely is a noise reduction graph found which would match the requirement curve. It must be remembered that the noise reduction graph of the selected construction should be at or above the required values in each and every octave band, even at its weakest point. Often, at most of the octave bands, the insulation will thus be more than necessary.

Fig 131
Noise criteria curves

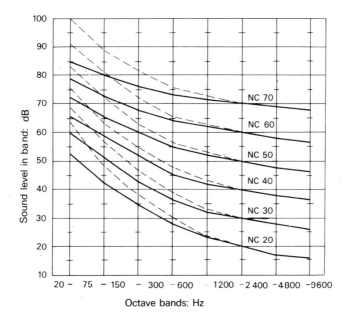

The corresponding subjective assessments of the sonic
environment are:

NC 20 – 25 very quiet
NC 30 – 35 quiet
NC 40 – 45 moderately noisy
NC 50 – 55 noisy
NC 55 and over very noisy

A slightly relaxed set of requirements is shown in dotted line
and is refferred to as NCA curves.

Fig 132
Noise spectrum
relative to a
requirement

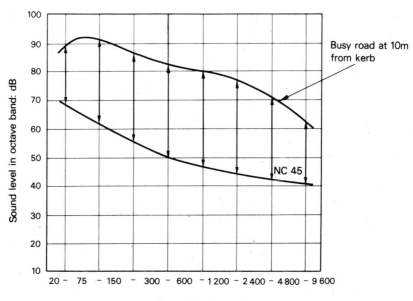

190 Fig 133
Noise reduction:
required versus actual

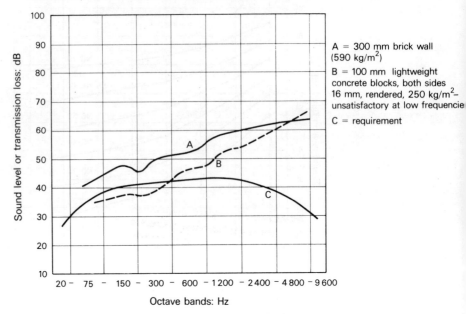

Distance between two lines transferred from Fig 132 –
measured up from base line in each octave to produce curve C

A = 300 mm brick wall
(590 kg/m^2)

B = 100 mm lightweight
concrete blocks, both sides
16 mm, rendered, 250 kg/m^2–
unsatisfactory at low frequencie

C = requirement

Octave bands: Hz

Fig 134
Residential insulation
requirements

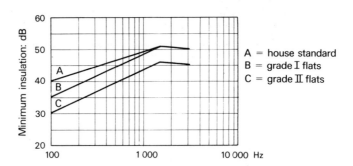

A = house standard
B = grade I flats
C = grade II flats

6.2.8
Noise control
performance

Once the noise control requirements have been established, the next step is to select a construction with the appropriate performance. In 6.2.6 methods were given for finding the TI (or noise reduction) value of massive walls – but this was an average TI value for the 50–5000 Hz range of frequencies.

To allow for changes of the TI with the frequency of sound, the formula is modified into:

$$TI = 18 \log M + 12 \log f - 25$$

where M = mass of wall (kg/m²)
    f = frequency of sound (Hz)

For example, a 230 mm brick wall, with M = 440 kg/m², will have the following TI values:

TI_{av} = 18 log 440 + 8 =   55·5 dB

TI_{160} = 18 log 440 + 12 log 160 −25 = 49 dB

TI_{640} = 18 log 440 + 12 log 640 −25 = 56 dB

TI_{2400} = 18 log 440 + 12 log 2400 −25 = 63 dB

These are theoretical values, valid only for solid, homogeneous, non-porous
walls. Porosity can reduce the TI values by up to 15 dB. On porous materials a
surface film (e.g. paint), which blocks the pores, can bring the TI up to almost the
above-mentioned theoretical values. Actual measured values for the 230 mm brick
wall are:

$$TI_{av} = 50 \text{ dB}, \qquad TI_{160} = 43 \text{ dB}, \qquad TI_{640} = 52 \text{ dB}, \qquad TI_{2\,400} = 59 \text{ dB}$$

When the resonant frequency (or natural frequency) of an element is at or near
the frequency of sound, coincidence occurs and the TI is reduced by up to 10 dB.
(Strictly speaking, resonance and coincidence are different phenomena: the former
occurs when the two frequencies are exactly the same; the latter occurs with sound
incidence at an angle to the wall, when the wavelength, projected onto the wall
surface, coincides with the wave motion of the wall. The latter will occur in a
broader band of frequencies. For our purposes this difference is not significant.)

Fig 135
Insulation of a solid
non-porous wall

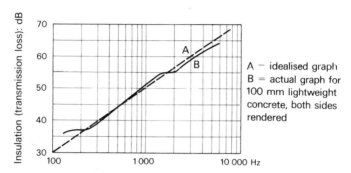

A — idealised graph
B = actual graph for
100 mm lightweight
concrete, both sides
rendered

Figure 135 shows the TI graph for solid, non-porous walls and Figure 136 gives
the TI graph of a partition wall, with the characteristic coincidence dip. Such a dip
occurs, in fact, with any wall, but in massive masonry walls it is shallower and
narrower, and it is positioned in the very low frequencies. It is, however, quite
significant in the case of lightweight walls and partitions.

The application of some coating with a vibration dampening effect, such as
rubber or plastic foam, would reduce the coincidence dip, both in width and depth.

Fig 136
Insulation of a
lightweight partition

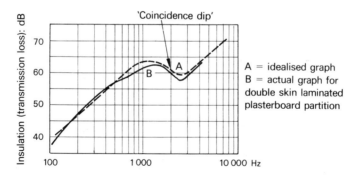

A = idealised graph
B = actual graph for
double skin laminated
plasterboard partition

6.2.9 Multilayer constructions

Where substantial noise reduction is required, but the use of massive construction
is impracticable (e.g. for windows) — two or more layers of light construction could
be used to advantage. The greatest resistance to sound transmission is provided
at the surface of the wall material. (The magnitude of this depends on the difference
in density between air and the material.) If the same amount (thickness) of material
is used in two independent layers, rather than in one, the TI will be doubled —
provided no vibration is transmitted directly between the two layers. This ideal case
will never be reached in practice, but it can be approached if there is no rigid con-

nection between the two (or more) layers and even the edge fixings or supports are flexible.

Figure 137 shows some practical constructional details. Faultless workmanship, hence strict supervision, is essential, as the slightest fault (for instance mortar droppings) can defeat the purpose of the effort and expense.

Fig 137
Double skin floors
and walls

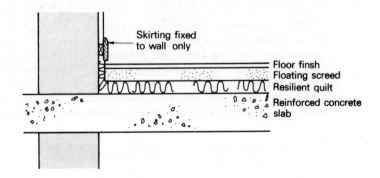

Skirting fixed
to wall only

Floor finsh
Floating screed
Resilient quilt
Reinforced concrete
slab

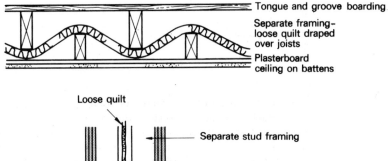

Tongue and groove boarding

Separate framing-
loose quilt draped
over joists

Plasterboard
ceiling on battens

Loose quilt

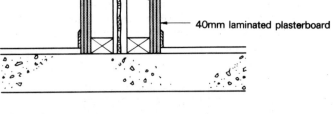

Separate stud framing

40mm laminated plasterboard

Placing an absorbent material in the cavity would reduce the build-up of reverberant sound within the cavity, thus it would further improve the TI value.

Windows are weak points in the building envelope from the noise insulation point of view (same as thermally). Their performance can, however, be improved by:

a ensuring airtight closure by using gaskets
b using double (or triple) glazing, where each pane with its frame is independent of the other
c placing absorbent material on the reveals, but this will only be effective if the reveal, i.e. the distance between the two panes, is at least 150 mm, but preferably 200 mm

Figure 138 shows some typical window details.

6.2.10 Ventilators

In many cases openings must be left for some reason, such as for ventilation. A ventilating duct may also pierce the noise insulating airtight envelope. These present a special problem which cannot be solved in a positive way, but can only be indirectly ameliorated by the use of absorption.

The method is based on the following principles:

Fig 138
Double 'acoustic'
windows

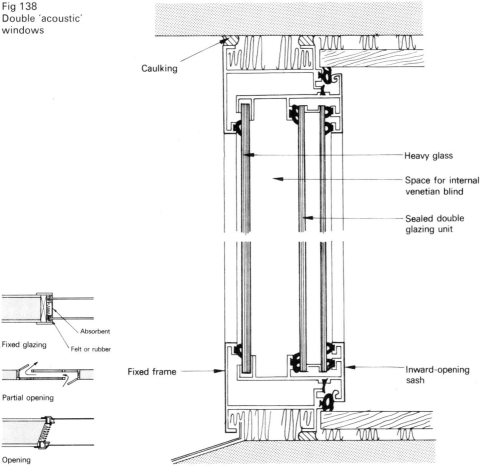

Caulking

Heavy glass

Space for internal
venetian blind

Sealed double
glazing unit

Absorbent

Fixed glazing

Felt or rubber

Partial opening

Opening

Fixed frame

Inward-opening
sash

1 the air is passed through not only an opening, but a length of duct (minimum length 1 m)
2 the duct is curved or shaped in such a way that there is no direct straight line path left for the sound
3 as the shape induces multiple sound reflections within this duct, all internal surfaces are lined with a highly absorbent material
4 to further increase the number of reflections and the total absorbent surface available, absorbent baffles can be placed inside the duct

Figure 139 shows some typical arrangements.

Fig 139
Ventilator and ducts
with absorbent baffles

ceiling

absorbent

6.3.1   Introduction
6.3.2   Noise conditions
6.3.3   Aural requirements
6.3.4   Means of control
6.3.5   Noise control requirements
6.3.6   Control by absorption
6.3.7   In hot-dry climates
6.3.8   In warm-humid climates
6.3.9   In composite climates

**6.3.1
Introduction**

Section 6.2 has established noise criteria and the means available for noise control, as a concise summary of present knowledge, developed for the industrial civilisations of moderate climates.

The questions can now be stated:

a   in what way is this applicable to tropical conditions? or
b   are noise problems and noise control different in the tropics and, if so, in what way?

Differences might be found:

1   in existing noise conditions
2   in aural comfort requirements, acceptable noise levels
3   in the means available for noise control
4   as a consequence of these — in noise control requirements

Each of these subjects will be examined in the following paragraphs.

**6.3.2
Noise
conditions**

The major noise sources in an industralised society are:

a   road traffic
b   railways
c   aircraft, particularly airports
d   industry: factories, workshops, etc.
e   office machines (typewriters, teletype, accounting machines, etc.)
f   people in residences: conversation, singing, music, radio, records, TV, etc.
g   motorised appliances in general use (lawn mowers, portable tools, kitchen implements, etc.)

All these can occur in tropical conditions, but perhaps to a lesser extent. In rural areas there seems to be no significant noise problem, but in an urban situation noise can be as bad in the tropics as anywhere. Most of the tropical areas are in developing countries, where urbanisation is gathering momentum. At present the ratio of urban to rural areas is much less than in more industrialised societies, but:

1   urban areas themselves present the same problems
2   with rapid urbanisation tomorrow's problems may be the same even on a national scale

The car ownership rate is much less than in western Europe, but traffic density in towns can reach the same level. The railway network may not be as dense, but near railways the problems are the same. At some major airports the density of aircraft movements reaches the level of secondary airports in Europe (e.g. Nairobi is about the same as Manchester), but this is rapidly increasing.

There is little heavy industry and even if there is, it is normally positioned with more foresight than in Europe — away from noise sensitive areas — therefore industrial noise is usually better contained.

The noise generated by people is probably higher than in Europe, due to more open-air activities, more uninhibited behaviour, love of music, etc.

6.3.3 Aural requirements

In some urban housing areas in the tropics, radios, children, people talking and singing, may produce noise levels up to 65 to 70 dBA, which in a western European society may be judged as annoying.* The social attitude of the people — their need for privacy — especially aural privacy, is, however, different. Their community spirit and social interdependence is greater. It is even suggested [94] that the degree of quietness required in western Europe would produce a sense of isolation, thus it would be socially undesirable. There may be a paternalistic attitude behind this contention, but there is no sufficient evidence available to reach a definite conclusion. It may well be the case, that the same standards of quietness would be preferred by people in the tropics, and that the less exacting standards are acceptable only because of economic necessity.

It is suggested that the designer operating in a given location should start with the norms published in the literature (see appendix 10.1) and, on the basis of local information, examine whether these norms should be modified.

6.3.4 Means of control

Referring back to the possible means of noise control listed in 6.2.1, the following differences may be found:

As protection against an external noise, all six ways of noise control are available, except the last one: the noise insulating envelope. Noise insulation can only be spoken of in relation to a fully enclosed space. The primary requirement is airtightness. Under tropical conditions (especially in warm-humid climates) full enclosure and airtightness can only be (and, indeed, should be) achieved with air conditioning. In non-air conditioned buildings openings must be left for ventilation, therefore the remaining five ways of noise reduction should be utilised.

Against noises generated inside the building, all eight ways of control (as listed in 6.2.1) can be used, except item 7: noise insulating construction. This may, in some cases, be achieved, if either the noise source area, or the receiving area could be fully enclosed and made airtight. Should this be impossible for some reason (as in the majority of cases), the relative importance of all the other measures is radically increased. Skilful use of absorbent surfaces will greatly help in reducing noise.

6.3.5 Noise control requirements

Statutory requirements for noise control are few and far between in tropical areas. The choice is left to the designer, but this also increases his responsibility.

Today, noise sources are less and generally noise level is lower than in industrialised societies. Human tolerance is greater; aural privacy requirements are less exacting.

---

* UK and German norms are 40 to 45 dBA.

So for both reasons the requirements for noise control performance are less. This is just as well, because the available means of noise control are also less effective.

In the future the noise is likely to increase. The improving standard of living and changing social patterns will bring about an increased demand for aural privacy. Then the designer will face a very serious challenge, a problem much greater than the problems in moderate climates.

The shelter, the building enevelope, should give a satisfactory performance in controlling heat and light, as well as sound. In tropical climates the aural and the thermal requirements may clash. The contradiction cannot be resolved in physical terms.

Firstly: aural and thermal factors must be weighted. The relative importance of good thermal and good aural conditions must be established. Clearly, this will be a function of building use. Generally in the tropics thermal factors will outweigh sonic ones, unless the activity housed imposes strict aural requirements (as in a lecture room). Time and duration of exposure conditions may help this weighting, e.g. if the out-doors is noisy all day, and overheating occurs only after 15.00 hours, the noise control requirement may become more important than the thermal control.

Secondly: the economic implications must be considered in relation to the weighted requirements. To continue the above example: if an inexpensive shading device could overcome the afternoon overheating, both aural and thermal requirements would be satisfied. If, however, it is found that thermal as well as aural comfort can only be ensured by full air conditioning, the cost of such an installation must be weighed against the benefit of full comfort, and indeed, against the capital available for investment.

6.3.6
Control by absorption

The conflict between noise and thermal control is due to the fact that the former requires full enclosure, whilst the latter may demand openings as large as possible. With large openings absorption may be relied on — if not to control, at least to reduce the entering noise. The principles are rather similar to those mentioned for ventilators in 6.2.10:

1 surfaces from which sound may be reflected into the building must be identified and made absorptive
2 the situation permitting, new surfaces may be introduced to prevent a straight passage of sound, and these surfaces must be made absorptive

Fig 140
Absorbent soffit to
canopy

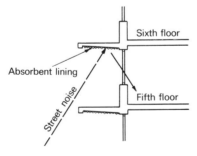

The method will best be illustrated by some practical examples.

Figure 140 shows an upper floor window, with a canopy above it (this may be a shading device or the balcony of the next floor). Street noise would be reflected into the room by this soffit and by the ceiling near the window. Absorbent lining would reduce the reflected noise. Ignoring other noise paths, if 70 dB was incident on these surfaces, this would correspond to an intensity:

$$I = 10^{-12} \times \text{antilog } 7 = 10^{-12} \times 10^7 = 10^{-5} \text{ W/m}^2$$

$$\text{as} \quad 70 = 10 \log \frac{I}{10^{-12}}$$

$$7 = \log \frac{I}{10^{-12}}$$

With an absorption coefficient of 0·05 (concrete), 95% of this would be reflected, giving a sound level:

$$N' = 10 \log \frac{10^{-5} \times 0·95}{10^{-12}} = 10 \log 0·95 \times 10^7 = 69·7 \text{ dB}$$

If the surfaces are covered by a perforated tile, giving an absorption coefficient of 0·75, only 25% will be reflected, giving a sound level:

$$N' = 10 \log \frac{10^{-5} \times 0·25}{10^{-12}} = 10 \log 0·25 \times 10^7 = 63·9 \text{ dB}$$

A reduction of some 6 dB would be achieved.

Fig 141
Absorbent lining to
louvres

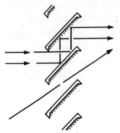

Figure 141 shows a louvre system, on a ground floor opening. A sound of horizontal direction will be reflected twice, once from the top and once from the underside of a louvre blade. By making the underside absorptive, an effect similar to the above may be reached. If both surfaces were to be absorptive, to the same extent, only 0·25 ×0·25 = 0·0625, i.e. 6·25%, would be reflected, which would give a noise level of:

$$N' = 10 \log \frac{10^{-5} \times 0·0625}{10^{-12}} = 10 \log 0·0625 \times 10^7 = 57·9 \text{ dB}$$

The total reduction would be some 12 dB.

Unfortunately the top surface of the blade is rather exposed and most absorbent materials are vulnerable to mechanical and moisture damage. If Figure 141 is taken to represent a plan view of a set of vertical blades, the use of absorbents on both sides would be more feasible, particularly in protected positions.

The effectiveness of absorption is improved if the louvre spacing to width ratio is reduced, that is, if the blade width is increased or the blades are positioned closer together. Z or S-shaped blades would also improve the effectiveness of a louvre system for sound reduction (Figure 142).

Fig 142
Noise reducing louvres
(absorption at each
reflection)

 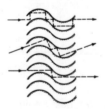

There are, of course, numerous other sound paths, thus the reduction may not be quite as great as calculated above. In the case of Figure 141, sound may be reflected from the pavement, and the inclined sound path would not be interrupted at all. In this case it would be advantageous (if possible) to introduce an absorbent ground cover instead of a hard pavement, e.g. a lawn. If, as in this instance, the freely entering sound would strike the ceiling, a part of the ceiling near the window could be made absorptive.

Typical building forms resulting from the various climate types should now be examined, on how they affect noise problems.

6.3.7
In hot-dry
climates

In hot-dry climates walls and roofs are usually of massive construction. Windows and openings are typically small and they often face an enclosed courtyard. All these are rather favourable from the point of view of external noise exclusion. Such a building would only be vulnerable to noise generated within the courtyard or by overhead noise sources (e.g. overflying aircraft). As the occurrence of the latter is infrequent (except near airports) and the former are 'familiar' noises, there will be no serious noise problems.

As it has been mentioned in 4.2.3, the very large thermal capacity of the building may necessitate the erection of a lightweight shelter on the roof, to be used for sleeping — at least in the first half of the night. Noise protection for this shelter will be practically impossible, but at least the users will have the option to choose between a thermally comfortable but noisy space, or a quiet but somewhat overheated one.

The only special measure which could be taken for the reduction of external noise penetration is the protection of the small windows or ventilators in the external walls, for the period when they are open. (When closed, the heavy shutters used for thermal reasons would provide adequate protection.) This can be achieved by methods described in 6.2.10 or 6.3.6.

As the only potential source of discomfort are the noises inside the courtyard, it may be helpful if soft surfaces are used as far as practicable, for instance, lawn instead of paving, or absorbent materials on the soffit of the verandah roof around the courtyard.

6.3.8
In warm-
humid
climates

In these climates the buildings would typically be of a lightweight construction, with very large openings exposed to wind and air movement. The building envelope will not be able to control noise. At the very best it can reduce the penetration of outside noise by skilful use of absorbent surfaces. From the point of view of inside noises, the situation may be somewhat better than in the hot-dry climate courtyard house: inside sounds are free to escape, will not be reflected from bounding surfaces and there will be no build-up of a reverberant sound.

Planning controls, such as distance, positioning or various forms of barriers will have to be relied on to a great extent. Fortunately there are two areas of concurrence between thermal and sonic requirements:

1   densities in this climate are and should be much less than in other climate zones. Distances between buildings must be kept greater, to allow air movement — this would also help the noise problem
2   as the positive control of humidity is only possible with air conditioning, the use of such an installation is much more warranted here, than in any other climate. Air conditioning implies a sealed envelope, which in turn makes positive noise control feasible. Noise control requirements, especially in the case of highly noise sensitive buildings, would assist or reinforce the case for the installation of air conditioning

6.3.9
In composite
climates

Buildings in this climate are likely to be of massive construction (7.3.7). Windows and openings would probably be reasonably large to provide air movement in the warm-humid season (7.3.9) but with provision for closure in the cold season and during the day in the hot-dry season. Generally the building would be closer in character to buildings in hot-dry climates, thus the noise problems would also be similar — not very serious. Window shutters and doors should be massive, both for thermal reasons and for noise reduction.

Problems may arise in the warm-humid season, when windows are open for ventilation. In such a situation it would be futile to attempt noise insulation. Absorption could be used to reduce the noise, as in warm-humid climates, but the benefit of this would not normally justify the cost, for three reasons:

1   the warm-humid season, when such ventilation is necessary, is usually short — up to about three months

2   absorption is not very effective in reducing noise penetration

3   absorptive materials are mostly rather vulnerable — exposed to changing climatic conditions they may rapidly deteriorate

In critical situations (e.g. lecture rooms), suitable aural environment can only be ensured with a sealed envelope, which would demand air conditioning. In fact, aural requirements may dictate the use of air conditioning, even if its use would not be fully justified by thermal reasons.

7.1.1 Nature of the climate

Hot-dry desert and semi-desert climates are characterised by very hot, dry air and dry ground. Day-time air temperatures may range between 27 and 49°C (normally higher than the 31 to 34°C skin temperature), but at night it may fall as much as 22 degC (see 1.3.5).

Humidity is continuously moderate to low. There is little or no cloud cover to reduce the high intensity of direct solar radiation. The clear skies do, however, permit a considerable amount of heat to be reradiated to outer space at night.

The dry air, low humidity and minimal rainfall discourage plant life, and the dry, dusty ground reflects the strong sunlight, producing an uncomfortable ground glare.

Local thermal winds often carry dust and sand.

7.1.2 Physiological objectives

Physical comfort by day depends mainly on a reduction of the intense radiation from the sun, ground and surrounding buildings. It is basically a problem of protection. A knowledge of periodic heat flow characteristics of various constructions will enable the designer to select walls and roofs which can, during the day, maintain inner surface temperatures less than the skin temperature. This will allow the body to dissipate some of its surplus heat to the surrounding surfaces by radiation, as well as cool the indoor air by convection.

At night the air temperature is frequently low enough to permit an increase in effective temperature by surface temperatures higher than this air temperature. Such an increase may even be beneficial.

Because of the constantly low humidity, evaporation is greater here than in any other climate and takes place so readily that special arrangement is quite unnecessary (provided the skin can supply sufficient sweat).

Breezes cannot be used to advantage indoors, unless the air is cooled and the dust filtered out.

7.1.3
Form and
planning

Out-door conditions are so hostile in this climate, that both the buildings and the external living spaces need to be protected as much as possible from the intense solar radiation and the hot, dusty winds.

An enclosed, compactly planned and essentially inward-looking building is the most suitable. Sensible application of planning principles, such as accessibility of water, fuel and food storage to points of use, easily cleaned surfaces, reduction of movement distances and avoidance of unnecessary stairs will all benefit the occupants by reducing physical movement, effort and fatigue [4]. By placing as much accommodation as possible under one roof, thermal loading from the sun and hot air will be considerably lessened.

Surfaces exposed to the sun should be reduced as much as possible. Site conditions permitting, the larger dimensions of a building should preferably face north and south, as these elevations receive the lowest heat loads from solar radiation. The worst orientation is the west. Although solar radiation is similar on the east and west elevations, peak intensity on the west coincides in time with the highest air temperatures, causing a higher total peak load. Non-habitable rooms (stores, toilets, etc.), can be effectively used as thermal barriers if planned and placed on the east and, especially, the west end of the building.

Shading of roofs, walls and out-door spaces is critical. Projecting roofs, verandahs, shading devices, trees and utilisation of surrounding walls and buildings are familiar techniques of solving this problem. There is a very great variety of possible shading devices and the prediction of their performance is a relatively easy task by using the solar charts and protractors or the heliodon. Care must be taken to use low thermal capacity materials for shading devices close to openings, to ensure their quick cooling after sunset.

Fig 143
A typical hot-dry
region settlement:
Marakesh

By aligning buildings close to each other, especially if east and west walls are placed close together, mutual shading will decrease the heat gains on external walls. For this reason in hot-dry climates the tendency is to have close groups of buildings, narrow roads and streets, arcades, colonnades and small enclosed courtyards, in order to get the maximum amount of shade and coolness [5] (Figure 143).

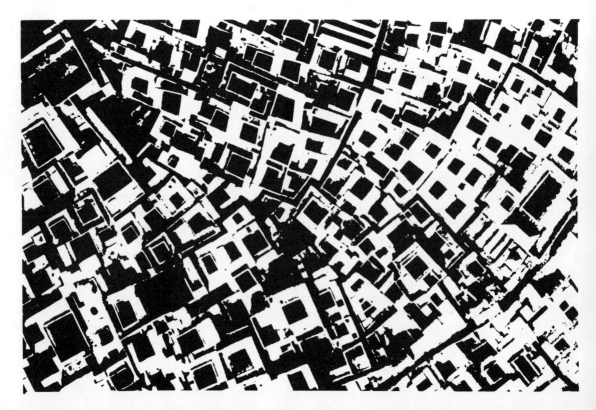

Shading of the roof is much more difficult. The most effective method is to construct a second roof over the first. Since the outer roof, gaining heat through radiation, will reach a very high temperature, it is imperative to separate it well from the main roof, to provide for the dissipation of heat from the space between the two roofs, and to use a reflective surface on both roofs. The surface of the lower 'roof' should be reflective for the low temperature (long infra-red) radiation, emitted by the upper roof. This would necessitate the use of a polished metal surface.

The cost of a 'double roof', in the true sense of the term, would be in most cases prohibitive. However, a simple ceiling, with a ventilated roof-space would be almost as effective.

7.1.4 External spaces

As in most warm climates much of the day-to-day activities take place out-of-doors. It is therefore necessary to treat the external spaces just as carefully as the building itself.

Adjacent buildings, pavements and dry ground heat up quickly, causing both a painful glare and reflected heat radiation towards the building during the day, and at night they will reradiate the heat stored during the day. Enclosure of out-door areas by walls which are themselves shaded will help to avoid such effects, and at the same time keep out dust and hot winds.

Trees, plants and water in the enclosed space will cool the air by evaporation, help to keep dust down and provide shade, visual and psychological relief.

Fig 144
The thermal system of a small courtyard house

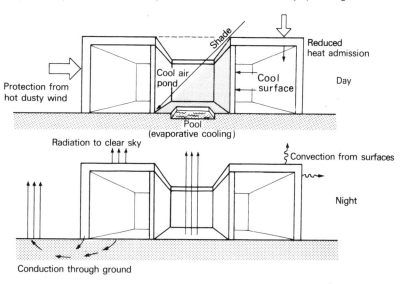

The best external space in this type of climate is a courtyard. Here a pool of cool night air can be retained, as this is heavier than the surrounding warm air. If the courtyard is small (i.e. the width is not greater than the height), even breezes will leave such pools of cool air undisturbed.

The small courtyard is an excellent thermal regulator in many ways [96]. High walls cut off the sun, and large areas of the inner surfaces and courtyard floor are shaded during the day. Cooler air, cooler surfaces, the earth beneath the courtyard will draw heat from the surrounding areas, re-emitting it to the open sky during the night. Figure 144 and 145 explain the thermal system of courtyard buildings.

7.1.5 Roofs, walls and openings

As mentioned earlier (4.2.3) the basic method of utilising the large diurnal temperature variations consists of the use of large thermal capacity structures. These will absorb much of the heat entering through the outer surface during the day, before the inner surface temperature would show any appreciable increase. To achieve this, walls and particularly roofs must be constructed of heavy materials, with a large thermal capacity.

Fig 145
The thermal system of
a larger courtyard
house

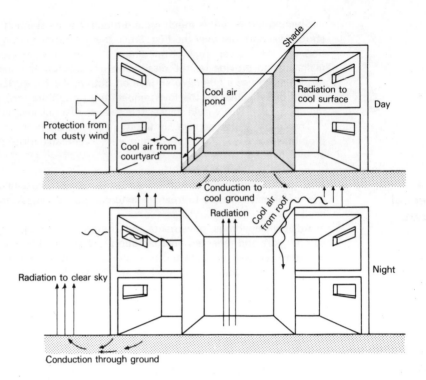

The method will be effective only if the morning heating-up period is started with as little heat content (as low a temperature) as possible. The heat stored during the previous day must be dissipated during the night. Cooling through the outer surfaces alone will not be sufficient for this purpose. Heat dissipation through the inside surfaces should be assisted during the night by adequate ventilation.

Thus the design of openings is governed by two requirements:

1 during the day the absence of openings would be most desirable, or at least openings as small as possible, located high on the walls
2 during the night the openings should be large enough to provide adequate ventilation for the dissipation of heat emitted by the walls and roof

A solution satisfying both requirements is the use of large openings, with massive shutters, with a thermal capacity approaching that of the walls. This could be a technological problem. If so, the next best thing would be the use of shutters with a high thermal resistance, e.g. heavy shutters made of wood. If these are kept closed during the day, the heat inflow is retarded, and if opened at night, the heat disssipation is not obstructed. This, however, involves a 'managerial control', the appropriate action of the occupants, which cannot always be relied on. It could happen that for communication and movement between indoor and out-door spaces the shutters are left open during the day, but for reasons of privacy or security they may be closed during the night, thus producing the opposite of the desired effect. This method of thermal control is as much a matter of living habits as of design and construction. The designer can adapt his design to living habits, e.g. where the occupants are for some reason security-conscious, they would not leave the shutters open at night, unless burglar-bars are fitted to the openings.

Before arriving at design decisions, the designer must study the occupancy pattern of the building. For example an office building occupied only during the morning and early afternoon will need to have a time-lag of 4 to 6 hours, just sufficient to reduce and delay the passage of heat until after the building is left by the occupants. A residential building would more probably need to have a time-lag of 9 to 12 hours, to delay the inside heat emission to the time of lowest air temperature, that is the after midnight and pre-dawn hours, when the extra heat may be welcome in the otherwise chilly conditions. Massive roofs will be particularly effective for this purpose.

In regions where diurnal ranges are less extreme, where the night-time temperature does not fall below the comfort zone, the large thermal capacity should be restricted to internal walls, partitions and floors, whilst the outer walls and roof would need to have a high resistive insulation.

Alternatively separate day and night rooms could be provided in the house, the former enclosed with high thermal capacity elements, the latter with thinner elements of lighter materials which cool quickly after sunset.

An intimate knowledge of the thermal behaviour of materials is necessary in order to select the most appropriate ones, or indeed the best sequence of layers, if multilayer construction is possible. For example, placing a lightweight insulating material on the outside of a massive wall or roof will give a time-lag almost four times as much as if the same insulation is placed on the inside of the massive layer. At the same time, the insulation, being on the outside, will effectively prevent the heat dissipation to the outside air from the massive part during the night. Ample internal ventilation at night will thus become imperative, or else over a period of only a few days the heat content of the massive part will build up to such levels, that the internal conditions will be even more intolerable than that out-doors.

The ground is also a valuable means of heat storage. To utilise it as fully as possible, the building should have maximum contact with the ground, i.e. ground-floors should be solid, not suspended, and in no case should the building be built on stilts. The heat will then be conducted from the building fabric to the ground. Best results will be achieved if the ground near the building is shaded during the day, but fully exposed to the night sky, so that the radiant heat emission is not obstructed.

7.1.6
Roof and wall surfaces

Surface treatment and the selection of surface materials will also influence the thermal behaviour of the building and can help in reducing the heat load. Light coloured or shiny external surfaces will reflect a large part of the incident solar radiation, thus much less heat will actually enter the building fabric.

Undoubtedly the most critical part of the whole building surface is the roof. In any location near the Equator this receives the greatest amount of solar radiation, thus the highest heat load. But it is also the surface most exposed to the clear night sky, therefore it will most readily emit heat by radiation to outer space. The selection of roof surface materials will have the greatest effect, far more than that of the walls.

It is worth recalling (see 3.1.16) that absorbance and emittance values of a given material are the same for the same temperature of radiation. They will, however, differ when the heat received comes from the sun, with a surface temperature of about 5500 °C, but the emitting temperature is that of the surface itself, rarely above 50 °C on the earth. This is most significant in selecting roof surfacing materials.

Although a bright metal surface, such as an aluminium sheet, and a white painted surface both will have an absorbance around 0·2 the latter will have an emittance value about eight times as high as the bright metal (0·8 as opposed to 0·1). If we consider that a white surface will not remain very bright for long, its absorbance may increase to 0·3, and if we compare this with a polished aluminium sheet, which may have an absorbance of only 0·1, it is seen that the aluminium will absorb much less heat. However, the difference in emittance remains the same — thus for a roof, which has a possibility for emission of heat to outer space, it will still be more advantageous to use a white surface. For a vertical wall, which is opposed by other surfaces of buildings and ground at a similar temperature and accordingly has little opportunity to emit any heat by radiation, the emittance value will be of little consequence; the use of a bright metal surface may give better results, even if its absorbance also increases in time to anything up to 0·25 (Figure 146).

Dark coloured surfaces should in all cases be avoided.

Fig 146
White versus bright
metal surface

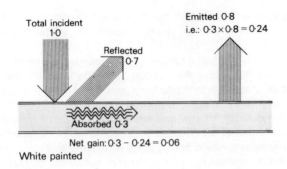

Total incident
1·0

Reflected
0·7

Emitted 0·8
i.e.: 0·3 × 0·8 = 0·24

Absorbed 0·3

Net gain: 0·3 − 0·24 = 0·06
White painted

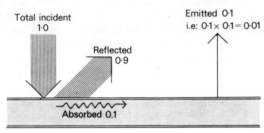

Total incident
1·0

Reflected
0·9

Emitted 0·1
i.e: 0·1 × 0·1 = 0·01

Absorbed 0.1

Net gain: 0·1 − 0·01 = 0·09
Bright aluminium
Where radiant loss is possible (for example to sky) a white
surface gives less net gain. Where opposing surfaces are warm,
there is no radiant loss, and aluminium is preferred

7.1.7 Ventilation and air flow

During the day-time openings should be closed and shaded. Ventilation should be kept to the absolute minimum necessary for hygenic reasons, to minimise the entry of hot and often dusty external air. Air intake openings should be located so that the coolest and most dust-free air is taken, and, if necessary, the air can be ducted to the points where it is needed. Thus the cool conditions existing at dawn can be maintained inside the building for the longest possible period.

Internal heat gains, the heat output of human bodies, cooking and lighting (often referred to as 'wild heat'), can present quite a problem. Ventilation can only remove 'high grade' heat (temperatures higher than the outside air). If possible, such heat sources should be isolated and separately ventilated. In assembly areas (e.g. schools, meeting halls, etc) it is almost impossible to keep the internal air cooler than the external, other than for a short period. When the bodily heat output exceeds the rate of heat absorption by the building fabric, the air temperature will increase. When it reaches the out-door air temperature, further increase can be avoided by ample ventilation.

Ample ventilation at night, as we have seen, is necessary where the stored heat is to be dissipated. It will be an advantage if the indoor air stream at night can be directed so that it passes the hottest inside surfaces. As the hottest surface is likely to be the ceiling or the underside of the roof, it is advisable to have the top of the openings level with the ceiling.

If double roofs, or a separate roof and ceiling is used, we must consider the heat transfer from the outer skin to the ceiling. This will be partly radiant (approximately 80%) and partly conductive. As the roof is warmer than the ceiling, and hot air rises to the roof, there will be no convection currents, only conduction. If the roof space is closed, the enclosed volume of air may reach a very high temperature, thus increasing the conductive heat transfer. This can be avoided by ample ventilation of the roof space.

Ventilation will *not* reduce the radiant heat transfer, but by lowering the temperature of the inside surface of the outer skin, it will reduce the radiant heat emission of that surface. Another way of reducing the radiant heat transfer between the two skins is the use of a low emittance surface on the inside of the outer skin (e.g. aluminium painted white on the outside but left bright on the inside) and a highly reflective surface on top of the ceiling. A bright aluminium foil can be used to advantage in both situations (see 7.1.6).

As adequate ventilation of the roof space is useful on both counts, attention must be paid to the design of the openings to this space and their orientation in relation to the prevailing breeze. Even if this breeze itself is warmer than comfortable, (it will therefore be excluded from the room itself), the roof temperature both on the outside and on the inside of the outer skin is likely to be much higher, thus it will still help in removing some of the heat.

A separate roof and ceiling is the obvious solution for warm-humid climates (7.2.5), but it will rarely be used in hot-dry regions. If for some reason it is used, the roof should be light and the ceiling should be massive. Roof slopes should be orientated towards the prevailing breeze, and any obstructions which would prevent the air flow next to the roof surfaces should be avoided. High solid parapet walls around the roof would, for example, create a stagnant pool of hot air, and should, therefore, be avoided.

Fig 147
Traditional mud houses
in Kano, Nigeria

7.1.8 Traditional shelter

The traditional shelter found in most desert regions has heavy walls of earth, brick or stone and roofs of the same material, often supported by a few timbers where vaulting is not used (Figure 147). Thick walls provide good thermal capacity, as well as security and protection against noise. These structures tend to be too hot at night during prolonged hot seasons. At these times roofs and courtyards are frequently used for sleeping out-of-doors.

Rooms are often built around a central courtyard, which provides a relatively cool private out-door space for family activities.

Windows and door openings are small in size and few in number. Windows are usually located high on the walls, admitting little heat and dust, reducing ground glare, but ventilation is often inadequate not only for the purposes of night-time cooling but also from the hygienic point of view, often to the extent where it endangers health and promotes the spread of epidemics through the closely built together houses.

Figure 148 shows a traditional Egyptian village house of the type which is used in desert regions both in rural and urban areas. Figure 149 gives a similar example from Morocco, whilst Figures 150 and 151 are more recent examples.

7.1.9 Maritime desert climate

These climates differ only slightly from the hot-dry desert regions — the main difference being the high humidity. The diurnal temperature variations are less but the maxima are also lower. It is the most difficult climate to design buildings for (see 1.3.6).

Fig 148
A traditional Egyptian
village house

(after Arthur J. Little
Inc.)

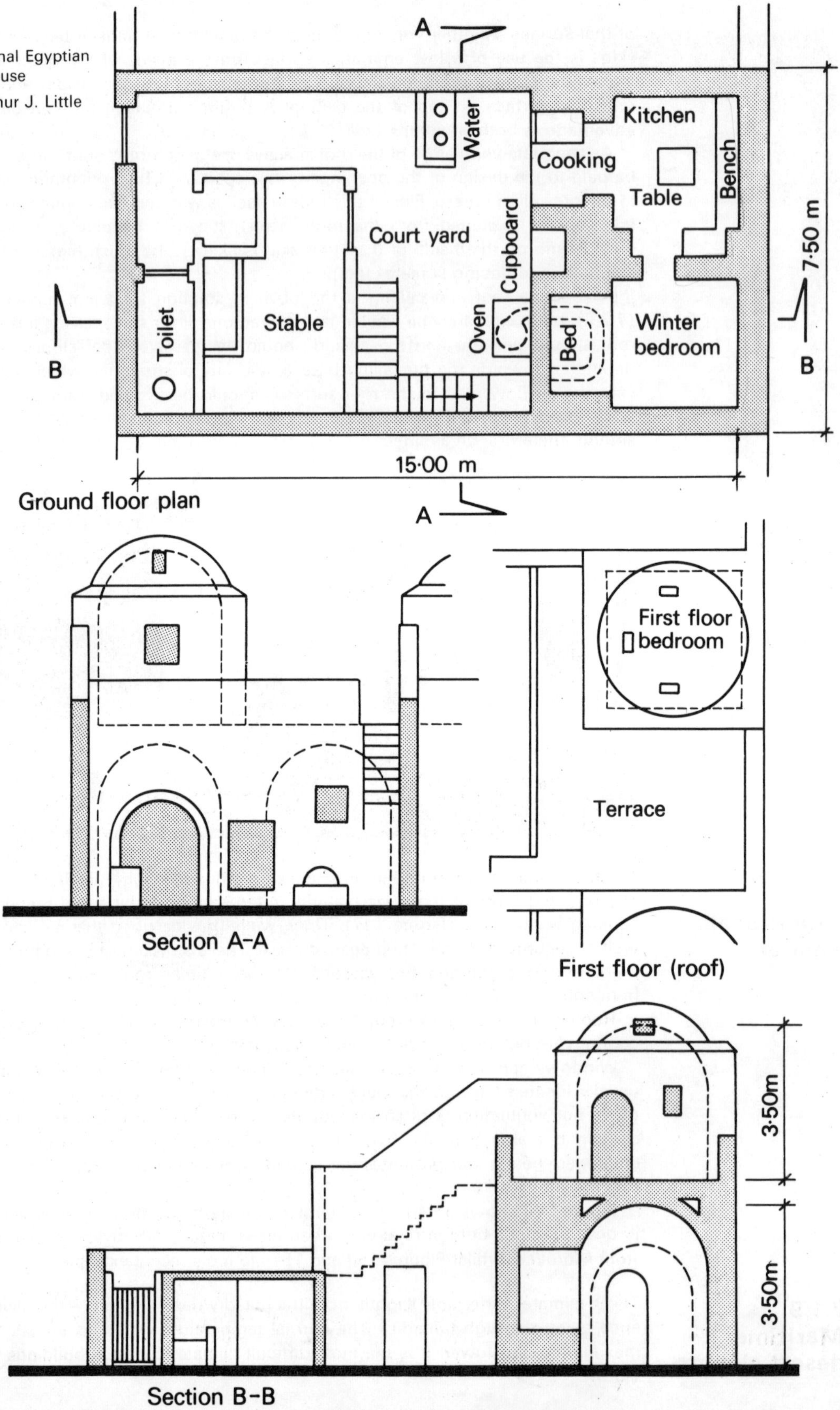

A

Water

Kitchen

Cooking

Bench

Table

Court yard

Cupboard

Toilet

Stable

Oven

Bed

Winter
bedroom

B

B

7·50 m

A

15·00 m

Ground floor plan

A

Section A-A

First floor
bedroom

Terrace

First floor (roof)

3·50m

3·50m

Section B-B

Fig 149
Traditional Berber houses in Morocco

Fig 150
Recent low cost housing in Touggourt, Algeria (compare with traditional lay-out, Fig 143. The old city streets are narrow and shaded, the new streets in Touggourt are wide, sun-drenched and dusty.)

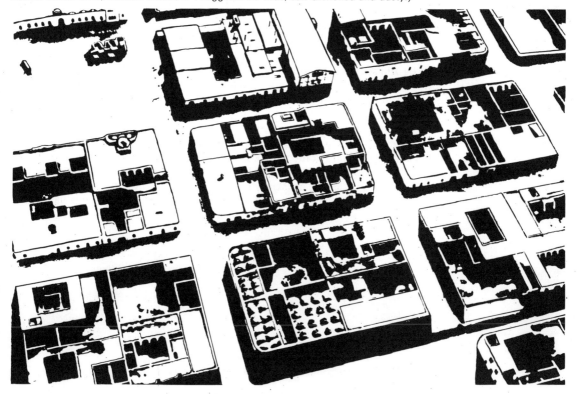

Fig 151
A middle class house in Kano, Nigeria, designed by
Architects Co-Partnership. Massive ground floor for
day-rooms. Lightweight structure with white
painted aluminium cladding for the first floor
bedrooms. Its performance, tested five years after
completion, proved to be highly satisfactory

The use of high thermal capacity structures (although still useful) will not be as effective as in hot-dry regions. The coastal wind blowing off the sea during the day may be utilised to ameliorate thermal conditions. The night-time wind blowing towards the sea, brings the hot inland desert air, possibly dust, and it can be decidedly unpleasant. Protection from this should be provided.

Perhaps the only solution is to provide alternative spaces:

a one with high thermal capacity walls and roof, for use at night, especially during the cooler part of the year. This should have no openings facing the inland direction

b one of lightweight construction, the roof only to provide shade, the side facing the sea, as well as the opposite side being almost completely open. This is the best solution for day-time use, especially during the hottest part of the year

It is in this climate that the wind scoop (4.3.16 and Figure 85) has its greatest benefit.

7.2.1 Nature of the climate

The most prominent characteristics of this climate are the hot, sticky conditions and the continual presence of dampness. Air temperature remains moderately high, between 21 and 32 °C, with little variation between day and night. It seldom exceeds normal skin temperature.

Humidity is high during all seasons. Heavy cloud and water vapour in the air act as a filter to direct solar radiation; it is thus reduced and mostly diffused – but clouds also prevent reradiation from the earth at night.

Moisture in the air combined with moderate heat and high rainfall is favourable to the growth of vegetation. The plant cover of the ground reduces reflected radiation, and lessens the heating up of the ground surface.

Winds are generally of low speed, variable in speed, but almost constant in direction (see 1.3.3).

7.2.2 Physiological objectives

Because the air temperature is continually very near to skin temperature, bodily heat loss to the air by convection or conduction is negligible.

To achieve physical comfort, there must be some heat dissipation from the body to its environment, at least as much as the metabolic heat production of the body. In high humidity air the evaporation of a small quantity of moisture from the body would form a saturated air envelope, effectively preventing any further evaporation, thus blocking the last resort of heat dissipation. This saturated air envelope can be removed by air movement. Some degree of comfort can be achieved by encouraging out-door breezes to pass not only through the building, but across the body surface of the occupants. This is, in fact, the only way of ameliorating thermal conditions.

As there is no significant cooling down at night, the wall and roof surface temperatures tend to even out and settle at the same level as the air temperature. This evening out is also promoted by the flow of outside air through the building.

214 Fig 152
A middle class house
in Northern Territory,
Australia (Housing for
Commonwealth
employees, Darwin —
standard type DI —
Design: Department of
of Works, Northern
Territory, 1953)

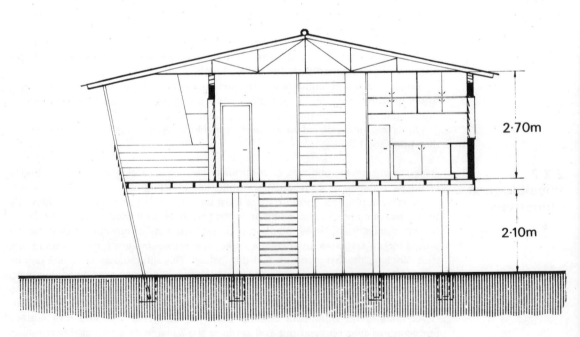

2·70m

2·10m

Section A-A

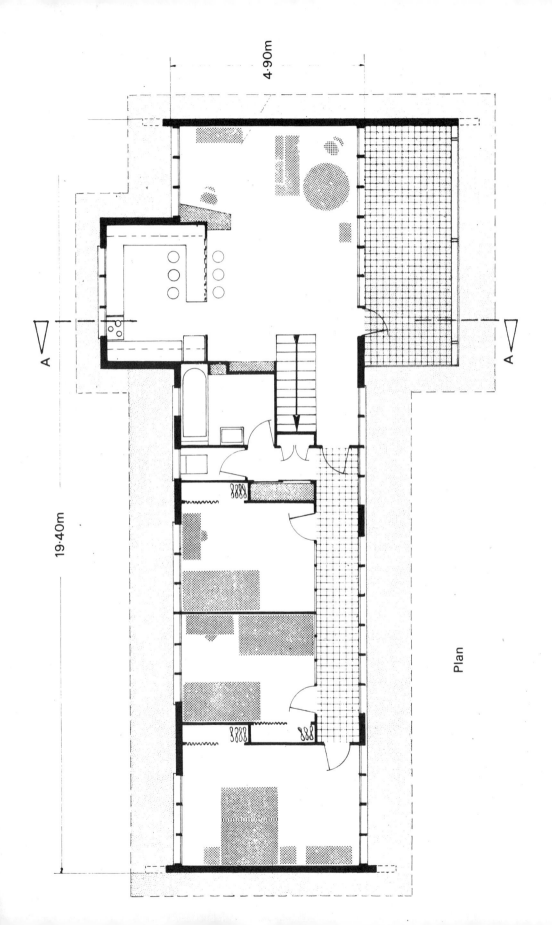

4·90m

19·40m

A

A

Plan

Radiant heat loss from the body will thus be negligible, as the surface temperatures are near to skin temperature. Radiant heat gain from the sun and sky should, however, be prevented.

7.2.3 Form and planning

As movement of air is the only available relief from climatic stress, therefore vital to indoor comfort, the building will have to be opened up to breezes and orientated to catch whatever air movement there is. Failure to do this would produce indoor conditions always warmer than a shaded external space which is open to air movement.

In this type of climate buildings tend to have open elongated plan shapes, with a single row of rooms to allow cross-ventilation (Figure 152). Such rooms may be accessible from open verandahs or galleries, which also provide shading. Door and window openings are, or should be, as large as possible, allowing a free passage of air. Groups of buildings also tend to be spread out. Extended plans, in a line across the prevailing wind direction, afford low resistance to air movement and is therefore the ideal solution.

If several rows of buildings follow, the air movement through buildings in the down-wind row will be substantially reduced by the first row.

Plant cover of the ground tends to create a steeper wind gradient than an open surface (see 1.4.11 and Figure 25), i.e. it restricts the movement of air near the ground, and it is often necessary to elevate the building on stilts, thereby avoiding the stagnant or slowly moving air at the ground surface, capturing air movements of a higher velocity (Figure 153). The ground itself tends to be of the same temperature as the air, thus conduction of heat away from the building into the ground would not be significant anyway.

Although the intensity of radiation is normally less than in hot-dry regions, it is nevertheless a significant source of heat, therefore its entry into the building should be prevented. Whereas in hot-dry climates, the radiation being mostly directional, shadow angles can be established in quite precise terms, here much of the radiation being diffuse, coming from the whole of the sky hemisphere, the shading devices should provide a greater coverage, obstructing most of the sky and not just the location of the sun. As the openings are far larger than in hot-dry climates, the shading devices will be much larger on both counts. Openness and shading will be the dominant characteristics of the building.

Shading of all vertical surfaces, of both openings and solid walls will be beneficial. This task will be much easier, if the building height is kept down. Very often the roof will extend far beyond the line of walls, with broad overhanging eaves, providing the necessary shading to both openings and wall surfaces.

From the point of view of solar heat gain, the best arrangement would be to orientate buildings with the long axes in east—west direction. This may often conflict with the requirement of orientation for wind. Such a conflict should be subjected to detailed analysis in every individual case, as there is no generally applicable rule. It must be remembered, however, that the solar geometry cannot be changed, but skilful use of elements built outside, e.g. screen walls or even the projecting wing of a building, can change the direction of air movement.

With low rise buildings, where the walls would not get much radiation, orientation for wind is more advisable. With high rise buildings the opposite is true, and avoidance of sun should be the decisive factor.

7.2.4 External spaces

The same principles apply to the design of external spaces as to the design of buildings. Shading and free passage for air movement are the two basic requirements.

Trees and planting can be relied on for shading, as plants carry full foliage all year round. Rarely will a structure be built just to provide shade to an open space, but pergolas and light framing to be covered by climbing plants can be provided quite cheaply and they can be very effective. Open spaces left under buildings elevated on stilts can also be put to use as shaded out-door spaces.

It is difficult to provide privacy as well as allowing for the passage of air, but

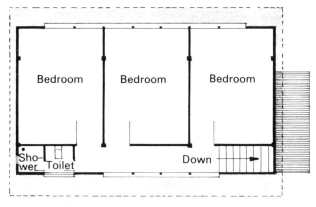

Upper floor

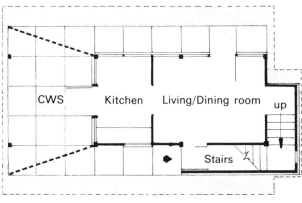

Ground floor

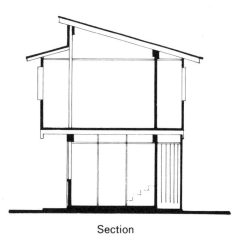

Section

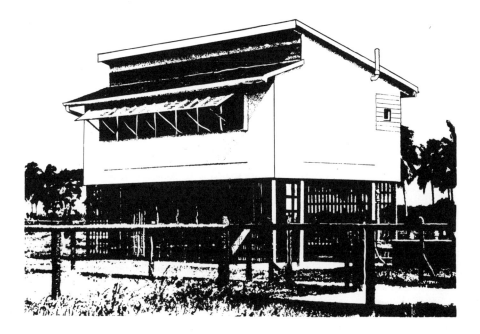

Fig 153
A recent low cost
house in Guyana
(Architect: Mihael
Costello)

various systems of paling fences and screen walls have been devised which do not permit direct view but allow the breeze to penetrate. Most of these consist of louvred timber boards or some overlapping arrangements of boards or planks. Unfortunately, most of these reduce the air velocity quite substantially.

The density of development in warm-humid regions is always far less than in hot-dry climates for three reasons:

1 to allow free movement of air through buildings and through spaces between buildings
2 to provide privacy by distance, as walls and screens cannot be used for this purpose (they would prohibit air movement)
3 many activities are carried on out-of-doors

7.2.5 Roofs and walls

Because the temperature of the outside air remains almost the same throughout the day and night, a building cannot cool off sufficiently at night-time to allow the storage of heat during the day. The principle of thermal storage cannot be relied on in this climate. It is, in fact, advisable to construct buildings of low thermal capacity materials, using lightweight construction.

By opening up the building to air movements, thus to outside conditions, the influence of structure upon indoor conditions is lessened considerably. The roof is practically the only element which has a very great significance. It cannot improve the conditions, i.e. it will not produce temperatures cooler than the out-door air, but at least, if well designed, it can prevent the indoor temperature increasing above the out-door air temperature, and keep the ceiling temperature around the same level as other surfaces.

This will be achieved by a reflective upper surface, a double roof construction, with roof space ventilated, a ceiling with its upper surface highly reflective, and having a good resistive insulation. Both the roof and the ceiling should be of low thermal capacity.

As rainfall is rather high in these regions, a pitched roof will most often be used — covered by corrugated iron, asbestos cement or bright aluminium. Alone, such a roof would create almost intolerable conditions indoors, with surface temperatures up to 30 degC higher than the air temperature.

It has been suggested [97] as a performance standard, that the ceiling temperature should not exceed the air temperature by more than 4 degC. This could be achieved by a ceiling of some kind of insulation board with a U-value around 1·5 W/m² degC (i.e. a roof-ceiling overall U-value of 0·8 W/m² degC).

Unfortunately, insulation of this quality is still rather expensive, exceeding the cost limits of most low cost housing schemes. However, even the cheapest kind of ceiling would produce substantial improvements. It has been reported [98] that in two identical houses, roofed with corrugated asbestos cement, a difference of 14 degC in ceiling temperatures has been found: in one case, 48 °C measured on the underside of an asbestos cement roof where there was no ceiling; in the other case, 34 °C on the kraft paper ceiling (faced with aluminium foil on the upper surface) stretched over the tie beams of the roof trusses (the out-door air temperature being 22 °C).

For solid vertical walls insulation is not necessary if they are shaded. However, if these walls are exposed to solar radiation (such as gable walls), good insulation will prevent the elevation of inner surface temperature above the air temperature. Reflective qualities on the outer surface of such unshaded walls will also be helpful.

7.2.6 Air flow and openings

Openings must be placed suitably in relation to the prevailing breezes to permit natural air flow through the internal spaces at body level, i.e. in the 'living zone' (up to 2 m). Such openings should be large and fully openable; there is no point in having windows with fixed glass panes.

The flow of air can be influenced by topographical features, by the orientation of the building and the position of surrounding buildings and other obstructions. All these must be considered carefully, as the openings should be free from the effect of outside obstructions. The air flow should not pass over hot surfaces (such as asphalt) before reaching the building.

One of the most difficult problems which a designer must attempt to solve is to provide large openings, but at the same time give protection from driving rain, insects, smells and noise, without radically reducing air movement. Some of the means available for the solution of this problem have been surveyed in Sections 4.3.10 to 14.

Ceiling mounted or other electric fans may be used when there is little or no breeze, but these will normally only provide an air movement (thus assist evaporative cooling), not induce the exchange of air.

7.2.7 Ventilation

Ventilation, i.e. the exchange of air, is also necessary. Without the exchange of air, both the temperature and the humidity of room air will increase above the out-door values, due to the heat and moisture output of human bodies and of various human activities (e.g. washing and cooking). Thus in this climate there is a need for both a frequent change of air (ventilation) and for a sensible air movement across the body surface.

Ventilation will also be necessary to the space between the roof and ceiling, and adequate openings must be provided for this purpose. Ventilation of the roof space can cause a ceiling temperature to drop 2 degC, without any other constructional change [99]. Care must be taken to avoid air which has passed through a roof space reaching the living zone (e.g. discharged onto a verandah) as this will be much hotter than the normal out-door air.

7.2.8 Traditional shelter

Two basic types of traditional shelters are found in warm-humid climates.

Where timber is scarce, single storey, earth-walled houses are typical, with the roof framed in timber, bamboo or palm frond and covered with thatch. Broad overhanging eaves shade the walls. There are several disadvantages with this form of shelter. Firstly, the poor or non-existent air movement inside the dwelling will create

Fig 154
Village house in
Malaya

220

unbearable conditions. Secondly, what little benefit may be gained from breezes is frequently prevented by the fenced or walled compound. The intense, heavy rains are likely to erode the bases and surfaces of earth walls, therefore annual maintenance is essential. Unventilated interiors often remain constantly damp.

In regions more favoured with timber or where earth is unsuitable for building, the traditional shelter is often elevated on stilts and is constructed from local timber or a bamboo frame with open-weave matting, timber or split bamboo walls, floors, doors and shutters. Thatch or built up layers of leaves cover a bamboo or timber roof-frame, which usually has broad overhanging eaves (Figures 154 and 155).

The lightweight timber construction holds little heat and cools adequately at night. The elevated position provides a better security and better air movement than single storey shelters. The thatched roof is an excellent thermal insulator, although it may not be quite waterproof when new. The broad eaves shade the walls and openings, provide protection from driving rain and sky glare and permit the openings to be kept open most of the time. One weakness is that the thatch is a convenient breeding ground for insects, and the entirely wood and vegetable matter structure gives food and easy passage to termites.

Both types of shelter perform reasonably well in their traditional rural context, where materials and labour for their construction and regular upkeep are readily available. In densely built up areas, such as towns, even the latter type loses its climatic advantages, and the thatch roofs create a serious fire hazard. It is difficult to employ any of the two types in towns.

7.2.9 Warm-humid island climates

This is a variety of the warm-humid climate — slightly more favourable than the former. Temperatures are slightly lower, but there is a steady wind of 6 to 7 m/s and of an almost constant direction to rely on for cooling. The orientation and construction of the building to catch the maximum amount of air movement will be even more imperative than in the warm-humid climate.

Most of these islands lie in the tropical cyclone belt. Construction and structure must be designed to withstand winds of up to 70 m/s (150 mph or force 12).

Fig 155
Houses on the river
in Thailand

**7.3.1
Nature of the climate**

Composite or monsoon climates are neither consistently hot and dry, nor warm and humid. Their characteristics change from season to season, alternating between long hot, dry periods to shorter periods of concentrated rainfall and high humidity. Significant differences in air temperature, humidity, wind, sky and ground conditions can easily be appreciated by comparing the descriptions of warm-humid and hot-dry climates. (see 1.3.7)

In many areas there is also a third season, with dry, sunny days and uncomfortable cold nights, which is referred to as 'winter'.

**7.3.2
Physiological objectives**

The physiological objectives set out for warm-humid and hot-dry climates apply to the respective seasons of composite climates. Additional problems are created by the third season. During this cold season effective temperatures are much lower than in the two warmer seasons, and physical comfort will depend on the prevention of heat loss from the body, especially at night. In the warm seasons the heat dissipation is inadequate, and the designer attempts to increase it as much as possible, but in the cold season it may become excessive, creating a sensation of cold discomfort — consequently measures for the retention of heat are necessary.

The situation is aggravated by the fact that during the warm season people get acclimatised to high temperatures, so their tolerance of cold conditions will be reduced.

**7.3.3
Design criteria**

Climates with changing seasons set a difficult task for the designer. Solutions suitable for one season may be unsatisfactory for others. Thermal design criteria recommended for hot-dry climates are applicable not only to the hot-dry season of composite climates, but also to the cold season, except for minor details. For the 'monsoon' or rainy season however, buildings should be designed according to the criteria of warm-humid climates, which would require entirely different solutions.

Many constructional features may serve equally well in all seasons. Difficulties arise with conflicting or incompatible requirements. In order to develop optimum design standards which are appropriate to composite climates as a whole, it is necessary to establish some form of weighting whereby priorities can be allocated. Such a weighting system can be based on the length of different seasons, on the relative severity of the conditions and their correlation with the living pattern. The method developed is best explained through an example.

Fig 156
Monthly effective
temperatures
(Islamabad)

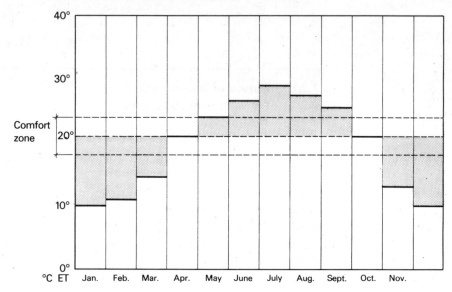

7.3.4
The
discomfort
index

Figure 156 gives the monthly average ET for Islambad. The comfort zone is also indicated on the graph, its centre line being 21 °C. The distance between this centre-line and the ET curve gives the 'discomfort level' for each month in + or −degC. The discomfort level multiplied by the duration of that condition gives the 'discomfort index'. For Islambad the following values can be read:

		discomfort level	duration	index	percentage
Hot-dry season	May	+ 3 degC	1 month	3	
	June	+ 5·5	1	5·5	
		seasonal total:		8·5 (+)	13·5
Warm-humid season	July	+ 8 degC	1	8	
	August	+ 6·5	1	6·5	
	September	+ 4·5	0·5	2·25	
		seasonal total:		16·75 (+)	26·5
Cold-dry season	November	−8 degC	0·3	2·4	
	December	−11	1	11	
	January	−11	1	11	
	February	−10	1	10	
	March	−6·5	0·5	3·25	
		seasonal total:		37·65 (−)	60
		annual total:		62·9	100
Total of hot seasons (hot-dry +warm-humid)					40
Total of dry seasons (hot-dry +cold-dry)					73·5

The results show that, taken singly, the cold season is the most important for thermal design. It outweighs the two hot seasons put together. However, where the design solutions are similar for the hot-dry and cold-dry seasons, their predominance over the warm-humid season is even more pronounced.

On the basis of such an analysis design standards can be formulated for the composite climate.

7.3.5 Form and planning

Moderately compact internal planning of houses will be of benefit for most of the year. Courtyard type buildings are very suitable. Buildings should be grouped in such a way as to take advantage of prevailing breezes during the short period when air movement is necessary. A moderately dense, low rise development is suitable for these climates, which will ensure protection of out-door spaces, mutual shading of external walls, shelter from the wind in the cold season, shelter from dust and reduction of surfaces exposed to solar radiation.

Houses with separate day and night rooms, which were suggested for hot-dry regions, are equally good for composite climates, except that they would only be used during the hottest months. Shading of walls is desirable but not critical. Provided that the roof has a low transmittance value and a good thermal capacity, the question of a double roof does not arise. Thermal loading of roofs in hot-dry and cold seasons is reduced by outgoing radiation to the clear sky. External openings, however, do require shading during the hot and warm seasons.

7.3.6 External spaces

Large projecting eaves and wide verandahs are needed in the warm-humid season as out-door living areas, to reduce sky glare, keep out the rain and provide shade. They can also be an asset in the dry seasons. *Brise-soleils*, louvres and other sun breaks used to protect openings during the hot-dry period, are also advantageous in the rainy season, serving as protection against rain and wind driven spray. Shading devices should preferably be of low thermal capacity.

During the cold season, when solar gain is welcome, all shading is undesirable.

For the dry seasons controlled landscape and enclosure walls are necessary to provide protection against dust and thermal winds. They are no great disadvantage in the wet season.

The high rainfall makes it easier to maintain vegetation around buildings, thereby reducing dust. A courtyard is the most pleasant out-door space for most of the year, because it excludes the wind and traps the sun. It should be designed in such a way as to allow sun penetration during the winter months, but provide shading in the hot season. Deciduous plants can serve a useful purpose. Courtyards may even be covered by a pergola, carrying deciduous creepers. These would provide shade in the hot season but admit the sun in the 'winter'. The building shown in Figure 157 has a variety of external spaces, some covered, some open.

7.3.7 Roofs and walls

The retention of night-time low wall temperatures is desirable in the hot-dry season only but the same thermal properties will be useful in the cold season to retain the heat of the day for the uncomfortably cold nights.

Roofs and external walls should, therefore, be constructed of solid masonry or concrete, to have a 9 to 12 hour time-lag in heat transmission. The thermal capacity will be of advantage in both the cold and hot-dry seasons. In the warm-humid season a low thermal capacity but good insulating wall and roof would be better — the large thermal capacity being of no great disadvantage, provided it does not impede the movement of air. However, the best arrangement is if the thermal capacity is provided in massive floors, partitions and ceilings, permitting the outer walls to be used more freely for large openings.

Resistance insulation should be placed at the outside surfaces of external walls or roofs. Insulation on the inside would only reduce the beneficial effects of high thermal capacity walls and roofs.

An advantage of low rise development is the greater contact of walls with the ground, thus the ground will also be utilised for thermal storage.

Fig 157
A recent house in
Northern India
(Design: Public Works
Department, New
Delhi, 1954)

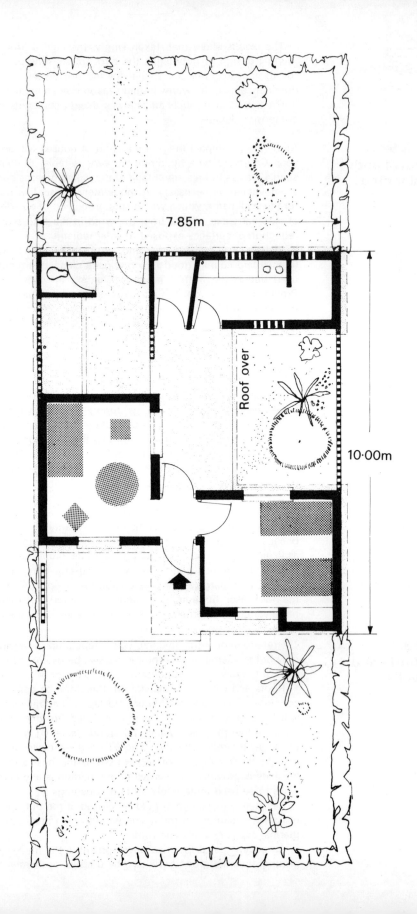

7.3.8
Surface
treatment

The prevention of heat entering through the outer surfaces of the walls and roof is a fundamental rule. Surfaces exposed to the sun during the hot and warm seasons should be light coloured or of shiny polished metal.

During the cold season the heat of the sun is important for improving indoor comfort, therefore absorptive surfaces will be required in place of the shading and reflective surfaces of the hot seasons. Variable surfaces may be devised, but the solar geometry may often permit permanent surfaces to be utilised in the appropriate seasons, e.g. north of the tropic of Cancer, the back walls of south facing verandahs will be reached by the sun in November to February, thus should be made highly absorptive. In some such locations (as labour is cheap) a new trade has developed — a man who whitewashes roofs at the beginning of the warm season and paints them black before the cold season arrives.

7.3.9
Openings

Orientation of openings is determined by two factors:

1   towards the breeze prevailing during the warm-humid season, to utilise its cooling effect
2   towards the sun during the cold season, to utilise the heating effect of radiation entering through the windows

If the two factors lead to contradictory solutions, the discomfort index (7.3.4) can assist in the final decision.

Reasonably large openings in opposite walls are suitable, preferably with solid shutters which can be opened when cross-ventilation is necessary, possibly during the warm-humid season or for evening cooling in the hot-dry season. The area of such openings should not normally exceed the area of solid walling on the same elevation (i.e. the walls facing the wind and the opposite). On the adjacent walls the windows (if any) should not occupy more than about 25% of the total area.

7.3.10
Ventilation
and
condensation

As buildings are frequently closed for long periods, ventilation requirements should be satisfied during the hot-dry season by special provisions (see 4.3.4, 4.3.16 and Figure 85). Two small openings, one high level and one low level, or ventilating stacks may provide a solution. When the indoor air is warmer than the out-door, for example, during the cold season, the air flow will be 'in' at low level and 'out' at high level. The reverse will occur when the out-door temperature is higher than the indoor, such as during the day in the hot-dry season. Figure 158 shows some ventilating stacks, which also serve as wind scoops.

Occasionally, during transitional periods (i.e. from one season to another), condensation may occur when two factors coincide:

1   when the relative humidity of the air is high
2   when the surface of a wall or ceiling is cold enough to cool the adjacent layer of air below its dewpoint

Very rarely such conditions may arise towards the end of the rainy season, when the moisture content of the air is still high and the night-time temperature suddenly drops. A more likely period of occurrence is at the beginning of the rainy season, when the cold night thoroughly cools the structure, and this is followed by the sudden influx of warm, humid air. More especially, elements of high thermal capacity will retain their low temperature for a longer time, thus their surface may be covered with condensation.

As there is no danger of frost, and as weather conditions producing condensation are only of a short duration, the danger of structural damage is negligible. Contrary to the methods of protection used in colder climates, the best protection in the tropics is to use porous and moisture absorptive materials (e.g. 'anti-condensation' paints), which will act as buffers, absorbing the moisture as condensation occurs and releasing it as soon as the air is sufficiently dry.

Fig 158
Wind scoops in
Hyderabad Sind (with
a maritime desert
climate, having a short
monsoon period, thus
it can be considered
as a composite
climate)

Fig 159
A village house in the
Punjab

7.3.11 Traditional shelter

The character of houses traditional to a composite climate of any particular region depends upon the relative predominance of hot-dry or warm-humid conditions during the course of the year (Figure 159). A familiar urban solution for housing in these climates is a ground floor with massive walls (earth or masonry) with large shuttered openings, laid out around a courtyard, and a first floor structure of light-weight materials. These cool quickly at night, to allow fairly comfortable sleeping conditions during the hottest part of the year. In such a hybrid structure the centre of family life shifts with the seasonal changes of climate (Figure 160).

Fig 160
A low cost house
with separate day and
night rooms

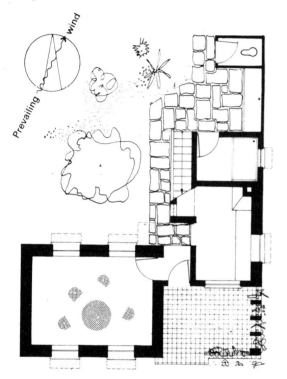

Day room – ground floor

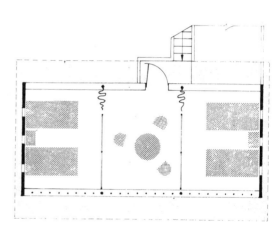

Night rooms – first floor

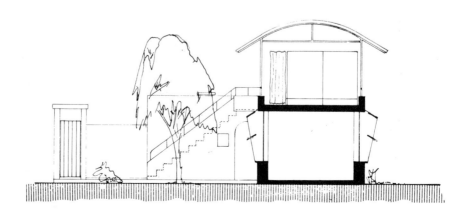

7.4.1 Nature of the climate

This climate is in many ways similar to the composite or monsoon climates, with its distinct rainy seasons. It is dominated by strong solar radiation, often with moderate to cool air temperature. Even in the warmest part of the year air temperature rarely reaches 30°C but the diurnal variation can be as much as 20 degC. There is a marked reduction in temperature in upland climates further away from the Equator. Humidities are not excessive and there is an almost constant air movement, never very strong.

7.4.2 Physiological objectives

As the air temperature rarely (if ever) exceeds the upper comfort limit, overheating would only be caused by solar radiation when it is incident directly on the body or by heating up the building fabric. Excessive glazed areas can be a source of overheating.

Protection against such overheating can be provided by several means:

1 The provision of adequate shading, both for windows and for external activity areas
2 by limiting the heat admission of buildings during the strongest sunshine hours (insulation, thermal inertia and reflective colouring)
3 if the building is overheated, this can be counteracted by the provision of adequate ventilation (air changes only for convective cooling; sensible air movement, i.e. physiological cooling, is unnecessary)

Cold discomfort can often occur at night, even in the warm season. People's clothing will be very different at night to that during the day. The building itself can ameliorate the cold night conditions by:

a providing a closed (or closeable) internal environment
b storing some of the heat gained from solar radiation, to re-emit it at night, during the cold period

c if the above two means fail to achieve thermal comfort, some small amount of heating may have to be provided

7.4.3
Form and planning

The building plan should be reasonably compact, as this would help in slowing down the response to changing thermal conditions. It would reduce heat gain during the day and heat loss during the night.

Windows and openings will have to be protected from solar radiation. Solar control devices will often be the most prominent features of the building (Figure 161).

Fig 161
Office blocks, with shading, in Nairobi

Orientation of the building and of its major openings can greatly influence the solar heat gain, thus it should be carefully considered. North and south facing vertical walls receive the least amount of radiation. Of these two less is received by the one facing away from the Equator, i.e. facing north on the northern hemisphere and facing south on the southern half of the globe. East, south-west and north-west walls will receive about the same amount of radiation and the west wall will receive the most. The chart (Figure 162) gives total annual solar heat gains on vertical walls of different orientations, on a comparative scale, for Nairobi. Other equatorial locations would give rather similar diagrams.

On this basis, with an oblong shaped plan, the longer walls should face north and south, and major openings should be located in these walls. Windows facing east would admit the sun, but at a time when the air temperature is still quite low. Windows facing west should be avoided, whenever possible, as the solar heat gain through these would coincide with the highest air temperatures.

This arrangement would reduce incident solar radiation and would also minimise the extent (and cost) of shading devices, as north and south facing windows can be shaded by the simplest of means.

7.4.4
External spaces

Well-shaded external spaces should be provided, as:

a many activities are going on out-of-doors – as in all warm climates
b the very strong radiation would create hot discomfort, even with quite low air temperatures

Shade could be provided by the building itself, by pergolas, awnings or by vegetation.

Fig 162
Relative magnitude of
solar heat gains on
different orientations
(Nairobi)

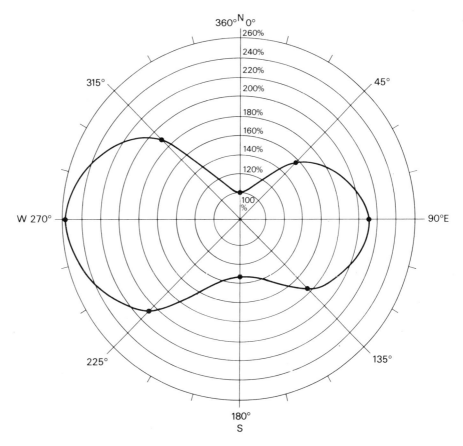

In the cooler period of the year sunshine may be welcome in external spaces. Two possibilities are open to the designer:

1 to provide some form of adjustable shading device to the external activity area
2 to provide alternative external spaces for use in the different seasons: shaded for the hot period and unshaded, wind protected for the cool part of the year

The former can be achieved by some form of canvas awning, cantilevered or supported by a pergola-like frame, or by matting spread on some framing. The cost of more elaborate devices would in most cases be prohibitive.

The latter arrangement may be wasteful of space, duplicating the out-door area, but where space is not at a premium, it may be the easier and more economical solution.

In some situations the same external space may be shaded or unshaded in different parts of the year, and luckily this may coincide with shading requirements. For example, if July to August is the cool period (as in many tropical upland areas), in an equatorial location the sun at this time is in the northern sky, thus a space on the north side of the building will receive solar radiation. The same space will be overshadowed by the building itself in the hottest part of the year (December to January) when the sun is in the southern sky.

7.4.5 Roofs and walls

Nights are cool and solar radiation can cause overheating of buildings during the day. For continuously occupied buildings the task is therefore two-fold:

1 to limit the heat admitted during the strong sunshine hours
2 to store some heat, to be re-emitted during the cool period

Both purposes would be well served by a high thermal capacity structure. A time-lag of 8 hours is advisable, as this would bring the maximum indoor heat emission to

20.00 to 21.00 hours, when it is most needed, before the occupants go to bed. (A 200 mm concrete slab, with screed and felt or a 150 mm concrete slab with an insulating screed would give this performance.)

The roof is by far the most important, as it receives the greatest amount of radiation. East, and especially the west walls should also be massive. North and south walls will not receive much radiation and they may be of a lightweight construction.

In buildings occupied during the day but not at night, only the first of the two above tasks must be fulfilled. In this case a lower thermal capacity may be quite sufficient. A time-lag of 5 hours would bring the maximum heat gain to 17.00 or 18.00 hours, which is normally past the working hours. A lightweight wall is also possible, especially in multistorey buildings, provided it is well insulated and the windows are shaded.

7.4.6 Surface treatment

Reflective surfaces would be useful in reducing the heat load. White or bright metallic surfaces would be most advantageous for buildings occupied only during the day-time. In cases of continuous occupancy, it may be desirable to admit solar heat into the fabric – to store it for the night. Therefore a darker, more absorbent surface finish may be more suitable. This should be used only with buildings of high thermal capacity. Where such heat storage is not possible, if for some reason a lightweight construction is used, the surfaces must be light and reflective.

Roof surfaces (especially of flat roofs) deserve particular attention, as horizontal surfaces receive a far greater amount of solar radiation than any vertical surface. A massive roof slab of at least 8 hours time-lag can become the most important heat regulator. A black bituminous or asphalt finish can serve a useful purpose in absorbing much of the solar heat during the day to be released after sunset. With lightweight roofs (with timber or metal decking) however good the insulation, the use of absorbent surfaces must be avoided. If bituminous felt is used for roofing, the top layer should be faced with aluminium foil. Alternatively, white marble chips can be used as a finish on bituminous or asphalt roofs. This is quite effective in reducing the absorption whilst new, but when it becomes dirty much of its reflectance is lost. Some self-cleansing surface would be preferable.

At high altitudes the ultra-violet component of solar radiation is much greater than at sea-level. This radiation can damage some materials and can cause decomposition of polymers. Only well-tested materials should be used.

7.4.7 Openings

As the air temperature rarely (if ever) reaches the upper comfort limit, there is no need for physiological cooling by air movement, and no need for cross-ventilation, as long as the problem of solar control is adequately solved. Where solar overheating does occur, cross-ventilation may provide relief, but most of the time, it would contribute to a feeling of cold discomfort.

It is essential to provide for the adequate closing of openings, windows and doors. As, on the other hand, there is no need to capture winds and cooling breezes and, on the other hand, there are no strong winds to be avoided, the wind direction need not be considered in deciding the orientation of openings. Solar heat gain will be the only factor governing the orientation of windows, as described in 7.4.3 (and possibly some non-climatic factors, such as aspect and prospect).

The size of openings will be governed by considerations other than thermal. From the point of view of solar heat gain the lesser the openings, the easier the control. For ventilation and daylighting, in most cases, a window of some 20% of the elevational area will be quite adequate.

7.4.8 Traditional shelter

The traditional rural shelter in these climates is the round hut, with mud-and-wattle walls and thatched roofs. The walls consist of vertical poles driven into the ground in a circle, horizontal twigs and branches threaded in between to form a basket-weave pattern. The whole is plastered with mud. Subsequent layers of mud are often built up to a thickness of 0·25 m, thus providing a substantial thermal capacity (Figure 163).

In some areas the mud-and-wattle construction is carried through the roof, which will also have a high thermal capacity (Figure 164).

In urban areas where stone is available, one can see masonry walling and slate roofs. Roofs may still be thatched or of wood framework plastered with mud. Openings are always small.

Fig 163
Village houses near
Nairobi

Fig 164
Masai houses in
Ngorongoro, Tanzania

8.1.1
The design process

Numerous research workers and theoreticians have attempted to construct a schema or model of the design process [101 and 102]. The proposed models may be schematic or highly refined and complex, may be derived from observation or may be built up in a rather abstract way, postulating a process 'as it should be'. Each model is more or less controversial. In all models the three notions:

analysis — synthesis — evaluation

occur, meaning either a distinct phase, or a type of activity in the design process. Many suggest a cyclic repetition of the three phases.

Without taking a stand in the controversy, the above three terms are accepted and used here, as depicting types of activity.

From the point of view of climatic influences on building design, the distinction of three stages is essential. These do not constitute a complete and continuous process of design, but indicate stages when climatic factors must be brought in and considered in conjunction with other factors:

a *forward analysis*, i.e. analytical work which precedes the formulation of a design solution (as opposed to analytical work applied to or directed by a design hypothesis, which may be described as 'backward analysis'). In this stage data are collected, sorted and processed, in order to accumulate and present all the information necessary for the synthesis of a formal solution

b *plan development*, which begins after a formal concept, or a design hypothesis, has been produced. This stage may include all three types of activity: evaluation may show the need for further analysis, which in turn may lead to a revised synthesis

c *element design*, which follows after the major design decisions have been taken, after the design as a whole is accepted as satisfactory. It may again involve all three types of activities, analysis, as well as synthesis and evaluation, with the difference of handling one element at a time and considering it in the context of the agreed overall design

Correspondingly the various aids to be described in this part will fall into two categories:

1 *design tools*, to be used in the forward analysis stage, or in any step directed towards producing formal solutions

2 *checking tools*, in evaluation, to assess the performance of an already produced solution

8.1.2
The task of analysis

In the synthesis a design solution is to be produced, to satisfy the psychological, social and functional, as well as the physical and physiological, needs of the occupants within the given topographic, climatic and economic constraints. The solution must be structurally sound, constructionally suitable and must fit into the broader planning context. All these problems must be considered simultaneously, as it is impossible to establish an order of importance, thus a sequential operation.

The problem in the forward analysis stage is to collect all the relevant information, recognising and establishing all the factual constraints, without unduly restricting the designer's freedom, and without prejudicing the solution to be produced in the synthesis.

This information must be collected, processed and presented to the designer (possibly to oneself) prior to the synthetic step – to the production of a sketch design.

8.1.3
Information transfer

In the synthesis the designer must consider a wide range of factors simultaneously. The capacity of his mind is limited. It is therefore essential to present the information in a readily comprehensible form. It should not be excessively detailed, but it should still take into account all that is relevant. The problem is one of information transfer. This body of information is the product of the forward analysis stage. It could be transferred in one of the following three forms:

a data, i.e. raw material, organised in a hierarchical order

b performance specifications

c design decisions

The first would be difficult to keep in mind when it comes to the synthesis. The last should only be used when a particular variable can be isolated, when all the factors influencing the particular decision have been surveyed and when no further factors will influence that decision. Perhaps the performance specifications are the most useful form, being sufficiently precise and concise without prejudicing the synthesis. At times it may be difficult to draw the line between a broad design decision and the specification of performance. Both are parts of the same continuum.

The following sections will clarify this theoretical framework.

Only climatic factors are dealt with in the present volume, but the method may well be useful for a whole range of other factors.

8.1.4
Climatic data

Meteorological stations publish a large amount of data. Observations by these stations are deliberately made in locations where readings are not affected by local topographical features (1.4.2 *et seq.*). Unless the magnitude, importance and timing of the project permits the establishment of a site observatory (anything less than a year would be useless), the designer must accept the data from the nearest meteorological station as depicting the regional climate. Deviations of the site climate from this are rarely large enough to affect the sketch design. Major features, if any, can be recognised and allowed for quite readily, and minor deviations can be considered later, in the element design stage.

The structural engineer must base his design on extreme conditions. The architect can only base his climatic design on typical or normal conditions. Such normal conditions are adequately defined by monthly mean minimum and maximum values (see 1.2.3).

8.1.5
The Mahoney
tables

When the climatic pattern emerging from the data clearly corresponds to warm-humid or hot-dry climate types (1.3.3 and 1.3.5), it is relatively easy to arrive at performance specifications. In composite climates the seasonal requirements may be contradictory. A weighting system must be used to assess the relative importance of conflicting requirements. The system must take into account the duration and the severity of the various climatic factors.

Based on such a system, a series of tables have been devised by C Mahoney.* Table 1 is used to record the most essential climatic data, directing and defining the extent of data search. Table 2 facilitates a diagnosis of the climate and develops a series of climatic indicators. Table 3 translates these into performance specifications or sketch design recommendations.

Although the tables have been developed for composite climates, they may be used for the diagnosis of any climate.

Fig 165
Mahoney table 1 —
first part (completed
for Baghdad)

The tables are described in the following paragraphs, step by step. A complete set of tables is given in appendix 11, which can be reproduced for use in practice.

TABLE 1

Location	Baghdad, Iraq
Longitude	44°24' E.
Latitude	33°20' N.
Altitude	34 m

Air temperature: °C

	J	F	M	A	M	J	J	A	S	O	N	D	High	AMT
Monthly mean max.	16	18·5	22	29	36	41	43·5	43·5	40	34	24·5	17·5	43·5	23·5
Monthly mean min.	4	5·5	9	14·5	20	23·5	25·5	24·5	21	16	10·5	5	4	39·5
Monthly mean range	12	13	13	14	16	17·5	18	18	19	18	14	12·5	Low	AMR

8.1.6
Temperature

Table 1 is used to assemble temperature, humidity, rainfall and wind data. Figure 165 shows the temperature part of table 1. After filling in the title block (location identification), proceed as follows:

1 from meteorological records enter the monthly mean maximum and mean minimum air temperature values in the first two lines. All values should be rounded to the nearest 0·5 °C.
2 find the mean range for each month by deducting the mean minimum from the mean maximum values (second line from the first) and enter these in the third line
3 in the separate box on the right enter the highest of the twelve maxima and the. lowest of the twelve minima respectively
4 by adding these two values and dividing it by two find the *annual mean temperature* and enter this value in the box marked AMT

* First published by the United Nations Centre for Housing, Building and Planning, in *Climate and House Design* as part of the series *Trends in House Design*. Permission of the Centre for inclusion of these tables in the present volume is gratefully acknowledged.

5 by finding the difference between these two values (deducting the lowest mean minimum from the highest mean maximum) get the *annual mean range* and enter it in the box marked AMR

Fig 166
Mahoney table 1 –
second part

Relative humidity: %

Monthly mean max. a.m.	87	78	74	68	46	34	32	32	38	50	67	89
Monthly mean min. p.m.	50	41	35	27	18	13	12	13	15	21	39	51
Average	68·5	59·5	54·5	47·5	32	23·5	22	23·5	26·5	35·5	53	70
Humidity group	3	3	3	2	2	1	1	1	1	2	3	3

Humidity group:	1	If average RH:	below 30%
	2		30–50%
	3		50–70%
	4		above 70%

Rain and wind

Rainfall, mm	24	25	28	15	7	0	0	0	0	3	22	26		150	Total

Wind, prevailing	NW.	NW.	NW.	NW.	NW.	NW.	NW.	NW.	NW.	NW.	NW.	NW.
Wind, secondary	SE.	SE.	N	N	N	N	N &W	N	N	N	N	SE.
	J	F	M	A	M	J	J	A	S	O	N	D

8.1.7
Humidity, rain and wind

Figure 166 shows the second half of table 1. Proceed as follows:

a from meteorological records enter the monthly mean maxima (early morning readings) and minima (early afternoon readings) of relative humidity (RH) in the first two lines

b find the 'average humidity' for each month by adding the above two values and dividing it by two. Enter these averages in the third line

c establish the 'humidity group' for each month (1, 2, 3 or 4) according to the following categories:

average RH: below 30% = group 1
             30–50%   = group 2
             50–70%   = group 3
             above 70% = group 4

Enter these in the fourth line

d enter the monthly average rainfall values (in mm) in the fifth line. Adding these twelve values find the annual total rainfall and enter this in the separate box at the end of the line

e in the last two lines enter the prevailing and secondary wind directions for each month, on the basis of first and second peaks in published wind frequency tables or figures (16 compass points should be distinguished, if available, i.e. N., NNE., NE., ENE., E., ESE., etc.)

Fig 167
Mahoney table 2 —
first part (completed
for Baghdad)

Comfort limits		AMT over 20°C		AMT 15–20°C		AMT below 15°C	
		Day	Night	Day	Night	Day	Night
Humidity group:	1	26–34	17–25	23–32	14–23	21–30	12–21
	2	25–31	17–24	22–30	14–22	20–27	12–20
	3	23–29	17–23	21–28	14–21	19–26	12–19
	4	22–27	17–21	20–25	14–20	18–24	12–18

TABLE 2
Diagnosis: °C

	J	F	M	A	M	J	J	A	S	O	N	D	
Monthly mean max.	16	18·5	22	29	36	41	43·5	43·5	40	34	24·5	17·5	23·5 AMT
Day comfort: upper	29	29	29	31	31	34	34	34	34	31	29	29	
lower	23	23	23	25	25	26	26	26	26	25	23	23	
Monthly mean min.	4	5·5	9	14·5	20	23·5	25·5	24·5	21	16	10·5	5	
Night comfort: upper	23	23	23	24	24	25	25	25	25	24	23	23	
lower	17	17	17	17	17	17	17	17	17	17	17	17	
Thermal stress: day	C	C	C	O	H	H	H	H	H	H	O	C	
night	C	C	C	C	O	O	H	O	O	C	C	C	

8.1.8 Diagnosis

Table 2 serves the purpose of diagnosis. The first half of this table is shown in Figure 167 and the steps to be followed are:

1 enter in the first and fourth lines the monthly mean minimum and maximum temperatures from table 1

2 find the upper and lower comfort limits for the day and night of each month, on the basis of the chart shown at the top of Figure 167, as defined by the 'annual mean temperature' and the 'humidity group' for each month. Enter these values in lines 2, 3, 5 and 6 respectively

3 compare the day comfort limits with the mean maxima and the night comfort limits with the mean minima and establish the nature of thermal stress by entering the following symbols in the last two lines:

H (hot) — if mean is above limit
O (comfort) — if mean is within limits
C (cold) — if mean is below the limit

8.1.9 Indicators

Certain groups of symptoms (nature of the thermal stress, some climate characteristics and the duration of both) indicate the remedial action the designer could take. The method developed uses six 'indicators' (three 'humid indicators': H1, 2, 3, and three 'arid indicators': A1, 2, 3), as defined in the notes at the foot of table 2 (Figure 168).

The process to be followed is to check from table 2 the termal stress indices (day and night) and from table 1 the humidity group, the rainfall and the monthly mean range of temperatures against the definition of the indicators and place a tick in the

Fig 168
Mahoney table 2 —
second part

Indicators

															Totals
Humid:	H1													0	Totals
	H2													0	
	H3													0	
Arid:	A1	√	√	√	√	√	√	√	√	√	√	√	√	12	
	A2					√	√	√	√	√				5	
	A3	√	√	√									√	4	

Meaning:	Indicator	Thermal stress		Rainfall	Humidity group	Monthly mean range
Applicable when:		Day	Night			
Air movement essential	H1	H			4	
		H			2, 3	Less than 10°
Air movement desirable	H2	O			4	
Rain protection necessary	H3			Over 200 mm		
Thermal capacity necessary	A1				1, 2, 3	More than 10°
Out-door sleeping desirable	A2		H		1, 2	
		H	O		1, 2	More than 10°
Protection from cold	A3	C				

line of the appropriate indicator where the month's data corresponds to the definition.

In the last column show the number of months in which each indicator is applicable (the number of ticks in each line).

8.1.10 Specifications

Table 3 gives to the designer the specifications resulting from the above indicators. Recommended specifications are grouped under eight headings:

Layout
Spacing
Air movement
Openings
Walls
Roofs
Out-door sleeping
Rain protection

The specification items are numbered and a brief description is given in table 3 (Figure 169). For detailed explanation see 8.1.11.

Fig 169
Mahoney table 3
(completed for
Baghdad)

243

Indicator totals from table 2					
H1	H2	H3	A1	A2	A3
0	0	0	12	5	4

TABLE 3
Recommended specifications

Layout

H1	H2	H3	A1	A2	A3	✓	No.	Specification
			0–10	5–12			1	Orientation north and south (long axis east–west)
			11, 12	0–4		√	2	Compact courtyard planning

Spacing

H1	H2	H3	A1	A2	A3	✓	No.	Specification
11, 12							3	Open spacing for breeze penetration
2–10							4	As **3**, but protection from hot and cold wind
0, 1							5	Compact lay-out of estates

Air movement

H1	H2	H3	A1	A2	A3	✓	No.	Specification
3–12							6	Rooms single banked, permanent provision for air movement
1, 2	0–5							
	6–12					√	7	Double banked rooms, temporary provision for air movement
0	2–12							
	0, 1						8	No air movement requirement

Openings

H1	H2	H3	A1	A2	A3	✓	No.	Specification
			0, 1	0			9	Large openings, 40–80%
			11, 12	0, 1		√	10	Very small openings, 10–20%
Any other conditions							11	Medium openings, 20–40%

Walls

H1	H2	H3	A1	A2	A3	✓	No.	Specification
			0–2				12	Light walls, short time-lag
			3–12			√	13	Heavy external and internal walls

Roofs

H1	H2	H3	A1	A2	A3	✓	No.	Specification
			0–5				14	Light, insulated roofs
			6–12			√	15	Heavy roofs, over 8 h time-lag

Out-door sleeping

H1	H2	H3	A1	A2	A3	✓	No.	Specification
				2–12		√	16	Space for out-door sleeping required

Rain protection

H1	H2	H3	A1	A2	A3	✓	No.	Specification
	3–12						17	Protection from heavy rain necessary

The steps to be followed are:

a transfer indicator totals from table 2 to the first line of table 3

b where the indicator total falls between values given in table 3, place a tick against the specification item in the same line

c there can only be one specification item recommended under each of the eight headings. It will be the first one arrived at when scanning from left to right

d in some cases the first coincidence will select two items. In this case continue further right, the next indicator will make the final choice

8.1.11 Items amplified

Specification items in the last column of table 3 are further explained as follows:

Layout

There are two alternative layouts:

1 buildings should be orientated on an east–west axis, the long elevations facing north and south, to reduce exposure to the sun

2 buildings should be planned around small courtyards if thermal storage is required for most of the year, i.e. when the hot-dry season is dominant

Spacing

Spacing has three options:

3 buildings should be broadly spaced for breeze penetration. As a rough guide: space between long rows of building should not be less than five times the height

4 if wind penetration is needed only for part of the year, item **3** still applies, but provision must be made for protection from cold or dusty hot winds. See diagnosis in table 2 and wind directions in table 1

5 compact planning is recommended if the air movement requirement is insignificant

Air movement

This is influenced by planning arrangements:

6 rooms should be single banked with windows in the north and south walls, to ensure air movement by ample cross-ventilation

7 rooms may be double banked, but the plan should allow for temporary cross-ventilation (e.g. large interconnecting doors). If wind is unreliable, or site limitations restrict planning for cross-ventilation, ceiling-mounted fans may be considered. These would require a room height of not less than 2·75 m, which will affect the basic built form

8 if air movement is never essential, and is desirable for not more than a month, rooms can be double banked and there is not much need for cross-ventilation

Openings

Openings in walls are classified in three categories:

9 'large', between 40 and 80% of the north and south walls. These need not be fully glazed, but should be protected from the sun, sky glare and rain, preferably by horizontal overhangs

10 'very small', less than 20% of the wall

11 'medium', between 20 and 40% of the wall area. Openings in the east wall may be desirable where the cold season is long. In west walls openings are acceptable in moderate or cold climates, but under no circumstances in the tropics

Walls

There are two broad categories of walls:

12 external walls should be light with low thermal capacity. Within this category there are two subtypes:

a internal walls should also be light where hot-dry conditions prevail for a short time only

b internal walls should be heavy and massive, where any occurence of hot-dry conditions is combined with a large annual mean range of temperature (over 20 degC)

13 both external and internal walls should be massive

Roofs	Two basic types are distinguished: **14** a light but well insulated roof, with low thermal capacity **15** a heavy roof, with substantial thermal capacity, giving a time-lag of at least 8 hours
Outdoor sleeping	Provisions for out-door sleeping is either required or not. If so: **16** it should be provided on roofs, balconies or in patios, so that sleepers are exposed to the coldest part of the night sky (the zenith) to increase heat loss by outgoing radiation
Rain protection	**17** special protective measures are needed if rain is frequent and heavy – such as deep verandahs, wide overhangs and covered passages

8.1.12 Summary

The tables should be considered as an aid to sketch design, but not a mechanically used substitute for thinking. The logic of the process must be understood and kept in mind.

In table 1 the dominant features of the climate and their duration have been recorded in a simplified form. In table 2 the nature of thermal stress has been diagnosed and the duration of need for certain thermal controls has been expressed by the indicators. In table 3 these indicators have been examined and correlated, producing some recommendations. It is immaterial whether these are taken as broad and basic design decisions or only as specifications of the required performance. In any case they are to be used as constraints (or aids, fixed points or starting points) together with many factors other than climatic, in formulating the sketch design.

The method is quick, broad and sketchy. It contains compromises. There may be instances or periods when the design thus formulated will be less than perfect. This, however, does not invalidate the method. It simply means that climatic design does not end with the sketch design stage.

In climate control through natural means compromises are often unavoidable. The later plan development and element design stages will provide the opportunity to enhance the favourable and mitigate the unfavourable features of the initial concept.

8.1.13 Mechanical controls

As discussed in 4.1.2 (and shown in Figure 44), precise control of indoor climate under all conditions is only possibly by mechanical means. In the tropics the mechanical control which may be relied on is *air conditioning*. The decision to use air conditioning for indoor climate control is one of the most basic ones, and it may radically influence the whole of the design.

Principles of operation and the basic systems have been described in 4.1.10 to 14. The design philosophy relating to the role of air conditioning has been outlined in 4.2.1. Here the choice parameters will be examined in some detail.

In hot-dry climates, however high the afternoon maximum temperature, as long as the daily mean is not higher than the comfort limit, satisfactory control is possible without air conditioning, purely by structural means.

In maritime desert climates it is more probable that air conditioning would be called for. In both cases constructional and structural requirements for an air conditioned building do not greatly differ from those for a 'naturally' controlled one. The building should be 'sealed', i.e. closed (or closeable), it should have small windows to reduce solar gain, good insulation and a large thermal capacity to reduce peak loads.

Specifications are valid whether the building is air conditioned or not.

Warm-humid climates create the greatest need for air conditioning. The air is both hot and humid, and it often remains warm overnight. A decision to install air conditioning will radically change the building design. Without it, ample air movement is the only way of ameliorating conditions. This will be achieved by designing a building as open and transparent for wind as is possible. If air conditioned, the building should be closed and cooled below the out-door temperature, thus the walls need to be well insulated: without it the insulating qualities of the walls are unimportant.

In composite climates the decision may be to install air conditioning but operate it only in the warm-humid season, whilst relying on natural controls at other times. A word of caution about over-conditioning, which is especially relevant where conditioning is not constant: a building cooled to the lower limit of comfort may acclimatise the occupants to the low temperatures, thus make the out-door over-heated conditions even more intolerable. The discrepancy between out-door and indoor conditions should not be excessive. As a rough guidance the comfort limits given at the head of Mahoney table 3 (Figure 169) should be used as a target.

In tropical upland climates, with a well-designed building, air conditioning will not normally be necessary. However, some external constraints (e.g. an urban site dictating a wrong orientation) or the attached 'prestige value' may swing the balance and bring about a decision for air conditioning. In some situations prestige value demand may be satisfied by creating the impression of air conditioning, without really providing it. For example, a department store may be mechanically ventilated only, but may have a set of local conditioners giving a cooled air curtain just inside of the entrances. This is a solution not advocated, but often used.

As can be seen, the decision for or against air conditioning will be based not only on comfort, climatic and physical parameters, but largely on social and economic factors.

8.2.1
Analysis and
development

The forward analysis stage ends with the formulation of specifications for the climatic performance of the building in general, mainly in qualitative terms. This will be followed by the production of a formal solution — a sketch design. Having done this, more precise specifications can be established in quantitative terms during the plan development stage. This will involve analytical as well as evaluative work.

Although it is advisable to go as far as practicable in specifying the building's performance during the forward analysis, without prejudicing the synthesis, many factors can only be analysed after certain design decisions have been made, when a design hypothesis exists.

The question of solar controls is a good example. The performance of these could be defined quite precisely by horizontal and vertical shadow angles (see 4.2.12) without designing the actual device. However, before this can be done, at least the orientation of openings (if not their size) should be decided. So, in the forward analysis stage shadow angles cannot be specified, unless the trouble is taken of specifying them for the whole range of possible orientations. It would be far more profitable to define only their performance in terms of the 'over-heated period' and leave the definition of shadow angles to the development stage. The actual device can be designed in the element design stage.

The depth of analysis by the use of the Mahoney tables is sufficient to permit the formulation of a sketch design or design hypothesis. Further refinement can be carried out in the development stage, when the design hypothesis already formulated can help to structure the data search.

Such further refinement may relate to:

a   the synchronisation of a space use pattern with the seasonal and daily change pattern of climatic conditions
b   extending the consideration of the building to out-door spaces
c   the precise definition of physical properties of the building, e.g. of:
thermal insulation
thermal capacity
solar control
ventilation and air movement

These subjects will be examined in 8.2.2. to 13.

8.2.2 Periodic changes

No room or open space is used all the time by all the occupants. Climatically no room or open space can be equally good at all hours of the day and night (unless mechanical controls are used). The designer's objective must be to synchronise the most intensive use with the best climatic conditions. To achieve this, two sets of information must be obtained and correlated:

1   occupancy or space use pattern
2   changes of out-door and indoor climate during the 24-hour cycle

For recording the occupancy and space use pattern a useful aid is the *activity chart*, introduced in 8.2.3.

Information on climatic changes is required for at least one typical day of each season. Sometimes hourly temperature data are available. If not, the following assumptions can be made:

a   the monthly mean minimum and maximum temperature (which has been recorded in the Mahoney tables) corresponds to the highest and lowest temperature of a typical day of that month
b   the daily temperature changes can be represented by a sinusoidal curve, the maximum occurring shortly after midday and the minimum in the early morning hours
Both assumptions are justified for the purposes of such a comparison.

This information will best be transferred to the activity chart, to allow direct correlation.

8.2.3 Activity charts

The activity chart consists of two parts, the top showing graphs of out-door and indoor temperature changes, with the comfort zone superimposed, and the lower part gives a record of activities in the various spaces of the building (including out-door spaces). Figure 170 shows a completed example. A blank form is given in appendix 12.

It is suggested that the activity chart be reproduced and duplicated, to be used in specific investigations. If the location investigated has distinguishable seasons, or if there are seasonal changes in the building use, a separate form should be used for each season.

In using the chart the following steps should be taken:

1   select a month which is typical of the season to be considered*
2   refer to Figure 37, (p.62) the diurnal temperature variation chart. Mark the mean maximum temperature of the month on the top scale and the mean minimum temperature on the bottom scale (it is useful to lay a tracing paper over the chart and work on this). Connect the two points by a straight line, and read off the hourly temperatures on the top or bottom scale, where the respective hour lines are intersected

* If hourly temperature values are available for a nearby station, these should be used for step **3** and step **2** should be omitted.

Fig 170
Activity chart
(Khartoum, Sudan –
hot season, June)

249

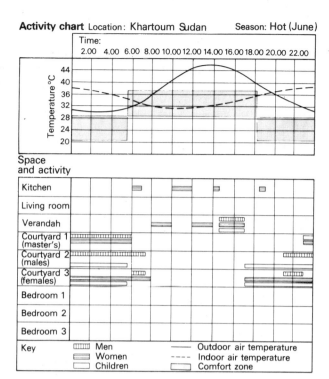

Activity chart Location: Khartoum, Sudan   Season: Hot (June)

NOTES

1. Men go to work at 7.30 and return at 14.30 hours (time spent at work is from 8.00 to 14.00 hours).
2. Children go to school at 7.30 and return at 14.30 hours (time spent at school is from 8.00 to 14.00 hours).
3. The verandah is used as a dining area at lunch time and as a sleeping space during the afternoon siesta.
4. Courtyard 1 is used at night as a sleeping area by parents only.
5. Courtyard 2 is used to entertain male visitors in the evening. At night it is used as a sleeping space by the male members of the household.
6. Courtyard 3 is used to entertain female visitors. The whole family takes breakfast and dinner here. At night it is used as a sleeping space by the female members of the household.

3 transfer these values to the activity chart and construct the out-door temperature curve

4 superimpose the day and night-time comfort limits (as established in the 'diagnosis' of table 2)

5 with lightweight building fabric and generous air movement the indoor temperature is not likely to differ from the out-door. For massive and closed buildings an indoor temperature curve should be constructed, using the information given in 3.3.2 and 4.2.3 (Figures 41 and 49 respectively)

6 enter the names of major out-door and indoor spaces in the first column of the lower half of the chart, reserving a separate line for each (the chart can be extended downwards)

7 establish simple symbols for the different persons (or types of persons) using the spaces, and indicate by horizontal lines the time and duration that he or she (or they) uses the space

The two parts of the chart can now be correlated. This would help in planning (e.g. where to position the various spaces in relation to orientation) and in deciding about the types of control necessary for each activity space (e.g. out-door sleeping).

**8.2.4
Outdoor
spaces**

In tropical climates many of the activities normally associated with indoor spaces in moderate climates (sleeping, washing, cooking, eating, playing, working, etc.) are performed out-of-doors. This is especially true for residential buildings, but can occur with other building types, such as schools. The shelter of the building is sought only when the need for privacy or unfavourable weather conditions demand it, and for the safe keeping of belongings.

The following considerations may influence the formulation of the initial design concept, or sketch design, but the obvious time for closer examination of and decisions about out-door spaces is the plan development stage.

As the area adjoining the building becomes an extension of the indoor space, it must be treated by the designer with equal care. For indoor spaces, natural conditioning is preferable to mechanical controls. For the out-door space this is the only form of control possible.

**8.2.5
Outdoor
spaces in hot-
dry climates**

For controlling the climatic conditions of out-door spaces in hot-dry climates the designer can rely on the following means:

Enclosure

Walls, often quite high, surrounding a courtyard or garden, serve practical purposes, such as protection from scorching hot wind, dust, stray dogs and goats, trespassers or the limitation of evaporation and retention of an air pool cooled by evaporation; but the psychological need for privacy, for a demarcation line between the man-made orderly space and the barren hostile world outside, is no less important.

*Inward looking
plan*

The building so arranged as to surround a courtyard or patio (possibly only partly, but completed by walls) serves a similar purpose. Even without water and planting, this will be a more desirable space to be in or to look at than the arid landscape or townscape outside.

Planting

This is restricted by the availability of water. It is more feasible in enclosed spaces than in the open. Evergreen trees, shrubs, cacti, creepers and a few types of grass can be used. Planting can pleasantly contrast paved areas. Even potted plants can play a role. Lawns are difficult to maintain. Creepers will give the best value, producing large green areas to look at, or (supported by light framing or stretched out wires) giving an overhead cover, a pleasant dappled shade.

Water

The smallest pond, basin or fountain adds to the sense of well-being of the occupants. The physical effect: evaporative cooling is quite significant in enclosed out-door spaces, but the psychological effect is far greater. The view of a surface of water and especially the sound of moving water brings relief long before any drop in air temperature could be measured.

Shading

Shading is essential for the day-time use of out-door spaces. Vertical elements (walls and the building itself) provide shade only in the morning and late afternoon hours. Horizontal elements, loggias, verandahs or purpose-made devices (e.g. matting on a frame, awnings and louvres), may be used more effectively, but plantage gives the most pleasant shade, reducing the contrast between bright light and solid shadow with its soft half-lights. The best results will be achieved by shading the floor of the yard during the day, but leaving it exposed to the zenith sky at night, without restricting outgoing radiation.

*Protected
circulation*

Pedestrians and parked cars also need shade. Narrow alleyways rather than wide open roads, arcades, broad overhangings awnings and covered ways serve the pedestrians. Protection of cars could be provided by creepers on pergolas or by special structures (which are expensive) within or under the building. This brings problems of access, affecting the layout.

Public spaces

The principles are the same as for private open spaces, but the question of maintenance is much more acute. Size must be related to resources of water and maintenance capacity. Oversized spaces tend to be turned into neglected no-man's-lands, dust-bowls and refuse dumps: 'less (well kept) is more'. Public open spaces should be enclosed, well planted, cooled by water and shaded for most of the day.

8.2.6 Outdoor spaces in warm-humid climates

Out-door spaces in warm-humid climates are even more important than in the hot-dry regions. More activities take place out-of-doors. It is easier to maintain comfort conditions out-of-doors than inside buildings. The out-door space will be pleasant if there is air movement, shade and protection from the rain.

Air movement

Air movement will be ensured if:
a   there are no enclosure walls. For demarcation of boundaries or visual privacy use open fences or screens which permit wind penetration
b   the 'five times height' rule for spacing is followed as a rough guide. For details see 4.3.9 and 15. Generally the building must be made as 'transparent' for wind as possible (elevated on stilts, open staircases to interrupt long rows, etc.)
c   there are no courtyards or closed rows of buildings, instead there should be free and irregular groupings
d   with greater densities the height is increased rather than the ground coverage

Shade

Vertical elements used in hot-dry regions are ruled out (they would restrict air flow). Roof overhangs, verandahs, porticoes, awnings and covered passages are useful. Most welcome is the shade of trees.

Planting

Shrubs or hedges must only be used with care, not to reduce air flow near the ground, where it is most needed. Tall trees, with clear trunks are preferable, as they would cast a broad shadow whilst permit penetration of the breeze. Ground cover is important, but can be a problem in two ways:

1   in some locations ground cover is so abundant, that it is hard to keep cutting it back, to allow free passage of air
2   in eroded areas, where the top soil has been washed away, it is hard to get anything to grow. Shrubs or hedges can be used here, at least until a healthy ground cover is re-established

Shelter from rain

As rains are frequent and often intensive and as it is warm even during rains, out-door spaces should be provided for use during rains. Verandahs, covered passages and broad, continuous awnings over the fronts of shops can serve this purpose as well as shading. A roofed area without walls may be provided for specific activities.

Public spaces

Open spaces without maintenance will usually remain green (unlike in hot-dry climates). The problem may, however, be:

a   overgrowing vegetation
b   refuse dumping
c   unintended irregular occupation by huts, shacks and shops, with the associated creation of unhealthy conditions

An open space must have a purpose and must be designed to serve that purpose — responsibility for its maintenance must be clearly defined.

8.2.7 Outdoor spaces in composite climates

The elements examined in 8.2.5 and 6 can be combined intelligently in composite climates, as the need arises: different external spaces can serve for use in the different seasons. The designer can think in terms such as 'hot weather yards', 'monsoon gardens' or 'cool season patios'.

A small enclosed yard on one side of a building can be made pleasant during an arid season and, on the other side, a large shaded space, open to the breeze, can be provided for use in the warm-humid season.

Deciduous trees, creepers and vines will provide shade when needed also allow sun penetration in the cool season when they lose their foliage.

**8.2.8
Thermal
insulation**

In a heated or air conditioned building it is quite a straightforward matter to define the optimum amount of insulation through a cost/benefit optimisation process.

The capital cost of insulation can be shown by a straight line graph as a function of thickness (Figure 171). Then the reduction in heat loss rate (or gain) due to this insulation can be computed, multiplied by the number of degree days and the cost of heating (or cooling) to get the saving per annum. This saving, calculated for a suitable amortisation period, can be shown on the same graph by a hyperbolic curve, also as a function of thickness. The intersection of the two curves will define the optimum thickness.

In naturally conditioned buildings such a calculation is impossible. Partial culations can perhaps aid the decision making based on qualitative consideration.

In hot-dry climates walls and roofs should be massive and heavy, to even out diurnal variations in temperature. Resistive insulation alone (see 4.2.3) will not be effective.

In warm-humid climates with adequate air movement the indoor and out-door air temperature will be the same. The task of insulation will only be the reduction of heat flow due to solar overheating of the outer surfaces. Roofs receive far more solar energy than walls. Walls would normally be shaded, thus the only element to be insulated is the roof. How much insulation is advisable for roofs?

The magnitude of the *sol-air excess temperature* (T_{se}) (i.e. the temperature equivalent of the radiant gain, of 3.1.18) can be calculated:

$$T_{se} = \frac{I \times a}{f_o}$$

where I = intensity of radiation
   a = absorbance of the surface
   f_o = outside surface conductance

and it can be compounded for any selected period (e.g. a year). The greater this value, the more benefit to be gained from the insulation. The benefit would, however, be in improved environmental conditions and not in any cost saving. Direct comparison is impossible. Any decision will be arbitrary or relying on value judgements. Koenigsberger and Lynn [97] have suggested a performance specification: the ceiling temperature should not exceed the air temperature by more than 4 degC. To achieve this, the U-value of the roof-ceiling combination will need to be around 0·8 W/m² degC (see 7.2.5) or the surface should be highly reflective. Some constructions giving such a performance are tabulated in appendix 13. This tabulation provides a comparison in performance, without which cost comparisons would be meaningless.

In composite climates, if the hot-dry season is dominant, lasting 6 months or more, a heavy roof should be used (as suggested by Mahoney table 3, item **15**). If this season is shorter, a lightweight, insulated roof is suggested. Definition of the borderline is rather arbitrary. As either a massive roof with high capacitive insulation, or a light roof with good resistive insulation would do almost the same job, the deciding factor will very often be the comparative cost, which in turn depends on local conditions, availability of materials and labour.

Fig 171
Optimisation of
insulation thickness

An instrument factory, roofed with asbestos-cement, $U = 8.00 \ W/m \ deg \ C$
Insulation costs 80p/cm thickness and m², $k = 0.1 \ W/m \ deg \ C$
Heating cost per kWh =1p
Building to be kept at a constant 18°C

Take the difference between 18°C and monthly mean temperature and multiply by
number of days in the month. Add for 12 months to get 'degree- days': 2 800. (approximately)
This gives $2\ 800 \times 24 = 67\ 200$ h deg C ('degree-hours').
Set up table and calculate (assuming 5 year amortisation):

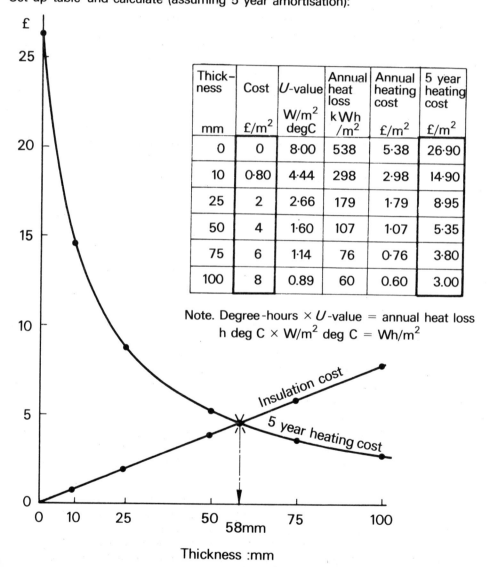

Thick-ness	Cost	U-value	Annual heat loss	Annual heating cost	5 year heating cost
mm	£/m²	W/m² degC	kWh /m²	£/m²	£/m²
0	0	8.00	538	5.38	26.90
10	0.80	4.44	298	2.98	14.90
25	2	2.66	179	1.79	8.95
50	4	1.60	107	1.07	5.35
75	6	1.14	76	0.76	3.80
100	8	0.89	60	0.60	3.00

Note. Degree -hours $\times U$-value = annual heat loss
h deg C $\times$ W/m² deg C = Wh/m²

8.2.9
**Thermal
capacity**

Mahoney table 3, items **13** and **15**, suggest the use of massive walls and roofs
respectively. In the latter item a minimum time-lag of 8 hours is recommended. Such
a broad statement is sufficient for the purposes of producing a sketch design, but in
the development stage the question arises: 'How much time-lag is desirable?'

It may be reasonable to assume that the air temperature is the same on any side of the building. The actual heat flow into the fabric will, however, depend also on solar radiation, as expressed by the sol-air temperature (3.1.18). At any moment the value of this will be different for each surface of the building and all values will change from hour to hour with the movement of the sun. For this reason the question of time-lag should be considered separately for each building surface — at least the four walls and the roof.

A method for defining the desirable time-lag has been described in 4.2.3 and Figure 49. This should be carried out for each surface in succession. The process is as follows:

a   draw a graph of the out-door air temperature variations over 24 hours for a critical day. Reproduce this in five copies — one for each surface.
b   compute the sol-air excess temperature at least for 2-hour intervals for each surface (on the basis of incident radiation data) and superimpose this on the air temperature graphs
c   for each surface establish the time of out-door sol-air temperature peak value
d   considering the space bounded by the particular surface, assess the time when the maximum heat inflow would be desirable or at least tolerable
e   the difference between the two points will be the desirable time-lag in hours

· Clearly, this can only be done when orientation (position of surface), surface finishes and positions of the various rooms have been decided. Results of this analysis during the development stage may, however, lead to a revision of the building plan, a rearrangement of rooms and a more efficient correlation of the three factors:

1   room use pattern
2   the heating cycle of outer surfaces
3   time-lag of the envelope elements

**8.2.10
Solar control**

The design of solar controls to windows and openings involves three steps:

a   definition of the overheated period, when shading is required
b   specifying the performance of the device in terms of shadow angles
c   detail design of the device

The first step could have been carried out in the forward analysis stage, but may be carried out now. The second step is clearly a task for the development stage, when orientation of openings is already established. Both are described below.

Design of the actual device is left to the element design stage.

**8.2.11
Shading time**

Shading time can be defined in three ways:

1   in terms of air temperature alone
2   in terms of effective temperature, combining air temperature and humidity, possibly air movement
3   in terms of sol-air temperature, separately for every surface of a different orientation

The first one is the simplest. Having completed the activity chart (see 8.2.3 and Figure 170) reference can be made to the top part of this. Shading will be required whenever the out-door temperature line is above the *lower* limit of the comfort zone. If activity charts are available for different dates of the year, the overheated period can be defined in terms of dates and hours. This information can be shown on an isopleth diagram (similar to Figure 38) or on a pair of sun-path diagram overlays (Figure 64) as described in 4.2.14, except that here only air temperature values would be used and not ET.

For definition in terms of effective temperature hourly ET values for each month of the year are needed. This could be assessed, even if there is no more information available than that contained in Mahoney table 1. The following steps are to be taken:

a take the mean maximum temperature (DBT) and the p.m. humidity value for each month (Mahoney table 1). Read the corresponding wet-bulb temperature (WBT) from the psychrometric chart (Figure 12)

For example if   DBT = 22°C
          and   RH = 60%
          read: WBT = 17°C

b using the effective temperature nomogram (Figure 30), assuming there is no air movement, read the ET value, which will be the maximum ET for the day.

For example connecting DBT 22°C with WBT 17°C, the line intersects the 0 air velocity curve at 25°C ET

c repeat this with the mean minimum temperature and morning humidity, to get the minimum ET for the day
d turn to Figure 37 and establish hourly (or 2-hourly) ET values. The use of this diagram is explained in detail in 2.3.8

A table, such as that shown in Figure 38, may help in carrying out this calculation.
The values obtained can be transferred to an isopleth diagram or a pair of sun-path diagram overlays, as described in 4.2.14 and shown in Figures 38 and 64.

Definition in terms of sol-air temperature would require the production of sol-air temperature isopleth diagrams for each orientation. This means that hourly sol-air temperature values are needed for one day of each month and for each orientation, each of which would depend on the incident radiation intensity. A very lengthy job, but certainly the most accurate method. (It could be used for the definition of the desirable time-lag, as discussed in 8.2.9.) Its execution would be warranted on important or repetitive projects, but also if many projects are to be carried out in the same location. The sol-air temperature values need to be calculated once and for all. For some locations the data is available in published form, as it is widely used by air conditioning engineers.

**8.2.12
Shadow
angles**

To specify the required performance of shading devices, the vertical and horizontal shadow angles should be established. The process is based on two sets of information:

1 a defined shading period
2 the orientation decided

and involves the use of sun-path diagrams (appendix 8) and shadow angle protractor (inside back cover). These have been discussed in detail in 4.2.12 to 14 and the step-by-step procedure is summarised below:

a select the sun-path diagram appropriate to the latitude
b delineate the shading period on tracing paper laid over the sun-path diagram. As each horizontal curve indicates two dates, mark both outlines. Generally the broader coverage should be adopted, but some intelligent compromise may be exercised
c lay the protractor over the diagram, with its base line crossing the centre and its centre line pointing to the required orientation
d the part of the shading period falling 'behind' the base line (behind the elevation considered) can be ignored
e select a combination of horizontal and vertical shadow angles, defining a shading mask, which would cover the shading period area with as close a fit as possible. This step is described in detail by Figure 65
f in most cases it will be found that a number of combinations of vertical and horizontal shadow angles would give shading masks to cover the shading period.

If so, it will be useful to list a few such alternatives, to preserve as much freedom of choice as possible for the detail design stage. For example, a certain shading period would be masked by either of the following:

(i)   vertical angle $\epsilon = 16°$
(ii)   vertical angle $\epsilon = 40°$ and
     horizontal angle $\delta = -47°$ to $-8°$
(iii) vertical angle $\epsilon = 60°$ and
     horizontal angle $\delta = -59°$ to $+17°$
(iv) horizontal angle $\delta = -70°$ to $+90°$

8.2.13 Ventilation and air movement

Ventilation, i.e. the supply of fresh air, is necessary under any circumstances. Estimation of requirements and the necessary provisions have been discussed in 4.1.6 and 4.3.2. These will be relevant if the building is basically closed, as in hot-dry climates. In no case will it strongly influence the built form.

Ventilation, as used for convective cooling, has been discussed in 4.1.8 and 4.3.3. It is only effective if the out-door air is significantly cooler than the indoor, thus it will rarely, if ever, be used in the tropics.

Air movement through the building, as opposed to ventilation, is essential in warm-humid climates. Mahoney table 3, item **6** has recommended that air movement through the building should be ensured. Now, in the development stage the recommendation would need to be quantified. The most useful basis for this would be the effective temperature isopleth diagram, as described in 8.2.11, **a–d**. These ET values have been calculated for still air. Figure 172 repeats Figure 38, but with both upper and lower comfort limits marked. When the ET value exceeds the *upper* comfort limit, reference to the ET nomogram (Figure 30) can establish what air velocity would bring the ET down to an acceptable value.

Fig 172
Effective temperature isopleths, with comfort limits (New Delhi, India – from Fig 38)

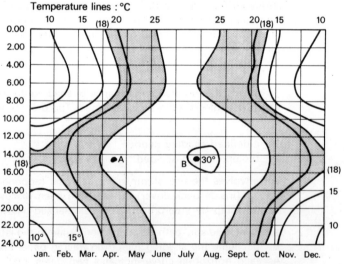

	From table, Fig. 38:			From nomogram, Fig. 30:
at 'A' (April)	ET=26·5°C	DBT=36°C	WBT=19°C	3 m/s brings it to ET=25°C 7 m/s brings it to ET=24°C
at 'B' (July)	ET=30°C	DBT=35·5°C	WBT=27°C	7 m/s brings it to ET=26·5°C remains above comfort limit

A simpler method can be based on the activity chart. Whenever the air temperature curve is above the *upper* comfort limit, air movement will be necessary. When the temperature excess above the comfort zone is established, reference can be made to the bioclimatic chart (Figure 29), which will show what air velocity will compensate for that excess.

For example   0·1 m/s would compensate for 1·5 degC
              1 m/s would compensate for 5·5 degC
              (at medium humidities)

Figure 29 shows 30°C as the upper comfort limit. Here, the comfort limit given in Mahoney table 2 should be used, but the temperature *intervals* given in Figure 29 for the effect of various air velocities are still valid (not in °C, a position on the scale, but in degC, a distance or interval on the scale).

By this means it will be established what air velocity there ought to be inside the room, at the body surface. The next step is to establish what the prevailing wind velocities are during the same period. After this the design of openings can be considered.

In Mahoney table 1 only wind directions have been recorded, thus reference should be made to meteorological data, to establish wind velocities. On the basis of information given in 4.3.7 *et seq.*, particularly in 4.3.13, the openings and associated control devices can be designed.

Unfortunately, it will be found that the highest temperatures often coincide with the least amount of breeze. As this would be the critical situation, the best that can be done is to provide openings as large and unobstructed as possible, to make the building as transparent for wind as practically feasible.

Indeed, the whole analysis should start with this point. If it is discovered that such coincidence of maximum heat and minimum wind is the case, further analysis would be unproductive.

The problem of contradictory orientation requirements for wind and sun-exclusion has been discussed in 7.2.3 and is referred to again in 8.3.3, item **6**.

8.3.1   **The task**
8.3.2   **Mahoney table 4**
8.3.3   **Items amplified**
8.3.4   **Shading devices**
8.3.5   **Walls and roofs**
8.3.6   **Long time-lag constructions**
8.3.7   **Openings**
8.3.8   **Consistency**

**8.3.1
The task**

When the overall design concept has been agreed and the design has been developed to a stage when everything 'works', not only from climatic, but from any other point of view, each element should be re-examined at a much closer, detailed level, to determine its form and dimensions with greater precision.

Indeed, it might have happened during the development stage, that some earlier established, climatically correct solution was modified, compromised or even ignored for the sake of some other factor, e.g. structural, constructional, economic or town planning requirements. The re-examination now may result in the design of elements which would improve (if not optimise) the climatic performance of the building, whilst accepting the non-climatic contraints.

Thus the element design stage has two major tasks:

1   to determine form and dimensions of elements which are not yet designed and for which only performance specifications exist
2   to re-examine elements which may have been agreed earlier, when design changes cast doubt on their climatic performance

A general review may be facilitated by Mahoney table 4, which is described in 8.3.2. and 3. In subsequent sections some techniques for the design of building elements will be reviewed.

**8.3.2
Mahoney
table 4**

As an extension of the series of tables described in 8.1.5 to 11, table 4 gives recommendations for the design of building elements. The table is shown in Figure 173, but it is also included with the complete set of Mahoney tables in appendix 11.

The last column of the table includes recommendations for six main features of building elements:

size of openings
position of openings

Indicator totals from table 2					
H1	H2	H3	A1	A2	A3

TABLE 4

Detail recommendations

Size of opening

H1	H2	H3	A1	A2	A3	No.	Recommendation
			0, 1	0		1	Large: 40–80%
				1–12		2	Medium: 25–40%
			2–5				
			6–10			3	Small: 15–25%
			11, 12	0–3		4	Very small: 10–20%
				4–12		5	Medium: 25–40%

Position of openings

H1	H2	H3	A1	A2	A3	No.	Recommendation
3–12						6	In north and south walls at body height on windward side
1–2			0–5				
			6–12			7	As above, openings also in internal walls
0	2–12						

Protection of openings

H1	H2	H3	A1	A2	A3	No.	Recommendation
				0–2		8	Exclude direct sunlight
		2–12				9	Provide protection from rain

Walls and floors

H1	H2	H3	A1	A2	A3	No.	Recommendation
			0–2			10	Light, low thermal capacity
			3–12			11	Heavy, over 8 h time-lag

Roofs

H1	H2	H3	A1	A2	A3	No.	Recommendation
10–12			0–2			12	Light, reflective surface, cavity
			3–12			13	Light, well insulated
0·9			0–5				
			6–12			14	Heavy, over 8 h time-lag

External features

H1	H2	H3	A1	A2	A3	No.	Recommendation
				1–12		15	Space for out-door sleeping
		1–12				16	Adequate rainwater drainage

protection of openings
walls and floors
roofs
external features

261

The recommendation items are numbered and a brief description is given in the last column of table 4. Items are further explained in 8.3.3.

In using the table the following steps are to be taken:

a repeat indicator totals in the first line, as in table 3
b where the indicator total falls between the values given below it in the same column, place a tick against the item to the right, in the same line
c items relating to the same feature are mutually exclusive – there can be only one item recommended under four of the six features (the exceptions are 'protection of openings' and 'external features')

**8.3.3
Items
amplified**

Should there by any discrepancy between recommendations of tables 3 and 4, the latter should take precedence over the former.

Size of openings

1 large, 40 to 80% of wall area. Applicable when thermal storage is needed for not more than 1 month (A1) and there is no cold season (A3)
2 medium, 25 to 40% of wall area. Applicable when thermal storage is needed for not more than 1 month and there is a cool season – or if thermal storage is needed for 2 to 5 months
3 small, 15 to 25% of wall area. Applicable when thermal storage is needed for 6 to 10 months
4 very small, 10 to 20% of wall area. Applicable when thermal storage is needed all year round (11 to 12 months) and the cool season is not more than 3 months
5 medium size openings are recommended also when thermal storage is required throughout the year and sun penetration is desirable during a cool season of more than 4 months

*Position of
openings*

6 when air movement (H1) is essential for 3 months or more, or for a lesser period, but thermal storage is needed for less than half a year (A1) the openings should be positioned so as to direct the breeze at the occupants (see 4.3.7 *et seq.* and to Figures 73 to 76). First preference is north and south orientation, but in this case the wind direction may take precedence over solar orientation
7 when air movement is essential for 1 or 2 months only and thermal storage is needed for more than 6 months – or when air flow is not essential, only desirable for 2 months or more (H2) – the rooms may be double banked, with the internal walls having adequate openings. In this case the optimum solar orientation (north and south) should take precedence over orientation for wind

*Protection of
openings*

8 complete exclusion of solar radiation throughout the year is recommended, when there is no cool season or it lasts not more than 2 months. If there is a longer cool season, the shading period can be determined as described in 8.2.11. The sun should be admitted during the cool period
9 protection of openings from rain penetration will be necessary when a rainfall exceeding 200 mm occurs in more than 1 month (H3). For the appropriate provisions see 4.3.14 and Figure 80
Note. Both **8** and **9** should be examined for their effect on air flow. See 4.3.13 and Figures 77 to 79

Walls and floors

10 when thermal storage (A1) is required for 2 months or less, a lightweight fabric is recommended. This may be provided by hollow blocks or bricks, with more than 40% void, by a thin solid wall, e.g. 50 mm dense concrete, or by sheeted walls enclosing a cavity (the latter may harbour insects and vermin). Outside surfaces should be reflective

11   when thermal storage is required for more than 2 months, a heavy fabric is recommended. Solid bricks, blocks, concrete or adobe of about 300 mm thickness should satisfy the requirement. A lesser thickness, down to 100 mm is satisfactory, if it is insulated on the outside (see 3.3.2, Figure 42 and appendix 6)

Roofs

12   with an air movement requirement (H1) for 10 to 12 months, if the thermal storage requirement is less than 2 months, a light roof should be used. Its time-lag should never exceed 3 hours. It should have a reflective surface and good insulation. A cavity within the roof or a roof-ceiling combination is advantageous. The roof-ceiling overall U-value should be in the region of 1 W/m² degC

13   with a similar air movement requirement, if the thermal storage requirement is more than 3 months − or with an air movement requirement for less than 9 months and thermal storage is needed for less than 5 months − the roof should still be light, but its insulation is even more important. An overall U-value not exceeding 0·8 W/m² degC is recommended. This performance could be provided by an external sheet with a reflective surface, a cavity and a ceiling incorporating at least 25 mm insulation and a reflective top (aluminium foil, for instance)

14   in all other cases a massive roof should be used, with a time-lag of hours or more (see 3.3.2, Figure 43 and appendix 6)

External features

15   when indicator A2 is one or more, space for out-door sleeping has to be provided. More often this will be on the roof, in which case the roof finish should be selected to withstand foot traffic

16   with heavy rainfall (H3) occurring even in one month of the year, special provisions for roof drainage will be necessary. Stagnant pools must be avoided (e.g. level gutters) as these will provide breeding grounds for mosquitoes. In low cost building spouts at roof level or eaves discharge is acceptable if the foot of the walls is surrounded by a concrete path or apron 0·5 m wide, sloping away from the building

8.3.4 Shading devices

The required shading performance has been specified (8.2.12) in terms of shadow angles or shading masks, thus there is no great difficulty in designing the actual elements, the shading devices.

These can be classified into four main categories:

a   a single overhang, canopy or awning
b   multiple horizontal devices: louvre blades
c   multiple vertical devices: louvres or fins
d   egg-crate devices, e.g. grille blocks

The information necessary for their design has been given in 4.2.13 and Figures 60 to 63. There will, however, be a number of factors influencing the design of these devices, other than their shading performance. Construction, materials and cost are some of the most obvious such factors, but there are others depending on the design intent, such as:

1   the options may be to use vertical or horizontal louvres. The former would obstruct all views except to one side at a very acute angle; the latter would permit a view of the ground up to the horizon. Is this view of any value? − a question of intent

2   a single canopy may provide the required shading, but the use of a grille-block screen, giving a similar performance, may serve other purposes at the same time, such as visual definition of a space (a space enclosing element), burglar-proofing and it may also give a better control of day-lighting

Some forms of building construction lend themselves to certain types of devices, such as:

a   if there are projecting columns, it would be quite easy to fit horizontal devices between these columns, whilst the fitting of any other kind of device may create

b if the roof is a reinforced concrete slab, with eaves projecting about 0·5 m, and the window is placed high, with its head at ceiling level, a slight extension of the roof slab may solve the shading problem. Constructionally advantageous, but the view may be lost and may adversely affect air movement (see 4.3.13).

The device must satisfy the established requirements. Which of the possible alternative combinations of shadow angles will be chosen and how the shading requirements will be satisfied, is up to the designer's discretion.

8.3.5
Walls and
roofs

The desirable thermal performance of walls and roofs should by now be specified, either in the forward analysis stage (at least in broad terms, e.g. by using Mahoney table 3, items **12** to **15**, as described in 8.1.11), or in the development stage, as discussed in 8.2.8 and 9. If not, or if a recheck is felt to be necessary, Mahoney table 4 above would also establish the required performance.

When the performance is specified in terms of a U-value and a time-lag value, the selection of the actual material (or materials) and construction must follow. This is clearly a task for the element design stage.

Transmittances or U-values could be calculated quite readily for any composite construction, following the method described in 3.1.10 and 11. The basic data necessary for this, such as conductivities (k-values) of materials, resistance of cavities and surfaces, can be found in appendix 5. Appendix 5.4, however, also gives the U-value itself for a whole range of most frequently used constructional elements.

Definition of the time-lag for a homogeneous constructional element is quite simple – it can be read off directly from the graph given in Figure 43. Calculation of the time-lag for a multilayer composite element is, however, a lengthy and complicated task. The practitioner would normally rely on published data, such as that given in appendix 6. The following may give some guidance.

8.3.6
Long time-lag
constructions

Some examples of constructions which would give a long time-lag performance are listed below.

Walls

Requirement: U-value = less than 2 W/m² degC
time-lag = more than 8 hours

1 absorbance: max. 0·50
300 mm adobe, mud bricks or soil-cement blocks
2 absorbance: max. 0·50
100 mm hollow or lightweight blocks, cavity of min. 25 mm +100 mm solid concrete blocks
3 absorbance: max. 0·65
any sheet material, cavity of min 25 mm +200 mm solid concrete blocks
4 absorbance: max. 0·75
any sheet material, 25 mm expanded polystyrene +100 mm solid concrete blocks

Roofs

Requirement: U-value = less than 0·85 W/m² degC
time-lag = more than 8 hours

1 75 mm 'solar slab' (concrete tile, with 75 mm cavity under) + two layers asphalt + 50 mm vermiculite-cement screed + 100 mm reinforced concrete slab
2 50 mm white chippings on bituminous felt + 40 mm expanded polystyrene +100 mm reinforced concrete slab
3 corrugated aluminium sheet +narrow cavity +40 mm expanded polystyrene +50 mm reinforced concrete slab

8.3.7
Openings

Already in the forward analysis stage (Mahoney table 3, in 8.1.10) some broad recommendations for openings have been made. In the development stage more precise specifications have been laid down (8.2). In the element design stage Mahoney table 4 gave another opportunity to check or supplement earlier recommendations. Now, when it comes to the actual design of the opening as a building element, several of the separately established criteria must be brought together:

size
orientation and position
closing elements (sashes, shutters, glazing, etc.)
associated shading devices
insect or fly screens
security devices, e.g. burglar-bars

All these attributes and components mutually affect each other. The opening, together with its control devices as a complete unit, must satisfy requirements of:

ventilation and air movement
closure for exclusion of air at times
daylight admission and glare control
solar heat exclusion
insect, pest and burglar proofing
view and visual effects

Of all elements, openings give perhaps the most complicated and difficult design task. Careful consideration and weighting of the above requirements is necessary before one can proceed. Climatic factors will dictate which of the requirements is the most important. The opening can then be designed in these terms. When all other factors are also satisfied (e.g. louvres, insect screens and burglar-bars are added) the designer must check back to see if the original requirement (for instance, for air movement) is still adequately provided for. Some adjustment (such as an increase in size to allow for partial obstruction) may be necessary.

The dependence of daylighting on climatic conditions has been discussed in 5.2.2 and 5.2.6 to 8. When this is considered together with, perhaps, ventilation requirements, some interesting points emerge.

In moderate climates the light admitting area would need to be larger than the area needed for ventilation. The solution is a fully glazed window, with some fixed glass panes and some (not all) of the window openable. In the tropics, particularly in composite climates, the reverse is true. A much larger opening is necessary for ventilation than for daylighting. The solution will be a large opening, fully openable: some of the closing devices being glazed sashes; others solid, opaque shutters.

The best — and most original solutions might be achieved through the application of the principle of 'separation of functions'. Instead of trying to design a window that fulfils the above six functions, one might provide four sets of openings: one for daylight, a second for view, a third for air movement and, if needed, a fourth for ventilation. All four would require protection against direct solar radiation, burglars and insects.

Separation of functions of this kind would end the long reign of that 'jack of all trades' the conventional window. It might become an important step towards a new — and essentially tropical vocabulary of architecture.

The membrane that separates an indoor space from the outside world in the hot dry tropics would then consist of four elements.

1   a heavy wall area of appropriate heat capacity,
2   heavily shuttered, burglar- and mosquito-proofed openings near walls and ceiling for night-time cooling,
3   a translucent wall area (for day-lighting made of hollow glass bricks or a light-transmitting foamed plastic, and
4   a small viewing frame (double or treble glazed and protected from direct sunlight) that could be carefully shaped and positioned to give the best visual link to the outside world.

A fifth element would not necessarily form part of the outside membrane. It would be a set of controllable openings connecting to a vertical shaft for day-time ventilation.

In the hot/dry tropics, element 1 would be the largest in surface area. In warm/humid regions, element 2 would be larger and the fifth element could be dispensed with entirely.

8.3.8 Consistency

Consistency of detailing is an age old principle of architecture. Every single detail should be designed in the light of the total solution, every single detail should reflect the overall design intent.

If this is true in general terms, it is even more so in terms of climatic design. It implies not only a formal consistency, but a consistency in function. However good and climatically apt the overall solution, bad and ill thought-out details can spoil the performance of the building. If for some reason (external constraints, for instance) the overall scheme is climatically less than perfect, good detailing can make it work: if not creating comfort, at least ameliorating discomfort conditions.

The ideal case, of course, is when both the overall concept and the details are formulated with the same aim in mind: the creation of comfortable conditions for humans and their activities.

8.4.1
Models

The term 'model' is used here in a generic sense, meaning the representation of one system by another, which is analogous with it from the given point of view.
    In this sense we can speak of:

a   *drawings*, being two-dimensional representations of three-dimensional objects
b   *physical models*, reduced size reproductions of objects, for a specific purpose, which may be representative:

visually
structurally
for air-flow studies
for lighting studies, etc.

c   *analogues*, e.g. electrical or hydraulic heat flow analogues, or a string analogue of a movement pattern. Analogue computers fall into this category
d   *mathematical models* representing any system. These may be used with or without the aid of computers

8.4.2
Design tools and checking tools

From the point of view of use, such models fall into two broad categories:

1   *design tools*, where no assumptions or hypotheses are needed, but the product or solution is arrived at through analysis, using the model — i.e. 'forward analysis'. System optimisation methods and algorithms are design tools
2   *checking tools*, where it is necessary to assume a design hypothesis, which is then represented by a model and tested, leading to possible modifications — i.e. 'backward analysis'. Many familiar trial and error methods and the less familiar iterative computer programs fall into this category

In many instances the same tool may be used for checking in one step and as a design tool in another step.

8.4.3
Drawings

Besides being the most general communication medium in architecture and building, drawings are often used by the designer as design aids. Most frequently the designer would use a drawing (be it a sketch or an instrumental drawing) to test or *check* an idea from the visual or constructional point of view. It would help him to answer the questions: 'How would it look?' or 'How does it work?'

Less frequently, but especially at the detail design stage, the drawing can be a positive design tool. If the already decided plan and elements are drawn up, it may help in showing all the constraints of the detail problem and thus generate a solution in the 'forward analysis' sense.

Rarely can drawings be used specifically for the purposes of climatic design, although at times sketches may help in clear thinking. Drawings are the most typical tools used in the synthesis.

8.4.4
Wind tunnel

Physical models and maquettes are often used for checking or presenting a scheme in the visual sense. If the scale is suitable, the same model can be tested in the wind tunnel (see 4.3.7 and Figure 70) to examine the *air flow around buildings*.

It is, however, advisable to carry out such testing at an early stage, before finalising the scheme on less elaborate, perhaps only rough block, models. Physical models are checking tools and the test results may lead to modifications, which may change basic features, such as volumes, shapes and disposition of buildings. Indeed they may be tools in decision making and in selecting one of several possible solutions. A variable model would allow the examination of alternatives.

The need for such testing arises especially in case of larger developments or schemes involving groups of buildings. It may be useful to test even a single building, from two points-of-view:

a how upwind objects affect the air flow reaching the proposed building
b how the proposed building affects the existing environment in the downwind direction

It is, of course, necessary to represent on the model not only the building being designed, but all the surrounding buildings and topographical features already existing.

Another subject of testing may be the *air flow through a particular space*. This requires a model not only larger in scale, but also giving a true representation of openings and objects within the space.

For both purposes the testing itself can take three forms:

1 visualisation of air flow patterns, using smoke traces. Smoke can be generated by an oil burner with CO_2 pressurisation, by titanium tetrachloride* or by incense burning ('Joss-sticks')
2 measurement of pressure distribution, normally using miniature Pitot-tubes† as sensors, connected to a sensitive manometer
3 measurement of air velocity at various points. Small hot-wire anemometers, linked to a potentiometer, are the most useful instruments. Absolute values of velocities at various points should be expressed as 'velocity ratios', relating each reading to the 'free air speed'

The wind tunnel is a very useful design aid and can be classified as a checking tool. Its importance is increased by the fact that mathematical models are only available for the prediction of air flow patterns and velocity distribution in relatively simple situations. For testing complex situations the wind tunnel is the only available tool.

---

* Titanium tetrachloride is a rather expensive chemical (a liquid); it can only be used in small quantities and not for longer runs of testing as the fumes given off are throat and nose irritants.
† Pitot-tube: a long tube with an 'L'-shaped head. It measures dynamic pressure due to air movement, over and above the static atmospheric pressure. Also used on aeroplanes as air-speed meter.

**8.4.5
Solarscope**

For the prediction of insolation and shading the stereographic sun-path diagrams (solar charts) and the associated protractor and overlays give a comprehensive and easy to use set of design aids (see 4.2.10, 8.2.12 and appendix 8). These can also be considered as 'models', representing the sun–building relationship in graphic form. They can be used as checking tools for a proposed solution, but are primarily intended as design tools.

A number of devices have been constructed to simulate the sun–building relationship and to facilitate insolation and shading studies on models. They may be used for several purposes:

a as a final check on the model of a completed scheme
b in case of a complex scheme, where only a few salient points have been determined analytically (to determine all details for all eventualities would have been too lengthy), to examine the behaviour of the whole complex and of the postulated details
c as a teaching tool, or helping to visualise the sun–building relationship, requiring a lesser degree of abstraction than the graphic methods

The sun-dial is a very simple and inexpensive tool (Figure 174). If it is attached to the model, the model can be turned and tilted until the dial shows the required date and time. Any light source can be used. Best results are obtained with sunlight out-of-doors.

Fig 174
The sun-dial

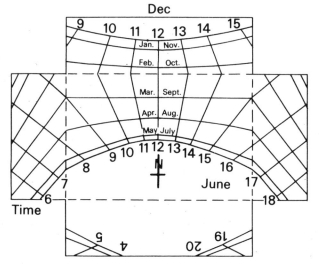

Fold and paste inside matchbox. Fix a 14 mm high stick at the 'N' -point; orientate to north point of model. Turn and tilt model and dial until tip of the shadow of the stick is at the required date and hour.

Fig 175
The heliodon

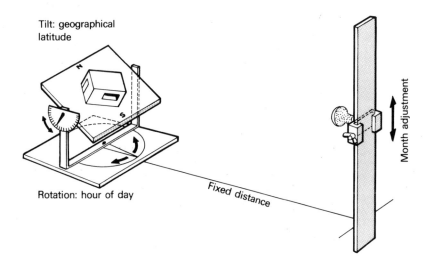

The heliodon (Figure 175) has a tilting and rotating model-table (latitude and hour adjustments respectively) also a lamp sliding up and down on a vertical rail at some distance away (time of year adjustment). *Advantage:* simple, inexpensive. *Disadvantage:* small table, model must be fixed as it will be tilted, difficult to visualise the relative position of sun and building.

Fig 176
The solarscope 'A'
(Developed by
Commonwealth
Experimental Building
Station, Sydney,
Australia)

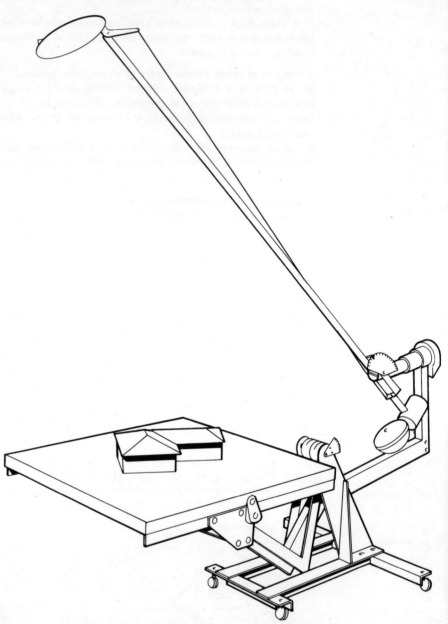

The solarscope 'A' (Figure 176) has a horizontal table and a lamp (or mirror) mounted at the end of a long arm, which has a three-way movement (for month, hour and latitude adjustment). *Advantage:* table remains level, can accommodate larger models, pieces can be left loose for adjustment. *Disadvantage:* precision engineering product, expensive, latitude adjustment limited.

The solarscope 'B' (Figure 177) has a three-quarter circle large radius rail, giving the sun-path, with a tilting (latitude) and parallel (time of year) movement, on which a lamp travels, giving the hour of day adjustment. *Advantage:* as above, plus the full sun-path is always indicated by the rail itself thus easier to understand. The

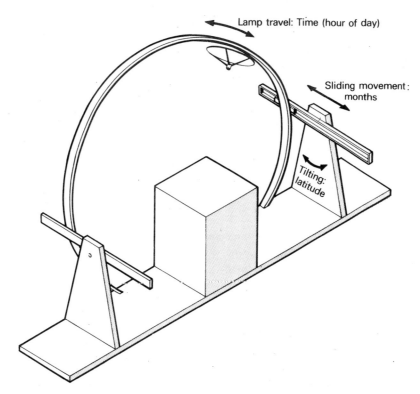

Fig 177
Arrangement diagram,
solarscope 'B'
(Developed by S V
Szokolay at the
Polytechnic of
Central London)

best for teaching purposes. *Disadvantage:* requires a large space, massive structure and rather expensive.

In any of these machines a visual model of a whole group of buildings can be tested to predict the duration and extent of shading of out-door spaces by buildings and of buildings by each other. A larger scale mock-up of a single window with part of the room it belongs to, can be best used for examining the performance of a shading device. It can be used to assist decision making in selecting one of several possible devices. With loose pieces it may be used as a positive design tool, to determine the optimum shape and position of a device.

8.4.6 Artificial sky

Artificial skies are used for model studies of daylighting. Two basic varieties, the hemispherical and the rectangular-mirrored types, have been described in 5.3.14 and shown in Figure 108. The purpose and method of use has also been explained. They are basically checking tools, as a model must be built first to an assumed hypothesis. Models with variable components can be used to optimise a choice between various possible solutions.

The daylighting protractor (5.3.4 and Figure 99) is a graphic analogue and can be used to predict the sky component of daylight factor on the basis of drawings (two-dimensional models) only. It is also a checking tool, as a design must be assumed before it can be used.

The 'pepper-pot' diagram (5.3.10 and Figure 103) is also a graphic analogue, but it can be used as a positive design tool.

The two graphic analogues give satisfactory results for typical and simple situations. Model tests can be relied on for complicated and unusual situations.

Artificial skies and the graphic analogues give results valid under overcast sky conditions or to predict the diffuse component of clear sky illumination (5.3.11). Direct sunlighting can be studied in models using the solarscope and the diffuse component measured in the artificial sky. No simple techniques have yet been established; the method is a research tool rather than a design aid.

A graphic analogue which has some limited usefulness for the prediction of sun plus clear sky illumination is the nomogram given in Figure 105 (5.3.11).

8.4.7
Heat flow
analogues

Heat flow through an element or through the entire building envelope under steady state conditions can be described quite simply by mathematical models. However, when the temperature is changing on one or two sides, the mathematical model becomes very complex and cumbersome in use. The problem lends itself to analogue simulation.

In the *electrical analogue* the indoor–out-door temperature difference is represented by a potential difference between two poles. The thermal resistance of surfaces and layers of materials is represented by electrical resistances. Thermal capacity of various elements are simulated by capacitors. Using plug-in resistor and capacitor elements on a plugboard base the thermal system of a complete building can be read by voltmeters, heat flow quantities measured by ammeters and a suitable time-scale can be established to measure the passage of temperature waves. This is basically a checking tool, but the elements being readily variable, the behaviour of a number of combinations can be examined which can assist in decision making.

In the *hydraulic analogue* the temperature difference is simulated by water level (thus pressure difference) in two vertical tubes. Connecting tubes of various narrow diameters (connected in line) represent the thermal resistance of surfaces and layers of materials. Parallel chains represent several elements. Vertical glass tube containers simulate the thermal capacities of layers of materials. The level of water in each tube gives the local temperature. The amount of water flowing through gives the heat flow quantity.

The assembly and rearrangement of tubes is rather cumbersome and no-one (to our knowledge) has yet produced a representation of a complete building. It is quite useful, however, for the representation of the thermal behaviour of a single element. It is a demonstration tool rather than a design aid.

8.4.8
Computers

A number of programs are available for heat flow studies by digital computers. Their number is constantly increasing; more and more new programs are being developed by research workers. Generally, if a system is described by mathematical models or graphic-geometrical analogues, there is no reason why the calculation could not be computerised.

Programs exist for heat flow calculations and for daylight prediction. Solar charts and shading device design have been computerised. All these constitute checking tools, used for backward analysis. After a solution has been postulated, its performance will be predicted by the computer.

The improvement of input–output devices, i.e. of the man-machine interaction (such as the 'sketch-pad', a cathode-ray tube screen, with light pen', facilitated a new family of programs of the INTUVAL type (intuition-evaluation). A solution is generated 'intuitively' and the computer prints out, or projects on the screen, a whole range of consequences, helping its 'evaluation'. The solution can then be immediately and easily modified, and the adjusted figures on the screen will show the consequences almost instantaneously. Thus the computer becomes a powerful design tool.

Programs have also been constructed on the basis of optimisation algorithms, e.g. for the planning of complex buildings such as hospitals. These not only check postulated hypotheses, but actually generate solutions. Their shortcoming at present is that the solution will be optimised in terms of one or a very few criteria. In one example a plan arrangement is produced, minimising the length of movements. It appears that subproblems can be solved, and subsystems can be optimised by such programs, but the synthesis is still left to the designer.

8.4.9
Computerised
Mahoney
tables

The Mahoney tables and their use have been fully described in 8.1.5 *et seq.* The method has a clear-cut logic, which lends itself to computer application. A program has been prepared and is in use.

The data input is only that contained in table 1, under temperature, humidity and rainfall. The program establishes the preferred comfort range, carries out a diagnosis, ascertains the indicators and translates this into recommended specifications. The last of these is produced as output.

Limitations of the method are those of the Mahoney tables, as discussed in 8.1.12. However, as the computer can produce the results very quickly, the method can be used for two further purposes over and above being a design tool:

1 for establishing climatic design zones: – not in terms of climate characteristics, but according to the actual design recommendations. This is done by processing meteorological data from a large number of locations in the region or country

2 for educational purposes: with its fast operation the program lends itself to conversational computing, which makes it possible to demonstrate how the variation and duration of climatic conditions creates a need for different solutions and different building forms

**8.4.10
Further
developments**

Computer methods now available tend to be either very specific, only dealing with narrow subproblems, or, if more comprehensive, they tend to remain at the level of broad generalisation. Future development is expected in the direction of combining both types.

On the one hand a method such as the Mahoney tables could provide a quick (however sketchy) forward analysis, establishing the broad parameters. On the other hand, based on these broad parameters, many possible solutions could be generated, almost intuitively, which could then be evaluated using rapid backward analysis routines. This way the road towards a comprehensive climatic design program could be opened up, from basic climate analysis right through to detail design.

1 KENDREW, W G. *Climatology*. Clarendon Press, 1957.

2 SUTTON, O G. *Understanding weather*. Penguin Books, 1962.

3 FLOHN, H. *Climate and weather*. World University Library, Weidenfeld and Nicolson, 1969.

4 LEE, D H K. *Physiological objectives in hot weather housing*. Washington, D.C., 1953.

5 BANHAM, REYNER. *The architecture of the well-tempered environment*. Architectural Press, 1969.

6 ATKINSON, G A. *Tropical architecture and building standards*. Conference on tropical architecture, 1953. Report of proceedings, 1954.

7 METEOROLOGICAL OFFICE (Air Ministry). *Tables of temperature, relative humidity and precipitation for the world*. 6 vols. HMSO, 1958.

8 LANDSBERG, H E. 'Microclimatic research, in relation to building construction'. *The Arch. Forum*, **86**, No. 3, March 1947, 114–119.

9 KOENIGSBERGER, O, MILLAR, J S and COSTOPOLOUS, J. 'Window and ventilator openings in warm and humid climates'. *Arch. Sc. Rev.*, **2**, No. 2, 1959, 82–96.

10 *An index of exposure to driving rain*. BRS Digest 23 (second series).

11 CUNLIFFE, D W and MUNCEY, R W. 'Thermal inertia effects on building air conditioning loads'. *Australian Refrig., Air-cond. and Heating*, May 1965, 18–28.

12 NATIONAL PHYSICS LABORATORY. *Changing to the metric system*. HMSO, 1967.

13 LANDSBERG, H E *et al. World maps of climatology*. Springer (Berlin), 1965.

14 PAGE, J K. *Climate and town planning, with special reference to tropical and sub-tropical climates*. BRS Overseas Building Notes, No. 52, June 1958.

15 ATKINSON, G A. 'An introduction to tropical building design'. *Architectural Design*, xxiii, Oct. 1953, 268.

16 GEIGER, R. *The climate near the ground*. Harvard University Press, 1957.

17 SEALEY, A. 'Local air flow and building'. *A.J.*, **142**, Oct. 1965, 983.

18 SHELLARD, H C. 'Microclimate and housing. 1: Topographical effects'. *A.J.*, **141**, Jan. 1965, 22.

19 CROWDEN, C P. *Indoor climate and thermal comfort in the tropics*. Conference on tropical architecture, 1953. Report of proceedings, 1954, 27.

20 FOX, R H. *Thermal comfort in industry*. Ergonomics for industry, No. 8. Ministry of Technology, 1965.

21 BEDFORD, T. *Environmental warmth and its measurement*. Medical Research Council, War Memorandum No. 17. HMSO, 1940/1961.

22 EDHOLM, O G. *The biology of work*. World University Library, Weidenfeld and Nicolson, 1967.

23 GIVONI, B. *Man, climate and architecture*. Elsevier, 1969.

24 BASSETT, C R and PRITCHARD, M D W. *Environmental physics: heating*. Longmans, 1968.

25 VAN STRAATEN, J F. *Thermal performance of buildings*. Elsevier, 1967.

26 OLGYAY, V. *Design with climate*. Princeton University Press, 1963.

27 HUNTINGDON, E. *Civilisation and climate*. Yale University Press, 1948.

28 A lecture by DR. THOMPSON to the Department of Tropical Studies, Architectural Association, 1963.

29 BEDFORD, T. *Warmth factor in comfort at work*. Medical Research Council, Industrial Health Research Board, Report No. 76. HMSO, 1936.

30 WINSLOW, C E A, HERRINGTON, L P and GAGGE, A P. 'Physiological reactions to environmental temperature'. *American J. of Physiology*, **120**, 1937, 1–22.

31 WEBB, C G. *Ventilation in warm climates*. BRS Overseas Building Notes, No. 66, March 1960.

32 McARDLE, B *et al. Prediction of the physiological effect of warm and hot environments*. Medical Research Council, RNP 47/391.

33 BELDING, H S and HATCH, T F. 'Index for evaluating heat stress in terms of resulting physiological strain'. *American J. of Heating, Piping and Air Conditioning*, **27**, No. 8, Aug. 1955.

34 DRYSDALE, J W. *Physiological Study No.* 2. Technical Study 32. C'wealth Exp. Blg. Stn. (Sydney), 1950.

35 OLGYAY, V. *Bioclimatic approach to architecture.* Housing and home finance agency (US). Report on project 1-T-130.

36 GIVONI, B. *Estimation of the effect of climate on man: developing a new thermal index.* Technion (Haifa), 1963.

37 PAGE, J K. 'Human thermal comfort'. *A.J.*, **137**, June 1963, 1306.

38 BILLINGTON, N S. *Building physics: heat.* Pergamon Press, 1967.

39 BILLINGTON, N S. *Thermal properties of buildings.* Cleaver-Hume Press, 1952.

40 SZOKOLAY, S V. 'Heating and thermal insulation'. *A.J.* **147**, March 1968; also *A.J. Metric Handbook*, 117–27; (2nd edn.) 147–57.

41 *Condensation*, BRS Digest 110, Oct. 1969.

42 SZOKOLAY, S V. 'Condensation and moisture movement'. *A.J.* **149**, Feb. 1969, 523.

43 PRATT, A W and LACY, R E. *Measurement of the thermal diffusivities of some single-layer walls in buildings.* BRS Current Papers, Research Series 64; also *Intern. J. of Heat and Mass Transfer*, **9**, No. 4, 345–53.

44 PRATT, A W and WESTON, E T. *Thermal capacities of structures.* Building Research Congress, London, 1951.

45 KUBA, G K. 'Climatic effect on buildings in hot-arid areas'. Ph.D. Thesis, University of Khartoum, 1970.

46 MACKEY, C O and WRIGHT, L T.
    a 'Summer comfort . . .'. *American J. of Heating, Piping and Air Conditioning*, **14**, No. 12, Dec. 1942, 750–7.
    b 'Periodic heat flow, homogeneous walls and roofs'. *ibid.*, **16**, No. 9, Sept. 44, 546.
    c 'Periodic heat flow, composite walls and roofs'. *ibid.*, **18**, No. 6, June 46, 107.

47 DANTER, E. 'Periodic heat flow characteristics of simple walls and roofs'. *I.H.V.E. J.*, **28**, July 1960, 136–46.

48 BILLINGTON, N S and BECHER, P. 'Some two dimensional heat flow problems'. *I.H.V.E. J.*, **18**, 1950, 297–312.

49 BALL, E F. *A simple transient flow method of measuring thermal conductivity and diffusivity.* BRS Current Papers, Research Series 65; also in *Proc. of Inst. of Refrigeration*, Feb. 1967.

50 LEE, D H K. 'Proprioclimates of man and domestic animals'. in UNESCO *Climatology.* (reviews of research) Paris, 1958.

51 KINZEY and SHARP. *Environmental technologies in architecture.* Prentice-Hall, 1963.

52 THERLKELD, T L. *Thermal environment engineering.* Prentice-Hall, 1962.

53 NATIONAL BUILDING AGENCY. *The economic and environmental benefits of improved thermal insulation.* Report No. 91, 1967/69.

54 COWAN, H J. *An historical outline of architectural science.* Elsevier, 1966.

55 COWAN, H J. Editorial in *Arch. Sc. Rev.*, Nov. 1959.

56 OLGYAY, V and OLGYAY, A. *Solar control and shading devices.* Princeton University Press, 1957.

57 WESTON, E T. 'The indoor and outdoor environment'. *Arch. Sc. Rev.*, **2**, 1959, 144–56.

58 PETHERBRIDGE, P. *Transmission characteristics of window glasses and sun controls.* BRS Research Papers, 72, Oct. 1967; also in *Sunlight in Buildings; Proceedings of the CIE Conference*, Bowcentrum (Rotterdam), 1967, 183–98.

59 NICOL, J F. *Radiation transmission characteristics of louvre systems.* BRS Current Paper, Research Series 53; also in *Building Science*, **1**, 1966, 167–82.

60 BURT, W *et al. Windows and environment.* Pilkington Brothers, 1969.

61 PERSSON, R. *Flat glass technology.* Butterworths, 1969.

62 SMITH, E G. *The feasibility of using models for predetermining natural ventilation.* Texas Eng. Exp. Stn., Research Report No. 26, 1951.

63 GIVONI, B. *Basic study of ventilation problems in hot countries.* Bldg. Res. Stn., Haifa, 1962.

64 CAUDILL, W W, CRITES, S E and SMITH, E G. *Some general considerations in the natural ventilation of buildings.* Texas Eng. Exp. Stn., Research Report No. 22, 1951.

65 CAUDILL, W W and REED, B H. *Geometry of classrooms as related to lighting and natural ventilation.* Texas Eng. Exp. Stn., Research Report No. 36, 1952.

66 WISE, A F E, SEXTON, D E and LILLYWHITE, M S T. 'Urban planning research: studies of air flow around buildings'. *A.J.*, **141**, May 1965, 1185–9.

67 WESTON, E T. *Air movement in industrial buildings: effect of nearby buildings.* C'wealth Exp. Bldg. Stn. (Sydney), Special Report No. 19, 1956.

68 EVANS, B H. *Natural air flow around buildings.* Texas Eng. Exp. Stn., Research Report **277**
No. 59, 1957.
69 OAKLEY, D J. *Tropical houses.* Batsford, 1961.
69*a* DRUMMOND, A J. 'Radiation and thermal balance' in UNESCO *Climatology* (reviews of research). Paris, 1958.
70 HOPKINSON, R G. *Architectural physics: lighting.* HMSO, 1963.
71 LIGHTING INDUSTRY FEDERATION (formerly British Lighting Council). *Interior lighting design*, metric edition, 1969.
72 GREGORY, R L. *Eye and brain.* World University Library, Weidenfeld and Nicolson, 1966.
73 VAN HEEL, A C S and VELSEL, C H F. *What is light?* World University Library, Weidenfeld and Nicolson, 1968.
74 LYNES, J. *Principles of natural lighting.* Elsevier, 1969.
75 HOPKINSON, R G, PETHERBRIDGE, P and LONGMORE, J. *Daylighting.* Heinemann, 1966.
76 *Recommendations for lighting building interiors – the 'IES Code'.* Illuminating Engineering Society, 1968.
77 PETHERBRIDGE, P. *Natural lighting prediction . . . for tropical climates.* P-59.20, CIE (Bruxelles), 1959.
78 SZOKOLAY, S V. 'Design of buildings for equatorial highland climates'. Master's Thesis, University of Liverpool, 1968.
79 LONGMORE, J. *BRS Daylight protractors.* HMSO, 1968.
80 *Estimating daylight in buildings.* BRS Digests 41 and 42 (second series).
81 MUNSELL, A H. *A colour notation.* Munsell Color Co. (Baltimore), 1961 (11th edn.).
82 BRITISH STANDARDS INSTITUTION. *Colours for building and decorative paints.* BS 4800:1972.
83 LYNES, J. 'Building Environment Handbook'. *A.J.*, **148**, 16 Oct. 1968, *et seq.*
84 PLANT, C G H, LONGMORE, J and HOPKINSON, R G. 'A study of interior illumination due to skylight and reflected sunlight, under tropical conditions' in *Sunlight in Buildings Proceedings of the CIE Conference*, Newcastle. Bowzentrum (Rotterdam), 1967.
85 PLANT, C G H. *Research in environmental design: tropical daylight and sunlight project, final report, stage* 1. University College (London), 1967.
86 KAUFMAN, J (ed.), *IES Lighting handbook.* New York, 1966; also 'Recommended practice in daylighting'. *I.E.S. J.*, **57**, 1962, 517–57.
87 *Evaluation of Discomfort Glare: the IES glare index system for artificial lighting installations.* Technical Report No. 10, Illuminating Engineering Society, 1967.
88 PAIX, D. *The design of buildings for daylighting.* Com'wealth Exp. Bldg. Stn. (Sydney), Bulletin No. 7, 1962.
89 KITTLER, R. 'An historical review of . . . daylight research by means of models and artificial skies'. *CIE Proceedings,* 1959, vol. B, 319–34.
90 LAWRENCE, A. *Acoustics in building* (Australian Building Science series). Hodder and Stoughton, 1962.
91 ALDERSEY-WILLIAMS, A. 'Sound' (Building Environment Handbook, pt. 5). in *A.J.*, **149**, 1969: 22 Jan., 259–278; 29 Jan., 321–344; 5 Feb., 395–410; 12 Feb., 455–474.
92 PARKIN, P H and HUMPHREYS, H R. *Acoustics, noise and building.* Faber and Faber, 1958.
93 *Some common noise problems.* Com'wealth Exp. Bldg. Stn. (Sydney), Notes on the Science of Building, No. 80, 1964.
94 *Housing and urbanisation.* Scientific Council for Africa South of the Sahara (CCTA), Nairobi, 1959.
95 NATIONAL PHYSICS LABORATORY. *The control of noise.* HMSO, 1962.
96 DUNHAM, D. 'The courtyard house as a temperature regulator'. *The New Scientist*, **8**, 663–6.
97 KOENIGSBERGER, O and LYNN, R. *Roofs in the warm humid tropics.* Architectural Association, paper 1. Lund Humphreys, 1965.
98 SZOKOLAY, S V. *Report on some thermal problems in low cost housing.* University of East Africa (Nairobi), 1966 (duplicated).
99 DRYSDALE, J W. *Summertime temperatures in building.* Com'wealth. Exp. Bldg. Stn. (Sydney), Special Report No. 11, 1952.
100 HARDY, A C and O'SULLIVAN, P E. *Insolation and fenestration.* Research Report, University of Newcastle upon Tyne. Oriel Press, 1967.
101 ROYAL INSTITUTE OF BRITISH ARCHITECTS. 'Plan of Work', *Handbook of Architectural Practice and Management.* RIBA, 1968.
102 BROADBENT, G H and WARD, A. *Design method in architecture.* Architectural Association, paper 3. Lund Humphreys, 1969.

Section 10 Appendices

Appendix 1.1

Saturation-point humidities

°C	moisture content g/kg	density of dry air kg/m³	moisture content g/m³
−20	0·63	1·396	0·879
−15	1·01	1·368	1·381
−10	1·60	1·342	2·147
−5	2·47	1·317	3·253
0	3·78	1·293	4·887
5	5·40	1·270	6·858
10	7·63	1·248	9·522
15	10·6	1·226	12·995
16	11·4	1·222	13·930
17	12·1	1·217	14·727
18	12·9	1·213	15·648
19	13·8	1·209	16·684
20	14·7	1·205	17·713
21	15·6	1·201	18·736
22	16·6	1·197	19·870
23	17·7	1·193	21·116
24	18·8	1·189	22·353
25	20·0	1·185	23·700
26	21·4	1·181	25·273
27	22·6	1·177	26·600
28	24·0	1·173	28·152
29	25·6	1·169	29·962
30	27·2	1·165	31·688
35	36·6	1·146	41·943
40	48·8	1·128	55·046

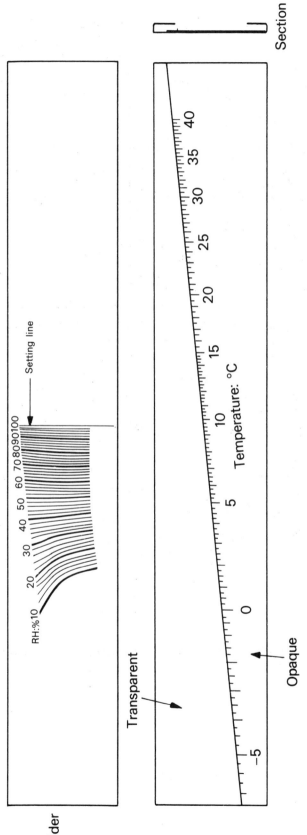

Section

Slider

Transparent

Setting line

RH:%10 20 30 40 50 60 70 80 90 100

Opaque

Temperature: °C

-5 0 5 10 15 20 25 30 35 40

To be used with whirling hygrometer. Adjust setting line against DBT (dry-bulb temperature). Select WBT (wet-bulb temperature) value; and, read against this on the slider the RH (relative humidity) percentage.

Solar radiation overlays

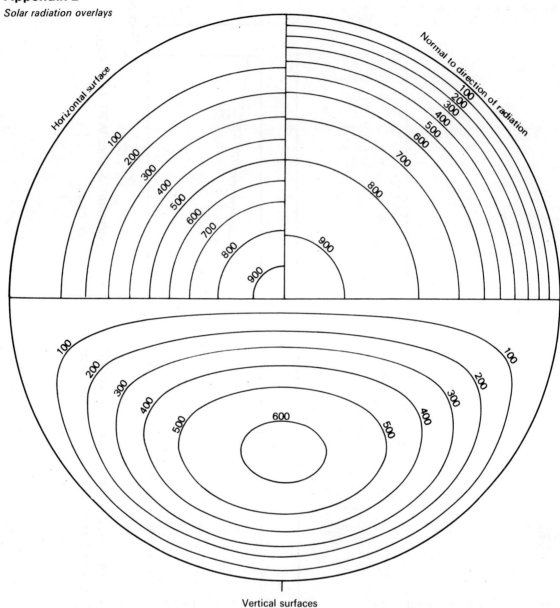

Intensity of direct solar radiation (in W/m²) – to be used as overlays with solar charts given in appendix 8.

Appendix 3

Estimating daily total radiation
incident on a horizontal plane on the basis of sunshine duration[*]

$$\frac{Q}{Q_s} = 0\cdot29 \cos\phi + 0\cdot52 \frac{n}{N}$$

where Q = radiation on horizontal plane, MJ/m²day
Q_s = same at upper limit of atmosphere (solar constant per day) MJ/m²day
n = number of hours of sunshine per day
N = possible sunshine hours per day
$0\cdot29$ = empirical constant, depending on transmission properties of the air mass
ϕ = geographical latitude

Q can be taken as a constant = 36 MJ/m²day

Example for Nairobi:

if $\phi = 0°$ $\cos\phi = 1$
$N = 12\cdot2$

$$\frac{Q}{36} = 0\cdot29 + \frac{0\cdot52}{12\cdot2} n$$

$Q = 10\cdot34 + 1\cdot53\, n$

then n should be obtained from meteorological records.

[*] Glover, J and McCulloch, J S G. 'The empirical relationship between solar radiation and hours of bright sunshine', *Q. J. of the Royal Meteorological Society*, **84**, 56.

Appendix 4

The Beaufort wind-force scale

force	observable effects	speed m/s
0	Complete calm, smoke rises straight vertically, lake surface smooth	up to 0·5
1	Slight movement, smoke slightly inclined	1·7
2	Slight breeze, leaves rustling	3·3
3	Slight wind, twigs moved, small ripples on water	5·2
4	Moderate wind, small branches moved	7·4
5	Strong wind, larger branches moved, booming noise, white crested waves	9·8
6	Very strong wind, leaves torn off, walking somewhat difficult	12·4
7	Storm, smaller tree trunks bent, twigs torn	15·2
8	Strong storm, branches may be torn, large branches bent	18·2
9	Very strong storm, smaller trees uprooted, roof tiles blow off, buildings damaged	21·5
10	Gale, heavy building damage, trees broken or uprooted	25·1
11	Gale, buildings destroyed, whole woods uprooted, men and animals may be lifted and carried	29·0
12	Gale, as above, but more so	above 29·0

Conductivity and resistivity of some materials

	conductivity k W/m degC	resistivity $1/k$ m degC/W
Asbestos: loose	0·034	29·40
sprayed	0·046	21·75
Asbestos cement sheet: light	0·216	4·63
average	0·360	2·78
dense	0·576	1·74
Asphalt	0·576	1·74
Brickwork commons: light	0·806	1·24
average	1·210	0·83
dense	1·470	0·68
in lightweight bricks	0·374	2·68
in engineering bricks	1·150	0·87
Concrete: ordinary, dense	1·440	0·69
clinker aggregate	0·403	2·48
expanded clay aggregate	0·345	2·90
foamed slag aggregate	0·245	4·08
Cork slab: natural	0·043	23·20
regranulated, baked	0·039	25·60
Eel grass blanket	0·043	23·20
Glass-wool: quilt	0·034	29·40
blanket	0·042	23·80
Mineral wool: felt	0·037	27·00
rigid slab	0·049	20·40
Onozote (expanded ebonite)	0·029	34·50
Plasterboard, gypsum	0·159	6·33
Plastering: gypsum	0·461	2·17
vermiculite	0·201	4·98
Plywood	0·138	7·25
Polystyrene foam slab	0·033	30·30
Rendering, sand-cement	0·532	1·88
Stone: granite	2·920	0·34
limestone	1·530	0·65
sandstone	1·295	0·77
Strawboard	0·093	10·75
Timber: softwood	0·138	7·25
hardwood	0·160	6·25
Wood chipboard	0·108	9·26
Wood fibre softboard	0·065	15·38
Wood wool slab: light	0·082	12·20
dense	0·115	8·70
Metals: lead	34	0·0294
cast-iron	50	0·0200
steel	58	0·0172
bronze	64	0·0156
zinc	110	0·0091
aluminium	220	0·0045
copper	350	0·0029
silver	407	0·0024
Air	0·026	38·45
Water	0·580	1·72

Appendix 5.2

Surface conductances and resistances

surface	conductance f W/m²degC	resistance $1/f$ m²degC/W
Internal surfaces (f_i):		
Walls	8·12	0·123
Floor, ceiling, heat flow up	9·48	0·105
Floor, ceiling, heat flow down	6·70	0·149
Underside of roof	9·48	0·105
External surfaces (f_o):		
Walls, South facing: sheltered	7·78	0·128
normal	10·00	0·100
severe exposure	13·18	0·076
Walls, West, Southwest, Southeast facing sheltered	10·00	0·100
normal	13·18	0·076
severe exposure	18·90	0·053
Walls, Northwest facing: sheltered	13·18	0·076
normal	18·90	0·053
severe exposure	31·50	0·032
Walls, North, Northeast, East, facing: sheltered	13·18	0·076
normal	18·90	0·053
severe exposure	81·20	0·012
Roofs: sheltered	14·20	0·070
normal	22·70	0·044
severe exposure	56·70	0·018

Appendix 5.3

Surface conductance as a function of wind speed

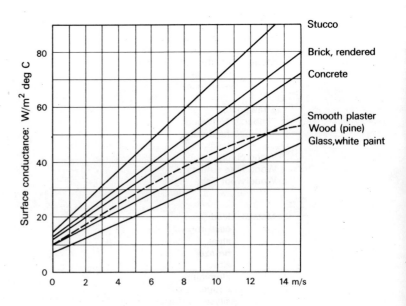

Transmittance (U-value) of some constructions (in W/m²degC)

Type of construction	

Walls

Brick:
solid, unplastered 114 mm	3·64
plastered both sides 114 mm	3·24
solid, unplastered 228 mm	2·67
plastered both sides 228 mm	2·44

Concrete, ordinary, dense:
152 mm	3·58
203 mm	3·18

Stone, medium, porous:
305 mm	2·84
457 mm	2·27

Brick, 280 mm cavity, fletton outer skin, commons inner, inside plastered	1·70

Brick with insulating boards, plastered:
25 mm corkboard	0·85
13 mm fibreboard	1·19
50 mm wood wool slab	0·85

Brick but 16 mm vermiculite plaster on inside	1·47

Brick but rigid boards on battens on inside:
13 mm asbestos board	1·19
13 mm fibreboard	0·95
50 mm strawboard, plastered	0·74

Brick but inner skin lightweight concrete blocks:
100 mm aerated concrete blocks	1·13
100 mm clinker concrete blocks	1·30

Concrete block, cavity, 250 mm (100 +50 +100), outside rendered, inside plastered:
aerated concrete blocks	1·19
clinker concrete blocks	1·08

Hollow concrete block, 228 mm, single skin, outside rendered, inside plastered:
aerated concrete blocks	1·70
clinker concrete blocks	1·59

Corrugated asbestos cement sheets on steel frame
Corrugated asbestos cement sheets on steel frame	6·53
+13 mm fibreboard	2·04
+50 mm straw or wood wool slab	1·19
+76 mm aerated concrete blocks	2·10

Roofs, pitched
Corrugated asbestos cement sheets	7·95
+13 mm timber boarding	2·16
+50 mm straw or wood wool slab	1·25
+25 mm quilt on 13 mm boarding	0·85

Corrugated iron sheets or tiles on battens	8·52
+plaster ceiling	3·18

Tiles or slates on boarding and felt with plaster ceiling	1·70

Aluminium deck, 13 mm fibreboard with two layers bituminous felt	2·16
Aluminium deck, 50 mm straw or wood wool slab	1·25

Roofs, flat
Reinforced concrete slab, 100 mm, screed 63–12 mm, 3 layers bituminous felt	3·35

As above – with insulation on the screed:
25 mm cork	1·08
50 mm straw or wood wool slab	1·13
two 12 mm fibreboards	1·25

As above – but lightweight screed (in lieu of normal):

Type of construction

127 mm to 76 mm aerated concrete	1·36
127 mm to 76 mm foamed slag concrete	1·47
Timber boarding, 25 mm on 178 mm joists with 3 layers bituminous felt, plaster ceiling	1·82
As above – with insulating slabs on boarding:	
25 mm cork	0·85
13 mm fibreboard	1·25
50 mm straw or wood wool slab	0·91

Floors

Concrete on ground or hardcore fill	1·13
+grano, terrazzo or tile finish	1·13
+wood block finish	0·85
Timber board on joists, underfloor space ventilated on one side	1·70
+parquet, lino or rubber finish	1·42
Timber board on joists, underfloor space ventilated on more sides	2·27
+parquet, lino or rubber finish	1·98
+25 mm fibreboard under boarding	1·08
+25 mm corkboard under boarding	0·95
+25 mm corkboard under joists	0·79
+50 mm strawboard under joists	0·85
+double sided aluminium foil, draped	1·42

Windows

Exposure South, sheltered:	single glazing	3·97
	double glazing, 6 mm space	2·67
	double glazing 20 mm space	2·32

South normal, West, Southwest, Southeast sheltered:

single glazing	4·48
double glazing, 6 mm space	2·90
double glazing, 20 mm space	2·50

South severe, West, Southwest, Southeast, normal or Northwest, North, Northeast, East sheltered:

single glazing	5·00
double glazing, 6 mm space	3·06
double glazing, 20 mm space	2·67

West, Southwest, Southeast severe, Northwest, North, Northeast, East normal:

single glazing	5·67
double glazing, 6 mm space	3·29
double glazing, 20 mm space	2·84

Exposure Northwest severe:	single glazing	6·47
	double glazing, 6 mm space	3·58
	double glazing, 20 mm space	3·00

Exposure North severe:	single glazing	7·38
	double glazing, 6 mm space	3·80
	double glazing, 20 mm space	3·18

Appendix 5.5

Conductance and resistance of cavities

cavity		conductance R_c W/m²degC	resistance $1/R_c$ m²degC/W
Vertical:	3 mm wide	14·50	0·069
	6 mm wide	8·74	0·114
	13 mm wide	7·04	0·142
	20 mm wide	6·63	0·151
	25 mm wide	6·52	0·153
	38 mm wide	6·52	0·153
Horizontal 76 mm:	heat flow up	7·48	0·133
	heat flow down	5·32	0·188
Values normally used in UK for:			
50 mm cavity		5·67	0·176
50 mm cavity, with aluminium foil		2·84	0·352

Appendix 5.6

Absorbance and emittance of surfaces

surface	absorbance for solar radiation	*a* and *e* 10 to 40 °C
Black, non-metallic	0·85–0·98	0·90–0·98
Red brick, stone, tile	0·65–0·80	0·85–0·95
Yellow and buff brick, stone	0·50–0·70	0·85–0·95
Cream brick, tile, plaster	0·30–0·50	0·40–0·60
Window glass	Transparent	0·90–0·95
Bright aluminium, gilt, bronze	0·30–0·50	0·40–0·60
Dull brass, aluminium, galvanised steel	0·40–0·65	0·20–0·30
Polished brass, copper	0·30–0·50	0·02–0·05
Polished aluminium, chromium	0·10–0·40	0·02–0·04

Appendix 6

Time-lag /φ − hours) and decrement factor (µ) of some constructions

thickness, mm	50		100		150		200		300	
	φ:h	µ	φ:h	µ	φ:h	µ	φ:h	µ	φ:h	µ
Concrete	1·3	0·67	3·0	0·45	4·4	0·30	6·1	0·20	9·2	0·09
Stabilised earth	—	—	2·4	0·48	4·0	0·34	5·2	0·24	8·1	0·12
Timber	2·5	0·48	5·4	0·23	8·3	0·11	—	—	—	—
Mineral wool	2·5	0·48	5·3	0·22	—	—	—	—	—	—

		φ:h	µ
Walls:	Cavity wall, two skins of 100 mm dense concrete blocks, both faces with 15 mm cement render	10·0	0·073
	Same, but with hollow concrete blocks	10·8	0·056
	Cavity wall, two skins of 100 mm hollow terracotta blocks, both faces with 15 mm cement render	8·7	0·100
Roofs:	100 mm reinforced concrete slab, bituminous asbestos felt finish, with 40 mm glass wool insulation *under* the slab	3·0	0·450
	Same, but insulation on top of the concrete slab	11·8	0·046
	240 mm hollow pot slab, underside rendered, 60 mm screed, bituminous asbestos felt membrane, 30 mm concrete paving slabs on 20 mm bedding	12·0	0·045

Appendix 7

Transmission characteristics of window glasses (per cent)

Type of glass			admitted	excluded
Ordinary 6 mm plate	$t =$	74	74	—
	$a =$	18	9	9
	$r =$	8	—	8
Totals		100	83	17
6 mm heat absorbing	$t =$	42	42	—
	$a =$	53	26	27
	$r =$	5	—	5
Totals		100	68	32
Double unit: heat absorbing outer, ordinary inner pane	$t =$	37	37	—
	$a =$	55	8	47
	$r =$	8	—	8
Totals		100	45	55
Single pane, ceramic coated	$t =$	26	26	—
	$a =$	56	15	41
	$r =$	18	—	18
Totals		100	41	59
Double unit, nickel coating on inside of outer pane	$t =$	25	25	—
	$a =$	52	13	39
	$r =$	23	—	23
Totals		100	38	62
Double unit, gold coating on inside of outer pane	$t =$	24	24	—
	$a =$	36	4	32
	$r =$	40	—	40
Totals		100	28	72

Changes with angle of incidence

Angle of incidence	Ordinary		Antisun		Calorex	
	t	a	t	a	t	a
0°	0·74	0·18	0·42	0·53	0·20	0·75
20°	0·73	0·19	0·41	0·54	0·19	0·76
40°	0·72	0·20	0·38	0·56	0·17	0·78
60°	0·65	0·21	0·32	0·58	0·13	0·78
70°	0·54	0·22	0·26	0·55	0·10	0·72
80°	0·32	0·20	0·14	0·45	0·05	0·55
85°	0·14	0·17	0·06	0·31	0·02	0·36
	t'	a'	t'	a'	t'	a'
Diffuse	0·67	0·20	0·34	0·55	0·15	0·75

Appendix 8

Solar charts (sun-path diagrams) for latitudes 0° to 44° north and south

The method of stereographic projection and use of the charts is explained in 4.2.10 to 14.

The shadow angle protractor to be used with these charts is attached inside the back cover.

For solar radiation overlays see appendix 2.

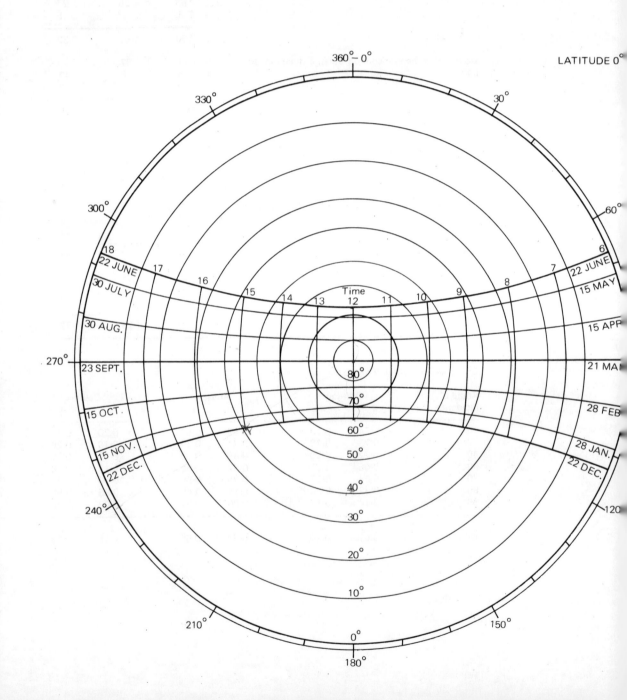

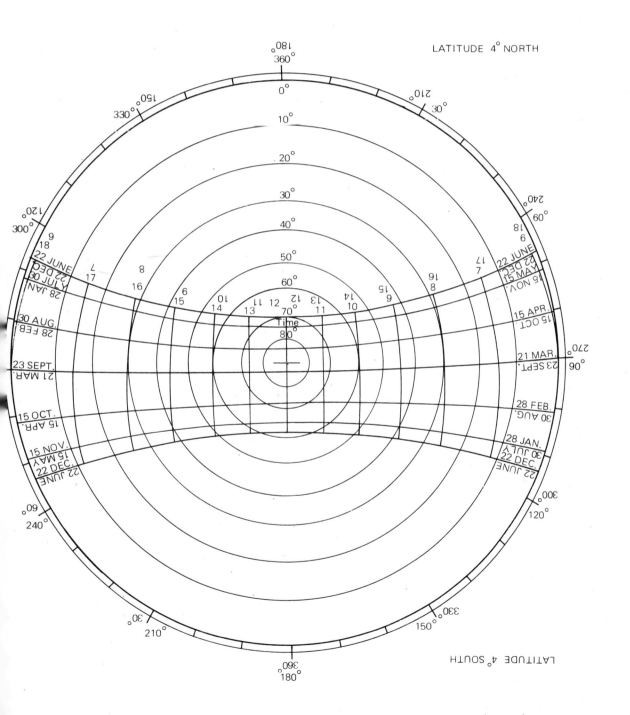

LATITUDE 4° NORTH

LATITUDE 4° SOUTH

294

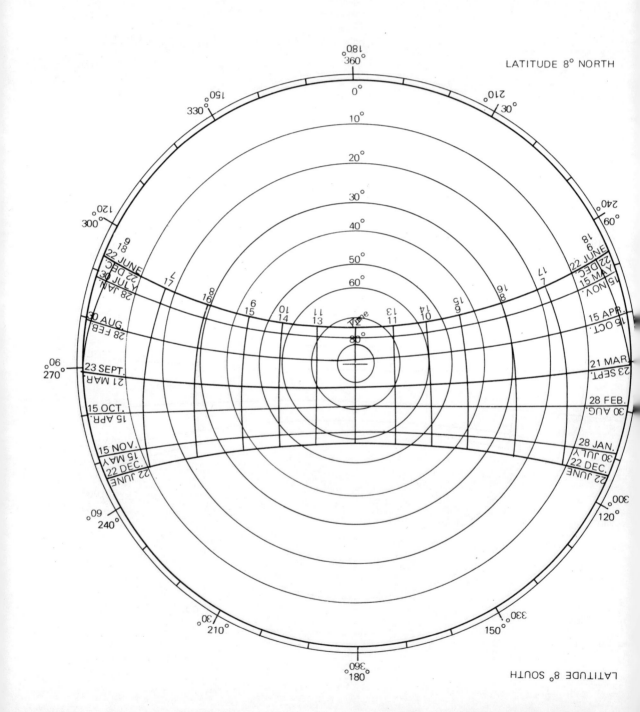

LATITUDE 8° NORTH

LATITUDE 8° SOUTH

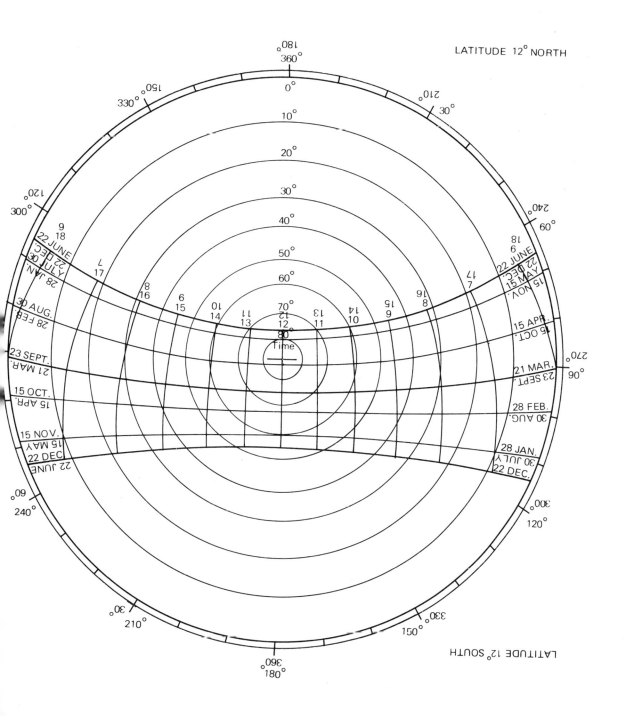

LATITUDE 12° NORTH

LATITUDE 12° SOUTH

296

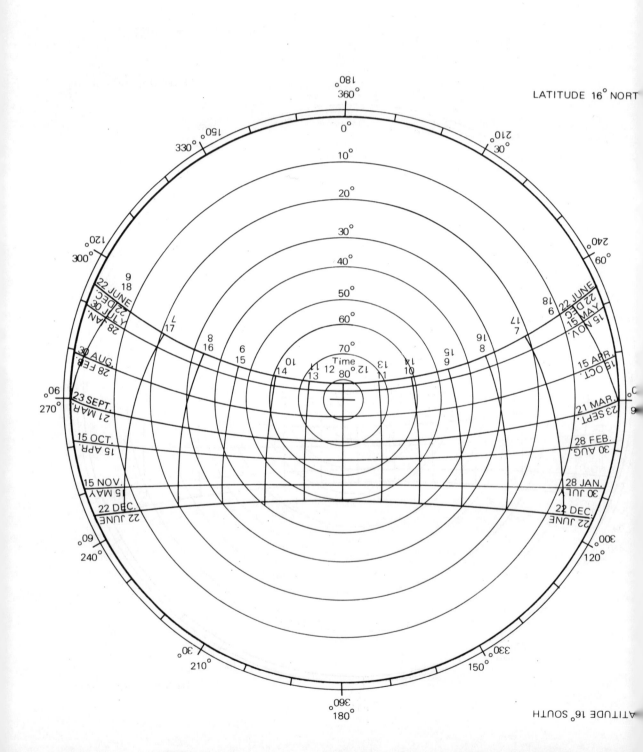

LATITUDE 16° NORTH

ATITUDE 16° SOUTH

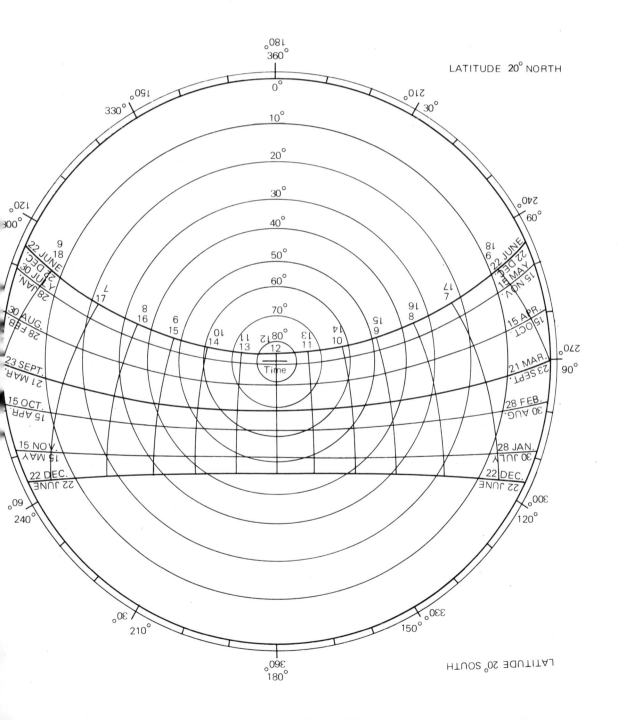

LATITUDE 20° NORTH

LATITUDE 20° SOUTH

298

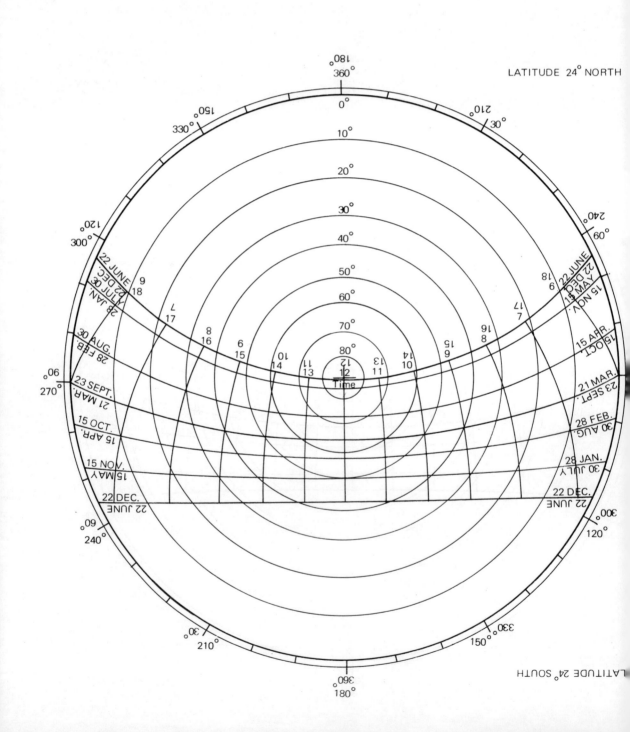

LATITUDE 24° NORTH

LATITUDE 24° SOUTH

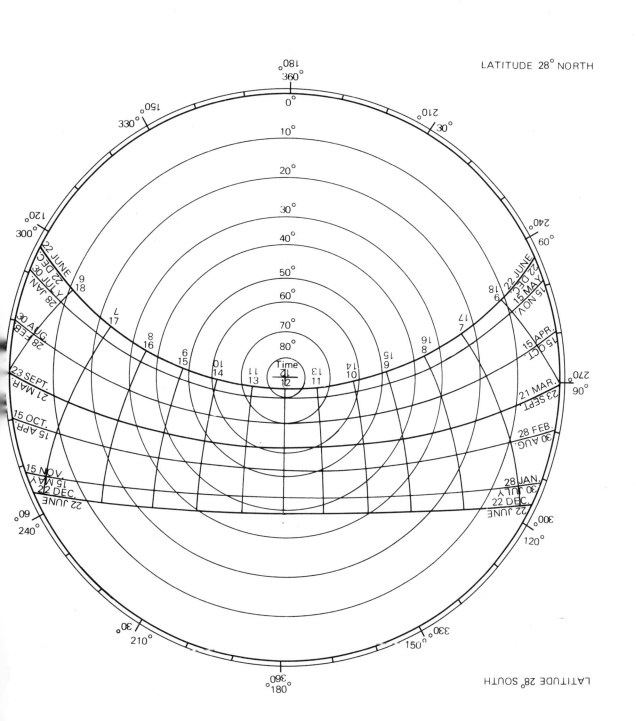

LATITUDE 28° NORTH

LATITUDE 28° SOUTH

300

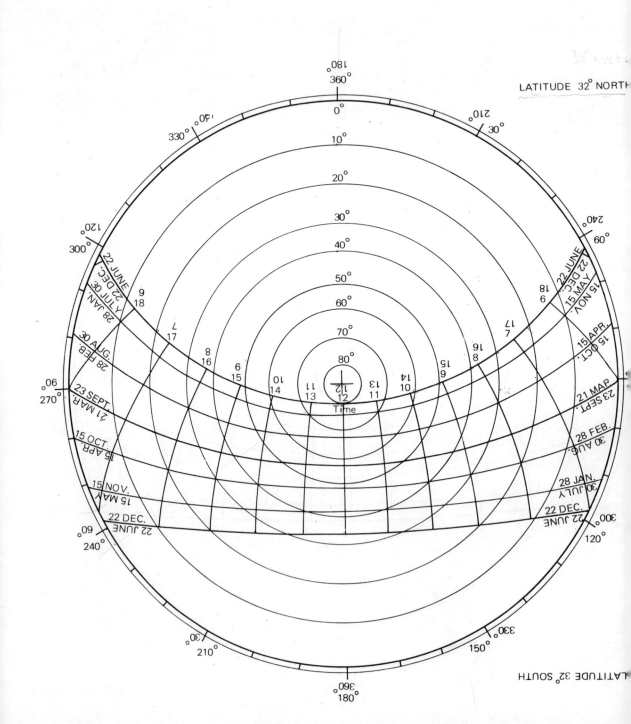

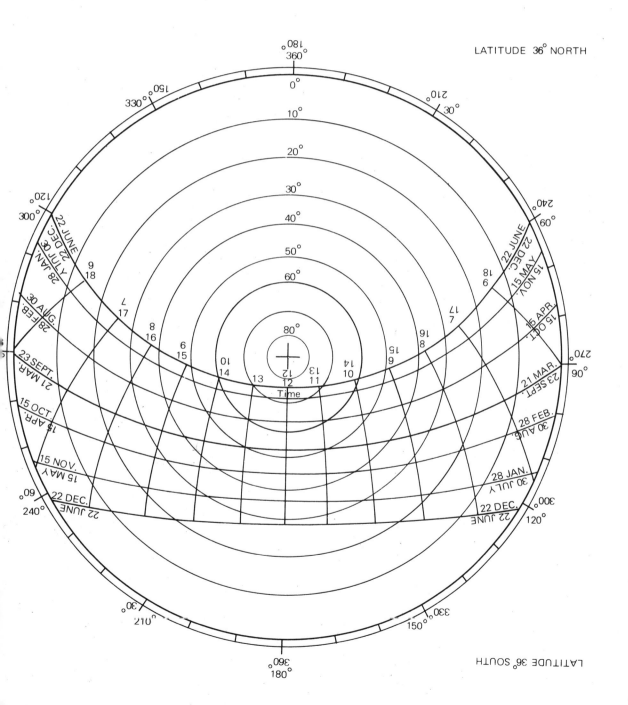

LATITUDE 36° NORTH

LATITUDE 36° SOUTH

302

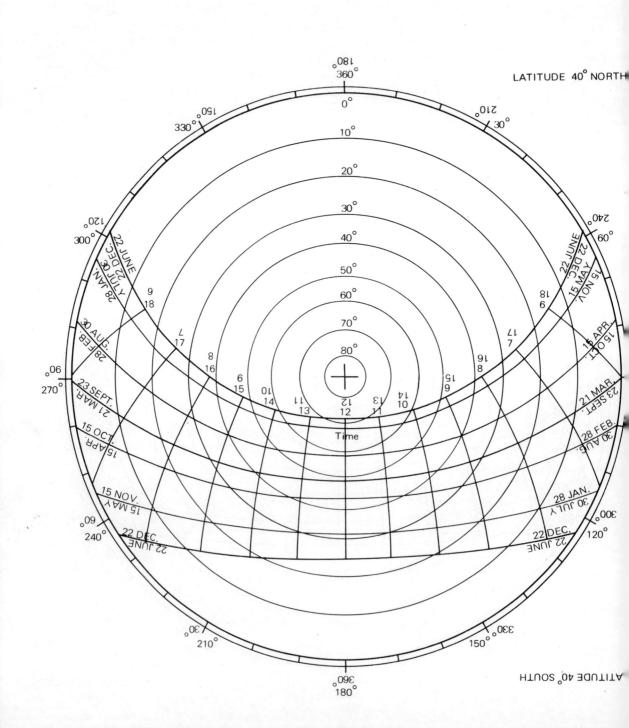

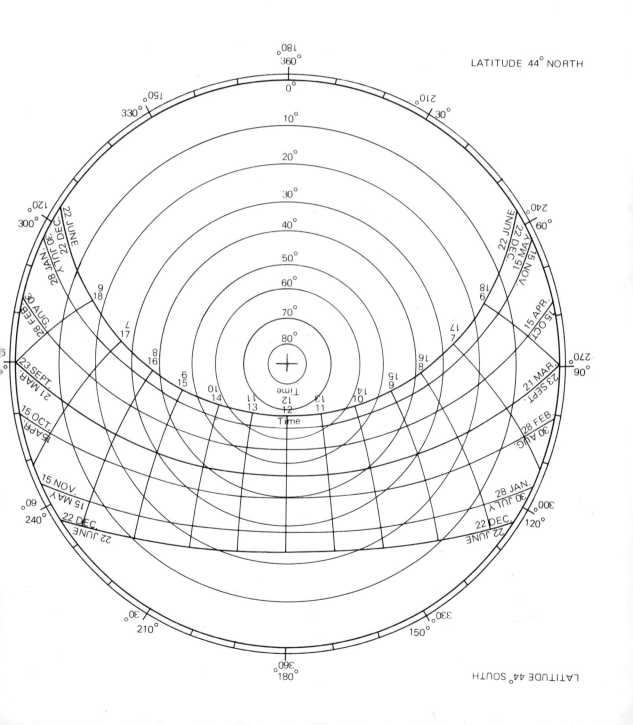

LATITUDE 44° NORTH

LATITUDE 44° SOUTH

Appendix 9.1

Recommended illumination and limiting glare index (based on IES Code, 1968)

visual task	illumination lux	glare index
Casual seeing	100	28
Rough task with large detail	200	25–28
Ordinary task, medium detail	400	25
Fairly severe task, small detail (e.g. drawing office, sewing)	600	19–22
Severe, prolonged task, small detail (e.g. fine assembly, hand tailoring)	900	16–22
Very severe, prolonged task, very small detail (e.g. gem cutting, hosiery mending, gauging very small parts)	1300–2000	13–16
Exceptionally severe task, with minute detail (e.g. watch and instrument making)	2000–3000	10

Appendix 9.2

Lamp lumen outputs

		watts	lumens
240 volt, standard incandescent lamps:		25	200
		40	325
		60	575
		100	1160
		150	1960
		200	2720
		300	4300
		500	7700
Tubular fluorescent lamps (warm white):	0·6 m	20	1050
		40	1550
	1·2 m	40	2650
	1·5 m	50	3100
		65	4400
		80	4850
	1·8 m	85	5550
	2·4 m	85	6400
		125	8300

Conversion factors for fluorescent lamps other than warm white

Daylight	0·95	Softone 27	0·55
Natural	0·75	Trucolor 37	0·55
Color matching	0·65	De lux natural	0·55
De luxe warm white	0·65	Artificial daylight	0·40
Colour 32 or 34	0·65		
Kolor-rite	0·65	Warmtone	0·70

Appendix 9.3

Minimum recommended daylight factors (based on BSCP* 3, chapter 1, part 1)

	%
Corridors	0·5
Entrance halls, lounges, stairs, churches, hospital wards	1
General offices, banks, reception areas, classrooms, surgeries, sports halls	2
Laboratories, pharmacies	3
Artists' studios	4

Homes:
living room	1%	over at least 8 m² and half the depth of room
bedroom	0·5%	over at least 6 m² and half the depth of room
kitchen	2%	over at least 5 m² or half the total floor area

381   * British Standard Code of Practice.

Acceptable noise levels (for general guidance only – in dBA)

Residential:	bedroom, private house	25
	bedroom, flat	30
	bedroom, hotel	35
	living room	40
Commercial:	private office	35–45
	bank	40–50
	conference room	40–45
	general office, shop, store	40–55
	restaurant	40–60
	cafeteria	50–60
Industrial:	precision workshop	40–60
	heavy workshop	60–90
	laboratory	40–50
Educational:	lecture room, classroom	30–40
	private study	20–35
	library	35–45
Health:	hospital, public ward	25–35
	hospital, private ward	20–25
	operating theatre	25–30
Auditoria:	concert hall	25–35
	church	35–40
	court room, conference room	40–45
	recording studio	20–25
	radio studio	20–30
	theatre for drama	30–40

Appendix 10.2

Transmission loss (TI) or sound reduction index of some common walls and floors (in dB)

frequency (Hz):	100	200	400	800	1 600	3 200	average
112 mm brick wall	31	36	38	50	55	60	45
225 mm brick wall	41	43	47	54	57	60	50
150 mm concrete wall	32	37	42	51	57	67	47
338 mm brick wall	42	45	48	54	62	61	52
130 mm concrete floor	32	36	40	45	55	62	45
130 mm floating scr'd	38	42	47	52	59	63	50
Wood joist floor, with tongue and groove boarding, plasterboard ceiling	14	23	34	39	45	45	34
As above, but floating boards	22	33	36	42	54	61	42
As above + 75 mm tock wool	23	35	41	47	53	59	43
Window, single	16	18	24	27	21	26	22
Double, 200 mm space sealed, abs reveals	26	33	41	44	46	37	39

Appendix 11

TABLE 1

Location	
Longitude	
Latitude	
Altitude	

Air temperature: °C

	J	F	M	A	M	J	J	A	S	O	N	D	High	AMT
Monthly mean max.														
Monthly mean min.														
Monthly mean range													Low	AMR

Relative humidity: %

	J	F	M	A	M	J	J	A	S	O	N	D
Monthly mean max. a.m.												
Monthly mean min. p.m.												
Average												
Humidity group												

Humidity group:	1	If average RH: below 30%
	2	30–50%
	3	50–70%
	4	above 70%

Rain and wind

	J	F	M	A	M	J	J	A	S	O	N	D		
Rainfall, mm														Total

	J	F	M	A	M	J	J	A	S	O	N	D
Wind, prevailing												
Wind, secondary												

Comfort limits	AMT over 20°C		AMT 15–20°C		AMT below 15°C	
Humidity group:	Day	Night	Day	Night	Day	Night
1	26–34	17–25	23–32	14–23	21–30	12–21
2	25–31	17–24	22–30	14–22	20–27	12–20
3	23–29	17–23	21–28	14–21	19–26	12–19
4	22–27	17–21	20–25	14–20	18–24	12–18

TABLE 2
Diagnosis: °C

	J	F	M	A	M	J	J	A	S	O	N	D
Monthly mean max.												
Day comfort: upper												
lower												
Monthly mean min.												
Night comfort: upper												
lower												
Thermal stress: day												
night												

AMT

Indicators

Humid:	H1		Totals
	H2		
	H3		
Arid:	A1		
	A2		
	A3		

Applicable when: Meaning:	Indicator	Thermal stress Day	Night	Rainfall	Humidity group	Monthly mean range
Air movement essential	H1	H			4	
		H			2, 3	Less than 10°
Air movement desirable	H2	O			4	
Rain protection necessary	H3			Over 200 mm		
Thermal capacity necessary	A1				1, 2, 3	More than 10°
Out-door sleeping desirable	A2		H		1, 2	
		H	O		1, 2	More than 10°
Protection from cold	A3	C				

Indicator totals from table 2					
H1	H2	H3	A1	A2	A3

TABLE 3
Recommended specifications

Layout

H1	H2	H3	A1	A2	A3	No.	Specification
			0–10			1	Orientation north and south (long axis east–west)
			11, 12	5–12			
				0–4		2	Compact courtyard planning

Spacing

H1	H2	H3	A1	A2	A3	No.	Specification
11, 12						3	Open spacing for breeze penetration
2–10						4	As 3, but protection from hot and cold wind
0, 1						5	Compact lay-out of estates

Air movement

H1	H2	H3	A1	A2	A3	No.	Specification
3–12						6	Rooms single banked, permanent provision for air movement
1, 2			0–5				
			▶12			7	Double banked rooms, temporary provision for air movement
0	2–12						
	0, 1					8	No air movement requirement

Openings

H1	H2	H3	A1	A2	A3	No.	Specification
			0, 1	0		9	Large openings, 40–80%
			11, 12	0, 1		10	Very small openings, 10–20%
Any other conditions						11	Medium openings, 20–40%

Walls

H1	H2	H3	A1	A2	A3	No.	Specification
			0–2			12	Light walls, short time-lag
			3–12			13	Heavy external and internal walls

Roofs

H1	H2	H3	A1	A2	A3	No.	Specification
			0–5			14	Light, insulated roofs
			6–12			15	Heavy roofs, over 8 h time-lag

Out-door sleeping

H1	H2	H3	A1	A2	A3	No.	Specification
				2–12		16	Space for out-door sleeping required

Rain protection

H1	H2	H3	A1	A2	A3	No.	Specification
		3–12				17	Protection from heavy rain necessary

Indicator totals from table 2					
H1	H2	H3	A1	A2	A3

TABLE 4

Detail recommendations

Size of opening

H1	H2	H3	A1	A2	A3		#	Recommendation
			0, 1	0			1	Large: 40–80%
				1–12			2	Medium: 25–40%
			2–5					
			6–10				3	Small: 15–25%
			11, 12	0–3			4	Very small: 10–20%
				4–12			5	Medium: 25–40%

Position of openings

H1	H2	H3	A1	A2	A3		#	Recommendation
3–12							6	In north and south walls at body height on windward side
1–2			0–5					
			6–12				7	As above, openings also in internal walls
0	2–12							

Protection of openings

H1	H2	H3	A1	A2	A3		#	Recommendation
				0–2			8	Exclude direct sunlight
		2–12					9	Provide protection from rain

Walls and floors

H1	H2	H3	A1	A2	A3		#	Recommendation
			0–2				10	Light, low thermal capacity
			3–12				11	Heavy, over 8 h time-lag

Roofs

H1	H2	H3	A1	A2	A3		#	Recommendation
10–12			0–2				12	Light, reflective surface, cavity
			3–12				13	Light, well insulated
0·9			0–5					
			6–12				14	Heavy, over 8 h time-lag

External features

H1	H2	H3	A1	A2	A3		#	Recommendation
				1–12			15	Space for out-door sleeping
	1–12						16	Adequate rainwater drainage

Activity chart Location: Season:

Time	2.00	4.00	6.00	8.00	10.00	12.00	14.00	16.00	18.00	20.00	22.00
Temperature °C 44											
40											
36											
32											
28											
24											
20											

Space and activity:

Key	Men / Women / Children						Outdoor air temperature / Indoor air temperature / Comfort zone				

Notes.

Appendix 13

Roof constructions and their performance

T_{ex} under 4 degC is acceptable — Density of heat flow rate (q) and ceiling *temperature excess* (T_{ex}) above air temperature under assumed conditions ($T_o = T_i = 30\,°C$ and $I = 920\ W/m^2$)

Roof material	Ceiling material	Construction	U-value W/m²degC	New q W/m²	New T_{ex} degC	Old q W/m²	Old T_{ex} degC
Corrugated asbestos cement	13 mm fibreboard	a/c* sheets on timber purlins, fibreboard nailed under rafters	1·7	29·3	4·3	62·4	9·4
Corrugated asbestos cement sandwiched with 25 mm fibreglass		sandwich sheets fixed on purlins and rafters	0·8	22·4	3·4	47·9	7·4
100 mm r/c slab 75 mm cement screed	13 mm fibreboard	*in situ* slab, fibreboard on battens	1·3	22·7	3·4	48·2	7·4
Corrugated asbestos cement	13 mm fibreboard	a/c sheets on purlins, fibreboard under horizontal ties	1·7	23·9	3·9	52·3	8·4
Corrugated iron sheets	13 mm fibreboard	iron sheets on purlins, fibreboard under horizontal ties	1·3	13·9	2·3	41·6	7·3
Corrugated iron sheets	13 mm timber board	iron sheets on purlins, timber board under horizontal ties	1·6	17·3	2·9	52·3	8·8
Corrugated iron sheets	5 mm a/c sheets	iron sheets on purlins, a/c sheets under horizontal ties	1·9	20·3	3·1	62·7	9·6
Corrugated asbestos cement	13 mm fibreboard + alum.† foil	a/c sheets on purlins, foil over fibreboard fixed under rafters	1·2	21·4	3·3	46·0	7·0
Corrugated asbestos cement	13 mm timber board + alum. foil.	a/c sheets on purlins, foil over timber boards fixed under rafters	1·6	29·3	4·4	62·7	9·5
Corrugated asbestos cement	5 mm a/c sheets + alum. foil	a/c sheets on purlins, foil over a/c ceiling fixed under rafters	1·7	29·3	4·4	62·7	9·5
Corrugated iron sheets	13 mm fibreboard + alum. foil	iron sheets on purlins, foil over fibreboard fixed under rafters	1·0	16·0	2·5	47·9	7·4
Corrugated iron sheets	13 mm timber board + alum. foil	iron sheets on purlins, foil over timber boards fixed under rafters	1·3	20·2	3·0	60·5	9·2
Corrugated iron sheets	5 mm a/c sheets + alum. foil	iron sheets on purlins, foil over a/c ceiling fixed under rafters	1·4	23·0	3·4	69·0	10·3
Red clay tiles	13 mm fibreboard 25 mm fibreglass + alum. foil	tiles on battens on rafters, foil on fibreglass on fibreboard under rafters	0·62	23·0	3·3	23·0	3·3
Red clay tiles	13 mm timber board, 25 mm fibreglass + alum. foil	tiles on battens on rafters, foil on fibreglass on boards under rafters	0·74	27·1	4·0	27·1	4·0
Red clay tiles	5 mm a/c sheets, 25 mm fibreglass + alum. foil	tiles on battens on rafters, foil on fibreglass on a/c under rafters	0·80	29·3	4·4	29·3	4·4
Corrugated asbestos cement	13 mm fibreboard, 25 mm fibreglass + alum. foil	a/c sheets on purlins, foil on fibreglass on fibreboard under under rafters	0·68	11·6	1·7	25·2	3·6

Roof constructions and their performance

T_{ex} under 4 degC is acceptable

Density of heat flow rate (q) and ceiling *temperature excess* (T_{ex}) above air temperature under assumed conditions ($T_o = T_i = 30°C$ and $I = 920 W/m^2$)

Roof material	Ceiling material	Construction	U-value W/m²degC	New q W/m²	New T_{ex} degC	Old q W/m²	Old T_{ex} degC
Corrugated asbestos cement	13 mm timber board, 25 mm fibreglass + alum. foil	a/c sheets on purlins, foil on fibreglass on boards under rafters	0·74	12·6	1·9	27·1	4·0
Corrugated asbestos cement	5 mm a/c sheets, 25 mm fibreglass + alum. foil	a/c sheets on purlins, foil on fibreglass on a/c ceiling under rafters	0·80	13·5	2·4	29·3	4·4
Corrugated alum. sheets	13 mm fibreboard	alum. on timber purlins, fibreboard under rafters	1·3	16·1	2·5	22·4	3·4
Corrugated alum. sheets	13 mm timber board	alum. on timber purlins, timber board under rafters	1·6	20·2	3·0	28·3	4·3
Corrugated alum. sheets	5 mm a/c sheets	alum. on timber purlins, a/c under rafters	1·9	22·1	3·3	31·2	4·6
Corrugated alum. sheets	100 mm reinforced concrete slab	alum. on timber purlins, reinforced concrete slab horizontal	1·6	20·2	3·0	28·3	4·3
Corrugated alum. sheets	13 mm resin bonded jute board	alum. sheets on timber purlins, board under rafters	1·4	16·7	2·5	23·6	3·6
Corrugated alum. sheets	50 mm strawboard	alum. on timber purlins, strawboard under rafters	1·08	11·0	1·8	15·4	2·5
Corrugated alum. sheets	25 mm wood wool slab	alum. on timber purlins, wood wool under rafters	1·42	14·5	2·2	20·5	3·1
Corrugated alum. sheets	10 mm plasterboard	alum. on timber purlins, plasterboard under rafters	1·88	19·2	2·9	27·4	3·5
Corrugated alum. sheets	25 mm cork slab	alum. on timber purlins, cork under rafters	1·27	13·2	2·0	18·6	2·7
Corrugated alum. sheets	100 mm reinforced concrete slab, 75 mm cement screed, 18 mm plastering	alum. on timber purlins, reinforced concrete slab horizontal underside plastered	1·23	17·3	2·4	24·6	3·4

Based on Koenigsberger and Lynn: *Roofs in the warm-humid tropics.*
* a/c = asbestos cement
† alum. = aluminium

BASIC SI UNITS

Quantity	unit symbol	name of unit	accepted units	obsolete units	
LENGTH	m	metre	km, (cm), mm, µm, nm	1 inch = 25·4 mm 1 foot = 305 mm	1 yard = 0·915 m 1 mile = 1·609 km
MASS	kg	kilogramme	tonne (= 1 000 kg) g (gramme)	1 ounce = 28·35 g 1 pound = 454 g	1 kip = 454 kg 1 ton = 1 016 kg
TIME	s	second	ms (millisecond) minute, hour		
ELECTRIC CURRENT	A	ampere			
TEMPERATURE	°K	degree kelvin	1 degC (celsius) = 1 degK N°C = N + 273·15°K	1 degF = 5/9 degC N°F = 5/9(N−32)°C	
LUMINOUS INTENSITY	cd	candela			

SUPPLEMENTARY UNITS

Quantity	unit symbol	name of unit	definition	accepted units	obsolete units
PLANE ANGLE	rad	radian	angle subtended at centre of unit radius circle by unit length of arc	° (degree), ' (minute), " (second) 1 r ≈ 114·6°	
SOLID ANGLE	sr	steradian	solid angle subtended at centre of unit radius sphere by unit area of surface		

Prefixes to units—Multiples and Submultiples

Fraction	Name	Abbreviation	Multiple	Name	Abbreviation
10^{-1}	deci	d)	(10	deca	da)
10^{-2}	centi	c)	(10^2	hecto	h)
10^{-3}	milli	m	10^3	kilo	k
10^{-6}	micro	µ	10^6	mega	M
10^{-9}	nano	n	10^9	giga	G
10^{-12}	pico	p	10^{12}	tera	T

DERIVED UNITS

Quantity	unit symbol	name of unit	dimension definition	accepted units	obsolete units
AREA	m²	metre squared	square with sides of unit length	1 mm² = 10^{-6} m² 1 ha (hectare) = 10^4 m² 1 km² = 10^6 m²	1 ft² = 0·093 m² 1 acre = 0·405 ha 1 mile² = 2·59 km²
VOLUME	m³	cubic metre	cube with sides of unit length	1 litre = 1 dm³ = 10^{-3} m³ 1 cm³ = 10^{-6} m³	1 ft³ = 0·028 m³ 1 gallon = 4·546 l
DENSITY	kg/m³	kilogramme per cubic metre	unit mass per unit volume	1 g/cm³ = 1 000 kg/m³	1 lb/ft³ = 16·019 kg/m³ 1 lb/in³ = 27·68 g/cm³
SURFACE DENSITY	kg/m²	kilogramme per metre squared	unit mass per unit area		1 lb/ft² = 4·882 kg/m²

Quantity	Symbol	Unit name	Base units	Definition	Conversions
VELOCITY, (LINEAR)	m/s	metre per second		unit length movement in unit time	1 km/h = 0·278 m/s · 1 ft/min = 0·005 m/s; 1 ft/s = 0·305 m/s · 1 mph = 1·609 km/h; 1 knot = 1·853 km/h
ACCELERATION (LINEAR)	m/s²	metre per second squared		unit velocity change in unit time	1 ft/s² = 0·305 m/s²
FORCE	N	newton	kg m/s²	causing unit acceleration of unit mass	kN, MN · 1 lbf = 4·448 N; 1 kgf = 9·807 N · 1 dyn = 10⁻⁵ N
WORK, ENERGY	J (N m)	joule	kg m²/s²	unit force acting over unit length	1 Wh = 3600 J; 1 kWh = 3600 kJ · 1 erg = 0·1 μJ; 1 cal = 4·187 J; 1 kcal = 4·187 J; 1 m kgf = 9·807 J · 1 Btu = 1055·06 J; 1 therm = 105·506 MJ; 1 hp-h = 2684·5 kJ; 1 ft lbf = 1·3556 J
POWER or ENERGY FLOW RATE	W (J/s)	watt	kg m²/s³	unit energy spent in unit time	megawatt, kilowatt · 1 erg/s = 0·1 μW; 1 cal/s = 4·187 W; 1 kcal/h = 1·163 W; 1 hp (metric) = 735·5 W · 1 Btu/h = 0·293 W; 1 ton refrig = 3·516 kW; 1 ft lbf/s = 1·356 W; 1 hp = 745·7 W
DENSITY OF ENERGY FLOW RATE (INTENSITY)	W/m²	watt per metre squared	kg/s³	unit energy flow rate through unit area	kW/m², μW/m², MJ/m².day · 1 Btu/ft² h = 3·155 W/m²; 1 cal/cm² h = 1 langley/h = 41·87 kJ/m² h · 1 kcal/m² h = 1·163 W/m²; 1 kcal/m² h = 11·63 W/m²
PRESSURE, STRESS	N/m² (pascal)	newton per metre squared	kg/m s²	unit force acting on unit area	kN/m², MN/m²; 1 bar = 100 kN/m²; 1 m bar = 100 N/m² · 1 kgf/cm² = 98 kN/m²; 1 kgf/m² = 9·8 N/m²; 1 atmosphere = 101·32 kN/m²; 1 m water gauge = 9·8 kN/m² · 1 lbf/in² = 6895 N/m²; 1 lbf/ft² = 47·88 N/m²; 1 tonf/ft² = 107·3 kN/m²; 1 ft water gauge = 2·99 kN/m²
THERMAL CAPACITY	J/degC			energy required by *body* for unit temperature increase	1 Btu/degF = 1899 J/degC · 1 kcal/degC = 4187 J/degC
SPECIFIC HEAT	J/kg degC; J/m³ degC			energy required by *substance* for unit temperature increase (per unit mass or unit volume)	1 Btu/lb degC = 4·187 J/kg degC; 1 Btu/ft³ degC = 67 kJ/m³ degC · 1 kcal/kg degC = 4·187 kJ/kg degC; 1 kcal/m³ degC = 4·187 kJ/m³ degC; 1 kcal/l degC = 4·187 MJ/m³ degC
THERMAL CONDUCTIVITY	W/m degC			heat flow rate through unit area of unit thickness of *substance* with unit temperature difference between the two faces	1 Btu.in/ft².h.degF = 0·144 W/m degC; 1 kcal/m.h. degC = 1·163 W/m degC
THERMAL TRANSMITTANCE	W/m² degC			heat flow rate through unit area of *body* with unit difference in temperature of air on the two sides	1 Btu/ft².h. degF = 5·678 W/m² degC; 1 kcal/m².h.degC = 1·163 W/m degC
LATENT HEAT, CALORIFIC VALUE	J/kg; J/m³			change in energy content at change of state, or heat produced by combustion (per unit mass or unit volume)	1 Btu/lb = 2326 J/kg; 1 Btu/ft³ = 37·26 kJ/m³; 1 Btu/gal = 232 kJ/m³ · 1 kcal/kg = 4187 J/kg; 1 kcal/m³ = 4187 J/m³; 1 kcal/l = 4187 kJ/m³
LUMINOUS FLUX	lm	lumen	cd.sr	emitted by unit intensity source in unit solid angle	
ILLUMINATION	lx	lux	lm/m²	unit flux incident on unit area	1 lm/ft² = 10·76 lx

Note **bold** numbers indicate the page where the word is defined
ital numbers indicate the page where the word occurs in a chapter or paragraph title

*The authors wish to express their gratitude to Miss Maria Kovacs for the preparation
of this index